Empirical Knowledge

Empirical Knowledge

ALAN H. GOLDMAN

UNIVERSITY OF CALIFORNIA PRESS
Berkeley   Los Angeles   London

University of California Press
Berkeley and Los Angeles, California

University of California Press, Ltd.
London, England

Copyright © 1988 by The Regents of the University of California

Library of Congress Cataloging in Publication Data

Goldman, Alan H., 1945–
Empirical knowledge.
Includes index.
1. Knowledge, Theory of. 2. Empiricism.
3. Realism. I. Title.
BD161.G64   1988   121   87-30143
ISBN 0-520-06202-7 (alk. paper)

Printed in the United States of America
1   2   3   4   5   6   7   8   9

For Michael and David—may they do better.

Contents

Acknowledgments

This book was long in the making. Probably the greatest influences on my thinking along the way were Arthur Danto, my advisor while I was a graduate student at Columbia, and Richard Rorty, with whom I studied during the year I spent at Princeton as a National Endowment for the Humanities Fellow. What impressed me about both men was not so much their opinions as their philosophical style, the broad range of their interests, and their deep attention to issues that struck me as fundamental. Rorty's effect was, if anything, enhanced by my disagreeing with all his philosophical views—a tribute, I think, to his openness and ability to challenge.

Gilbert Harman's influence on my adoption of an explanationist framework (which he does not use in the same way) should be obvious. I am grateful for more recent and specific improvements to William Lycan and Frederick Schmitt, who offered helpful criticisms of the entire manuscript.

A major part of the final draft of Part III was written at the University of Colorado while I was on sabbatical from the University of Miami. I thank James Nickel for providing such a pleasant atmosphere in which to work and Stephen Leeds for many stimulating and edifying discussions.

Sections of Part II appeared previously in *Philosophy and Phenomenological Research, Nous, Metaphilosophy,* and the *Journal of Philosophy;* sections of Part III in *Mind, Philosophia,* and the *Southern Journal of Philosophy;* and sections of Part I and the Appendix in *American Philosophical Quarterly.* I thank all these journals for permission to expand upon and reproduce portions of those articles.

Finally, I am grateful to the University of Miami Word Processing Center for an excellent job in preparing the final manuscript and to Nancy Atkinson of the University of California Press for improvements in style with never a loss in content.

Introduction

Broad strokes befit introductions. I should like here to locate the defense of foundationalism and realism to follow in a briefly sketched historical context.

THE CARTESIAN-LOCKEAN APPROACH
AND ITS CRITICS

Beginning with Descartes and Locke, epistemologists typically fashioned their theories as answers to skeptical challenges. By attempting to show how our ordinary and scientific claims to knowledge could be supported and vindicated in the face of real or imaginary doubts, they hoped to reveal the logical structure of empirical knowledge. They took this structure to be grounded in the original source of such knowledge: perception, or more specifically, perceptual experience of objects. The central question was whether experience partially caused by emissions from physical objects accurately reveals real properties of those objects.

The skeptical challenges arose from two sources. The first was the realization from examples of perceptual error in ordinary contexts that experience is no infallible guide to the nature of its objects. Most significantly, experience indistinguishable in itself from that which is taken to reveal the nature of objects in the environment can occur when the objects are very different from how they appear or when no objects are there at all. This realization was bolstered by the developing scientific theories of the causal chains involved in perceiving. The complex processes between objects and percepts indicate a far more indirect contact than that naively assumed.

The new science generated a second major source of skeptical worry as well: the recognition that the emerging scientific model of physical reality differed strikingly from the interpretation of physical objects natural to ordinary perception. Gone were colors, tastes, smells, etc. Faced with this apparent rift between perceptual experience and its source and target in independent physical reality, as described by means of our most reliable methods for investigating it, the epistemologist's task was to reconcile these two pictures, to show how suitably refined perceptual beliefs might at least partially rescue the common-sense view and ground the scientific. Subsequent theories of knowledge remain footnotes to the struggles and shortcomings of the classic Cartesian approach to this challenge.

Shifting forward several centuries, dominant trends in contemporary epistemology have sought to dismiss the skeptic's challenge as misguided or unintelligible, rather than seeking to answer it. The Cartesian formulation of the problem has been attacked from every side, many sallies deriving from the multifarious musings of the later Wittgenstein.

Least radical in their departure from the tradition are those neo-Wittgensteinians who accept the formulation of the problem as concerning the relations between ways objects appear in experience and their objective properties, but who argue that the key connection is not empirical but conceptual.[1] According to them, while no set of statements about appearances strictly entails statements about (nonrelational) properties of objects, it is part of what we *mean* by saying that an object has certain perceptible properties that it appears in certain ways under certain conditions. Phenomenalism, the traditional ancestor of this position, according to which perceptible objects simply reduce to collections of experiences, is agreed to be defeated by our inability to translate object statements into statements referring only to appearances. But the key relation between the latter and the former remains logical or semantic. Skeptical doubts then remain nonsensical in violating rules of language. One cannot sensibly acknowledge claims regarding experiential evidence and dismiss claims for which they necessarily are evidence.

According to these philosophers, the Cartesian tradition went wrong in construing the relation between objective properties and ways they appear (and, in general, relations between the physical and the mental) as causal. This construal permits skeptical doubts regarding the inference from the experienced effects to their supposed causes. We should rather construe the relation as conceptual, or, more precisely, as *criterial:* when an object normally appears red, for example, it is conceptually settled that it is red, since the former is our only criterion for meaningfully asserting (or denying) the latter. Psychological theories regarding the causal variables involved in perceiving may be of interest in themselves or for purposes of prediction and control; but they remain epistemologically irrelevant, since they cannot falsify ascriptions of properties that are based on appearances in normal conditions, and they are not required to verify those ascriptions. Psychologists' theories become useful for explanation when things go wrong, when the context is abnormal. Then we seek causal explanations for perceptual errors. In normal conditions the explanation for an object's appearing red is simply that it is red, and our knowledge that it is red is based not on a causal inference but simply on our knowledge that the criterion for ascribing the property is satisfied.

This Wittgensteinian notion of a criterion as necessary evidence conceptually linked to a state of affairs, of central importance to this current school of epistemologists, will be explicated and criticized much later in our story. I shall argue that the notion is ultimately incoherent in itself. There simply is no fully coherent position between a phenomenalism or idealism that does away with the physical world as we conceive it and a full-blooded realism that acknowledges the world's independence from our efforts to know it. For the realist, the argument against phenomenalism on linguistic grounds rejects a wrong view for the wrong reason; and the attempt to save some noncontingent, conceptual connection between perceptual evidence and knowledge of objective properties retains the weakest premise of only one version of the older position. The relation between properties of objects and ways they appear is indeed causal. Our ascriptions of objective properties on the basis of perception do rest epistemically on certain (sometimes naive) assumptions regarding the causal connection between objects and perceivers, although ordinary perceptual judgments do not normally involve actual inferences. Psychology is informative and relevant to epistemology in clarifying the structure of this connection, but its theories must be placed in a broader epistemic context in order to complete a logical reconstruction of empirical knowledge, the

full task of the epistemologist. I hope to indicate the broad outlines of the fuller picture in the following chapters and to expand
on the relations between cognitive psychology and epistemology
in the Appendix.

Next in the line of recent anti-Cartesians is the materialist,
who rejects the dualist view of perceptual evidence.[2] For him
skepticism becomes inevitable once we erect in our theory of
perception an impenetrable shield of mental experience between perceiver and object. The fact that perceptual beliefs can
be mistaken in various ways does not force recognition of sensu-
ous appearance as an object or process in perceiving. Contemporary materialists offer epistemic accounts of perception, according to which perceiving is the direct acquisition, via the sensory
systems, of perceptual beliefs or inclinations to beliefs. This
nonrealist or reductionist attitude toward perceptual experience eliminates one of the terms in the formulation of the skeptic's problem, and so eliminates the problem itself, according to
the epistemically most sanguine materialist accounts.

I shall argue in Part II that ways of appearing are both irreducible and required for grounding the structure of empirical
knowledge. The account of perception as the acquisition of
belief encounters counterexamples in the perception of infants
(among other areas), which is most plausibly analyzed in the
light of evidence from developmental psychologists as nonepistemic perceiving, seeing without believing. The nonepistemic
psychological component in perceiving turns out to consist in
ways objects appear, which come to function epistemically as
the grounds of perceptual beliefs before being conceptualized
as appearance. Moreover, the elimination of this element from
the account of perceiving does nothing to avoid the skeptic's
challenge. To meet or avoid that challenge, one must still provide reasons for thinking perceptual beliefs generally true. In
fact it is more difficult to provide such reasons without appeal
to this originally nonepistemic component of perceiving.

The positive accounts of the nature of appearances, of the
immediate justification of beliefs about appearances, and of the
place and functions of such beliefs in a theory of knowledge,
which I shall offer in Part II, depart significantly from more
standard versions of Cartesian foundationalism. I hold these

beliefs to be self-justified without being self-evident, infallible, or incorrigible; and I hold them to be capable of serving as foundations for knowledge without its being possible to trace all other empirical beliefs directly back to them as ultimate sources of justification. The latter requirement of strong foundationalist theories is not necessary for these beliefs to ground empirical knowledge in the real world.

Yet more profound in their rejection of Cartesian premises than materialists, who remain realists in their view of physical reality, are those contemporary philosophers who oppose all realisms on semantic grounds.[3] For realists the objects of our percepts and concepts remain independent of our perceptual and conceptual schemes (in a sense of 'independence' to be made precise). For them the challenge of skepticism is therefore intelligible and genuine, since the question is open whether our percepts and concepts (indeed our entire conceptual scheme) reveal or capture their objects as they are in themselves. Semantic antirealists deny that this question can be meaningfully raised. According to them meaning and truth attach themselves to assertions only as these relate to others within a conceptual scheme or theory.[4] Semantic values of beliefs are relative to whole systems of belief, whether there is ultimately only one conceptual scheme for us or many, as the more thoroughgoing relativists maintain.

Here the coherence theory of truth, according to which those beliefs are true that cohere with others in a system, replaces the correspondence theory that is the mark of realism. According to the coherence theory, questions can be posed only from within a conceptual scheme: the veracity of our whole cognitive view of the world cannot be sensibly questioned. Truth conditions for statements are equated with conditions of justification or warranted assertibility. Justificatory conditions in turn are held to be either socially or psychologically determined. The uniquely philosophical character of epistemology, its task of critically exposing the ultimate grounds and premises of the sciences by inquiring into the relations between their semantic vehicles and the world, is lost. Either epistemology becomes "naturalized," its legitimate questions and functions taken over entirely by cognitive psychology, or the sociology of knowledge gains prominence as the queen of sciences. On the former variation, psychology is no longer simply relevant to epistemology in filling in the final stages of explanations for the epistemic data that consist in beliefs about appearances; rather, by providing the best tested theories of the relations of cognitive "inputs" to "outputs," it altogether replaces philosophical armchair versions. On the latter variation, psychology, like philosophy and the other sciences, becomes one more or less coherent story among others, its methodological development itself needing to be explained in sociological terms.

This final antirealist position is more thoroughgoing than that of the criteriologists mentioned earlier. The latter appear willing to accept the distinction between justification and truth, arguing only that conditions in which assertions are taken to be justified or verified partially determine the meanings of the assertions' empirical terms. Semantic antirealists deny the possibility or functionality of concepts that transcend those contexts in which language users deem it correct to apply them, contexts in which they may be publicly taught and learned. Without such concepts, philosophically interesting skeptical questions cannot be raised. The equation of truth with warranted assertibility renders this position more difficult to attack than the criteriological because it is more internally consistent. There is not the same tension between the concept of justification and the ordinarily more fundamental notion of truth, to which justification must be subordinate on the realist's view. This tension creates the chink in the armor of the criteriologist, a flaw absent from semantic antirealism.

There remains a different tension in the latter position: the threat of collapse into older, repudiated versions of idealism, verificationism, or phenomenalism. Again, the positive goal of the semantic antirealist appears to be the enunciation of a philosophy that falls between the extremes of standard idealisms and full-blooded realism,[5] but without the skeptical implications of the Kantian unknowable thing-in-itself that plagued the monumental first modern attempt at such a compromise. Whether this yet more troublesome skeptical bugaboo can be avoided by philosophers sometimes seemingly motivated by the desire to avoid all contact with the more mundane skeptical critics of realism, without their retreating to strongly counterintuitive forms of idealism, is a key question. I shall argue that the answer is negative.

TASKS FOR THE CARTESIAN-LOCKEAN REALIST

For the realist to exploit these tensions in opposing positions, he must show not only that belief in a fully independent reality is rationally supported or probably true (in his sense of 'true') but also, as a prior step in the argument, that such belief is possible, intelligible, and functional. In light of the semantic antirealist's arguments it must be shown how we can conceive of objects beyond conceiving of ways of verifying their existence and properties, how the reference of such concepts extends beyond experienced conditions in which they are learned, how such reference functions in discourse, and how it makes a difference to our theories and language. The realist must show also how the systemic falsity of our perceptually grounded belief system is an intelligible (but rationally indefensible) possibility. We must see why and how we refer to verification-transcendent objects about which we could conceivably believe only falsehoods. Such is the notion of independence intended in the realist's thesis of an independent physical reality. I shall broach this large task in the latter part of Part IV.

Once we understand how realist concepts are possible and sensible, we can argue that they are instantiated, or that it is rational to believe so. I will defend the latter claim via an inductive argument. In my view only inductive arguments are available to the thoroughgoing realist, for whom all epistemically interesting connections between beliefs and the world that ultimately verifies or falsifies them are contingent. In fact, an argument of the same structure as that presented in Part II to establish the experiential foundations of empirical knowledge will also be taken to support the initial realist inference and to extend that inference into a defense of scientific realism. Realism regarding science is the view that the best scientific theories are to be provisionally accepted as referring via some of their theoretical terms to real entities and as approximately true. According to this view the picture of the world that emerges in physical science corrects that of naive perceptual consciousness (although explanations appealing to natural selection in evolution may be offered for the relative success of each picture within its own domain).

The defense of scientific realism, necessary once we accept the principle of inductive inference I shall advocate, again requires blocking those skeptical inferences that realism makes possible. Such inferences appear to become more plausible in the scientific context if a realist view is maintained along with Thomas Kuhn's recently influential view of scientific development and the history of science.[6] The relations among theories of theory development, skepticism, and realism will also be examined in the fourth chapter. The currently dominant theories of relativity and quantum mechanics raise problems in themselves for realistic interpretations, which the scientific realist must address. Finally, there is the hoarier question of the extent to which the realist attitude toward science requires abandoning the natural or commonsense picture of the perceivable world, especially in regard to secondary qualities, especially colors.

I will then defend certain features of a tradition in epistemology that dates to Descartes and Locke against recent radical departures from it. Specifically, I will introduce a theory of knowledge that is realist, foundationalist, and inductivist. These three strands should be perceived as logically connected. For the realist the structure of empirical knowledge must be anchored to the world. There must be grounds other than coherence with other beliefs for maintaining that certain beliefs within the structure are true or in correspondence with their objects. Without some such privileged set of beliefs it would appear that many internally coherent systems of statements could be constructed with only tenuous connections to reality, connections not satisfying the realist's notion of truth. Developed myths are good examples. This requirement for true theories implies that a knowledge has a foundational structure, although the base need not be as extensive in relation to the superstructure of commonsense belief and scientific theory as has been traditionally thought. A new foundational theory, and a defense of the need for one, will be developed in the third chapter.

The realist must also demand some sort of inductive justification for both the foundations and the remainder of the structure of knowledge. If objects are conceived as logically independent of our perceptions and conceptual scheme, then connections among beliefs, ways objects appear in perceptual experience, and intrinsic properties of the objects must be contingent. The realist's philosophy of perception will be concerned with the natural relation of perceiver to object, and the justification for a normative epistemological theory will resemble that for a scientific theory. Differences will lie in the scope and generality of the former, its lack of concern for the causal details, its having initial premises or starting points at stages of knowledge long surpassed and taken for granted by scientists, and its self-conscious preoccupation with the most fundamental justificatory principles themselves. Those principles must justify inferences from beliefs and experienced qualities to the intrinsic nature of objects that transcend them, if skepticism is to be avoided.

We begin to see here the intertwining of epistemological issues (what we know) with metaphysical issues (what there is). Sometimes the epistemologist must carefully distinguish these philosophical realms, especially when a metaphysical debate lacks important epistemic implications. Such is pretty much the case, I shall argue in chapter 6, with the debate in the theory of perception between advocates of sense data and advocates of the adverbial or appearing terminology. But in the grander picture the metaphysical commitments of the epistemologist become crucial for determining the structure of his theory, and the philosopher's reaction to the threat of skepticism may determine his metaphysical commitments. (As indicated earlier, on some nonrealist views, skeptical questions become uninteresting if sensible, and nonsensical if seemingly interesting.) In contemporary philosophy both sorts of issues have been connected in turn with issues in the philosophies of language and science: questions regarding meaning, truth, and reference and regarding the semantics and content of scientific theories and their development. It has become almost standard, as my discussion of antirealism reflects, to pose the metaphysical issues in semantic terms, that is, in terms of arguments about reference and truth. And these arguments are sometimes motivated by reflections on the use and development of theoretical concepts and terms in science. Thus an epistemologist in the present context can hardly avoid forays into these other areas.

Radical departures from the Cartesian tradition are motivated also by difficulties intrinsic to Cartesian epistemological theory. Opponents despair of supporting inferences from the foundations of knowledge and share an equal contempt for attempts to explicate the foundations themselves and their immediate justification. They dismiss the idea of a privileged knowledge of experience, of the mental as opposed to the physical, with the metaphysical problems of dualism thereby engendered. Even aside from the problems of Cartesian metaphysics, the idea of an immediately justified yet only contingently true belief may appear incoherent. (I shall grant that beliefs made true by stipulation are unsuitable as grounds for knowledge.) A contingently true belief might have been false. How then could one show it to be true without producing evidence that it is not in fact false? But if evidence must be produced, then it seems that the belief is not immediately justified, but justified only in relation to the evidence. Such puzzles will have to be solved in Part II. We must demonstrate that foundational beliefs are immediately justifiable—that is, without producing evidence for the beliefs in question.

Many opponents of the tradition, including Kant, Wittgenstein, and Wilfrid Sellars, have also rejected the idea that there is a fixed order within justification and knowledge that places knowledge of experience before knowledge of publicly perceptible objects. They point out that we cannot first conceptualize an order to experience independent of the realm of objects and then infer to that realm as the explanation for this order. I shall argue that their valid point regarding conceptual priority is epistemically irrelevant. Epistemic foundations need not be conceptual foundations also.

Descartes, himself, of course, sought indubitability for his foundations, the logical impossibility of first-person error. Since the stock of empirical propositions meeting that criterion is far too small to serve as our epistemic foundation, he sought to grant this exalted status to all first-person claims about experience, claims that do not, in fact, satisfy his stringent demand. Nor did he fare better in the inference *from* foundations, taking the circuitous route through a benevolent deus ex machina.

Critics argue that successors to Descartes can meet with no greater success. The problem with this sort of inference is held to be endemic to the whole approach. Construing the inference as deductive or conceptual loses us the independent world we seek; inductive reasoning seems unable to bridge the gap between radically disparate epistemic levels—from the directly known or observable to the transcendent, from experience and perceptual beliefs to what lies beyond them. We have no sample class of observed correlations between beliefs and objects in which to ground an enumerative induction, since we can never move outside our beliefs to compare them directly to the world (or even to unconceptualized experience of the world). Induction of the scientific kind, in this case inference to the best explanation for the characteristics of our beliefs and experiences, can in principle never be verified or corroborated, either directly by observing connections to objects or indirectly by testing novel predictions. Since we cannot escape from the circle of our beliefs, and since we cannot test for correspondence with an independent reality even indirectly (no novel predictions are forthcoming from rival theories), our criterion for justification or acceptance or validation of beliefs cannot but be coherentist. And if acceptability consists in coherence, of what use could a notion of truth as correspondence be? On what grounds could we hold that an explanatory inference to the physical world leads to truth in that sense, even assuming that such an inference is unproblematically better than alternatives?

Such questions as these regarding both the empirical foundations and those inferences from the foundations that demonstrate knowledge of the physical world will be answered in the chapters to follow. Inference to the best explanation will be taken to establish the foundations and support the superstructure. I shall provide an argument at the close of Part III that the use of the best-explanation principle tends to be truth preserving, even when inferences to best explanations cross epistemic levels from belief to experience, from experience to its objects, and from observed objects to the unobserved or unobservable.

Our ultimate criterion is indeed (explanatory) coherence; but this criterion itself, together with basic realist inferences that follow from its application, affords reason to believe that it allows us access to truth about a world to which we are naturally related. The grand argument will be circular, as must be all justifications of ultimate justificatory or validating principles, but I hope not viciously so. (To seek moral or pragmatic justification for epistemic principles is to change the subject.) In any case I hope to show that the realist's position is superior to the coherentist's even on the latter's own terms.

PROGRESS AND THE BROADER CONTEXT

Descartes's and Locke's illustrious successors—Berkeley, Hume, and Kant—all argued against their predecessors' approach to the theory of knowledge, each in ways that parallel the more contemporary objections. Berkeley argued, as does Wilfrid Sellars, against the possibility of an inductive inference from experience to an independent reality. Berkeley held that nothing could correspond to an idea except another idea and that causation was a category applicable only within experience itself. To the contemporary arguments that we cannot acquire concepts that transcend conditions in which their correct applications can be verified and that we cannot refer to objects without causally interacting with and acquiring true beliefs about them, corresponds Hume's central argument that all our empirical ideas must arise from and be limited by our sense impressions. And Kant held that we cannot conceptualize experience in an ordered way except via concepts of objects; we do not first know the nature of our experiences and then infer from that basis to the realm of their objects. Wittgenstein and his followers echo that argument.

To philosophers who recognize these parallels, a defense of even the major structural features of the Cartesian-Lockean approach may appear doubly archaic. For those who take seriously the arguments of this book, the impression might be reinforced that debate on these fundamental philosophical issues moves in circles, repeating itself in changed vocabulary without progressing to higher levels. Others more radical in philosophical outlook might find the problems themselves less than fundamental, perhaps only a creation of the Cartesian framework itself. Certainly philosophy in the present century, as in the previous one, is replete with efforts to overcome the dichotomies of the traditional framework in lieu of defending particular sides of them.

In my view these attempts tend under critical scrutiny to collapse into not-so-novel variations on the old themes, while attempts to change the subject completely often presuppose some position on the standard metaphysical and epistemological grids. To me it is not surprising that those philosophical geniuses present and involved in the birth of modern science should have grasped the genuinely basic philosophical issues and even had some inklings of approaches to solving them. Of course matters have progressed in both philosophy and science. While the spectacular development of physical science in this century has made scientific realism both easier and harder to defend, there has been progress as well in philosophical argument. Certain Cartesian premises, regarding indubitability and the nature of the "given" for example, have been successfully refuted; and certain alternative positions, such as Berkeleyan phenomenalism, would no longer be seriously considered. Although in their frankest moments many philosophers might admit that for every argument there appears to be a counterargument, it is not difficult to separate the strong ones from the weak, and the broad and consistent positions from the picayune and contradictory.

One relatively recent development in the theory of knowledge from which future argument can benefit is the detailed attention to the analysis of our concept of knowing. Like ethics, the subject can now be divided legitimately into levels: meta-epistemology and normative epistemology. The former is concerned with stating criteria for knowing, and the latter with the questions when and how those criteria are satisfied. As in ethics, exclusive concern with conceptual analysis at the metalevel can become tedious and unfruitful. There is a tendency for argument to degenerate into a hair-splitting search for precision in the concept, which, as Wittgenstein warned us, is most often not to be found (and to be legislated only at the risk of loss of consistency or relevance). That exclusive concern may have been necessary originally for sharpening the analytical tools, but the real use of analysis is at the normative level. The most interesting issues there are never broached when an analysis out of touch with the social nature of the concept of knowledge, an analysis far too demanding in its criteria, is presupposed. I shall offer an account of the concept in Part I that avoids this pitfall. The conceptual analysis will suggest ways to proceed with the normative argument so as to achieve a consistent and unified picture of our place in the world as knowing subjects. The influence between the meta- and normative levels will also flow in the opposite direction: the inductive style of inference that permeates the realist's normative account will enter prominently into the analysis of knowledge itself, tightening the explanatory coherence of the system that results.

The historical context suggested thus far is for the most part philosophically self-contained, although I have suggested some connections to developments in physical science and psychology to be explored later. Although it is no longer fashionable (perhaps because it is beyond anyone's competence) to link epistemological theories explicitly to social philosophy in the grand manner of Plato, Hobbes, Locke, or Hegel, one might wish to explore also those more indirect connections that might obtain between philosophical movements and broader historical and social forces. While I generally reject strictly sociological explanations for developments in the sciences and philosophy and believe in the genuinely motivational force of the rational search for truth, I would not deny that subtle influences might operate in both directions. The influence of social forces on science depends on the bluntness of those with political and economic power, and the reverse influence depends on their sophistication. A full exploration of these connections in various historical eras would require another book and a knowledge of historical detail certainly beyond my scope. But I would suspect that metaphysical and epistemological idealism would not gain in attractiveness from such a study. For the correlations between the most ardent idealist philosophies of the last century (together with their immediate successors) and the most objectionable political movements on the Continent (not to mention ancient Greece) would, I suspect, be shown to be, to some extent, nonaccidental.

Full-blown idealism is a most arrogant thesis, doing away with those hard facts that can falsify our seemingly most successful theoretical pretensions (even when these are not frustrated by later experiences). While elevating theory to the status of dictating the nature of reality, this philosophy remains out of line with some of our most entrenched scientific theories, not simply in that a realist interpretation is natural for physical science but also in that our accepted cosmological and biological theories reveal us to be relative latecomers even to the tiny speck in the universe we inhabit. How is acceptance of such theories as literally true to be reconciled with the thesis that the universe as we know it is a developing product of our minds? Granting the response that the philosophical theory occupies a higher metalevel in relation to the empirical theories, the tension remains.

It should be mentioned in this context that current antirealists appear to have clean hands not only politically but also when it comes to the pretensions of their theories. None argues straightforwardly that reality itself is a mere product of our minds. As indicated, theirs is a more subtle, compromise thesis, that reality as we can know it is at least partially structured or determined by our experience, theories, language, or conceptual scheme. This thesis may in the end, from the realist's viewpoint, approach nearer to skepticism than to old-fashioned nineteenth-century idealism. Its epistemological vice may lie not in hubris but in excessive modesty.

We can hope to do better in defending our status as knowers by beginning to cash some of the promissory notes already issued.

PART I
THE CONCEPT OF KNOWLEDGE

1
THE ANALYSIS

Some of the most recent discussion of the analysis of knowledge has taken on a glass-beads-game quality—counterexamples dazzling in their originality, designed to capture intuitions few of us recognize as such, generating additional criteria for knowledge so complex in their application as to be of no use in deciding when and what we know. We seek in this chapter an analysis that will point the way toward a unified account on the level of normative epistemology. The analysis to be proposed bears some resemblance to certain earlier ones, and we will need to consider some of the usual exotic examples and variations to bring out the similarities and differences. But I shall expend little effort in devising new examples: the recent literature in epistemology is replete with them, and I will avoid further epicycles in the analysis itself. My proposal is considerably simpler in its motivating idea, if not in its full explication, than are those that add conditions to the traditional view of knowledge as justified true belief in light of the counterexamples.

Preliminarily we may extract a moral from the recent history of the study of ethics. The real fruits of the movement toward metaethics in the first half of this century have been born only lately in normative ethical theories that are conceptually more sophisticated as a result of the earlier philosophical labor. Sustained reflection on the nature of moral argument and on the conceptual foundations of ethics, sometimes tedious in itself, has led to better moral argument on real social issues and to more adequate normative theories. Those writers in the latter fields who might have taken themselves to be rebelling against the exclusive emphasis on metaethics—the exclusive concern with the analysis of moral concepts and the unwillingness to offer normative principles or draw moral conclusions—could not help but benefit from that earlier emphasis.

The same shift is now beginning to occur in epistemology. Philosophers who offer metalevel analyses of the concept of knowledge must begin to look at their use on and implications for the normative level of the subject. Conceptual accounts must facilitate the job of the normative epistemologist in separating mere belief and conjecture from knowledge and in reconstructing, through justificatory argument, both the broad outlines of knowledge at various levels and a defense of those principles that underlie it. Just as a metaethical theory ought to capture the structure of moral argument, ought as a minimal requirement not to render moral debate useless or unintelligible, and ought at best to suggest ways to proceed fruitfully on the normative level, so parallel goals and requirements should animate the task of the metaepistemologist.

An analysis of knowledge should be helpful in revealing the structure and limits of knowledge. It should neither beg the skeptic's questions nor grant him too easy a victory. It will be guilty of the former if its criteria require only coherence among beliefs. The analysis itself can remain neutral on this score by including a criterion of truth and awaiting subsequent argument on coherence versus correspondence theories of truth. An account will be guilty of granting the skeptic too easy a victory if its criteria for knowledge are too stringent, if they are out of line with our concept as we apply it. In seeking the proper analysis we must be guided initially by our intuitions regarding the possession of knowledge in particular instances. As in ethics, intuitions that guide the initial formulation of the concept are not sacrosanct and may be defeated by argument at the normative level. Indeed they are more vulnerable here, where we take ourselves initially to be speaking of knowledge of an independent world (it would take powerful antirealist arguments to drive us from that presumption, which must nevertheless be justified by the normative epistemologist). It may turn out that we have no good reason to believe that beliefs intuitively taken to be knowledge of that world capture its real features. Or, even worse, we may discover inconsistencies in our initial ascriptions of knowledge or discrepancies in light of newly discovered scientific evidence (I shall argue that this is the case in our ascriptions of certain qualities to objects). Nevertheless, an initial analysis on the metalevel must capture central features of our concept of knowledge as we apply it. We must therefore guard against stipulation of criteria so strong that they not only guarantee skeptical outcomes of normative arguments but specify a concept irrelevant to epistemic practice.

As important as the requirement that our account capture specific intuitions in normal and favorite exotic situations is the demand that it render intelligible the quest for knowledge in other disciplines. One way in which the connection to the normative level and to the quest for knowledge in the particular sciences can be secured is by having those forms of inference that we take to be fundamental and knowledge preserving reflected in the analysis of the concept. Such will be the case with the account proposed here. The principle of inference prevalent in scientific reasoning, inference to the best explanation, will be incorporated as a central part of the concept of knowledge itself.[1] This will indicate immediately why science should be our model of a knowledge-seeking endeavor and why it must have the last (if not the first) word on empirical knowledge, on the real nature of the world. (Another reason for its status, as will be explicated in the following chapter, is its fidelity to the empirical data.) Despite this implication, the analysis does not beg the important normative issues in epistemology as long as the epistemic principle of inference to the best explanation itself is defended at some point, as it will be later, and as long as the concept of knowledge captured is indeed our own. It is to be expected that our model of knowledge seeking should reflect our concept of knowledge. An analysis that did not capture this normative implication would so far fail to provide for coherence on the normative level.

As a secondary requirement, an analysis should reveal whatever looseness exists in our concept of knowledge. Our criteria for assessing specific knowledge claims, while sharing certain formal features, differ in their stringency in different contexts of application. What counts as empirical knowledge in a casual conversation might not count in a court of law, in a philosophy classroom, or in a physics laboratory. And of course empirical knowledge differs from mathematical knowledge, ethical knowledge, and other types. The analysis should capture what is common across contexts and types while allowing for variation in application. It should accept that the concept of knowledge is social, that its criteria must be applicable without being overly rigid and, in the case of empirical knowledge, without cutting the knower off from the real world he seeks to know.

The analysis I wish to suggest in light of the above considerations is this: *a belief counts as knowledge when appeal to the truth of the belief enters prominently into the best explanation for its being held.* This account retains two of the requirements of the standard analysis of knowledge as justified true belief—that the knower must believe and that his belief must be true. But it substitutes for the requirement of justification (a notion that in its most common use refers to a subjective condition of the believer in relation to his evidence) the demand that his belief be connected to its truth condition, that is, to the fact to which it refers. (I shall argue that a believer need not be justified in the ordinary sense in order to know.) This demand differs from the demand that the belief be connected causally to its truth condition, although it captures the causal analysis, where valid, as a special case.[2] (I shall argue that the causal analysis, another proposed alternative to the account of knowledge as justified true belief, is both too narrow and too broad.) Explanations need not be causal, although appeal to causes is a common way of explaining in certain contexts.

In saying that the truth of a belief enters into its explanation, I mean that the fact to which the belief refers helps to explain both its content and the way it is held—for example, via perception, with a certain degree of confidence, and so on. In the absence of the fact in question, the chances are less that the same belief would be held in the same way. It might be objected at the outset that such an analysis seeks to account for a somewhat elusive concept, knowledge, by appealing to one yet more mysterious, explanation. Similarly, it might be claimed that the account presupposes what it is trying to elucidate, in that an explanation is best only when the explanans is known to be true. Analyses, like definitions, must elucidate difficult concepts by means of clearer ones and must not presuppose what they are trying conceptually to explain.

Regarding the second objection, I agree that the best explanation must be a true one but disagree that it must be known to be true. Indeed the best explanation for a given state of affairs need not be known at all in order to be best. We search for the best explanation before we know what it is, and we must find it rather than manufacture it. Thus the concept of explanation does not presuppose that of knowledge and may enter into its analysis. Regarding the first objection, it can be replied that, even if we accepted the notion of explanation as primitive, still one unanalyzed concept would be better than two, especially if our ascriptions of knowledge are found to vary with our intuitive grasp of explanations for beliefs. That the concept of explanation itself is philosophically controversial does not prevent its functioning in analysis. Its epistemological centrality, not only here but at the normative level, renders its use unavoidable and accounts for the philosophical attention and controversy surrounding it. More to the point, however, is that we need not leave the analysans itself totally unanalyzed but can specify further some features of the relevant concept of explanation.

EXPLANATION

Our intuitive notion of explaining in this context is that of rendering a fact or event intelligible by showing why it should have been expected to obtain or occur. Factors that enter into explanations for states or affairs help to show why those states were predictable in the context in question. More precisely, if B is to be part of the explanation for A, then B must be distinct from A, the probability of A given B must be greater than the antecedent probability of A, and there must not be some third factor C in the set of relevant background conditions that wholly accounts for this difference. Formally this partial analysis is as follows:

$$((P(A/B) > P(A)) \cdot \sim ((P(A/B) \cdot C) = P(A/C))).[3]$$

The last clause is necessary to rule out pseudoexplanations, as when we explain the coming of spring to a child by noting that winter has lasted several months. If B is a prominent part of the explanation for A, then it must have raised significantly the antecedent probability of A. If S knows that p, then p is a prominent part of the explanation for his believing that p. The fact that p, or p's being true, must have raised the antecedent probability of his believing it in the way that he does.

Part of the looseness or variability in our concept of knowledge derives from variation in the extent to which the probability of a belief's being held must be raised by the fact to which it refers in order to count the belief as knowledge. What does it mean to be stringent in our evaluations of knowledge claims, for example in the context of evaluating the testimony of witnesses in criminal trials? It means that we are required to establish that the belief of the witness had far less probability of being held in the same way in the absence of the facts he alleges. If a defense attorney can show that a witness's belief was equally or almost as probable in the context in the absence of the alleged facts, then the testimony loses value. It no longer counts as knowledge. The lawyer will seek to offer alternative explanations for the witness's belief and argue for the equal plausibility of his explanations. He will maintain that other factors in the context, perhaps the witness's desires or expectations operating in an unclear perceptual environment or over time on his memories, in themselves rendered his present beliefs highly probable. In other contexts we are not so demanding. We require only that the truth of the belief enter into one plausible explanation for its being held. Most readers would grant my claim to know that my wife is in the next room on the basis of my hearing her move about there, even though those same noises might with almost equal probability have been produced by other causes, causes themselves almost equally probable in the context. At least they would grant that claim as long as little rides on it.

There are other sources of variability in explanations that must be mentioned as well. Explanations or particular events or states of affairs vary with choices of reference classes and with factors presupposed or held constant as field or background conditions. The reference class for an explanation consists of those states of affairs relative to which the explanans raises the probability of the explanandum. Background or field conditions are other factors that also raise that probability but are not emphasized for the purposes of the particular explanations being considered. I can explain the large number of casualties in the town hit by the hurricane by pointing out the lack of adequate precautions, the severity of the storm, errors in the long-range forecast, failure of the populace to heed last-minute warnings to evacuate, or the poor construction of the houses. Which factors I assume as background conditions and which I cite as explanatory will depend on whether my interests are meterological or relate to public safety procedures or housing construction. Any of these factors can be genuinely explanatory, since each raises the probability of the sorry state of affairs relative to the others as background conditions.

Explanations for beliefs could differ in similar ways in different contexts of inquiry. A future neurophysiologist might seek to explain belief states by appealing to immediately antecedent brain states. (It might be thought that such brain states would always screen out prior states in probabilistic explanations. I will later add a condition to the analysis that shows why this is not so.) For purposes of epistemic evaluation we assume a more sweeping view, holding constant antecedent internal and certain external conditions and asking whether the fact specified by the belief explains the belief's having arisen in those conditions. Given antecedent states that do not in themselves account for the belief, we want to know why the subject now believes as he does. If prior standing conditions are sufficient to explain the belief alone or together with external conditions other than the fact in question, then there is no knowledge of that fact. If, for example, John sees red when presented with any visual stimulus and believes everything before him to be red, then he does not know that the red patch before him is red, since the fact that it is red does not raise the probability of his believing it to be so. It does not explain why he sees red in this particular instance.

PROBABILITY

While the explanation for a belief relevant to its evaluation as a claim to knowledge may not be the explanation uniquely best for all explanatory purposes, the probability relations that emerge when other conditions are held constant I take to express objective relations. In speaking of B's raising the probability of A, I intend to assert more than a statistical correlation between them. The correlation must be nonaccidental, although obviously it need not express a deterministic law. One recent account of probability that appears capable of capturing the sense I intend is that which uses the model of possible world semantics. According to this model, the probability of a proposition's being true is measured by the number of close or accessible possible worlds in which it is true (or by the ratio of those in which it is true to those in which it is false).[4] Adapting this idea to our topic, we can say that, if B raises the probability of A, then the ratio of close worlds in which A obtains is higher in the set of worlds in which B obtains than in the entire set of worlds.

We need to specify *close* worlds, since a connection between A and B in very remotely conceivable circumstances may not much affect the relevant probability relations. This restriction may appear to create a problem in the account, since at present I know of no clearly defined function that properly gauges degrees of closeness in assigning probabilities. I assume that such a function can be found. Until then, there are simpler expedients, such as simply limiting the universe of discourse to close (or reasonably similar) worlds and counting all these equally. This expedient will give us a rough measure of the relevant probability relations.

Why must we insist on lawlike connections that hold across close possible worlds? One reason is that only such connections render events to be explained truly more predictable. A particular frequency correlation may reasonably be expected to extend beyond past observations into the future only if we infer from the observed correlation to a lawlike connection.[5] Second, insistence on such connections accommodates cases in which explanatory or causal factors appear not to raise the probabilities of their explananda because such factors are correlated with others that lower those probabilities. If p raises the probability of q, it may not do so when r is added to it. If p is correlated with r, then its presence may not appear to raise the probability of q, even though in particular circumstances it may cause and therefore explain q.[6] Suppose, for example, that my being nervous about tennis matches causes me to practice harder before them, which usually helps me win the matches. Still, on a particular occasion my nervousness might cause me to miss an important shot and lose. One might insist that in such a case there must be some other factor present that explains the effect of my nervousness here. Given that factor, even together with the earlier extra practice, being nervous raises the probability of a costly error. But it is conceivable that the relations here are irreducibly statistical, such that nervousness only sometimes causes errors without there being additional factors that determine when it does. This case nevertheless poses no problem for the account, if we measure the frequency of losing across worlds in which nervousness and longer practice vary. Then we shall find that nervousness raises the probability of losing both when longer practice occurs and when it does not, a connection sufficient for nervousness to enter into some explanations for losing. (One must look at the factors in each case in order to decide which ones can be cited in explanation.) Thus insistence on lawlike connections across worlds saves the account from this kind of seeming counterexample.

We can use the model in more complex examples to compare the strength of connections between different potential explaining factors and explananda. Such comparisons in these terms allow us to avoid further seeming counterexamples to the probabilistic account of explanation. Consider a case in which A brings about B fifty percent of the time, such that whenever it does so, it brings about C immediately afterward. Here the probability of C given B seems higher than that of C given A, so that B would seem to screen out A in the probabilistic account of C, although A and not B is the proper explanans for C in the example as defined. But to say that A rather than B brings about C is to suggest a lawlike connection between A and C that does not hold between B and C, although clearly the connection is not deterministic. This connection is reflected in the possible worlds model in that the set of close worlds in which C is connected to A is larger than the set in which it is connected to B. On this level it is A that screens out B and hence constitutes the proper explanans, as it should.

It might be objected here that a lawlike connection does appear to exist between B and C in the example as defined, such that the set of worlds in which C is connected to B is about the same size as the set in which it is connected to A. But I believe that the reason why we say that A and not B brings about C in this context, and the reason why we appeal to A but not B in explaining C, is precisely that A is more closely connected to C than is B across close worlds. If, as the objection has it, this were not the case, then we would say that B causes C after itself being caused by A, or we would explain C by appealing to B (itself explained by appeal to A). As a variation on the latter possibility, consider the case in which A is a particle that divides into two others with opposite spin, where this expresses a deeper conservation law. Then, since B and C (the resulting particles) are related in a lawlike way, we can explain the existence of one of them by appealing to the creation of the other and to the law in question. Such cases then support my interpretation of probabilistic explanation rather than constituting counterexamples.

Pragmatic interests aside, of two competing explanations we prefer the one citing factors that raise the probability of the explanandum more across close possible worlds. This claim will figure in my justifications of realism in the third part of the book. There may still appear to be counterexamples, however. If a particle of U-238 decays, then the fact that it was uranium may seem to raise the probability of decay more than the fact that it was U-238 (a slow-decaying isotope). But the better explanation appears to be the more specific one.[7] We may accept this claim, however, without admitting a counterexample. The reason why it fails to contradict the above thesis about our preferences is that there are no close possible worlds in which the particle was not U-238 but some other isotope of uranium. A particle of any element has the same chemical composition in all close worlds. Thus in this case the fact that it is uranium raises the probability across possible worlds to the same degree as the fact that it is U-238.

The possible worlds model also handles seeming difficulties for the probabilistic account arising from the asymmetry between explanans and explanandum.[8] Consider the standard examples of the flagpole and its shadow and of the barometer and the approaching storm. The length of the flagpole explains that of its shadow, and the approach of the storm explains the falling barometer. The converse explanations are not acceptable, although the probability relations might appear to be symmetrical. The storm is more likely given the falling barometer, as well as the converse; the height of the flagpole can be computed from the length of its shadow (and the angle of the sun). If the probability relations here are purely symmetrical, such that each term raises the probability of the other equally, while the explanatory relations are not, then at best our account is seriously inadequate, even as a partial account. But reference to possible worlds reveals the falsity of the antecedent. In many close worlds in which there are no barometers, the storms still come. (Otherwise, avoidance of storms in our world would be a simple matter.) But in close worlds without approaching storms, barometers do not fall. (Otherwise, weather forecasting in our world would be even less reliable than it is.) Similarly, in close worlds in which the flagpole casts no shadow, where it is cloudy for example, the pole nevertheless retains its height, while the shadow cannot retain its length without the pole. Thus asymmetries in explanation are matched by asymmetries in probability relations across possible worlds.

Avoiding apparent counterexamples requires attention also to the proper reference classes or background fields for particular explanations. Wesley Salmon concludes, upon consideration of a case involving a mixture of uranium and plutonium, that an explanans need not raise the probability of its explanandum.[9] The probability of decay within a specified time is higher for the plutonium, hence lower for the uranium than for the mixture. Drawing a particular sample of uranium from the batch will lower the sample's probability of decay relative to the initial condition, although the fact of its being uranium explains the decay when it occurs. Here we seem to have a case in which the explanans lowers rather than raises the probability of the event to be explained. But, while the fact that a particular element (or metal or material) decayed can be explained by the fact that it is uranium, the latter fact cannot explain why a particular piece of uranium (or a selection from a batch of uranium-plutonium) decayed. Relative to the latter reference class, there is no explanation for why the uranium decayed. Attention to the reference class that renders the explanation possible and proper fails to reveal a counterexample, since, relative to that reference class, the probability of the explanandum is raised.

In the case of beliefs and the facts that help to bring them about via perception or communication, we can appeal to frequencies as indicators of the deeper, lawlike probability relations. To determine whether a particular state of affairs raises the antecedent probability of a belief, we can ask how frequently this type of belief arises, first in the background conditions minus the state of affairs to which the belief refers, and then in the total conditions including that state of affairs. If the truth of the belief is unconnected with its being held, then the first set of conditions, perhaps together with some degree of free choice, will have been sufficient to produce it.

The use of probability here in explicating explanation of beliefs is quite different from another use common in the literature of epistemology, in writings on rational acceptance of hypotheses on the basis of evidence. There, where there appears to be no independent means of judging the truth of the hypotheses, the enterprise rests upon the rationality of subjective assignments of antecedent probabilities of their being true. In our case we can estimate rough frequencies of beliefs coming to be held in various conditions, and that is all we need do. The truth of the beliefs is a separate requirement in ordinary contexts (although we shall, using the same kind of explanatory inference, establish the general truth of key types of belief when we turn to normative epistemology. There we shall find that the process begins with certain beliefs that are evidence for their own truth according to this principle of inference.) The question whether your belief counts as knowledge depends not on my estimation of the relevant probabilities but on what they in fact are, although my evaluation of your knowledge claim will of course depend on my estimate of them.

In thinking of frequencies and of possible world probabilities, we must again abstract from certain specific features of beliefs and the facts to which they refer that render them unique, so as to focus on the content of the beliefs and the

manner in which they are held. Although the probability relations in this account are taken to be objective, we should not
attempt to eliminate them in favor of talk of nonstatistical laws
or necessary or sufficient conditions. Regarding the latter, it
would not be sufficient for knowledge of a particular fact, whenever such facts obtain in like conditions, for beliefs that such
facts obtain to be formed, since this would be true also in the
situation described above (John seeing red) in which internal
conditions alone are sufficient. Still not satisfactory is the more
plausible requirement that the fact must be a necessary part of a
sufficient condition for the belief. To speak of the material
conditions, external and internal, as having to be sufficient is to
beg the question against choice or indeterminism in the formation of beliefs. If we ever do have genuine choice in believing
(or in convincing ourselves to believe), then the facts believed in
those cases are not sufficient to produce the beliefs, even holding other conditions constant. Yet I see no contradiction in the
idea of such beliefs' counting as knowledge. That a person
could choose not to believe some fact, and therefore in some
sense choose to believe it, does not in itself imply that he does
not know it to be the case. While I am not myself a believer in
free will, I do not believe that the application of our concept of
knowledge requires the refutation of that doctrine.

In regard to the more interesting question of necessity, it is
not necessary, when a person has knowledge, that his belief
would not have been formed if not for the fact to which it
refers. The fact need not be necessary for the belief's being
held, although it must render it more probable in the relevant
context. If I am playing tennis with my son when an assassination occurs at some distant location, then I know for certain that
my son is not the assassin. That I would not have believed him
to be the assassin if he were is irrelevant, given my irrefutable
evidence in the real situation. The fact that he is not the assassin
(or whatever positive facts—for example, that someone at the
scene of the crime far distant from us is the culprit—explain
that negative fact) can increase the probability of my so believing without being necessary for my having formed the belief.
There are two reasons why this case satisfies our criterion for
knowledge without the fact's being necessary to the belief. One

derives from the fact that belief contrasts not only with disbelief but with suspension of belief and with simple lack of belief. In this example I might have had no beliefs about any such matter at all if those positive facts about the assassin that help to explain my son's not being guilty had not come to my attention, but I still would not have believed my son guilty if he were. Thus the facts in question increase the probability of my believing without being necessary for my belief.

The second relevant factor here, given various facts about my son (that he is only fourteen years old, generally well behaved, politically unmotivated, and so on), is the extremely low probability of the situation in which both he is the assassin and I nevertheless disbelieve it. In general, whether relevant facts do increase the probability of a belief's being held when they are not necessary for its formation depends on the likelihood of the counterfactual situation in which the belief is formed in their absence. I will shortly cite examples in which such counterfactual situations defeat claims to knowledge, although, as we see here, they need not do so if their antecedent probability is very low. The possible worlds model of probability, together with the probabilistic interpretation of explanation and the explanatory analysis of knowledge, support the intuitive verdict on my knowledge in this assassination example. Although the closest possible world in which my son is guilty may be a world in which I still do not believe him to be so, all those worlds in which he is the assassin are very distant from the one described, in which he is fourteen years old, politically unmotivated, etc. The number of close possible worlds in which my belief is correlated with facts that imply his innocence is far greater than the number of worlds in which it is correlated with other facts, specifically with those that would cause me to believe him innocent in this world even were he guilty. While all those close worlds in which I believe him innocent may also be worlds in which I love my son, there are many worlds in which I love him but have no beliefs at all about such an assassination.

COMPLICATIONS

When beliefs are overdetermined by several causal chains, we require only that one contain the fact to which the belief refers if it is to count as knowledge. A more interesting case is that of causal preemption, the situation in which a cause is prevented from operating by an alternative chain of events that brings about the same effect. Consider first a nonepistemic example of a hospital that maintains a backup generator for its electrical system. Suppose we want to explain the operation of the system. In normal circumstances the explanation for the equipment's working in the hospital appeals to the power supply from the public utility, despite the existence of the backup system. Such cases raise a serious problem for counterfactual or conditional analyses of causation, according to which a cause is necessary to its effect, or it is counterfactually true that, if the cause had not occurred, the effect would not have occurred. The example appears to generate a similar objection to our probability account of (partial) explanation, since here the explanation for the equipment's working will appeal to the cause of its working. The problem is that the actual cause in such circumstances does not appear to be necessary for its effect or even to raise the probability of the effect's occurring, given the backup causal mechanism. If that mechanism itself is extremely reliable, as we would hope and expect in a hospital system, then the probability appears to be antecedently very high that the system will operate, and the current from the usual source of power does not appear to increase that probability significantly. Thus we seem to have the counterexample of an explanans that does not increase the probability of the explanandum.

I believe that the probability account can be defended with respect to cases of preemption by noting again that explanations are provided relative to background conditions or fields. In these cases, if the preempted cause is included within the background field or context for the explanation, then appeal to the actual cause will not constitute a satisfactory explanation for the effect. It will not significantly raise the probability of the effect's occurrence. But if the preempted cause is excluded from the context, when the causal explanation will be acceptable, since then the actual cause will raise the probability of the effect relative to the background conditions. Additional probability considerations determine whether or not the backup cause should be included within the background field. In our example, whether appeal to the normal power supply is a sufficient explanation for the equipment's running depends on the likelihood of having to use the alternative source instead. If failures are extremely rare, then it is not necessary to mention the alternative source. We explain the system's operation by pointing out the ordinary source of power. But if the backup source is very often the actual cause of the power's being on, a full explanation for its being on at particular times should describe the whole system.

This distinction is implied again by the possible worlds model of probability as it relates to the account of explanation. If the normal power supply is unreliable, this indicates almost as many close worlds in which the operation of the system is connected to the backup cause as worlds in which it is caused by the normal supply. Given reliability in the backup mechanism, the probability of the system's working is not significantly increased by the normal cause. But if the normal mechanisms are extremely reliable, this indicates that those worlds in which they break down are more distant, that they involve more radical departures from actual physical conditions in this world. In this case the proportion of close worlds in which the system works is higher where the normal power supply exists, the backup cause operating only in relatively distant worlds. Hence the normal power supply is what primarily raises the antecedent probability of the system's working.

This difference can be made clearer still by analogy to a further example. Consider explanations by historians for the outbreaks of wars. Sometimes the best explanation appeals to a particular event or decision and sometimes to a broader historical context. The more specific is best when the war probably would not have broken out if not for the event in question. The more general is preferred when any number of events were equally likely to set off hostilities in the political context. In the hospital case, when the backup generator is commonly used, an explanation that omits mention of this alternative source is misleading in the same way that a historical explanation of the origins of a war is misleading when it cites the one among many equally likely events that actually triggered the hostilities. The full antecedent situations are the preferred explanans in both these contexts. In the hospital example the entire power system accounts for the probability of the equipment's running; but in one version of the case the normal supply in itself renders that probability sufficiently high, while in the other version the backup supply significantly raises the probability, and the actual cause had no higher antecedent possibility of occurring than did the backup. We shall return shortly to epistemic contexts in which intuitions about knowledge vary in parallel fashion. Our point will be that the close correlation between the ways our intuitions vary in examples involving knowledge claims on the one hand and preferred explanations on the other supports the analysis of knowledge in terms of explanation.

Before turning to other similar examples, we must complicate our analysis somewhat further. If the account is to be widely applicable, we must allow not only direct explanations of beliefs by facts but chains of explanation. This expansion was implicit in our earlier discussion of the assassination case. There those facts that helped to explain why my son was not the assassin also helped to explain my beliefs about the matter. Our criterion for knowledge will be satisfied, then, if that which explains a belief also ultimately explains or is explained by the fact to which the belief refers. Consider as a further example knowledge of universal propositions, for which explanatory but not causal chains can account. What typically explains my belief that all A's are B? In one type of case, in which my knowledge is most direct, my belief is explained by further beliefs about particular A's that are B. All the A's I have directly observed have been B, and I infer that the best explanation for these observations is that all A's are B. (The explanation is not directly causal, although it may presuppose appeal to a law of nature that helps to explain causally why all A's are B.) This explanatory inference, together with the observational beliefs that ground it, explains my belief in the universal proposition. In other cases I have been informed by others, whom I take to be knowledgeable, that all A's are B. These others may in turn have been informed, and their informers may have been informed . . ., but ultimately their knowledge must depend on those with direct knowledge of particular A's. Thus in both types of cases the truth of the universal proposition explains the evidence that ultimately helps to explain my belief.

Beliefs about the past and future can exemplify similar chains. On one variation a past fact explains subsequent perceptions and beliefs that, together with communication, explain a present belief about that fact. This type of chain can be expanded to include more intermediate links consisting of beliefs and desires to communicate, up to some present believer whose beliefs are explained by that chain or by its last link. On a second variation a past fact leaves material traces (that it explains), which constitute present evidence that, together with beliefs about the explanatory relations themselves, explains present belief about the past fact. Knowledge about the future derives from similar chains. Currently observed facts can help to explain some belief about the future, and these facts can also explain, via causal chains, the coming to pass of the future events now believed on the basis of this evidence to be forthcoming.

Later examples will reveal a further, more complex requirement on these chains. This condition is as follows:

> The explanans for a belief, which explanans explains (type 1) or is explained by (type 2) the fact to which the belief refers, must be such that: if it is a type 1 explanans, its raising the probability of the belief is itself made more probable by its raising the probability of the fact to which the belief refers; if it is a type 2 explanans, its raising the probability of the belief is made more probable by its being made more probable by the fact to which the belief refers.[10]

Call this requirement Condition C. When it is met, explanatory chains are strengthened, in that each probabilistic link is made more probable by the others. When it is not met, there can remain an element of accident in the connection between a belief and the fact to which it refers. We may translate this requirement for second-order probabilistic connections among probabilistic connections into the possible worlds language, although there may be little or no gain in clarity from doing so. If A's making B more probable is itself made more probable by C's making A more probable, then we can say that the proportion of close galaxies of worlds in which B's truth varies with A's given that A's truth varies with C's, is higher than the overall proportion of galaxies in which B's truth varies with A's. (A similar translation could be given for type 1 cases.)

Application of Condition C determines when knowledge claims based on causal chains are justified or defeated. In cases of genuine knowledge of facts obtained through causal chains, its application shows why later links in the chains do not screen out earlier ones. When the later links are made more probable by the earlier ones, then knowledge extends back to the latter. When this relation fails to hold, however, there is a screening out of probabilities, and knowledge of the prior states of affairs fails. We have already seen one such case, that of the perceiver who sees only red. In contrast to the situation with ordinary perceivers, the fact that his sensory state makes more probable his belief that a red object is before him is not itself made more probable by that state's being caused (being made more probable) by the presence of a red object. Thus our new condition is violated in this case. Its function in positive and negative evaluations should become clearer in relation to more complex test cases for the analysis. I now turn to such cases.

2
TEST CASES

We may begin with the simplest cases and proceed to more complex ones that involve explanatory chains or dual sets of relevant probabilities. These complex cases parallel the case of causal preemption discussed in the previous chapter.

JUSTIFICATION

The first class of relevant cases involves knowledge on the part of the unsophisticated, who lack the philosophical and psychological insight to reconstruct their methods of knowing various kinds of facts. Certain analyses, for example those that require subjects to be able to justify their beliefs, are too strong in ruling out such cases. These accounts must violate ordinary language by inventing new epistemic categories, e.g., "proto-knowledge," to cover what we all count as knowledge of particular facts possessed by children and other epistemically naive subjects. In nonphilosophical moments we all grant that a young child knows all sorts of particular facts—that his room is on the second floor, that his dog is named Rocky, that he likes chocolate ice cream, and so on almost *ad infinitum*. There is no intuitive reason to deny that a child knows such things as well as and in the same way that we all do. I mention such trivialities only because some philosophical theories would have us deny the obvious here on the grounds that the child cannot justify his beliefs. While ordinary language intuitions are not sacrosanct, an analysis of a concept so untrue to our ordinary practice would have to show some inconsistency in that practice that warrants the departure. There is no inconsistency in our practice with regard to children.

Indeed I suspect that few adults would know where to begin to justify knowledge claims regarding the locations of their bedrooms and other such mundane matters. It is not required for an adult any more than for a child that he know how he knows or how to justify his claims in order to know various facts. To make this requirement reveals the philosopher's bias in favor of the intellectually sophisticated. Our being right in our psychological and epistemological theories is not a precondition of our knowing simpler matters. My analysis allows for such knowledge in the absence of *any* ability to reconstruct methods. Even those with some philosophical savvy may fail to satisfy the stronger requirement in some cases in which they have knowledge. My not having found any satisfactory theory about how we come to have mathematical knowledge or about the nature of mathematical truth (which explains the title of this book) and my not remembering anything about my learning of arithmetic do not preclude me from knowledge of that subject.

Granting that a requirement of showing justification is too strong, other accounts appeal to a distinction between being justified and being able to demonstrate justification, and they continue to require the former. But if being justified has to do in the majority of cases with the relation of a believer to his evidence (this seems to be part of the ordinary meaning, if there is an ordinary meaning in epistemic, as opposed to moral, contexts), then the demand is still too strong. We may bring this out by the perhaps unlikely example of a child psychic who picks the right horses in the next day's double every time. Such a sensational psychic soothsayer must eventually be said to know the winners in advance and to have known them all along, although no one knows exactly how he knows them. It is not simply that he knows the winners after a number of right guesses sufficient to justify him or us in believing what he predicts. There need be no difference in his method early and late in the series; if he knows, he knows from the beginning.

What might tempt some to draw a false distinction here is the fact that we know that he knows only after a sufficient number of right guesses. Only at a certain point, say after several hundred consecutive correct predictions, can coincidence be ruled out as an alternative to explanation by truth. Only at that point must we assume that whatever explains the child's belief also somehow explains why the predicted winners win. On my account, only then can we show that he knows, and in this case, given its bizarre character, only then would we come to believe that he knows (if, as responsible epistemic subjects, we try to withhold belief until we have adequate evidence to justify us in believing) and hence come to know that he knows. But the child's knowledge does not await our second-level, reflective knowledge of his knowledge. The best explanation for his beliefs from the beginning involves their being true, although we do not know this explanation to be best from the beginning. (I argued earlier that an explanation need not be known to be best in order to be so.) In general, believers whose beliefs connect to facts in the proper way but who do not know that their beliefs are so connected are not justified (in the ordinary sense) in their beliefs, which nevertheless qualify as knowledge.

The epistemic notion of justification derives from ethics and must retain its normative force if the term is to remain univocal. We may distinguish stronger and weaker normative senses in epistemology. In the weaker sense, if a person is unjustified in holding a belief, then he ought to give it up. The stronger sense demands more than the "right" to have a certain belief: if a subject is justified in holding or has justification for a belief, she must be capable of meeting challenges to it in a rational way. Thus justification in this sense carries an obligation as well as a right (although the obligation is not to form the belief, which may be beyond voluntary control).

Justification in this stronger sense is not required for knowledge. If a subject is to be capable of meeting challenges, he must be able to appeal to inferential relations to other beliefs within his doxastic system. This system must itself consist of justified beliefs accessible on demand. Such accessibility is implausible in many cases, and still not sufficient for complete justification. The subject must also recognize the connection between these inferential relations and a high probability of truth within the system. He must further be able to justify whatever criterion of truth he uses to identify this connection. In other words, he must be a rather skilled epistemologist.

To avoid making epistemological skill a requirement for

knowledge, many epistemologists would want to press again the distinction between being justified and showing justification. I accept this distinction in the sense that a subject who has justification for his beliefs need only be capable of meeting challenges. But if the concept of justification is to retain its connection as an evaluative term with general normative theory, then in epistemology it must refer to the obligations of truth seekers in relation to available evidence. And complete justification must require them to be able to establish the likely truth of their beliefs vis-à-vis such evidence. If one instead calls a relation external to the subject 'justification' simply in virtue of its being proposed as a (third) condition for knowledge, then one loses this normative force, which typically defines the concept. The only remaining moves for those who hold justification to be necessary for knowledge are to appeal to "accessibility in principle" of belief systems or to think of ordinary knowledge as an approximation to some higher ideal that alone deserves the title. Neither of these moves is well motivated. If entire belief systems are not accessible, then it is unclear what it can mean to call them accessible in principle. If ordinary knowledge does not include ordinary justification, it is nevertheless our primary interest. We want to know whether beliefs are true and properly connected to their objects.

The position of the epistemologist, however, differs from that of other knowers. While others can have knowledge without being justified in their beliefs, epistemologists, in showing what knowledge people have, will be demonstrating the justification for beliefs. The use of the principle of inference to the best explanation illustrates this difference. Anyone has knowledge when one's beliefs are explained by their truth, whether or not one has independent evidence for their truth. The epistemologist, however, must demonstrate the structure of knowledge. In so doing she uses the principle to establish the foundations and to extend the structure to explanatorily deeper levels. In this context the principle exhibits our evidence and sanctions inferences from it: if p is accepted or established, and q best explains p, then p is evidence for q. Finally, the normative epistemologist must justify the use of such epistemic principles themselves by showing them to be generally truth preserving. (As should be obvious, if these are ultimate principles, such justification must be in some sense circular, or else be nonepistemic, and hence irrelevant.)

I said above that the long tradition of including a requirement of justification in analyses of knowledge as the extra ingredient to be added to true belief, borrowing the concept from its proper home on the normative level, reveals the bias of the philosopher in favor of the epistemically sophisticated subject. This bias may be explained by the natural confusions of the epistemologist between her obligation to show justification for belief and the obligations of an ordinary knower, and between having knowledge and finding the best methods of obtaining it, another of her concerns. The tradition was so well entrenched in discussions of knowledge that even when Gettier refuted the standard analysis, most philosophers retained the basic recipe of adding subjective justification to true belief to produce knowledge. They simply began to include new and more exotic ingredients along with the old. Some who did move to other criteria, such as the reliability of the source of the belief, still paid lip service to the tradition by referring to their new requirements as 'justifications', although it now had nothing to do with the subject's epistemic responsibility. One moral of Gettier's examples and of the ones I have cited in this section is that subjective justification is indeed irrelevant to having knowledge, as the proposed analysis implies.

GETTIER CASES

I have been referring, as all contemporary students of the concept of knowledge must, to an article by Edmund Gettier.[1] By showing that a person could be justified in inferring a true belief from a false but justified belief as a premise, he showed that the standard analysis of knowledge as justified true belief is faulty. The analysis I am proposing handles the usual Gettier cases, whether or not they involve reasoning explicitly from false premises. If, for example, I am justified in believing that *Smith owns a Ford or Jones is in Barcelona* because I am justified in believing the first disjunct, when only the second disjunct is true, then it is clear that the fact that makes my belief true does not explain and has not raised the probability of my so believing. I will not review further Gettier examples of this type. Others have pointed out that in each case it is only accidental that the believer is right. This lack of connection between belief and truth is what defeats the claim to knowledge in these cases. In general, satisfaction of the truth requirement of the analysis is external to the believer: it is the world, not his subjective condition, that makes his belief true. The state of affairs that makes the belief true must be connected to it for the belief to qualify as knowledge; but subjective justification does not forge the required connection, as Gettier cases show.

My analysis makes explicit the sense in which it must be nonaccidental that the knower is right in his belief. There must be a nonaccidental probabilistic connection between the belief and the fact that makes it true, one that holds across close possible worlds. In the case of empirical beliefs about particular matters of fact, the connection, if sufficient for knowledge, will be causal, although not all such causal connections are sufficient for knowledge, and knowledge of other kinds of facts requires other kinds of connections. But if there is no genuine connection, causal or otherwise, between the belief and the fact in question, then other factors in the properly described relevant field will fully account for the probability of the belief's being held, and the fact will not have raised that probability. (The only other relevant factor is the decision, if any, of the subject.)

Next in order of increasing complexity are examples involving the ability to discriminate truth from falsity in contexts of belief. Consider cases of perceiving a barn in an area in which barn facsimiles (cardboard structures that look like barns) abound, and of perceiving friend Judy without knowing about her identical twin, Trudy.[2] If the perceiver comes to believe he sees a barn in the first context and his friend in the second, he may have Gettier-type true beliefs that fail to qualify as knowledge. As the author of these examples points out, the beliefs fail to qualify as knowledge when the subject lacks the ability to discriminate truth from falsity in the context. Such cases again defeat the causal analysis of knowing, according to which a causal connection of belief to fact believed is necessary and sufficient for knowledge, since here the normal causal-perceptual relations between perceiver and objects obtain despite the lack of knowledge. It is most interesting to note that, while barn facsimiles in the immediate vicinity defeat knowledge claims regarding barns, facsimiles in far distant areas and merely possible facsimiles appear to be irrelevant. Just when do such indiscriminable possibilities defeat claims to knowledge?

Our analysis implies an account of the relevant variables in such evaluations. According to it the crucial question is whether the fact that the barn or Judy is perceived significantly raises the probability of the perceiver's believing there to be a barn or Judy there. If barn facsimiles or Trudy are in the immediate vicinity, then the probability is high that the same belief will be acquired in the absence of the fact believed, which therefore does not significantly raise the probability of the belief's being held. In terms of the possible worlds model, there will be more close possible worlds in which the belief is caused by facsimiles than close worlds in which it is caused by real barns, and the percentage of close worlds in which the belief correlates with a barn will be no higher than the overall percentage of worlds in which there is such a belief. In such cases, as in the earlier example of the historian, the proper explanation for the belief appeals to the broader context of the perceiver's being in the vicinity of all these look-alike objects, any of which would produce the belief in question. But if the perceiver is in Miami, the facsimiles are in Sweden, and Trudy is in California, then the relevant facts do explain the beliefs, since they alone among the external conditions render them highly predictable. The possible worlds in which the beliefs are caused by facsimiles are in this case distant.

The reader may object that reference classes are being chosen here simply to match our intuitions regarding knowledge. My point is rather that our intuitions match my account under choices of reference classes that the intuitions suggest or determine. Such dependence is legitimate rather than vicious in conceptual analysis. As long as the reference classes themselves are intuitive, the notion of explanation in question can be seen to underlie our evaluations of claims to knowledge.

HARDER CASES

We may turn to beliefs that exemplify more complex explanatory chains by studying possible counterexamples to the analysis
and how they might be handled. Consider the following purported counterexample to an explanatory account of justification.[3] If genuine, the counterexample would count against the
proposed analysis of knowledge. In this example I know that a
mouse is three feet from a four-foot flagpole with an owl on
top, and I deduce that the mouse is five feet from the owl. I
then know this fact, although I have no explanation for the
mouse's being five feet from the owl (I have no idea why he has
stationed himself there) and the fact does not explain my belief
(my use of the Pythagorean theorem and my beliefs about the
other distances explain this belief). We seem here to have a case
of knowledge in which the belief is not explained by the fact
that makes it true, showing the analysis to be too strong. Appeal
to explanatory chains, however, allows us to assimilate this case
to others within the scope of the account. The theorem of geometry is the common element in the relevant chains here.
First, the truth of that theorem explains why, *given that the mouse
is three feet from a four-foot pole*, it is five feet from the top, although it does not explain that fact *simpliciter*. Someone who
accepts the other two measurements but does not know why,
given them, the mouse is five feet from the owl, has only to be
informed of the theorem of geometry. Second, the truth of the
theorem helps to explain why mathematicians believe it to be
true,[4] which ultimately explains my belief in it. My belief in the
theorem in turn helps to explain my belief about the distance of
the mouse from the owl. Thus what helps to explain my belief
in the fact in question also helps to explain that fact, given the
appropriate background conditions, which include the other
distances. The case fits our account.

Consider another example of this type that again might be
taken to indicate that the analysis is too strong, excluding cases
of genuine knowledge.[5] In this example I know that comet B
always follows comet A by five years. Observing comet A, I then
come to know that comet B will appear in five years. Again
explanatory relations may be obscure. The future appearance

of B does not directly explain my belief, and what does explain it, the appearance of comet A and my belief in the generalization, does not explain the future fact of B's appearance. Our paradigm model for knowledge of the future, in which what explains my belief also explains the coming to be of the future fact, appears not to fit. Yet here too there is an explanatory link between my belief and the future fact in question. The universal proposition about the time interval between the appearances of the comets, or the laws of motion and the initial conditions that make that proposition true, explain why, *given that A has appeared,* B will follow on the predicted date. The proposition that the comets always appear five years apart also explains the past observations of the time interval that ultimately explain my belief in that proposition. The latter in turn explains my knowledge of comet B's future appearance, given my observation of comet A. Thus once more what helps to explain my belief, here the truth of the universal proposition, also helps to explain the fact believed, given the relevant background conditions. Only by ignoring the latter conditions, including the appearance of the first comet, do we fail to locate the explanatory link.

The previous two examples attempt to show that the explanatory analysis is too strong. We might also consider some that purport to reveal it as too weak, as admitting unacceptable knowledge claims.[6] Consider first a case in which ingestion of a poison causes brain damage, which in turn causes the victim to believe he has been poisoned. Suppose that his belief is based on no reason but results from his insanity alone. We do not acknowledge knowledge on his part, although the poison appears to explain, via the causal chain, his belief that he has been poisoned. If the fact believed explains the belief without there being knowledge, then our analysis is defeated.

We might think that the victim here lacks knowledge because he has no good reasons for his belief. But I rejected above the idea that a believer must have sound reasons for his belief in order to know, and the many examples of naive knowers continue to persuade me to remain true to this feature of our ordinary concept of knowledge. What convinces us in this case that the victim does not know he has been poisoned is not simply his lack of reasons (for the child psychic also lacked reasons) but the fact that the brain state's explaining his belief seems completely independent of its being caused by poison. While the poison accounts for the pathological condition and the latter for the belief, the first connection is unrelated to the second. The same pathological condition would cause the same belief whether or not it were caused by poison: its being caused by poison does not make it more probable that it will cause the belief (the lack of reasons enters indirectly here). The case therefore violates our Condition C and fails to qualify as knowledge.

Consider next along the same lines the case of a totally gullible person's being informed of the same fact. Normally total gullibility would defeat a knowledge claim, since falsity would be as readily believed as truth. The truth of a gullible person's beliefs does not explain their being held for the same reason that the redness of an object does not explain the belief that it is red in a subject who believes objects of all colors to be red. But now add to this example the fact that the informer is totally honest and would not have communicated his belief unless he knew it to be true. Then again we appear to have a chain in which the truth of the gullible person's belief enters into its ultimate explanation, having raised the probability of its being held. Once more our account seems to have admitted an illegitimate claim as knowledge.

But the question again is whether explanation in this case is transitive, as it must be for the entire explanatory chain to be relevant. Here, that the fact in question obtains helps to explain its being communicated, but its communication in itself explains the final belief. The truth of the belief in this case again becomes merely part of the background conditions rather than part of the explanation proper. The reason why this fact remains in the background rather than becoming prominent in the explanation itself relates again to Condition C. The belief is made no more probable by the fact that the communication was made more probable by its being true. At the later stages in the causal chain the truth of the belief does not contribute to the probability of its being held and becomes irrelevant to its explanation. For this reason gullibility defeats knowledge as usual. This example can then be handled in the same way as the poison case. It resembles as well the case of the perceiver who sees only red and is presented with a red object. In fact we can make these cases exactly parallel if we think of the perceiver entering the room of a person who decorates rooms with only red objects. This addition to the examples does not change the status of his beliefs, nor does it change their proper explanations. In this new situation as well the perceiver's condition alone accounts for his beliefs about the color of the objects in the room, despite the fact that he would not be perceiving them if they were not red.

Finally, these cases resemble another in the literature that might be proposed as a counterexample to my account. It was offered to refute the idea that the problem in Gettier-type situations lies in the fact that the believer is only accidentally right in his belief.[7] I accepted that interpretation of Gettier examples and pointed out that the explanatory analysis implies it. The case in point involves a philosophical trick in which a perceptual context is created to cause a subject to have justified true belief without perceptual knowledge. Imagine, for example, a setup with candles and a mirror, in which the perceiver sees a mirror image of a candle and so acquires the perceptual belief that there is a candle before him, when a second candle is behind the mirror and thus before the perceiver, although hidden from him. His belief fails to qualify as knowledge, even though it appears to be nonaccidental that he is right, given the deliberate way in which the trick situation is constructed.

Despite this appearance, explanation for this belief again fails to reach the truth of the belief. While the deceiver sets up the situation so as to create a true belief, his intent to deceive is what explains his setting up the apparatus. The fact that a candle is before the perceiver, which makes his belief true, does not make more probable the action of the deceiver or the apparatus that results, the seeing of which explains the perceiver's belief. One might claim that a different chain here satisfies our criterion, in that the intent and subsequent action of the deceiver might be taken to explain both the fact of a candle's being before the perceiver and his belief that there is a candle there. But the intent of the deceiver explains the perceiver's belief through explaining only that part of the apparatus that causes the belief, which does not include the candle that makes the

belief true. That the action of the deceiver increases the probability of the perceiver's belief is not made more probable by its
increasing the probability of the truth of the belief. Condition C
is therefore violated. The link between the belief and its truth is
not strong enough, and in this sense it remains accidental that
the belief is true.

We may contrast these cases with another that resembles
them except for a difference in respect to knowledge. Consider
a historian who believes some historical fact on the basis of
present evidence. Let us say that the evidence is correct but is
such that it would have produced his belief even if it were in
fact misleading or not causally connected to the fact believed. If
we assume that the historian is a good one, that he bases his
beliefs only on reliable evidence, then the counterfactual need
not defeat his knowledge claim. The key variable is the probability that the evidence would have derived from some other
source while he continued to believe it. If that probability is low
enough, his knowledge remains intact. In that case Condition C
is met, since his believing on the basis of the evidence is made
more probable by the fact that the evidence is made more probable by the historical fact. More simply (but somewhat too
strongly), the historian would not believe as he does if the evidence were not evidence for the truth of his belief. In the case
of the gullible believer, on the other hand, the information
would have been believed whether or not it was (probabilistically) linked to the fact in question.

The same kinds of connections among links in explanatory
chains hold in ordinary perceptual situations (but not in Gettier-
type perceptual situations). Consider my present belief that
there is a typewriter before me, which belief is based on the
causal chain from the object through my perceptual system. We
might wonder[8] why the retinal image, for example, does not
screen out the typewriter in the explanation for my belief, given
that the probability of my believing can be determined by appeal
to the retinal image alone and that it occupies a place later in the
causal chain. The answer is that explanation is transitive here,
since Condition C is once more satisfied. That the retinal image
makes my belief more probable can itself be explained by the fact
that the retinal image is much more probable given the type-

writer. (This second-order connection among probabilities can itself be explained on a third level by appeal to the evolution of human visual systems. Beliefs based causally on retinal images presumably have been selected because of the connections between retinal images and the objects of those beliefs.)

To conclude this section I shall mention a class of cases that I take to indicate again the looseness in our concepts of knowledge and explanation. These cases involve belief in the context of evidence one does not possess. Suppose I read an accurate news report of an assassination, when all other local reports are censored and therefore deny the success of the assassination attempt.[9] Do I know of the assassination? I am not sure without additional information. Is my belief explained by my having read the accurate report, and is the report explained by the reporter's having witnessed the event; or is my belief explained by my not having read the other reports, and the accurate report explained by its having slipped past the censors? Again the key variables involve probabilities: the probability that I would have read the other reports and the probability of this report's slipping by the censor. If the first is high and the second low, then my knowledge claim is suspect. But its acceptance will depend also on the context in which it is put forth and on how demanding we choose to be in that context. The initial definition of the case thus leaves us uncertain, and our lack of firm intuition regarding knowledge here again supports the proposed analysis in terms of probabilities, themselves doubly uncertain in this context.

3

OTHER ANALYSES

CAUSAL AND RELIABILITY ACCOUNTS

Criticisms of certain earlier analyses of knowledge were scattered in the previous chapters. We have seen that the present account captures the causal analysis as a special case: it applies when we explain a belief by appealing to the fact to which the belief refers (or to the event contained in or corresponding to the fact) as its cause. We also saw that sometimes the particular cause of a belief does not satisfactorily explain its being held, that we must sometimes appeal to the broader context in which the cause operated. This shows the causal analysis to be too weak in allowing knowledge where none exists but where the usual causal relations between subject and object obtain. It is obvious too that the causal analysis does not fit intuitions in other areas for which our broader analysis is required, for example, knowledge of universal propositions and of logical or mathematical truths. In excluding these types of knowledge, the causal analysis is too strong.

This book does not directly concern knowledge of logic or mathematics; its normative account will be limited to empirical knowledge. But a conceptual analysis of knowledge should be adaptable to all kinds, revealing what is common among them. Our account can be adapted with slight modifications to non-empirical knowledge. In the case of mathematics, there is normally no direct explanatory link between what makes a mathematical proposition true (we need not be concerned here with the question what that is) and belief in it. What normally explains a mathematician's belief in a theorem is his having found or been exposed to some proof. It would also appear strange to say that the truth of the theorem explains, or even that it helps to explain, its proof. But I believe we can say that what makes a mathematical proposition true helps to explain the possibility of a proof for it. If a mathematical proposition is true, then we should expect a proof to be possible. (I ignore here problems raised by incompleteness.) Thus the explanatory (but not causal) link is established, only with a different modality (as we might expect) from the case of empirical knowledge. The possibility of that which ultimately explains knowledge of the necessary truth is explained by the truth of the proposition believed.

Thus, to return to our proper topic, causal analyses prove to be both too weak and too strong, defects corrected by the explanatory account. Both charges can be leveled also at various reliability accounts, according to which knowledge is true belief based on a reliable source. Here, as in our account, there is an attempt to substitute an objective criterion (the requirement that the source of the belief generally lead to true beliefs) for the notion of subjective justification offered by the standard analysis. Here too the requirement is broader than the demand for strictly causal relations between beliefs and their objects. Nevertheless, reliability accounts are too weak if the reliability of sources in their general operation is interpreted straightforwardly in terms of probability and probabilities of less than one are allowed. This becomes clear in lottery examples. We can make the reliability of the inductive source of my belief that my ticket will not win a lottery as close to one as we like by increasing the number of tickets. Yet no matter how high the number, I still do not know it will not win.[1] Compare this case with that in which expectant parents know on the basis of a chromosome reading that their child will be a boy. Why this difference, when the amniocentesis may be slightly less reliable than my inductive inference in a large lottery? The answer lies in the direct explanatory link between belief and truth in the case of the parents: the best explanation for the chromosome reading is the male sex of the fetus.

The use of probability in interpreting the general reliability of sources is very different from its use in my analysis. If we evaluate the lottery case according to the latter, we find that our judgment of the claim to knowledge is negative. Neither the future fact that my ticket will not win nor what explains it, the fact that another ticket is drawn at the later time, explains my belief that I will not win. Neither fact raises the antecedent probability of my holding this belief, which is explained rather by my knowledge of the number of tickets and my ability to infer inductively on that basis. While raising the number of tickets raises the probability of my not winning, the number of tickets normally is a background condition for the best explanation of my not winning, the explanation itself appealing to the drawing of another ticket. Thus there is no explanatory chain linking belief to fact believed, and our analysis excludes knowledge as it should, in contrast to the weaker reliability account.

That account is too weak because it validates knowledge claims when the beliefs in question remain unconnected to the facts they specify. Its failure to require an actual connection leaves it open to Gettier-type cases, despite the substitution of a requirement of objective reliability for subjective justification. Nor can we demand perfect reliability from the source in its general operation, for that demand would disallow all knowledge of objects gained from perception or inductive reference.

We must therefore think of the sources of belief only as they operate in particular contexts. This is clear from other examples as well. Suppose that I am not good at identifying barns (I cannot differentiate them from other structures), but I am good at identifying *red* barns. Then on a given occasion I can know that there is a barn in a field by knowing that there is a red barn there. A source of belief is reliable in context *iff* it produces true beliefs all or most of the time in such contexts. Given the source of a belief in a particular situation, facts of the same type as that to which the belief refers must tend to obtain. Properly elaborated, this requirement singles out a particular kind of (indirect) connection between fact and belief that turns out to be an instance of our more general explanatory relation. That is, this most plausible way of spelling out the notion of reliability turns out to instantiate one type of permissible explanatory chain, in which the source of belief explains both the belief and the fact to which it refers (or it is explained by that fact). The reliability of a source is important only because it connects the believer in the right way to the fact believed. Why not focus on this connection directly?

According to a second version of the reliability account, it is not the source of the belief but the belief itself that must be a reliable indicator (though not necessarily a sufficient condition) of the fact to which it refers.[2] Once more a straightforward interpretation in terms of probability is out of place. We cannot require that the belief raise the antecedent probability of the fact to which it refers, since on any reasonable interpretation of that notion the probability normally will be fully determined by other factors. Although the straightforward interpretation has the relation between belief and independent fact backward, we can say that the belief is evidence for the fact it specifies when a person has knowledge. I mentioned early in this part (p. 41) that if p is accepted and q best explains p, then p is evidence for q. Thus when a person knows, his belief is evidence for the fact that explains it. To say this is not to endorse a coherence theory of truth, which holds that beliefs normally provide in themselves evidence for their truth. On our account we must first know that a belief is best explained by its truth—that the person knows—before we can count the belief as evidence for the fact to which it refers. (In some cases we may have independent reasons to believe that this connection exists, for example, when the believers are experts.) Thus the evidential relation from belief to fact is not normally usable as such. In the usual sense of 'evidence', the term refers to accessible data from which we may infer to the less accessible. But the broader sense of 'evidence' applicable here does serve to assimilate the second notion of reliability to the explanatory account.

DEFEASIBILITY ACCOUNTS

Another major trend in the post-Gettier literature involves the addition to the standard analysis of fourth conditions that specify when justified true beliefs are defeated by counterevidence. The most obvious advantage of the present proposal over such analyses lies not in its scope but in its utility as a practicable criterion of knowledge. At this point we may begin to compare the value of the meta-accounts for the normative level of epistemology. Defeasibility analyses view knowledge as justified true belief that is not defeated by counterevidence. But not all counterevidence defeats; some is simply misleading, irrelevant, and therefore to be disregarded. For instance, in our second assassination example we saw that the false news reports, though always counterevidence to the success of the attempt, only sometimes defeat the claim to knowledge of the person who reads the true report. According to the most prominent of the defeasibility accounts,[3] in order to separate counterevidence that defeats from that which is both misleading and irrelevant, we must appeal to what the believer would believe, or would be justified in believing, if he were ideally situated or believed only truths. The question is whether such an ideal epistemic subject would continue to be justified in believing as the subject whose claim is being evaluated believes. If the answer is yes, then the real subject has knowledge; if no, then his knowledge claim is defeated. This type of fourth condition derives also from the recognition that victims in Gettier-type situations often rely in some sense on false presuppositions. While subjectively justified in their beliefs given their situations, they would neither believe as they do nor be justified in so believing if they were better situated epistemically or believed all or only truths. The person who believes that Smith owns a Ford or Jones is in Barcelona on the basis of believing the first disjunct when only the second is true would not be justified in believing as he does if his false beliefs were corrected.

The first problem for accounts that require indefeasible justification is that this notion implies that of justification (*simpliciter*), and in my view that is already too strong. In further evaluating such accounts, consider the following pair of cases, offshoots of the second assassination example. In the first I know, by having the usual kind of evidence, that Smith, who works in my office, owns a Ford. Unknown to me, Smith has an enemy in a distant city who might deceive me, if I met him, into believing that Smith stole his car. The second case is similar, except that Smith's enemy is also in my office and has deceived everyone else there but me into believing that Smith is a notorious car thief.

According to my analysis, I have knowledge in the first of these cases but not in the second. The fact that I would no longer believe as I do now in that distant possible world in which I meet the enemy of the first case is irrelevant to my knowledge claim, which must be evaluated only across close possible worlds. In the second case, the connection between fact and belief is broken in close worlds, and I therefore lack knowledge. The defeasibility account would evaluate both cases in the same way—either both would be or both would fail to be cases of knowledge—but which alternative it would imply would depend on its interpretation and on other facts that I take to be irrelevant. On the first interpretation, we allow the subject omniscience or belief in all true propositions in the counterfactual situation. That criterion would have us confidently grant me knowledge in both cases, since I would know not only of the existence of the enemy but of his duplicity. This approach entails, however, that no one's knowledge claims can be defeated by misleading evidence he does not possess (since the ideally situated epistemic counterpart will possess all evidence). This implication is implausible, especially in cases in which the person should have known of the evidence but would have no way of knowing that it is misleading.

If we use a second interpretation of the defeasibility account to analyze this example and, in judging my knowledge claim, correct only whatever original false beliefs I held, if any, then we derive opposing evaluations depending on whether I have actually formed beliefs that there are not conflicting reports. If I have formed such (false) beliefs, then I do not know that Smith owns the Ford, since I would not be justified in continuing to believe so once I believed the negations of these beliefs. But if it has never occurred to me to form such beliefs, then my knowledge is intact. We cannot correct beliefs not actually held on this interpretation; hence justification and knowledge remain intact in the absence of formulated false beliefs. This is again implausible. How can a person's failure to think about the situation in these ways save his knowledge?

Consider finally the following example. Suppose that I have (misleading) evidence that Smith owns the Ford he drove to work this morning, but I am very cautious. I therefore believe the disjunction: either Smith owns a Ford or he does not own the car he drove to work this morning. The real situation is that Smith rented the Ford he was driving but that, unknown to him (or me), he has won that very car in the rental company's annual lucky giveaway lottery.[4] Here I do not know the disjunction to be true, since I know neither disjunct (and there is a close world in which he has won a different Ford). Yet it seems that any available defeater of my belief in the first disjunct would justify me in believing the second, and conversely. Thus I would continue to believe truly and be justified in believing when seeming defeaters are added. The true propositions of which I am unaware would not prevent me from being justified in believing (truly) the disjunction, and yet I do not know it. The only defeasibility analysis that could handle such cases would be Keith Lehrer's latest version, in which we correct beliefs in distinct stages, first eliminating the false ones and then substituting true ones for them. The first step might rule out the knowledge claim in this case. But, aside from its complexity and ad hoc quality, this analysis still falls prey to cases involving misleading evidence about which the subject has no beliefs, as in the previous example.[5]

COUNTERFACTUAL ACCOUNTS

We may now return, in closing this critical section, to more direct counterfactual analyses suggested by Fred Dretske and Alvin Goldman and recently developed in most detail by Robert Nozick.[6] According to Nozick, S's belief that p counts as knowledge when the following counterfactuals hold: if p were not true, then S would not believe it; and if p were true (in nonactual close worlds), then S would believe it. When these conditions hold, S is said to *track* the fact that p. This relation need not obtain over all possible worlds, only over the closest worlds in which the antecedents are true.

Nozick adjusts this analysis to accommodate the example of a grandmother who sees her grandson and therefore knows he is well, but who would be deceived by other relatives as to the grandson's health were he sick. Here she knows that her grandson is well even though she would not believe him to be sick if he were. Because this counterfactual violates the first condition of Nozick's analysis, he amends the condition to require that the source or method of knowing be held constant in the counterfactual situations: if the grandmother were to *see* her sick grandson, she would not believe him to be well. But our first assassination example shows that the first counterfactual criterion remains too strong even as amended. That the father who is playing golf with his son at the time of a distant assassination might somehow deny to himself that his son is guilty in that highly improbable world in which he witnesses him doing the deed does not destroy his knowledge in the real world. (Remember that we are to consider the closest world in which the antecedent of our counterfactual is true, even if that world is very distant.) Otherwise none of us could know that his or her loved ones are not guilty of crimes so horrendous that their perception would drive us to distraction or result in hysteria or insanity. Yet we do know this of our spouses and children. Nozick's amendment would fail even in his own grandmother example, if the sight of her sick grandson would cause her so much *tsuris* that she could not bring herself to believe him really sick.

An example of similar structure was suggested to me by Risto Hilpinen. I am looking at a thermometer that is accurate within the range of 0° to 100°F. At all temperatures below 0° the thermometer registers 0°. By observing its reading of 70° I come to believe that it is not −50°. I thereby know that it is not −50°, even though if it were, I would not believe it to be. We see that a measuring instrument that links an observer to facts within its range can produce knowledge when it helps to explain true beliefs in that range. (The visual system can be thought of as such an instrument in the assassination example.) If the closest world in which such a fact fails to obtain is distant, then the lack of tracking in that world is irrelevant to that knowledge claim. (If, however, the thermometer is registering a temperature close to its threshold of accuracy and is not always accurate around that point, then my beliefs based on it regarding values just outside its range will not qualify as knowledge. In such cases there are close worlds in which the link between fact and belief is broken.)

Thus Nozick's first tracking condition is too strong. In other cases it proves to be too weak, failing to disallow bogus claims to knowledge. Such is the case when the truth of propositions is counterfactually linked to beliefs, but only via (explanatory)

chains that are defective. Consider again a Gettier case inten-
tionally set up to deceive its subject. I have been tricked into
believing that someone in my office owns a Ford by Smith's
having given me evidence that Jones owns one, when Smith is
the owner. If my belief were not true, then Smith would not
have led me to hold it. Yet I do not know that someone in the
office owns a Ford, since the usual Gettier conditions obtain.
(My inferring it is not made more probable by its being true—
Condition C is violated.)

Nozick's second condition is also both too weak and too
strong. Imagine first a brain in a vat programmed to have visual
experiences of a vat surrounding it. In the closest worlds in
which the brain continues to believe on the basis of its visual
experience (in which its method of arriving at belief is held
constant), it continues to believe truly that there is a vat around
it. Yet it doesn't know this. Thus the second condition is too
weak. To see that it is also too strong, imagine an old logician
with failing mental capacities. He is still capable of deriving the
correct conclusion in a particular proof, hence of knowing it,
but there are close worlds in which he can no longer do so. He
has knowledge, but the second condition is violated. We see
again that a method which links a subject to facts within its
range need not always do so outside its range. (According to my
analysis, as long as there are sufficient close worlds in which fact
and belief are linked, knowledge is intact, despite some close
worlds in which the link is broken.)

Another, equally grave problem with the counterfactual
analysis is its implications for normative epistemology. It will be
useful in making the transition to the normative level to compare the analyses on this score. On Nozick's account we cannot
know that either pervasive or more local skeptical alternatives
to our beliefs do not in fact obtain. Consider the theses that our
everyday perceptual beliefs systematically err because we are
deceived by Descartes's demon, or the thesis that we are all
brains in vats being programmed to have the experiences we do
by superscientists. If these skeptical possibilities were real, we
would not believe they were. Hence we do not track the fact that
they are not real. The same holds for more local skeptical possibilities regarding other minds (that other people are mindless

automata), memory (that the universe came into existence five minutes ago exactly as we know it), and so on.

Having granted this sweeping concession to the skeptic, Nozick attempts to save our everyday knowledge from skeptical refutation by denying logical closure, even in cases of obvious implications known to hold. According to him, I can know that p, know that p implies q, and yet not know q, even where p and q are replaced by relatively simple sentences and I believe q on the basis of my knowledge of the implication. I can therefore know various propositions to be true without knowing the skeptic's alternatives to be false, even though the truth of the former implies the falsity of the latter. In fact on his account I do know the former without knowing the latter, because I track the former but not the latter. I can track the truth of various propositions without tracking the denial of the skeptical theses because the skeptic's worlds are not the closest in which the everyday propositions I believe are false. If they were false, I would not believe them, although in the skeptic's possible worlds they are false and I do believe them. If my pipe were not in my mouth, for example, I would not believe it to be (since it would be on my desk and I would believe that); although if a demon tricked me into thinking I were smoking when I am not, I would believe as I do.

I see two major problems with this position regarding the scope of our knowledge, the most plausible position that Nozick can achieve given the strong criteria of the counterfactual analysis. The first problem relates again to specific knowledge claims allowed and disallowed when tracking is required and closure denied. According to Nozick, I cannot know, for example, that my son is not a brilliantly constructed robot, although I can know that I do not have a brilliantly constructed robot son. The distinction is epistemically crucial according to his account, since in the closest world in which my son is such a robot, I would not believe he is, while in the closest world in which I have a robot son, I would know I have one. I believe that our initial reaction of rejecting any thesis that implies such apparently incompatible evaluations is correct. According to the explanatory account, I certainly know that both propositions concerning my son are true, since in both cases the explanation for my beliefs that appeals to some enormously complex deception is far less plausible than that which appeals to the truth of the beliefs or to what makes them true (that my son is human). The former explanation leaves many more questions unanswered and many more speculations unsupported and unexplainable. As we intuitively should expect, there is little difference in this regard in the strength of the two claims to knowledge. I know just as well that my son is not a robot as that I do not have a robot son. Only a philosopher would think otherwise.

The second problem with the normative position implied by Nozick's analysis concerns the more general debate with the skeptic. Nozick saves the mere possibility of common knowledge by simply stating that the skeptic's worlds are not closest to the actual world. This premise is essential to his argument, since it is the basis for his claim that we would not hold particular perceptual and memory beliefs if they were false (they would not be false because the skeptic's alternatives were true, but for more accessible reasons). But how can we know that skeptical alternatives do not constitute close possible worlds, when we cannot know that they are not themselves actual? Nozick's account implies that I cannot know the latter, yet his argument against the skeptic (if intended as such) seems to assume that I do know it. At best, given across-the-board nonclosure under implication, he can show that common knowledge is possible in the face of skeptical challenge. He cannot show that it is real. He can offer no argument to this epistemically crucial conclusion, since the possibility of knowledge depends on the distance of the skeptic's alternative worlds, a measurement we are in no position to make if we accept Nozick's analysis. My answer to the skeptic also depends upon his world's being distant, but on my account we can know this on the basis of an inference to the best explanation.

It might be thought that Nozick can do better against the skeptic by moving from claims about knowledge to considerations of rational belief and evidence.[7] He in fact points out that there are asymmetries between the evidence for the existence of the real world and evidence for the existence of the skeptic's worlds.[8] There is evidence for the real world, since, if there were no such world, our experience would not be what it is; but there is no evidence for the skeptic's worlds, since, if they did not exist, our experience would be exactly as it is. Our experience as evidence tracks the hypothesis that there is a material world, but it does not track the skeptical alternatives. Thus, if rational belief is to be based on the evidence, it might appear more rational to believe in the real world than in the skeptical alternatives. This outcome might suffice to grant the victory to the nonskeptical epistemologist in his debate with the skeptic.

The problem here, however, is that the evidential relation is defined by Nozick in counterfactual terms similar to those in the analysis of knowledge. E is (strong) evidence for *h* if it tracks *h*. According to Nozick, our experience tracks the real world but not the skeptic's worlds. But since the evidential relation is as external to our point of view as the knowledge relation itself, we again have no way of knowing this. We have access to the supposed evidence but not to the evidential relation. In the end the latter must simply be stipulated or assumed to obtain. Thus we are left again with only the possibility of knowledge, not with anything approximating to its demonstration.

Nozick may respond that refutation of the skeptic is not among his purposes or that it is indeed impossible. For him the lure of the skeptic's arguments seems to lie in this very impossibility of refutation. But there is an alternative explanation of the skeptic's persistence, one that will satisfy the true believer more. This explanation points to the link between skepticism and the tendency to make the conditions for knowledge too strong, a link with a strong tradition in epistemology. The stronger the analysis of knowledge (and of evidence), the easier the skeptic's task. We saw above that Nozick's analysis appears too strong to capture our concept of knowledge as reflected in convictions regarding particular cases. It therefore may well fit the tradition that renders skepticism more plausible and immune to refutation than it need be.

One final ground of comparison may distinguish the counterfactual from our explanatory analysis of knowledge. In explaining the significance of knowledge for knowing subjects, Nozick argues that evolution or natural selection could be expected to result in subjects not simply with true beliefs but with sensitivity of beliefs to (changing) facts.[9] He takes this sensitivity to consist in the ability to track facts. Thus he takes evolutionary theory to support his analysis, which helps to show how the ability to know is an important achievement for the species as well as for the individual. Knowledge as tracking is the type of cognitive state that might be selected (or rather the ability to achieve such states might be selected). An analysis of knowledge should suggest why individuals and species benefit from its acquisition, and Nozick claims that his account satisfies this desideratum.

But in fact tracking is not quite the relation we would expect between believer and fact as the result of natural selection. We would not expect or require this relation to propositions that are false only in distant possible worlds. The ability to survive is not enhanced by sensitivity to counterfactual occurrences in those worlds. In fact, as we can see from several earlier examples, sensitivity to such distant counterfactual situations might distract us from knowledge in the real world. Facts must be (probabilistically) connected with beliefs across close possible worlds, however, and not simply in the actual world. We must be sensitive to likely changes in empirical conditions that might falsify our beliefs in close possible worlds, i.e., those that might well become actual. From this theoretical viewpoint too we require a connection weaker than Nozick's tracking, which takes us to distant worlds in many cases.

The explanatory analysis requires a probabilistic connection across close possible worlds, the type of connection that we could expect to have been selected. Similar considerations will be applied later on the normative level. We may now make the transition to that reconstruction.

TOWARD A NORMATIVE RECONSTRUCTION

I have contrasted the proposed analysis of knowledge with others not only in regard to specific intuitions captured but also in regard to more general normative implications, especially concerning skeptical challenges. The former condition of a successful analysis is the more obvious, but the latter determines its usefulness. While I agree with many recent epistemologists that the refutation of skepticism is not their sole or primary task, I would not dismiss the importance of this task or the seriousness of the problem for an analysis of knowledge that by implication grants the skeptic too easy a victory or a draw. As noted in the first chapter, acceptance of the realist's view of the objects of knowledge involves recognition of the genuineness of skeptical doubts. In my view the best answer to the skeptic is one that takes his doubts seriously without succumbing to them, one that seeks inductive validation for our claims to knowledge of independent reality. A priori refutations, those that posit conceptual or necessary connections between our experiential criteria and the objective facts for which they are evidence, must relinquish the realist view of the world that I shall argue most deeply explains the observational beliefs with which we begin.

In constructing the best inductive answer we can supply to skeptical doubts, we begin to reveal the structure and scope of our empirical knowledge and the rationale for its development, which in turn enables us to view more critically our methods of extending it. An analysis of knowledge is helpful in this context if it suggests a coherent account of the structure of knowledge as we seek to develop it. In my view the rationale for that development in the empirical realm lies mainly in our quest for explanations, as grounded in the requirement of fidelity to the phenomena as they appear. The model of knowledge as belief best explained by truth best coheres with this rationale. Knowledge is extended according to this model when we seek to extend explanations for an initial class of beliefs to deeper levels. We seek to explain these beliefs, then to explain what explains them, and so on.

Our analysis leads smoothly into our normative reconstruction because of the way it builds the principle of inference to the best explanation into the structure of knowledge. We said that when a belief is best explained by its truth, the belief is evidence for the fact that makes it true. If p is made more probable by q and p has been established or deemed acceptable, then p is evidence for q. We also said, in the first section of this chapter, that normally we must first know that a belief is true or type of belief generally true (and best explained by its truth) before we can know that the belief or type of belief is evidence for its truth. But there is one class of beliefs which we establish as true and at the same time as knowledge. These beliefs are evidence for their own truth because they are explained by their own truth alone. For them, truth can be established on no other basis than that the beliefs are held. Such beliefs are the only evidence, and the only evidence required, for their own truth. To say that they are explained by their truth alone is to say that they are self-explanatory. At this level the meta-account most clearly motivates the normative argument, since what establishes knowledge at the same time establishes the truth of the belief in question. It is this task of demonstrating truth as an external relation between belief and that to which it refers that has proved most difficult in the face of skeptical challenge. Traditionally the bridge has been constructed by a class of foundational beliefs referring to experience rather than to wholly external fact. That part of the standard normative picture will be retained here but subsumed under the explanatory model. Once we see that the acceptance of these beliefs too depends on the application of the principle of inference to the best explanation, it becomes easier to extend the argument to deeper levels, where it encompasses beliefs about physical reality.

Our model of knowledge then suggests first a defense of phenomenal, foundational beliefs (to be developed in the next chapter), one immune to standard objections to Cartesian accounts of foundations in terms of infallibility. On our model a belief is self-justified if it is self-explanatory, if it is explained by its truth *alone*. I shall argue that this criterion is satisfied by certain phenomenal reports of how things appear. Given the truth of foundational beliefs established on this basis, we seek to explain why things appear as they do and to see which beliefs about the causes of appearances are best explained in part by appeal to the alleged facts they specify. Once we demonstrate the truth of foundational beliefs about certain appearances, we must also accept the reality of that which best explains their truth (the facts about ways things appear), especially if the entire rationale for accepting the foundations lies in inference to the best explanation. Thus our model suggests second a defense of scientific realism that appeals to its explanatory depth, the topic of our fourth chapter. We are led to both physical science and psychology as providing together our most deeply coherent explanations and thus our ultimate empirical knowledge according to the criterion proposed.

I have been arguing that the ability to capture specific complex intuitions is only the first test for an analysis of knowledge. Such intuitions constitute a legitimate starting point because we seek to clarify *our* concept of knowledge. The ways the concept is applied in everyday discourse should not be overthrown without good reason, simply on the basis of an analysis out of line with those applications. But intuitions regarding knowledge, like moral convictions, may be found in the course of normative reconstruction to be inconsistent with each other or with the underlying rationale behind the application of the concept. While our everyday intuitions, some of which reflect an initial naive realist viewpoint, are not sacrosanct, indeed are sometimes systematically overthrown in the later pictures, they must be replaced not by skeptical doubts or idealist myths but by superior inductive theories. It is an old but continuing story in epistemology that hopelessly strong criteria for knowledge result in skepticism or idealism.

An analysis that places impossibly high demands on the justified application of the concept prevents us from making the transition from knowledge of subjectively accessible evidence (if indeed it allows for this) to knowledge of independent reality. To avoid this notorious stumbling block for normative epistemology, we require not only reference to a foundational class of beliefs about appearances (as relations between objects and subjects) but also a criterion of knowledge and a (knowledge-preserving) principle of inference falling under it that spans the internal and external viewpoints. We must be able to apply our criterion socially, from our collective subjective viewpoint, yet be able to argue that it provides access to the truth we seek about the real world. I believe that the concept of best explanation can provide the link. Best explanations are those that most increase our understanding of the nature of the world. To forge the link, we must argue, as I will, that inference to the best explanation leads (in the long run) to (approximate) truth. Within the realist framework a naturalist view suggests itself, together with a second-level evolutionary explanation for the connection between our quest for explanations and our success in the pursuit of truth. The principle of inference iterates, in that it becomes more explanatorily coherent to believe that explanatory coherence marks at least approximate truth.

The function of the analysis proposed here is to point the way toward this larger normative argument. I hope the following chapters will fulfill some of its promise in that regard.

PART II
FOUNDATIONS

4
THE NEED FOR FOUNDATIONS

We noted in chapter 2 a difference between the ordinary knower and the epistemologist regarding the requirement for justification or for showing the justification for beliefs. This distinction implies a second one regarding the need for foundations of empirical knowledge. The ordinary epistemic subject, requiring no ability to demonstrate justification in order to know, need never trace the justification for his beliefs back to any fixed base. If the truth of her belief in fact enters prominently into its best explanation, then she has knowledge. Neither she nor others need to know the truth or superiority of this explanation. But while the ordinary knower has no need of the philosopher to validate his knowledge claims, the normative epistemologist's interest lies precisely in demonstrating the extent and justificational structure of various types of knowledge. Our present interest is empirical knowledge, and here the need for foundations becomes manifest from at least two directions.

THE VALIDATION OF PERCEPTUAL BELIEFS

The first argument concerns the validation of ordinary perceptual claims to knowledge, a major area of interest for us. Consider my belief that there is a typewriter on the desk before me. Despite the facts that this belief is normally noninferential (I do not normally infer the presence of a typewriter from premises referring to appearances or physical stimulations) and that the truth of the belief seems to enter quite directly into the explanation for its being held, we still require an explanatory chain to validate the belief or establish its status as a case of knowledge. This chain leads to a fixed foundation in perceptual experience.

The direct explanation for my perceptual belief is that I see the typewriter. Given this explanation, we may not seem to require any explanatory chain to arrive at the fact of the typewriter's being there. Its being there is implicit in my seeing it, as indeed is my perceptual belief (perception by adults normally involves the acquisition of such beliefs). If the propositions that the typewriter is there before me and that I believe it is there enter into the analysis of the proposition that I see it, then there would seem to be a most direct connection between the fact and my belief. This initial explanation for my belief simply relates two parts to the same whole process: my believing is explained by my seeing because my believing is part of my seeing, as is the fact that is believed.

But the full validation of such knowledge claims nevertheless does involve appeal to slightly longer explanatory chains. The crucial point here is that, for an explanation to be best, it must be true, that is, it must appeal only to true propositions or genuine facts. Some philosophers might dispute this,[1] and we must pause a moment to consider it. The irrelevance of truth to explanation is suggested by analyses that define the latter solely in terms of implicative relations among propositions. Such relations, of course, hold independently of the truth or falsity of the antecedents or premises. If a set of propositions is said to explain another if the latter is deducible from the former, for example, then the truth or falsity of the explanans remains irrelevant to its function of explaining. I have suggested an account of explanation in terms of probability relations rather than relations of deducibility. Since our account is intended to support the idea that best explanations appeal only to genuine facts, it may seem most plausible for us to maintain that a fact must be actual (or proposition specifying it true) in order for it to have raised the antecedent probability of another state of affairs. In reply we could point out that for the purposes of the analysis of the concept of explanation, probability relations unpacked in terms of possible world connections need not relate only actual states of affairs. This is perfectly consistent with the claim that the occurrence of any actual state of affairs should be fully explained, have its probability fully accounted for, by antecedently actual conditions.

We need not pursue this facet of the analysis of explanation further, since our present concern is not simply the concept itself but the evaluation of explanations as good or best. Such evaluations normally involve very clear assumptions of truth for the propositions of the explanans. Indeed, at least in most contexts, the idea of searching for the best explanation for a given state of affairs is practically synonymous with that of seeking the true explanation. Even if explanations explain independently of their being true, for an explanation to be best, it must both explain and be true. The best explanation is the correct one, and the correct one must be true. The one conceivable exception would exist in cases in which the truth is too complex to be understood by us. Even then, the best explanation would be the one that is comprehensible and most clearly approximates to the truth. Less close approximations might be better for some purposes but not better simply as explanations. (The notion of 'best *simpliciter*' here does not contradict the earlier point that what counts as explanans proper and what as background condition is relative to interest and point of view. Best explanations specify background and explaining conditions by means of true propositions.)

Ordinary language is clear on the truth requirement for evaluations of explanations, although it may be slightly ambiguous on that for explanation itself. The ambiguity derives from the fact that ordinarily, when we talk of seeking an explanation, it is understood that we are speaking of seeking the best explanation. When a detective seeks the explanation for the known facts of a case, he should be interested in finding only the true explanation. We would not say in this context that some other explanation explains better; in fact we normally would not say that other possible explanations explain the facts at all—they only appear to explain them. If, in light of this common usage, we are nevertheless to deny the strict implication from explaining to being true or actual, we can do so only by maintaining that it is understood that the detective seeks not simply any explanation of the facts but the best one. In any case, the implication from explaining best to being true is clear.

If one wonders, then, how there could be a philosophical problem for the realist in establishing that inference to the best explanation generally leads to truth, the answer of course is that what is called 'inference to the best explanation' is really inference to what appears to us to be the best explanation. 'Seeming best explanation' is a purely epistemic concept, while 'best explanation' is not. We seek the latter and attempt to infer to it by seeing which possible explanation appears best to us. In drawing this distinction we may begin to note also the relations between probabilistic connections on the one hand and epistemic criteria for evaluating explanations on the other—criteria such as simplicity, depth, fruitfulness, and so on. While I take the best explanation to be the one that is true and actually accounts for the probability of the explanandum, citing factors that raise this probability to one in deterministic contexts, I also take it that in inferring to the best explanation we use the epistemic criteria, including depth of explanation. The latter will be linked to truth and probability later, via an argument that appeals to environmental selection both of forms of reasoning or inference patterns and of particular explanatory theories.

We may now return to our validation of a common perceptual belief, our inquiry into the explanation for my belief that there is a typewriter before me. The immediate explanation for this belief, as we saw, is that I see the typewriter. I have argued that for this, or any, explanation to be best, it must be true. The epistemologist must show this explanation to be best and hence must show it to be true. He must do this even for so obvious an explanation for my perceptual belief about the typewriter as the fact that I see it. The belief that I see the typewriter must be validated in order for the fact of my seeing it to be established as entering into the best explanation for my original perceptual belief.

One might try to validate the belief that I see the typewriter simply by inferring that I do as the best explanation for my perceptual belief, which is already accepted as a belief, though not yet as knowledge. It was pointed out above that if p is accepted and q best explains it, then p is evidence for q. But here this direct line will not do in itself, despite the evidential status of the belief. From just the fact that I believe there is a typewriter before me I cannot infer with any certainty the explanation that I see a typewriter. Even if we fill out the perceptual

belief with details about the color, position, and other perceptible properties of the machine, the fact that I see it does not
follow as the true explanation—I might have been informed of
or, more likely, remember these details. In the example as defined, the fact that I see the typewriter does enter into the
explanation for my belief that it is before me, but I would not
know this from reflecting merely on the belief itself. I must
rather consider the grounds for the belief, which also constitute
grounds for my belief that I see the object in question. These
grounds consist in my perceptual experiences, in the ways that
the shapes and colors appear to me. (If we take the third-person
point of view of another epistemologist evaluating my perceptual belief, then we require a longer route through his belief
that he sees me seeing the typewriter, but the structure of the
argument is the same.) It is the fact that I am appeared to in
certain ways that explains my belief that I see the typewriter
and that therefore helps to explain my belief that the typewriter
is before me.

Even at this level, however, it must be shown that this explanation is true. To validate the claim that I am appeared to in certain
ways, I do not simply infer to the nature of my experience as the
explanation for my belief that I see the typewriter and for my
perceptual beliefs about it. I also look more directly to the explanation for my belief that I am appeared to in those ways and ask
whether the truth of that belief enters prominently into its explanation. Even here the epistemologist must engage in the process
of validation; he cannot appeal directly to experience independent of all beliefs about its characteristics. There is no direct
escape from the web of beliefs for the epistemologist. The foundations themselves must consist in beliefs. While I shall argue in a
later section that appearing itself may be nonepistemic (something may appear to a subject without his acquiring any beliefs
about it), appearances must be conceptualized as such in order to
function in a process of epistemic validation. (There is also an
intermediate epistemic function of perceptual experience, in
which the way something appears to a subject is his reason for
believing that it has a certain property, without his conceiving of
the way of appearing as an appearance.) Unconceptualized appearing cannot be consulted directly; and inference to the na-

ture of appearance from beliefs with other contents—for example, as part of the explanation for beliefs about objects and their properties—is less certain than inference from beliefs about appearances themselves.

Let us pause and review the first argument to this point. We have explained my everyday perceptual belief that the typewriter is before me by appealing to the fact that I see it. But for this explanation to be best, that fact must be genuine: we must therefore validate the belief that I see it. This belief is explained in turn by appeal to ways I am appeared to. But again my beliefs about these appearances must be true for the next link in the chain of explanation to be strongest. Hence we next must look to the explanation for these beliefs. But here there is a difference. At this point the beliefs in question are no longer explained by facts beyond those to which they refer. We no longer require an explanatory chain for the full validation of these beliefs. I shall argue in detail below that they are fully and best explained by the very facts to which they refer alone. My belief that I am appeared to grayly, for example, is best explained solely by the fact that I am so appeared to. (What explains my being able to form such beliefs in the appropriate circumstances remains a general background condition for explanations of particular beliefs of this type.)

Thus we arrive at the most intimate connection of belief to reality, a type of belief explained by its truth or correspondence to fact alone (substantiation for this claim awaits chapter 7). We have established two closely related senses in which such beliefs function as empirical foundations. First, the validation of ordinary perceptual beliefs by appeal to other beliefs ends here: beyond this level in constructing explanatory chains we no longer appeal to further beliefs whose truth must be validated. Rather we infer from here directly to facts as the explanations for beliefs, where the latter constitute the only evidence available or needed to establish the facts in question. Second, these beliefs ground others most directly to the world to which they refer. The grounding requires two (types of) steps: the first from beliefs about appearances to appearances themselves, and the second from the appearances to the properties of the physical world that best explain them.

In a third, more traditional sense, beliefs about appearances are not foundational. The process of validating ordinary perceptual beliefs by inference to the best explanation does not terminate with beliefs about ways of appearing. While the validation of the latter beliefs marks the transition from belief to reality outside it, the explanatory chains required to demonstrate the knowledge expressed by ordinary perceptual claims about objects continue beyond beliefs about appearances and appearances themselves to the properties that explain them. The self-validation of claims about appearances is an intermediate step in this process that establishes the facts about ways things appear. The question then becomes whether the alleged facts specified by the original perceptual beliefs enter into the best explanations for these established ways of appearing. This will be the case with explanations for some types of apparent qualities but not others. That our foundational beliefs are not foundational in the traditional sense points up that we are not concerned here with the standard issue of subjective justification for beliefs. We focus here rather on the process of validation by inference to the best explanation, in which beliefs about experience function as foundations of a different sort.

I have assumed so far in this first argument that the best explanation in the context for my perceptual belief that there is a typewriter before me is that I see it. Certainly this would be the common assumption, and perhaps the correct one. Before concluding this discussion, however, we might take account of some considerations deemed relevant in the previous chapter to determining best explanations. On the one hand, it was argued that appeal to the specific cause of the explanandum does not always explain best. It does not explain best when other factors in the relevant set of conditions might equally have brought about the state of affairs to be explained, when this state of affairs is connected to those other factors in as many or more close possible worlds. (Recall the example of a historian explaining the origins of a war.) In the present context of explaining an ordinary perceptual belief, appeal to the fact that I see the typewriter brings out the specific causal origins of my belief. My seeing it includes the fact that it is there, that it appears to me, that I acquire some perceptual beliefs, and that a causal connection helps to determine the way it appears. But there is a broader (less specific) context that would have produced this belief without the causal connection or my actually seeing the typewriter, namely, the way I am appeared to in itself. Having these experiences, I acquire the perceptual belief, whether or not I actually see the typewriter. Perhaps, then, the best explanation is the less specific one. On the other hand, the probability of my being appeared to in this way without my actually seeing a typewriter appears to be quite low, the possible worlds in which I hallucinate in this way being relatively few and distant. We also argued previously that possibilities with very low probabilities of actualizing can generally be ignored in explaining actual events or states. Hence the best explanation here again seems to be my seeing the typewriter, if we remember still that this explanation itself must be validated by appeal to appearances and beliefs about appearances. (Recall also that explanation is transitive through the causal chain and visual experience to the object of perception because Condition C of the previous chapter is met.)

We must acknowledge finally that not all perceptual beliefs are explained in the same way as my belief about the typewriter. When it comes to visual beliefs about specific qualities or types of qualities of objects seen, actually seeing these qualities only sometimes enters into best explanations. Explanations for such beliefs sometimes appeal only to being appeared to in certain ways. While this distinction will be crucial for acceptance of realist versus nonrealist interpretations of the properties in question, it is not crucial in the present context. Where the appearing explanation for perceptual beliefs is best, it preserves the route to perceptual foundations, differing from the seeing explanation in a subsequent stage (namely, in inferring to the best explanation for the appearances). In all cases, alleged facts to which perceptual beliefs refer must be established or dismissed via the validation of beliefs referring to appearances, and then by explanation of the appearances as established in this process of validation. In all cases the connection with reality secured by beliefs about appearances is fundamental in determining the best explanations.

One might also argue that, while appeal to ways of appearing figures in the validation of perceptual beliefs at the present stage of the art, such appeal will become superfluous with greater knowledge of the physical sequences in the brain that produce such beliefs. Appeal to the physical causal chains from stimuli to the relevant brain states will replace appeals to experience in the best explanations for perceptual beliefs. This objection mislocates the role I have assigned to beliefs about appearances and inferences to the nature of appearances themselves. The full specification of the causal processes in question simply expands upon what is involved in seeing objects and their qualities, and I have agreed that in many cases appeal to seeing objects and their properties constitutes the best explanation for beliefs about them. In fact, fuller specification of the causal processes helps to separate instances in which appeal to seeing actual properties explains best from those in which perceptual beliefs refer only to appearances. The distinction is determined by the presence or absence of the properties in question at the inception of the causal chains specified by the best causal explanations for the beliefs being evaluated. But in both cases the epistemologist (or scientist) must establish the truth of the causal explanations. He does this not simply by showing that they explain beliefs about actual properties of objects. He must be equally interested in explaining how things appear to the subject, based on the latter's beliefs about how things appear (and, in the case of the scientist, he must explain how things appear to him as he observes the causal process in other subjects).

This task of explaining the grounds on which persons must form their perceptual beliefs is epistemically the more fundamental, because greater respect must be shown in the account to beliefs about appearances. The scientist's causal explanations could explain ordinary perceptual beliefs by showing how they systematically err; but when it comes to beliefs about how things appear, his explanations must accept the beliefs' reliability or general truth (this will be argued in detail later). Having accepted these beliefs as generally true, he must go on to explain the appearances themselves, as specified by such beliefs. Thus these beliefs, as those most immediately in contact with their referents, constitute a foundational constraint on the acceptability of scientific explanations, including explanations for ordinary perceptual beliefs. (We will consider the elimination or replaceability of reference to appearance further in following sections.)

INCOMPATIBLE, COHERENT BELIEF SYSTEMS

Consideration of ordinary perceptual beliefs then demonstrates the need for perceptual foundations to ground their best explanations and distinguish them from other possible explanations. Our second argument leads to the same conclusion from the opposite direction. Here we consider the outcome of a process of validation beginning with beliefs other than those deriving from perception. Such a process either never will lead to actual beliefs about ways things appear or else will lead to beliefs about appearances that conflict with another, broader class of beliefs of this type. Suppose in the former case that we can do without foundational beliefs or simply posit those that fit in when necessary to fill out the picture. Suppose in the latter case that we can simply throw out those beliefs about appearances that are incompatible with our explanatory account (most actual belief systems are not fully consistent, so that some beliefs need to be discarded or negated). Or suppose that we accept the appearances as posited by actual foundational beliefs but explain them away with accounts that would not be impartially accepted as best. If we are permitted such moves, then we are free to construct as many explanatorily coherent, broad belief systems as we like (at least if we have the ingenuity of a good fiction author).

Imagine specifically that we begin with the belief that Cinderella lost her slipper. We accept this as a genuine fact. Those familiar with the story know already how a full explanatory account of this supposed true belief and the fact that it posits would go. To blend this account smoothly with the rest of our world picture, we need only dismiss that evidence consisting in appearances best explained ultimately by the fact that the story is fictional. We can negate such evidence by ignoring beliefs about these appearances, by explaining away the appearances themselves, or by adding to them other evidence, for example, evidence indicating that the story was closely based on fact. The possibility of constructing an explanatorily coherent account for any belief by tinkering with the foundations in these ways shows that coherence without genuine foundations is insufficient for truth or for its demonstration.

The abstract possibility of fully coherent belief systems having no contact with reality, or therefore with truth, is even easier to illustrate. We simply begin a sequence of the following sort: p; $q \cdot q \supset p$; $r \cdot r \supset q$. . . Others have used such sequences to argue against the idea that an infinite regress of subjective justification could be genuinely justificatory.[2] If we think not simply of justification but of explanation (simply reinterpret the implication signs in the above scheme as signifying probability relations), the threat of a regress diminishes. Either explanation must end somewhere with an unexplained explainer or else we must construct explanatory circles with mutually supporting propositions or states of affairs. The latter are not inconceivable. To cite one example, a person's continuing desire to win at tennis might explain his hours of practice, his practice explain his fine play, his fine play explain his winning, his winning explain the pleasure he derives, and the pleasure he derives explain his continuing desire to win. Thus sequences of the type schematized above may be genuinely explanatory if r is replaced by an unexplained explainer and the other variables by states of affairs that stand in the proper probability relations, or if we close the circle with $p \supset r$ and replace the variables with explanatory sequences like the one just cited.

While such sequences may be genuinely explanatory, they may never touch reality if the initial state of affairs to be explained is not actual or, even if it is, say, an actual belief, if the belief is false and no genuine foundational beliefs enter the sequence. I argued above that propositions cannot enter best explanations unless they are true (or states of affairs enter such explanations unless they are actual). This allowed for false explanations, false but genuinely explanatory propositions. Even the connection between being true or actual and explaining best holds only when the fact or state of affairs to be explained is actual (an assumption that governed the earlier argument). Fictional states of affairs may be best explained by other fictional states of affairs, at least in certain contexts. Cinderella's losing her slipper is best explained in one context by her (fictional) nervousness and haste (or by her Freudian desire to leave a trace for the Prince), in another context by the storyteller's real desire to construct a bridge to his happy ending. A similar distinction arises among explanations for false beliefs. From the external point of view, as an actual state of a subject, a false belief will be explained by other actual states of affairs, perhaps by earlier errors of the subject, by his unfortunate epistemic position or faulty reasoning. But from the internal perspective, from the point of view of the subject himself or of those who agree with the content of his belief, the belief will be explained by alleged facts themselves probably falsely believed and posited by the explanations. It is the possibility that such accounts will form explanatorily coherent systems that demands some guarantee of conduct with reality beyond that afforded by explanatory coherence itself.

One might object to the abstractness of the argument and the artificiality of the examples so far cited. It could be argued that a convincing demonstration of full explanatory coherence without truth must begin with actual beliefs, not hypothetical beliefs about fictional characters. A philosopher who maintains that only coherence among actual beliefs is a mark of truth might defend this difference in epistemic status by appeal to a naturalist, evolutionary framework. The relevant point from that framework—an initial reason for the realist to accept that coherence is a mark of truth—is that our brain type originated through a process of adaptation that guarantees survival value to its normal products. This reason is weakened by the recognition that "useful fictions" may sometimes aid in the struggle to survive as well and that mere survival does not appear to require more than a very rough accommodation to the immediate environment. More important is the point that beyond the biological level of mere survival, our belief systems themselves have been shaped by interaction with their objects in pursuit of the goals of internal coherence, pragmatic success, and truth itself. The simplest explanation for our degree of success in actions requiring enormously complex coordination and adaptation to the physical environment appears to lie in the approximate truth of key elements in the belief systems or theories that guide those actions. Needed expansion of this argument and counterarguments will be considered later in the sections on realism. I mention it here because of the distinction it implies between the epistemic implications of coherence among actual beliefs and those of coherence among merely possible beliefs. So, the coherentist can argue, our pointing to a hypothetical belief system that exhibits explanatory coherence (in which all that needs explaining is explained) but is riddled with falsity fails to demonstrate the requirement for foundations. (The coherentist who distinguishes real belief systems on these grounds must apparently be a realist as well, since he speaks of adaptation to an external reality. We may consider this position first, in order to show that realism requires foundations.)

I shall endorse the broad outlines of the argument from adaptation in the next chapter, and I agree that it establishes only coherence among actual beliefs as an (inductive) indicator of truth. But even coherence among actual empirical beliefs, we may reply, signals truth only when the beliefs are properly grounded to the world in a way shown by appeal to foundational beliefs about appearances and the appearances themselves that directly explain and validate these beliefs. It is not much more difficult to exemplify coherence among false beliefs actually held than to find such examples in the realm of fiction. Widely believed political and religious myths, replete with alternative histories and cosmologies that provide broad internal explanatory coherence, afford ready cases in point. Adherents to such belief systems employ all three strategies mentioned above for nullifying counterevidence. In some cases such evidence is ignored, as is much of the evidence for Darwin's theory by Christian fundamentalists. In others conflicting evidence is fabricated, for example, to support the Nazi myth of a worldwide Jewish conspiracy. In yet others evidence is accepted but explained away by further, sometimes ad hoc, extensions of the underlying theories, as in later socialist explanations for the evidence that capitalist economies had not failed as Marx had predicted, or explanations for evidence of extreme poverty in capitalist societies by free market advocates, or explanations for experiences of gratuitous pain and suffering by deist theologians.

The cavalier treatment of seemingly relevant counterevidence by adherents to certain widely endorsed ideologies of the past and present is too banal to be of philosophical interest in itself. For this practice to have philosophical import in the present context, two further, related claims must be defended. These are, first, that such ideologies retain internal coherence, so that their fault lies not in any lack of coherence in itself; and second, that they do so precisely by avoiding contact with what I have called foundational beliefs, the sensory evidence established through such beliefs, and its best explanations. The latter claim may seem the more controversial, but is not really so. Its defense demands neither that such statements as those about the survival of capitalism or the origins of species be translatable into statements about appearances nor even that their justification derive solely from relations to such statements. More plausible premises are that (all) ultimate evidence for empirical knowledge (including whatever may be contained in the theories mentioned above) derives from ways things appear in sense perception, and that complete validation of belief systems having empirical content as a whole must make appeal to some actual beliefs about appearances, beliefs that establish those appearances that explain perceptual beliefs contained or implicit in viable theories. Given the failure of the ideologies mentioned to confront counterevidence squarely, and given also that such counterevidence must derive from perception, it becomes plausible to maintain that our inability to establish the truth of these theories derives from their failure to explain broad classes of appearances and the foundational beliefs that establish them. (The term 'ideology', aptly applied in such cases, itself suggests both internal coherence and lack of grounding in empirical fact.)

A full analysis of any such belief system along these lines would make an interesting exercise, but one far beyond our scope. I mention them here only to answer the objection to examples from fiction, to provide instances of all-too-actual belief systems that preserve internal coherence only by severing adequate empirical grounding. The claim that it is their lack of foundations, rather than a foundationless coherence criterion, that explains our reaction to these systems may still be questioned. While we cannot doubt that their breadth of internal explanatory coherence, their apparent ability to answer all questions, in part explains their wide appeal, the coherentist will remain unimpressed by such examples, even if he agrees with my lightning assessment of their method for preserving internal coherence without truth. *We* may judge such belief systems to be rife with falsity; but our criterion, he will maintain, is their failure to cohere with *our* beliefs, foundational or otherwise. I have simply assumed that my examples exhibit both coherence and falsity in the deeper sense of failure to correspond to independent fact. How can it be shown that the real complaints against these belief systems do not reduce to their lack of coherence with a set of beliefs about evidence and its explanation that I simply take to be inviolable within my system? (A related but different response by the coherentist would be to argue that our examples must demonstrate not only coherence among actual beliefs but also coherence with our shared epistemic beliefs, beliefs about the nature of evidence, etc.[3] This reply will not help him if the latter reflect implicit belief in foundationalism, as I think they do. He must, then, rather question the objectivity of these epistemic beliefs, as I am now having him do.)

My first response is to point out that failure to demand validation by appeal to foundational beliefs results in systems deemed false from many other perspectives because it allows construction of as many mutually incompatible but internally coherent belief systems as we care to consider, all with equal claim to validity. Were all such systems admissible as empirical knowledge, the status of the latter would be entirely assimilated to that of moral and other value judgments. Internally consistent systems of value judgments cannot be dismissed as false. Only particular judgments that fail to cohere with others that are more securely agreed upon or accepted can be held false or mistaken. Value systems in which independently endorsed general principles explain specific judgments, and in which the latter agree and differ in ways that match generalized judgments of relevant similarities and differences among situations, can be attacked only from the point of view of competing values within some other system with no objective claim to superiority.[4]

Empirical theories differ, at least if they are given realist interpretations, in that only one of a mutually incompatible set can be true of a single independent reality, and in that perfect

internal consistency therefore cannot guarantee truth or acceptability. According to the realist, all inquirers can agree on a
consistent and successful empirical theory that may in fact be
false, an indictment not applicable to nonempirical theories in
similar contexts. (Political and religious belief systems are more
complex, containing empirical and moral components. Only
the former component, in my view, requires foundational
grounding, in that only the former refers to a subject-independent reality. To draw this fact-value distinction is not to imply
that every sentence and term can be placed clearly in one category or the other. The pragmatic functions of speech often
require assertions and terms that straddle the distinction. Nor
does the distinction imply an absence of rational constraint on
moral and other value arguments. See note 4.)

For the realist epistemologist to escape skepticism, he must
find a way of differentiating among internally coherent but
mutually incompatible empirical belief systems. He must be
able to validate one such system as opposed to others. To do so
he must appeal to some privileged set of beliefs with which
others must cohere—hence his need for empirical foundations.
Such beliefs must be privileged in their manner of validation.
They must be acceptable not on grounds of explanatory coherence with other beliefs but via the demonstration of a more
direct connection to their objects, of the sort exemplified by
those beliefs about ways of appearing singled out as well by our
first argument as empirical foundations. Once such foundations are fixed in place, the prospect of many conflicting belief
systems, all equally coherent (according to our criteria for best
explanations) with them, becomes far less plausible.

A less pure coherentist system might retain the key premise
that all justification derives from relations among beliefs while
demanding input to the system in the form of noninferential
perceptual beliefs. The demand for such beliefs would be intended to fulfill the grounding function of foundations, but
here the justification for them would derive entirely from other
beliefs, those about the reliability of perception, for example.[5]
But if all beliefs, even those about appearances, are to be justified only in terms of their coherence with the subject's system of
beliefs, then the mere demand for perceptual beliefs cannot

solve the problem of incompatible but equally coherent belief systems. A person with wildly deviant perceptual beliefs could be entirely justified in them according to this account if he has equally deviant but internally coherent beliefs about their reliability.

Perhaps the coherentist could grant such justification, arguing that this subject's lack of knowledge would be due entirely to the falsity of his beliefs rather than to his lack of justification. Although I have held that justification is not necessary for knowledge, I do not believe that this answer suffices. We as epistemologists must demonstrate knowledge from within our own belief systems, and we must have some way of showing that we are not in the position of the envisaged madman. Our beliefs about the reliability of our perceptions do not suffice for this task, since the madman will have similar beliefs. We are therefore driven back to the demand for self-justifying beliefs involving a type of predicate that distinguishes them from the madman's perceptual beliefs. If we can isolate a set of such beliefs about appearances, then we can argue that the perceptual beliefs of a madman would not best explain them, no matter how otherwise internally coherent.

This second argument has eliminated the position of the coherentist (nonfoundationalist) who is also a realist by demonstrating the realist's need for empirical foundations. The less rare breed of nonrealist coherentist, who is willing to relativize truth to acceptability within a belief system, remains unaffected. The completion of this argument for foundationalism therefore awaits the defense of realism on grounds acceptable to the latter coherentist. It will have to be argued that a realist interpretation of empirical theories is preferable on grounds of (explanatory) coherence itself. Prior to providing this argument in the following chapter, we must consider more closely first the nature of appearing that I take to constitute grounds for empirical beliefs, and second the justification for beliefs about appearances that I take to be immediate. This further defense of these claims will guarantee the availability of those empirical foundations that we have seen to be required for the epistemologist, if not for the average unreflective knower, who may be secure in his knowledge without being able fully to defend or demonstrate it.

5

APPEARING AS IRREDUCIBLE

I said in the previous chapter that a subject's seeing an object consists normally in the object's standing in a causal relation to him, a relation involving stimulation of his sense organs, such that it appears in some way to him and he acquires some beliefs about it. The ways it appears, it was held, constitute the grounds for and help to explain the subject's perceptual beliefs. His beliefs about these appearances (if he has any such beliefs) constitute empirical foundations, in that they immediately establish the characteristics of these relations between the object and himself and therefore ground his perceptual beliefs in the world in the epistemologist's reconstruction. The epistemologist validates the claim that subjects actually see physical objects and various of their properties by showing that appeal to this causal account best explains how things appear to perceivers, the appearances themselves having been established immediately as the best explanations for beliefs about them.

EPISTEMIC ANALYSES OF PERCEIVING

Both the claim that ways of appearing constitute grounds for perceptual beliefs and the contention that beliefs about appearances are immediately justified require further explication and defense. The former, which runs counter to the major recent trend in philosophical analyses of perception, will concern us in this section. Its defense requires repudiation of materialist-reductionist accounts of perceiving, which limit perception to the epistemic or belief component alone.[1] As we shall see below, epistemic analyses are not the only reductionist accounts of perception, but they have been the dominant and perhaps most plausible ones.

According to these accounts, the locution 'S perceives x' is to be analyzed (roughly) as: 'S causally receives through his senses a belief or inclination to belief, at least partially true of x, that it has properties F . . .'[2] The simple locution 'S perceives x' must always be expanded in this account to 'S perceives x as (having the property) F', since the acquisition of belief about x entails believing that x has some property or other. Perception is identified here not with the possession of belief, often unconscious, but with the acquisition of belief via suitable stimulation of the sensory systems. The schematic analysis offered above includes a clause stipulating that the acquired beliefs must be partially true of x. This is included to ensure that it is x that is perceived. While a subject need not believe that it is an x that he perceives in order to perceive an x, if perceiving the x is simply a matter of acquiring beliefs about it, then it is plausible that it is not perceived at all unless some of the acquired beliefs, say about its location or other relational properties, are true of it. This issue relates to the determination of referents for beliefs, a topic to be treated later. Here the important issue concerns the omission in these accounts of reference to perceptual experience.

It must be shown that such analyses are inadequate in omitting independent reference to appearances. We must emphasize 'independent reference' here, since proponents of reductionist analyses do not deny the propriety of such locutions as 'The fire engine appears red to me'. They do maintain that such expressions are used only to assert tentative beliefs or inclinations to belief. If this were their only use, if reference to appearance always reduced in this way to reference to (guarded) belief, then clearly the ways things appear would not constitute grounds for perceptual beliefs, as I have maintained. The expression of tentative belief is certainly one use of 'appears', as in 'It appears that it will rain today'. We must indicate a different sense as entering into any adequate account of perceiving.

Before criticizing reductionist analyses, we should try to appreciate their motivation. In order to understand what motivates them and to assess their adequacy, we must first state requirements for an acceptable philosophical account of perceiving. These requirements are (A) that it state the necessary and sufficient conditions for a subject's perceiving something, that is, that it be capable of accommodating all different types of perceptual states and the phenomenological and psychological data concerning them; and (B) that it have acceptable metaphysical and epistemological implications, that is, that it not lead in itself to skeptical conclusions or insoluble puzzles that could be avoided simply by sifting the data into a different conceptual apparatus. These two criteria, when applied to particular analyses, may well have to be weighed against one another, but an acceptable analysis must first of all and at least meet the first.

Our concept of perceiving evolves to reflect and incorporate phenomenological, psychological, and physiological data regarding the processes involved. As with other empirical concepts, there must be complete integration between our most reasonable interpretations of new data (in this case our best explanations for how perceptual processes appear to investigators and for how perceptual inputs, as described by our best physical theories, relate to outputs) and the continuing refinement of the concept. The conceptual analysis first must capture, or at least be capable of accommodating, not only obvious phenomenological characteristics but the currently best theories and experimental data regarding perception. It is sometimes objected that such sophisticated matters cannot affect the concept itself, since the average man in the street knows perfectly well what perceiving is without knowing very much psychology or physiology. This objection assumes a false dichotomy between conceptual and empirical matters. The average person may not know *perfectly well* what perceiving is, and our educated concept need not be his. If our best theories and the data they explain together imply certain counterintuitive metaphysical or epistemological conclusions, so be it, as long as such conclusions do not issue from an initial conceptual framework not required for consistent interpretations of the bulk of empirical data.

While I place requirement (A) first, the reductionist analysis seems to be strongly motivated by supposed advantages relating to (B). Its purpose is to avoid metaphysical and epistemological puzzles associated with dualist accounts. Having been developed for that purpose, it is then argued after the fact to satisfy criterion (A), to accommodate the phenomenological and psychological facts. More specifically, the order of priority among goals for the reductionist, as I interpret him, is (1) to limit the referents of the analysis to physical objects and events, thus avoiding the problem of having to stipulate the relation of a nonphysical mind or mental objects or events to physical bodies; (2) to avoid reference to sense data, which involves special puzzles as to their nature beyond those connected with mental events and processes; (3) to avoid epistemological skepticism, held to be implicit in any account that interposes perceptual experience between the subject and the physical world as the grounds for his beliefs about it; and (4) at the same time to provide an analysis that will account for phenomenological facts and psychological data, especially the phenomenological similarity between illusory and veridical perception (which motivates sense data theories as well) and the psychological data on the causal influences upon ways things are perceived.

I shall argue first that the epistemic account fails to live up to (4), our criterion (A). Phenomenological, and especially psychological, data fail to fit this conceptual framework. Such data reveal first the phenomenon of nonepistemic perception, perception without the acquisition of belief, showing that the analysis fails to state even a necessary condition for perceiving. Not surprisingly, the acquisition of belief via sensory stimulation fails to be sufficient as well. Even when applied to normal adult perception, which includes acquiring such beliefs, the account fails to differentiate perceptual beliefs from certain other (possible) beliefs, fails to accommodate the perception of various secondary and aesthetic qualities, fails to differentiate among various (possible) perceptual states, fails to accommodate psychological data on the causes of differences in perceptions, and, by removing the grounds from perceptual beliefs, prevents an explication of the rationality of both veridical and illusory perceptual beliefs. The latter fault will prompt the argument that the reductionist analysis falls below alternatives in relation to goal (3), our main interest, as well. Goal (2) can be satisfied by alternative analyses also, leaving (1) as the sole advantage of the reductionist-epistemic account. This lone advantage cannot override the account's failures, given our reordering of the priorities. Dualist accounts generate major and perhaps insoluble puzzles, which I shall try to minimize in the following section. Unfortunately, they seem unavoidable.

NONEPISTEMIC PERCEPTION

Let us first exemplify the phenomenon of nonepistemic perception, seeing without believing. There may appear to be numerous everyday situations whose phenomenology suggests the phenomenon in question. We see so many things and parts of things in a matter of seconds that it seems implausible to claim that we are simultaneously acquiring beliefs about all of them. Unfortunately these cases prove to be untrustworthy for making our point. The reason they do not clearly demonstrate nonepistemic perception is that we are not always aware of all the beliefs we have or of their acquisition as such. There may be beliefs acquired in these contexts, of which we are unaware at the time. Hence their acquisition will not be part of the phenomenological data. The materialist will unpack the concept of belief in either dispositional or central-state terms. Beliefs are either tendencies to certain behavioral responses, verbal or otherwise, or states of the brain that underlie those tendencies.[3] In either case it is clear that belief and its acquisition may be unconscious, since we are not always aware of our dispositions or our brain states, or of their coming to be. It will be objected that perception is a conscious process, so that the acquisition of belief must be conscious too if it is to be equated with the process of perceiving. The objection is correct but misplaced, however, since we may be conscious of the process through which we acquire beliefs, and conscious of the objects of those beliefs, without being aware of the acquiring of the beliefs as such.

We may consider more closely some situations of this type suggested in the literature as examples of nonepistemic perception.[4] Take the situation in which we see things without paying any attention to them. It seems in such cases that we do not believe we see the objects we do see or acquire any beliefs about them at all. If we hold that paying attention is a necessary condition of acquiring beliefs but not of seeing, then reductionist analyses are defeated by such cases. I am now, for example, seeing various objects on my desk peripherally while concentrating on getting my thoughts down on the paper before me. I might very well later ask my wife where my coffee cup is and she reply, "You must have seen it; it was on the desk right in front of you." If the reply is accepted at face value, it implies that perception can occur without attention, that in such cases objects can be perceived without being noticed and without beliefs being acquired regarding their location, existence, or any of their qualities.

Unfortunately the reply can also be translated as, "It seems impossible (but is nevertheless true) that the cup failed to draw your attention, failed to register or to be seen, when it was so prominent in your visual field." So construed, it accepts that I did not see the cup, attributing my failure to see it to my unusual degree of concentration and obliviousness to all else but this chapter. This seems the proper way to construe it in light of other evidence that attending to objects at least in a minimal way is necessary for perceiving them. People trained to attend to certain details of objects, for example imperfections in materials or jewels, can see them when others do not. An object's being in one's visual field is not then a sufficient condition for perceiving it. Perceiving objects involves discriminating them from backgrounds, and this in turn requires a degree of attention. Thus an alternative interpretation of the phenomena here is that they do not exemplify seeing without believing because they do not include seeing. Yet a third interpretation of the case as described would be that I saw the cup, acquired beliefs about it, but later forgot seeing it and lost the beliefs I had acquired.

A reply similar to this last applies to a second purported counterexample to the epistemic account of perception. Consider cases in which a large number of items are seen in rapid succession, in which it therefore seems implausible to hold that beliefs are acquired regarding each. Think specifically of reading this page, a necessary condition of which is seeing or discriminating hundreds of letters. It seems unlikely from the phenomenology of this experience that beliefs are acquired regarding each letter. But again the phenomenology may mislead. In order to read the words and sentences correctly, you not only have to discriminate the letters but also recognize or correctly identify them (although such identification obviously will not consist in conscious pronouncements). Just as this required identification does not have to be in each case a conscious event, so neither must you be conscious of acquiring a belief about each letter as such. If I misidentify the 'x' as a 'p', I will misconstrue the title of Roosevelt's biography. If we grant that beliefs need be neither conscious nor long enduring, we can hold that in correctly identifying the 'x' when I read the title *The Lion and the Fox,* I acquire the fleeting belief that it is an 'x'. This seems to be shown by the fact that I would readily answer an inquiry as to the last letter of the title just read.

Thus both purported counterexamples fail, the first because it may not involve seeing and the second because it may involve believing as well as seeing. What we need are cases in which objects are attended to at least in a minimal way while the subject neither identifies them nor acquires any beliefs about them. I believe the most plausible cases involve developmentally primitive perception, that of newborn infants for example. In that context we attribute visual perception of objects when they are fixated to some degree by the eyes in decent lighting conditions, and yet it is implausible to attribute beliefs about what is perceived to such subjects. The operation of the infant's sensory system puts the claim that he is capable of perceiving beyond dispute, although he clearly does not yet perceive things as adults do. His perception is necessary for his learning anything about his environment. If the reductionist then admits that the infant perceives at all, he must claim also that he acquires beliefs, almost from the moment he opens his eyes. The defender of the epistemic account will then argue that just as the infant's perceptions are disorganized and confused (a claim based on the disorganization of the infant's perceptual attention), so his initial beliefs will be primitive and unspecific.[5] Perhaps a plausible candidate for such a belief might be "That over there is somehow different from that." Even primitive perception must involve discrimination, that is, some degree of organization and differentiation within the perceptual field, and such minimal discrimination could be expressed in beliefs such as that.

This response to the alleged counterexample slurs a relevant conceptual distinction, underestimates what is involved in acquiring beliefs, and seems therefore inapplicable to the data on early perceptual development. The distinction is that between perceptual discrimination on the one hand and identification or recognition of perceived objects on the other. The latter can be expressed by a proposition that can express also a belief about the object in question. Identification involves the application of a concept to the object perceived; the object is classified as an instance of some type. The identification can then be equated with a belief that the object is one of that type. But perceptual discrimination does not require identification or recognition of the objects discriminated. It need not then presuppose the possession of concepts of those objects. The acquisition of perceptual beliefs, unlike mere discrimination, does require concepts. Perceiving objects as having certain qualities presupposes some concepts of the objects, of the qualities in question, and of quality possession. To acquire the belief that the book I am perceiving is red, I require the concepts of a book and redness. Even to acquire the perceptual belief that this is different from that, an infant must possess a concept of qualitative difference. Since discriminating does not presuppose concepts and acquiring beliefs does, and since perceiving seems to require only discriminating and not identifying or recognizing, the possibility of perception without belief is established.

That this possibility is actualized in the perception of infants is suggested by the data evidencing a gradual development toward the recognition of objects as objects having certain properties.[6] While not all philosophers or psychologists would emphasize or even accept the distinction between discrimination and identification or recognition, my claim is that it is descriptively required to provide an account of this early development. The disorientation of the infant's initial perceptual attention and his lack of differential response to discrete objects in the perceptual environment provide evidence against the claim that the infant can identify or recognize objects from the beginning. Without any ability to recognize or identify what is seen, it is impossible to attribute perceptual concepts; and without such concepts, necessary conditions for the possession or acquisition of beliefs are lacking. Since there is no evidence of innate empirical concepts (as opposed to capacities to discriminate), these recogni-

tional capacities must themselves be acquired. Their acquisition
must be accomplished through early interaction with the perceived environment. 'Perceived' is of course to be emphasized,
for without perception there is no interaction, and without interaction no gradual development of those concepts necessary for
the acquisition of perceptual beliefs.[7]

Thus, in the absence of innate empirical concepts, there must
be perception prior to the acquisition of belief, perception that
cannot be fit into the reductionist-epistemic mold. The infant
perceives as soon as objects or their parts or combinations appear to him, i.e., are discriminated from the background field.
Once they begin to appear, he can begin the process of acquiring concepts of them and later beliefs. (The old empiricist thesis
that "impressions" must as a class precede "ideas" still appears
to be correct, although the psychological corollary that association constitutes the primary force behind the developmental
process was mistaken, and the strongly analytical use to which
Hume put the thesis was often misguided.) The order of this
process defeats the epistemic account of perception, showing
that it fails to state a necessary condition of perceiving.

Something more may be said regarding the concept of concepts with which I have been operating in claiming that perception must precede empirical concepts and these precede the
acquisition of perceptual beliefs. According to one fairly standard analysis of concepts, their possession would seem to require beliefs on the part of the subject. That analysis holds that
to have a concept of F is to know what it is for an x to be F.[8] The
latter presupposes beliefs about x's that are F, belief being included in the analysis of knowledge. Thus it would be entailed
by this interpretation of concepts that their acquisition must
involve the acquisition of belief as well, since having them
would always involve having knowledge and hence belief. But
the analysis itself is highly implausible if not paradoxical, since
beliefs contain concepts, or their representational instantiations, as constituents. If concepts enter into beliefs and are
therefore necessary for having beliefs, then they cannot also
presuppose prior beliefs. Having the concept of F-ness cannot
be equated from the beginning with believing truly or knowing

that certain things are F, although having such beliefs can be a criterion for having the concept at a later stage.

I have been assuming a more liberal analysis of concepts, according to which we attribute possession of a concept of F as soon as we attribute recognition of instances of F. Recognition can be exemplified in responses other than the formation of beliefs, which require representational capacities. Manifestations of concept possession range from primitive differential motor reactions to instances falling under the concept to complex representations. In my analysis the earliest concept acquisition does not presuppose possession of beliefs, only the acquisition of a differential behavior pattern toward instances, developed from previous perceptual encounters. For example, when an infant's sucking reflex begins to differentiate so that he exercises it more readily in the presence of the nipple, we can attribute an incipient (motor) concept without attributing belief at the beginning that any particular thing is a nipple or that a nipplelike thing exists at a particular spatial location or in any particular direction, etc. The earliest differentiation of reflex schemas, which comes about gradually in relation to early encounters with the perceived environment,[9] suggests incipient conceptualization without the necessity of attributing beliefs.

Even if we do attribute a belief that something is an F as soon as we attribute the empirical concept of F, prior perceptual experience will still be required for the acquisition of the concept and hence the belief. The only line left to the reductionist here is to claim that basic empirical concepts are innate and thus, while presupposed in the earliest acquisitions of belief, need not be acquired through perception prior to belief. If such concepts can be plausibly considered innate, then we cannot argue for a time prior to their acquisition when perception cannot consist in the acquisition of beliefs that presuppose them. This defense of the epistemic account requires, in relation to the psychological evidence, yet another analysis of what it is to have a concept. One possibility is to view concepts as capacities to form beliefs.[10] If we analyze the concept 'red', for example, as a capacity for having beliefs about red objects, then it seems plausible to hold that this concept or capacity can exist before red objects act on the subject to produce beliefs about them. We can have the capacity to acquire beliefs about a certain class of objects before encountering any of them, although we will not acquire the beliefs until some are encountered. The capacity can be claimed to be part of our innate physical makeup.

But the last claim itself is plausible only under a weak interpretation of what it is to have a capacity. If having the capacity to form a belief that something is an F means being able to form the belief as soon as an F thing is encountered, then it again becomes implausible, in light of the evidence, to hold that such capacities, or the concepts equated with them, are innate. The lack of inborn differential responses once more counts against the claim of innateness. If, on the other hand, we adopt a weaker interpretation of having a capacity, such that one has the capacity to form beliefs if one will come to form them at some time in the future, then, although this interpretation of empirical concepts renders their innateness plausible, the interpretation itself is not. For under it, *all* our empirical concepts, even complex ones like the concept of general relativity, must always be construed as innate, since we can never acquire any beliefs that we did not always have the capacity to acquire, in this sense of 'capacity'. I have adopted a stronger analysis of concepts such that their possession entails that the subject can already recognize or react selectively to instances. The application of this account to the evidence implies that empirical concepts are acquired rather than innate, and acquired via perceptual experience. If they are neither all innate nor all acquired immediately and simultaneously with beliefs, then we are left with the thesis that some are acquired through perception but prior to the acquisition of perceptual beliefs.

THE INFORMATIONAL ACCOUNT

There is one more recent philosophical account of perceiving, put forth by Dretske, that accepts nonepistemic perception, perception without the acquisition of belief, but remains reductionist in omitting appearing as an irreducibly necessary condition of perceiving. According to this account an object is perceived when information about the object is transmitted through the senses. The subject receives information perceptually before transforming it into belief—perception simply makes information about the physical environment available for the subject to transform into beliefs, which may then guide actions. According to Dretske perceptual belief formation involves the conversion of sensory information from analog to digital form, a process of abstraction and selection, that is, conceptualization.[11] If this account of the difference between perceiving and acquiring perceptual beliefs holds up, then my earlier criticism of epistemic analyses of perception does not establish appearing as irreducible. Here an object's appearing may itself be reduced to the subject's receiving sensory information about it, so that perception without belief formation would not demonstrate the epistemic importance or indispensability of the appeal to appearing.

The main problem with the informational account stems from the lack of bivalence in our ordinary notion of information itself. I refer to the fact that information does not admit of falsity. If one receives information about an object, this must be information about at least some of its actual properties. Information can be misleading in leading one to make false inferences from it, but it cannot be itself false. In Dretske's view, for a signal to carry the information to S that x is F, the conditional probability of x's being F, given the signal (and what else S knows) must be one. There must be a lawlike connection between properties of the signal and properties of the source for information to be conveyed. While this feature of information makes the account ideal for refuting skeptical doubts regarding perceptual knowledge (since we must abstract basic concepts from contact with genuine properties), it makes the account itself inapplicable in conceivable situations. It is simply not the case that a subject must receive information about an object's real properties in order for him to perceive the object. I have suggested that a subject perceives an object when it appears to him, when it causes him to have perceptual experiences. The object must appear discrete, must be discriminated, in order to be perceived. But despite this requirement, all the object's intrinsic, nonrelational, or real properties can appear other than they are while it is being perceived. I can see a white cube against a black background, for example, when the object appears red, irregularly shaped, smaller than it is, etc. When an object appears, it need not appear as it is. Combining that premise with the premise that its appearing is sufficient for perceiving it, we may conclude that information regarding its (real) properties is not necessary for perceiving it. It is conceivable that our senses systematically distort what we perceive, giving us no genuine information about objects, while nevertheless allowing us to perceive them.

It might be said in defense of the informational account that, even when an object appears entirely other than it is, the subject still receives information about it when perceiving it, specifically, information about the way it appears. But it is clear that this reply would remove the reductionist force of the informational account and render it benign from my point of view. Dretske's own version is more radical, as he clearly views its reductionist character as an advantage. He argues, for example, that we cannot specify the object of perception as the cause of perceptual experience or appearance. Rather, the object of perception can be identified only as that about which our senses provide primary information.[12] Thus he takes the acquisition of information about the object *as opposed to* its causing the subject to be appeared to as criterial for perceiving.

His argument against the causal criterion is that there is no way to distinguish the object as the cause of the experience from other elements in the causal chain. The object is not the only differential cause of the perceptual experience, for example. His argument that the informational criterion does work points out that information fails to be conveyed about other elements in the causal chain, specific features of the retinal image or of the signals in the visual cortex, for example. The operation of the perceptual object constancies of size, shape, and color—identificational properties perceived as relatively constant through changing perceptual conditions—involves processes of abstracting from certain specifics in the proximal stimuli so as to convey information about distal stimuli more useful to the function of guiding behavior. If differential proximal stimuli become encoded in the same way (represented in the same way in the visual system), then the system fails to provide information about them while encoding information about the object perceived. The latter then seems to be uniquely picked out by the informational but not the causal criterion.

Even accepting this criterion for the perceptual object and therefore admitting the acquisition of information to be necessary for perceiving, one could again avoid the reductionist implication by arguing that only information about the way an object appears is necessary for perceiving it. Deeper criticism is warranted here, however, requiring retention not only of appearing as irreducible but of the more traditional causal account of perceiving objects. Despite the empirical facts cited in behalf of the informational criterion and the objection to the causal account noted above, the causal account can be modified so as to specify the object of perception correctly, while the informational criterion fails in conceivable situations. The causal account can be made adequate by the specification of more details about the causal chains appropriate to each sense modality. The visual object, for example, is that which appears by emitting or reflecting light from its surfaces (or by contrasting with surrounding areas that emit or reflect light). The transmission of information about a source in the sensory system does not always make that source an object of perception, on the other hand. There is some evidence, for example, that the perceptual constancies must develop through early interaction with the perceived environment, that they are not equally present at all stages. If appearances accord more with properties of the retinal image than with those of the distal stimulus initially, it would follow from the informational account that the infant at first sees his own retinal image rather than the objects around him. This would follow since information would be conveyed about properties of the retinal image not yet abstracted or ignored. Such information would be conveyed, although not processed or transformed into belief by the infant. But this implication is clearly false, since the infant sees the objects around him and not his own visual system, although he does not see the former *as* objects or acquire beliefs about them at first.

The same sort of counterintuitive implication would arise for the informational criterion of the perceptual object if it turned out that certain perceptual representations come about in only one way in the nervous system. If there were only one set of differential conditions in the initial configurations of neurons responsible for these representations, it would follow from the informational account that the neurons would be objects of perception, would themselves be perceived. Between these configurations as sources and later signals would exist the lawlike necessary relations for the latter to convey information about the former. According to the more traditional account, however, objects of perception are perceived because they appear, their appearances being psychologically accessible in a way that the physical causal chains are not. Stages in the causal chains may be indistinguishable with regard to the information that is available for extraction from conceivable points of view; but there is a difference in the accessibility of the ways objects appear from the subject's point of view. Thus the appeal to appearing as irreducible is required for the specification of the perceptual object, and the informational account fails on this score.

The reductionist version of the informational analysis of perceiving fails also to provide a correct account of the acquisition of basic perceptual concepts. According to Dretske, when the concept of F cannot be analyzed into simpler concepts, its acquisition depends on the development of internal structures sensitive to information that particular x's are F. On his view such concepts must be acquired in the presence of such information.[13] The obvious objection to this is that simple perceptual concepts, of colors for example, can be acquired through contact with objects that appear F but are not F. If, as I shall argue in the next chapter, colors do not qualify objects themselves but only ways objects appear, then all color concepts will be acquired in the absence of information about (literally) colored objects. Dretske maintains that we can acquire only the concept of appearing red from objects that are not really red, although one may not distinguish this concept from that of red itself. But this reply is incorrect, since we have both concepts, contrast them with each other, and, if there are literally no red objects, have acquired both in relation to appearances only. (I shall argue later against the view that red objects are simply ones that appear red under certain conditions.) In any case, if the account is to remain reductionist and yet contrast information that objects are red with information that they only appear red, then it must seemingly appeal to some epistemic sense of appearing in terms of tentative belief or dispositions to such belief. Appearing itself cannot be reduced to the acquisition of information in the absence of dispositions to belief. We may then return to the epistemic version of reductionism for further evaluation.

APPEARING AS NECESSARY FOR PERCEIVING

My argument that an infant perceives when elements of the environment appear to him shows that the epistemic account fails to state a necessary condition of perceiving. To the nonreductionist it will be more obvious that the account is not sufficient, that it omits an essential aspect of the perceptual process. But since the independent phenomenal aspect of perceiving apparently does not strike the reductionist with the same force or clarity, argument by means of problematic cases is again required here. That the type of perception involving only the appearance of objects is eventually incorporated into the more sophisticated type that involves the acquisition of beliefs as well becomes clear not only from the implausibility of thinking that, despite phenomenological intuition, the first type of perception drops out at a certain stage but also from a more thorough unpacking of the notion of belief in materialist terms. The reductionist, we said, is either a behaviorist or a central state materialist. We may begin with the former. The ways things appear on this interpretation ultimately reduce to those types of discriminatory behavior that subjects are disposed to display toward them.

Let us begin by trying to apply the full behaviorist-reductionist picture to the perception of secondary qualities, specifically colors. The color that an object appears to a subject must ultimately reduce on this account to his dispositions to match and discriminate the object from others. Many problems arise here. First, it is certainly logically possible for there to be only one object of a particular shade, or even only one object for each shade of color.[14] If he wants to talk of matching, the reductionist must then analyze the color appearance of an object in terms of how the subject would match it with other possible, rather than actual, objects. But which possible objects? Obviously the reductionist cannot say, 'those that appear the same color'. He will, of course, include discriminating responses as well, and argue that uniqueness of shade can be analyzed in terms of dispositions to distinguish an object of that shade from all other actual objects. But while this criterion will reveal an object to be uniquely colored in appearance, it will not tell us which unique color it appears to be. In the possible world in which there is one object for each shade, the same discriminating response will be made to all, yet we will not know from any of these responses what color a particular object appears to have.

Finally the behaviorist can include not simply those responses that match or discriminate in all-or-nothing fashion but those that indicate degree of similarity and difference (for example, those that locate orange objects closer to red ones than to blue on a color scale). Here we might find enough responses to locate each color for each subject within a full spectrum by its relations to others. But we still would not know how each object appears in relation to the color scale—whether objects whose colors are located in the same place on the scale appear the same to different subjects. At least, sameness of appearance would not be entailed by sameness of position on the scale as located by behavioral response, as it must be on the behaviorist account. Imagine, for instance, a subject, perhaps an extraterrestrial, who is red-green color-blind but who has some other sensory means to detect all differences in shades in that range and has learned to locate them as normal humans do in the spectrum. Perhaps his brain is able to transmit verbal messages to him regarding wavelengths of reflected light. Objects will not appear to him as they do to us in relation to color, but his dispositions to discriminatory responses may be the same. We would hesitate to say that the alien perceives colors in that range, despite the sameness of response (I am assuming we could detect or induce a difference by noticing the difference in central states). This shows that a belief with the same behavioral expressions, perhaps even identical in content and in manner of acquisition (by means of sense organs) to a perceptual belief of a human may not even be a perceptual belief in our sense if nothing appears or appears in ways similar to ways things appear to us. The behaviorist cannot account for the conceivable difference.

Similar points have been made by reference to the possibility of spectrum inversion. It seems possible for two subjects to perceive colors in totally opposite ways—what appears a particular shade to one always appears the complementary shade to the other—and yet for their learned behavioral responses to be the same. (Ignore complications relating to black-white and brightness perception.) The behaviorist must either deny the intelligibility of this possibility or seek some way to describe it in behavioral terms. Denial of the possibility of spectrum inversion is difficult to swallow, not only because it *seems* obviously intelligible (if not for us, then for creatures with simpler spectra and fewer discriminations among shades) but also because the behaviorist appears to land himself in contradiction here. He must seemingly accept that it is possible for a single person to undergo a spectrum inversion between times t_1 and t_2. He must accept this possibility because it is describable in behaviorist terms and therefore intelligible according to his own criterion. A spectrum inversion for S can be described in dispositional terms as follows: at t_2, S is disposed to match with t_1 fire engines, ripe apples, etc. (as he now remembers them) what he was disposed to match with healthy grass, leaves, etc., at t_1. (Let us ignore our earlier point that it is only contingently true that there is more than one green object, and hence that it is not what we mean by saying something appears green that we are disposed to match it with grass, leaves, etc.) This shift in dispositions will be manifest initially in verbal behavior, confused color labeling, and so on, making the spectrum inversion undeniable on the behavioral evidence. But the acceptance of the single-person possibility makes acknowledgment of the same possible relation between two different subjects seemingly mandatory. For if one person previously like the rest of us undergoes such an inversion, then his spectrum will be inverted relative to ours. (In speaking of *ours,* I assume that the skeptical challenge posed by the possibility of inversion—that one can never know that the colors one experiences are the same as those experienced by others—can be met by appeal to the best explanation for our degree of behavioral agreement regarding colors, given our physical similarities and a common evolutionary history.) Finally, if it is possible for a person to become different in this way by undergoing such a change, then it seems not only possible but more likely that one might be born different in this way.[15] In that case there would be the difference that his difference would remain behaviorally undetectable. But for the behaviorist to deny the possibility on that ground, it seems he must also deny the behaviorally detectable single-person case as well.

We may assure ourselves further that he cannot seize the second horn of the dilemma posed for him by describing the two-person case in behavioral terms. Let us try an analysis of this case similar to the one offered above in the single-person case. The behaviorist can try to say, if S's spectrum is inverted relative to T's, that if T were in the state that S describes as an object's looking green, then T would be disposed to match the object with ripe apples, fire engines, etc.[16] This description appears to translate the difference between S and T into behavioral terms in much the same way that our earlier behavioral description captured the difference between S at t_1 and at t_2. The problem in the two-person case is that the description assumes a way to identify T's perceptual state independently of his dispositions to match and discriminate objects. If that state is instead exhausted by the dispositions in question, then S's being in that state must consist in his having the same dispositions, and the difference between them disappears. On the behaviorist account perceptual states are exhausted by the dispositions into which they are ultimately analyzed. If such states were not defined exclusively in terms of beliefs, or if the latter were not analyzed exclusively into dispositions to behave, then we would be able to pick out perceptual states on the basis of other criterially sufficient properties. But for the behaviorist there are no such properties on the basis of which to identify the states, and so the distinction between subjects with inverted spectra cannot be captured.

Of course the behaviorist can point out that one who holds an experiential account of appearing is in no better position to find out about the contrast between S and T, since he too can learn of the mental states of others only through observing their behavior. But unless we are verificationists, unless we hold that distinctions that fail to show up in public evidence must be unreal, this point does not argue that the nonreductionist is on no firmer ground in making sense of the imagined contrast. He has a way of referring to the different perceptual states directly in terms of the different ways of appearing they embody. The case of the inverted spectrum, with its argument from the one-person context, which the verificationist can accommodate, to the two-person context, which he cannot, raises serious difficulties for verificationism in general and not simply for its behaviorist manifestation. If the possibility of inversion is real, then a reductionist analysis of perception that unpacks belief in purely dispositional terms fails to state sufficient as well as necessary conditions (the latter having been shown in the previous argument, concerning the color-blind alien).

The application of the full behaviorist analysis to other phenomenological contexts is even more counterintuitive than its application to the perception of colors, if not as demonstrably paradoxical. Consider the perception of aesthetic qualities of great works of art. Is the beautiful sound of the opening bars of Mozart's Fortieth Symphony to be analyzed in terms of disposition to discriminate it from the Thirty-ninth or choose it over the Forty-first? These behaviors would evidence beliefs about the symphonies, but the acquisition of such dispositions is surely not identical to the complex and wonderful ways they sound. The suggestion sounds facetious if not sacrilegious.

Finally, the dispositional account does not fare well in relation to psychological evidence. Dispositions to respond to the perceptual array are much more easily influenced by verbal information, for example, than are the ways things appear. A subject who is informed in advance of perceiving the Müller-Lyer illusion that the horizontal lines are equal in length will then be disposed to respond to the lines as equal (to match them with lines of equal length, etc.). Yet when he perceives them, they will appear unequal despite his behavioral disposition. The way they appear is distinct from the way he is disposed to respond to them and certainly distinct from his beliefs about them, with which the behaviorist identifies these dispositions to respond.

Even the psychological evidence that appears at first to support the epistemic-dispositional account—by demonstrating correlations between changes in responses toward the perceived environment and changes in ways it appears—on further reflection supports a distinction between the two relata. The most dramatic demonstration of these correlations is found in Ivo Kohler's experiments with distorting lenses.[17] The spectacles utilized by Kohler and his subjects consisted in reversing mirrors, prisms, and lenses of various colors, which caused up-down and right-left reversal, downward deflection with distortion of curves, and bisecting complimentary colors in the perceptual field, respectively. With prolonged wearing of these spectacles, all distortions tended to correct themselves after the subjects' actions had adapted to the new situations, but to reappear in the opposite directions once the glasses were removed. Here we have a striking example of perceptual transformation as a function of adaptive action in the environment, an illustration of the fact that perceptual experience can be conditioned through behavior.

But, while the experiment establishes the adaptively valuable dependence of appearance on behavior, details of the experimental results support a thesis of causal dependence rather than identity, stipulated by the dispositional analysis. All subjects reported that their behavior completely adapted to the changed visual array well before the array itself changed its appearance. The former normally took a day or two; the latter several weeks. The gap makes it difficult to accept an identification of the appearance with the behavioral dispositions. If the relation is instead causal and complex, requiring gradual rearrangement of the neural basis for the appearance, then a gap is to be expected. Indeed our surprise at the dramatic outcome of these experiments indicates once more that we do not accept any such identification, that it does not fit the phenomenology of our experience. The capacity to adapt behavioral dispositions is not striking; the subsequent change in appearances is. We all recognize the difference.

Reductionists who unpack beliefs in terms of brain states rather than the behavioral dispositions that manifest them avoid some of the problems of their behaviorist counterparts.

The inverted spectrum possibility, for example, cannot demonstrably refute their view, since they, like nonreductionists, have a way to identify the difference between subjects with inverted spectra. Since differences in ways things appear presumably always correlate with differences in central states, we cannot demonstrate the independence of the former from epistemic states so interpreted by finding obvious failures to correlate. At least we cannot do so in the case of adult perception, which does involve the acquisition of beliefs. The demonstration of a lack of sufficiency in the central state epistemic account relates more directly to matters epistemological, to the failure of the account to include the evidential grounds for perceptual beliefs.

We may begin to reveal this weakness by turning to a standard test for analyses of perceiving, the ability to capture the phenomenological similarity between veridical, illusory, and hallucinatory perception. For the nonreductionist this similarity is captured by the likeness of the experience in all three cases. The reductionist will say that, while we acquire true beliefs about the environment in the first case, in the latter two we acquire false beliefs or inclinations to belief (in the case of illusion, the false belief that the object perceived has a certain property and in hallucination, that there is an object perceived).[18] I mentioned above the possibility of informing a subject in advance that he will perceive an illusion, giving him true belief about it from the start. Here the epistemic reductionist will have to say that the subject nevertheless acquires an inclination to the opposite belief when he perceives the illusion, an inclination that he might suppress given his knowledge of the situation. It seems, however, that if we explain the nature and basis of the illusion carefully enough in advance, we can remove all inclination to false belief when it is perceived. It will nevertheless retain its illusory appearance.

In reply the reductionist will simply deny that the inclination to false belief is ever obliterated, arguing that it is only suppressed or overcome by the conflicting knowledge. The lack of a behavioral criterion on the basis of which to decide the issue might require us to declare this particular debate a draw (the reductionist will dismiss counterexamples in which subjects testify that they have no inclination to believe the fingers are as they appear). But there is a more serious defect with the materialist account of hallucinations and illusions, namely, its failure to indicate or capture the reasons why subjects believe as they do when in these states. According to the reductionist, a subject who is hallucinating or perceiving an illusion believes as he does because he is in a state similar to the state in which he veridically perceives objects or properties that he only seems to perceive at present. The similarity is between the brain states; the difference, between their environmental causes. The problem with this account is that it fails to state the reason why the subject falsely believes as he does in the perceptual context; it states only a physical cause for his belief and not its evidential grounds. It fails, that is, to account for the rationality of the subject's false belief when he hallucinates or perceives an illusion.

Hallucinations themselves often result from irrational frames of mind or from physical causes that also cause irrational behavior. Nevertheless, even in such a case the subject's perceptual belief, while false, is not in itself irrational, given his perceptual experience at the time. He has a good reason for believing as he does. He does not simply find himself possessed by this belief, irresistibly caused to have it as he might be caused to exhibit purely physical symptoms of a disease. In this respect suffering a hallucination, while perhaps a symptom of a mentally deranged state, differs from other such symptoms. If asked why they exhibit various symptoms of disease, mental or physical, most subjects are at a loss, unless they have independent knowledge of the causes of their symptoms. But if a hallucinating subject is asked why he perceptually believes as he does, he will not hesitate, if he is articulate, to appeal to appearances, to the way the environment looks to him. In so appealing he states the reason or grounds for his belief.

Of course, the facts that such a subject has grounds for his belief and that he is not aware of these grounds as states of his brain do not show that these grounds cannot be so identified. To argue from those premises alone against the reductionist thesis would be to commit the intensional fallacy. One can know one's brain states without knowing them *as* one's brain states (rather, one knows them *as* ways of appearing). But, since the

epistemic reductionist identifies these perceptual beliefs themselves with the brain states in question, and since the beliefs do
not constitute their own grounds, he does have a problem here.
Perhaps he can find different sets of brain states to identify with
appearances and with the perceptual beliefs for which they are
grounds. But such distinctions at the neurophysiological level
would appear arbitrary at best. Probably for this reason epistemic reductions have ignored the grounds for perceptual beliefs
in appearances, rather than identifying them also with states of
the brain.

If even hallucinatory beliefs exhibit a rationality beyond the
conceptual means of the reductionist account to capture, the
possession of similar grounds for other perceptual beliefs is
more obvious. In the case of illusion, for example, the subject's
reason for believing as he does about the perceived object is
perfectly transparent to him. He may know also that the present state of his brain is similar to other states in which he perceives objects that are as this one looks. But if he knows this, his
knowledge will derive from an inference from the way the object currently appears. He has grounds for both his perceptual
belief and his belief, if any, about this state of his brain, and
these grounds are the same.

In normal perception too we possess grounds for our perceptual beliefs to which we can appeal if challenged or asked to
provide justification. We defend claims to perceptual knowledge of objects and their properties by reference to ways they
appear. It is appropriate for a witness to answer a challenge to
his claim that his assailant wore a blue coat by pointing out that
his coat appeared blue, that the lighting conditions appeared
favorable, and that only blue coats appear that way in such
conditions. The defense lawyer will not question the relevance
of this response, but rather question the witness's memory of
the appearance of the coat or suggest a different explanation
for the way it appeared. There can be no question that the way
something appears is a relevant ground for believing it to have
a certain property, whether or not the appearance is ultimately
best explained by appeal to that property. In so appealing to the
ways things appear we cannot be appealing to our perceptual

beliefs about their properties, since such appeal would be redundant rather than justificatory. Nor can we be appealing to our brain states if these are identified with these perceptual beliefs.

Ignoring the grounds for perceptual beliefs not only renders the epistemic account of perception less usable for normative epistemology, it also runs directly afoul of our original criterion (A), the requirement that an analysis state necessary and sufficient conditions for a subject's perceiving something. Even in cases in which perceiving involves acquiring beliefs, the epistemic account fails to characterize adequately the beliefs acquired. It is part of our notion of what it is to be a perceptual belief that it have certain grounds, that it be appropriate to defend the belief in a certain way if challenged. A belief that cannot be defended initially by appeal to ways things appear is not a perceptual belief, even if it is somehow acquired by use of sense organs and refers in its content to normally perceptible properties. We have seen that the reductionist analysis, whether elaborated in behaviorist or central state terms, cannot accommodate in a plausible way the appropriateness of such appeals. The central state version cannot do so without distinguishing in seemingly arbitrary ways among states of the brain. For the behaviorist, ways of appearing and perceptual beliefs may be indistinguishable, unpacked in terms of identical dispositions.

As mentioned at the beginning of this chapter, the reductionist's epistemic analysis of perception is sometimes seen to have an advantage over other analyses in its implications for normative epistemology. Reductionists argue that the attempt to base perceptual knowledge on an irreducible ground of experience or appearance leads to skeptical outcomes, since, as Berkeley argued against Locke, we have no reason to think that appearance resembles reality in the absence of any way to compare them. Experience becomes an opaque screen that prevents us from ever directly acquiring objective knowledge and therefore from verifying the truth of beliefs based upon it. If we can eliminate this screen from our view of perception and see it rather as an immediate contact between subject and object involving the direct acquisition of empirical knowledge, it seems we can rescue ourselves from a philosophically pernicious skepticism.

Whether we have grounds for inferring from the nature of

appearance to the nature of reality remains to be seen in the following chapter. But it should be clear at this point that reductionist accounts fare no better in the face of skeptical challenge. They may analyze normal perception as the direct acquisition of empirical knowledge without any need for independent experiential grounds, but the claim to knowledge of reality remains open to question. Eliminating the grounds from perceptual beliefs leaves them no better founded than do experiential accounts. The question still arises as to the reason for thinking perceptual beliefs true, for holding that they constitute knowledge, which parallels the question how we could know that appearance faithfully represents reality.

If empirical foundations are required to answer this question about perceptual beliefs, as I argued in the previous section they are, then such foundations must be validated without having to appeal to other beliefs for support. Ordinary perceptual beliefs about the properties of perceived objects are not self-validating in this way. If we use the model of self-validation by self-explanation, it is clear that my belief that the typewriter before me is gray is not explained simply by the fact that it is. The belief is rather explained by the way the object is reflecting light to my eyes, by the subsequent processes in my brain, by the way it appears to me, etc. The former two causally explain the belief; the latter is *my* reason for believing as I do. The physical causal explanation itself remains grounded in appearances and beliefs about them, in that the best causal explanation for a perceptual belief must explain also the ways the object appears. Removing the grounds from perceptual beliefs and their physical explanations, as does the reductionist analysis, not only leaves the epistemologist no better off vis-à-vis the skeptic's challenge; in my view it blocks the way to the most satisfying answer to it.

6
THE NATURE OF APPEARING

Our argument has established that an object's appearing is sufficient for perceiving it, and that the acquisition of beliefs about it
by means of sensory stimulation, while necessary for perceptual
knowledge, is not sufficient for perceiving. Appearing in itself
need not involve the application of concepts to what appears,
requiring only discrimination and not identification or recognition. (Even discrimination is necessary only for the perception
of objects or their parts: a uniformly colored field can appear
without a background from which to discriminate it.) We may
be more explicit about the nature of appearance by distinguishing three levels in its conceptualization.

APPEARING AND CONCEPTS

The first level, the nonepistemic, involves no application of concepts to what appears. An object's appearing F, we said, does not
presuppose the concept of F-ness; otherwise it could not be a
source of the concept. Many empirical concepts seem to be acquired in relation to early perceptual experience of objects that
instantiate those concepts. Appearing, which is necessary for
perceiving, is always appearing in some way. If an object's appearing F to a subject always required that he possess the concept of F,
then either some empirical concepts would have to be innate or
subjects could never begin to perceive. We have noted the lack of
evidence for innate empirical concepts. If the perceptual concept of F-ness is not innate, then unless it can be acquired by
perceiving objects that do not (yet) appear F, some objects must
appear F before being conceptualized as F objects. One can be
trained to notice features of objects that one had not noticed

before by having their relations to previously noticed features pointed out. In this way one can acquire a concept of F-ness by perceiving an object that had not previously appeared F. But such training cannot be the source of basic empirical concepts, since one cannot be trained to be perceptually conscious from the beginning. Thus appearing F cannot always presuppose a subject's possessing the conceptual category of F-ness.

An object's appearing *to be* F—the second level of conceptualization—which involves identification, correct or incorrect, of the object as an F object, does require the concept of F-ness. For an object to appear to be F, it need not appear F. It can appear G, and the subject can infer that it is F from the additional premise that F things appear G in such conditions as obtain. But for an object to appear perceptually to be F, it must appear F. Perceptual beliefs are noninferential: perceptually believing is to be contrasted with believing as a result of inference. That a belief must be noninferential in order to be a perceptual belief can be seen most easily in reference to perceptual knowledge and its acquisition. The acquisition of perceptual knowledge consists in simply noting an observable fact. But to note an observable fact is not to infer one—these are contrasting ways of acquiring knowledge. Inference "goes beyond" the immediately observed facts: to infer is to expand upon what is directly perceived, to arrive at a belief regarding a property not currently perceived. My colleague would think it a bad joke if, when looking directly at his blue jacket, I were to say, "I infer that you are wearing a blue jacket."

An object may appear F and appear perceptually to be F without the subject's being aware of it *as* appearing F. Awareness of its appearing F as an appearance requires the concept of appearing F as opposed to being F. Thus we have a third level in the conceptualization of ways things appear, that in which the appearance is categorized as such. The concept of appearing F is more sophisticated than that of being F, the former normally being parasitic upon the latter. Children learn to ascribe properties to objects well before they learn to qualify or limit such ascription to the ways they appear. We may grant for the sake of argument that this order of concept acquisition is necessary rather than accidental. Some philosophers have argued on this ground that perceivers are not normally aware of how things appear, that such awareness requires conceptual sophistication and an abnormally analytic frame of mind, the "painter's attitude."

From the same premise it has been argued also that beliefs about actual properties of objects cannot be justified ultimately by appeal to the ways they appear. We cannot, it is said, infer inductively from the order within experience to the nature of objects as its explanation without begging the question, since we cannot formulate that order without presupposing its objective basis.[1] It is not simply that we learn to ascribe qualities to objects first. The deeper problem for the inductivist indicated by that sequence is that concepts of appearances and of the order within them remain entirely parasitic upon their instantiation within the objective order. There is not one language for appearances and another for objective properties, but one language whose predicates apply primarily to objects themselves. If the ascription of properties to appearances logically presupposes the ascription of properties to objects, then the latter cannot be justified by appeal to the former. So goes the anti-Cartesian argument here.

These objections to claims I have made regarding the role of appearances and beliefs about them in validating perceptual beliefs can be met by maintaining a clear view of the nature of appearance and its relation to concepts as outlined above. I answered the claim that awareness of how things appear requires conceptual sophistication by arguing that it requires no conceptual ability at all in its function as a source of empirical concepts. In order to function in the justification of perceptual beliefs, appearances must be conceptualized as such. But just as a subject can have empirical knowledge without being able to justify his claims, so he can be aware of an object's appearing when he perceives it without conceptualizing the appearance as such. (We also granted to the epistemic analysis that a subject can acquire beliefs without being aware of acquiring them as such.) For an object to be perceived it must appear in some way; and the fact that the concept of an appearance is a sophisticated one no more affects the perception of an object than a rock's lacking the concept of force affects its striking another.

THE RETINAL IMAGE

The claim that perceivers are aware of the way something appears only when they adopt a painter's attitude, or restrict their attention to that perspective whose representation would most faithfully capture the perceived scene on canvas, belies a serious error regarding the phenomenology and psychology of perceiving. The error, an old one in psychology and philosophy, consists in identifying ways things appear with features of the retinal image, with the properties of light projected from the distal stimulus onto the retina. Experiments such as those by Kohler (described above) decisively refute the model of the visual system as a camera. They show that the retinal image lacks privileged psychological status in the causal chain involved in perceiving. Objects do not normally appear in ways fully predictable from the ways they reflect light from their plane surfaces. A subject is aware of the way an object appears if he is perceptually aware of it at all, and he is aware of the way it appears as an appearance if he conceptualizes it as such. Both claims are compatible with recognition of the difficulty of trying to make the properties as they appear approximate to those of the distal stimulus as indicated by measures of light waves, a feat of interest mainly to painters, who must reproduce the latter properties on their canvases if they seek realistic representation.

The temptation to elevate the importance of the retinal image beyond its capacity to transmit usable physical information as one link in the perceptual causal chain, the identification of properties therein with ways of appearing, derives not only from the model of the eye as a camera but from the epistemic desire to locate a purely objective level of data for perceptual belief. The retinal image is as yet "uncontaminated" by subjective factors, perhaps the last link in the causal chain to remain so. Its properties are a function of the reflected pattern of light alone. It is itself readily visible, at least to others, again the last link in the chain before its disappearance and radical alteration in the paths of the visual nervous system. These features render it a natural locus for "the given"—objective data available for the sensory system to process. To be "given" in a psychological sense, however, the properties of the retinal image must be accessible to the perceiving subject, as they normally are not. Hence the initial mistaken identification of properties of the retinal image with ways of appearing is followed by the misplaced objection that appearing (in this mistaken sense) is not normally an element of perceptual awareness.

One reaction to the divorce of phenomenologically accessible appearances from physical properties of the retinal image is to continue to speak of the latter as providing perceptual data, while dropping reference to appearances altogether. The proximal stimulus is to take over the foundational epistemic function from appearances once the latter are revealed to be dependent on the subject's behavior and on other subjective and contextual factors. The physical input to the sensory system becomes the data from which the brain infers to the nature of the perceived environment. Rather than validating perceptual beliefs by appeal to appearances as their foundations, we are to measure them as outputs against their physical data as inputs. Speaking of processes in the brain in terms of inferences has become prevalent among those interested in the way the brain processes sensory signals. The topic is of concern to both psychologists and neurophysiologists, who together try to map functional descriptions of this process onto physical descriptions. In this context it is useful to speak functionally of physical data and neural inference, for example, the inference of depth from certain visual cues in the physical information. Such terminology is useful also in the explanation of certain systematic perceptual errors or illusions, for example, those that result from the presence of depth cues in the absence of the physical configurations that they normally signal.

The use of terms like 'data' and 'inference' becomes misleading only in epistemic contexts, where, if taken literally, it is apt to confuse purely causal processes with justificatory or validating arguments. Physical stimulation, as "data" for the brain, cannot replace appearing or beliefs about appearing as foundations in the epistemologist's reconstruction. The former is from the epistemic point of view, a sophisticated theoretical posit; properties of appearances, in contrast, can be established immediately on the basis of beliefs about them alone. Views of the former change with developments in physical and physiological theory; all such theories, however, must remain true to appearances as established by subjective reports. Theory builders infer to best explanations for ways things appear; brains no more literally infer to best explanations for physical inputs than do elevators or turntables, although ascriptions of inferences may be heuristically useful as functional descriptions in all these cases. Subjects are normally unaware of physical stimuli and do not infer perceptual beliefs from them. As argued above, perceptual beliefs are not inferential at all, although their validation requires chains of explanatory inferences with central reference to appearances. These appearances can be neither identified with physical stimuli nor replaced by reference to them.

THE EPISTEMIC PRIORITY OF APPEARING

I have distinguished three types of priority sometimes confused in the literature of epistemology: (a) priority among elements in the causal chains leading to perceptual beliefs, (b) priority among levels in the acquisition of concepts, and (c) epistemic priority in the validation of beliefs. We have seen that the identification of ways of appearing with properties of the retinal image confuses (a) with (c). The claim that perceptual beliefs cannot be justified by appeal to appearances because ascription of properties to appearances presupposes their ascription to objects confuses (b) with (c). A belief whose possession or expression requires sophisticated concepts can figure in the validation of one that requires only more elementary concepts. Even the dependence of concepts in the former upon concepts in the latter remains irrelevant to their epistemic priority or degree of mediacy in validation. That a person must conceive of objective properties before conceiving of appearances does not show that the objective concepts are instantiated or that beliefs utilizing them are true. That concepts of and hence beliefs about appearances are sophisticated does not imply that such beliefs cannot be immediately justified or validated once held. These beliefs,

immediately validated, can be used in the validation of conceptually simpler perceptual beliefs, which must be shown to be
true. The objection to the foundationalist account fails.

It is also irrelevant to their foundational role that ways of
appearing can be affected by various subjective factors such as
attention and expectation, as well as by environmental factors
such as surrounding colors in the case of color perception. There
are no "uncontaminated" phenomenological data that vary only
with physical properties at each spatial point. While the brain
does not literally infer, it does process visual-behavioral information as if constructing hypotheses about behaviorally relevant
features of the environment rather than recording wavelengths
of light projected on the retina. But the fact that appearances
vary in these ways does not affect the validation of beliefs about
them, as long as the beliefs vary with the appearances. I shall
argue in the next section that we are justified in believing that
they do so vary, that is, that such beliefs are normally true. We
are justified in believing them true in the absence of evidence for
their truth. It is this immediacy in validation that renders such
beliefs foundational or epistemically basic. Because of the
epistemic status of these beliefs, reference to appearances in
their explanations marks the transition to reality beyond beliefs
in the epistemologist's structure. Causal influences upon appearances do not affect that status, although the separation of subjective from objective causal factors in the subsequent explanations
for ways of appearing is crucial in the final appraisal of perceptual beliefs.

We have distinguished the epistemically relevant sense of
'appear' from its use in expressing tentative belief and from the
mistaken use in referring to properties of the retinal image.
There is another unusual and irrelevant use, amply criticized
elsewhere,[2] that can be mentioned in passing, what is sometimes
called the comparative use. Here 'x appears blue' is supposed to
mean the same as 'x appears the way blue things do'. This use
actually approximates to that of 'x appears to be blue' rather
than to that of 'x appears blue'. Furthermore, the term would
not normally be used in this way to refer to perceptually appearing to be blue but rather to appearing to be blue by inference
from appearing some other color. One would normally talk of

the way blue things appear only in conditions in which they do not appear blue. Certainly the ordinary meaning of 'appears blue' makes no reference to blue things, since it is an open question whether that which appears blue is blue (or whether blue qualifies only ways things appear). In regard to nonrelational perceptible properties that indisputably qualify objects in themselves, it is only contingent, if true, that these properties also qualify the ways the objects appear. It may be that most or all objects with a particular property are disguised to hide it. Thus, where F is a perceptible property, it is not necessary that F things normally appear F or that things that normally appear F are. (The latter claim will be defended further in the next chapter.)

Having differentiated our intended sense of 'appears' from other uses, we may indicate it in a more positive way for those still in doubt by pointing out that what changes when perception is altered with alterations in conditions in which objects are perceived, when the properties of the objects themselves do not change, are the ways the objects appear. This characterization suffices to pick out appearances once changes in appearing have been clearly distinguished from changes in belief and inclinations to belief.

APPEARING AS INVOLVING THE MENTAL

I have concentrated so far in this section on the epistemic status of appearing, its relation to empirical concepts and beliefs. Clarification of the nature of appearing normally pertains more to its metaphysical status. Given that our interest is epistemological, I shall be brief on this issue, since there is little difference in epistemic implications of the different ways of specifying the metaphysical category into which appearances fit.

Once the materialist agrees in rejecting the epistemic account of appearing, once he accepts that appearances constitute grounds for perceptual beliefs rather than being tentative beliefs themselves, and once he admits that beliefs about appearances figure independently in the validation of perceptual beliefs, I would be very happy if all these epistemically independent elements could be unpacked in terms of physical states and processes alone. Unfortunately, I see little chance of success for this materialist project.

The main problem is a very old one: what to do about the secondary qualities that qualify ways things appear, for example, phenomenal colors in the case of visual perception. If qualities that qualify the ways things appear are not those falsely or truly believed to be intrinsic properties of perceived objects, as they are not if appearances do not reduce to beliefs, then they must, if physical, qualify some parts of the physical perceptual process or of the material entities related in that process. If visually appearing is a physical process, it must be identified with the process by which light is transmitted or reflected, or with subsequent processes in the brain, or both. Colors that appear, if physical, must be ascribed either to these processes or perhaps to the objects involved in them. The latter include perceived objects and the physical subject, specifically his retina and brain. The problem is that no physical properties in any of these loci seem identical with apparent colors.

If apparent colors were located in perceived objects themselves, they would have to be distinguished at least sometimes from intrinsic properties identified with actual colors, since objects sometimes appear other than we take them to be. It is clear that both real and apparent colors cannot be found in the same objects. In fact, I shall argue later, as others have,[3] that physical theory and psychological evidence render it implausible to ascribe *either* type of property to physical objects in themselves. Appeal to real colors does not enter into best physical explanations for how objects appear, and perceived colors do not vary with intrinsic properties of objects alone. The best candidate in the physical array external to the perceiver for a constant correlate with the ways objects appear colored seems to consist in certain complex relations among wavelengths of light reflected from the entire array.[4] But, in addition to the difficulty of identifying colors perceived at particular locations with physical relations obtaining elsewhere, there is the problem that perceptions of color vary also with states of adaptation in the retinal cells, which in turn vary with immediately prior perceptions of color. Identification of discrete colors as ways objects appear with relational properties spanning not only the space of the entire perceived array but a stretch of time extending to earlier perceptions of other colors, borders on unintelligibility.

If we were to identify apparent colors with such physical relations, the question would remain why these relations appear *as colors*. That this remains an open question indicates the failure of the enterprise, since, if the physical relations in question were colors, the question would not arise why they appear as colors. Thus this demand for further explanation would make it clear that we had not really succeeded in reducing the properties in questioning to their complex physical correlates. Any such reference to the physical relations alone leaves out what it is like to perceive colors, to have colors appear in one's experience. Identifying all the ways objects appear to the different sense modalities with the subjective and objective physical processes that cause them to so appear leaves out what it is like to experience, that is, the very ways in which these physical processes and their properties appear.[5] Such reduction leaves open the question of why the physical relations specified appear as they do to human subjects. This regress in my view defeats the attempted physical reduction. Its threat explains why materialists stick to epistemic accounts of perception. Only by offering such analyses can they eliminate apparent properties (properties that qualify ways things appear) by arguing that, when objects appear other than they are, this is just a matter of subjects falsely believing them to have those properties. The refutation of the epistemic account greatly reduces the chances for the reduction of experience to physical terms.

A materialist might claim that my reasons for rejecting the ascription of secondary qualities as they appear to physical relations apply to mentalist interpretations of appearances as well. First, just as we asked why certain physical relations appear as colors, so we may ask why irreducible appearances appear as they do. It might be claimed that we cannot answer the latter question any more satisfactorily than the former. But there is a difference. If we ask why irreducible appearances appear as they do, this is a request for a causal explanation, not a rejection of the identification of the appearances as appearances. While the completion of this causal explanation faces notorious difficulties, there is not the same regress or expression of incomprehension at the explanation of what the appearances or apparent qualities are. The identification of apparent color properties with complex physical relations obtaining between ratios of wavelengths and nerve cells fails because the question 'Why do these relations appear as colors?' shows that the apparent colors have not really been eliminated or reduced. The request for a causal explanation of experience, however, can receive at least a partial answer. Physical causal factors can be investigated by comparing (best theories of) inputs with outputs at each interval in the causal chain. The final output is epistemically most easily ascertained, although the mechanism of the final step in the causal chain eludes us so completely that it seems to set permanent limits to the scope of explanation. Despite this gap in comprehension, the complete specification of causally necessary and sufficient conditions, or of all factors accounting for the probability of things appearing as they do, should suffice. Causal inquiry in all areas must find its limits in regularities that cannot be further explained.

One might question also whether the apparent location in physical space of irreducible properties of appearances is any more comprehensible than the apparent locations of physical relations obtaining elsewhere. The answer seems to me affirmative. In the first case, properties appear to qualify objects at particular places when they do not really do so but, rather, qualify only the ways the objects appear. In the second case, by contrast, discrete properties that appear as, or appear to be, located in a given place are identified with complex relations located elsewhere. If they simply appear *to be* located in a given place, then we return to the attempt to reduce properties that appear to false beliefs, a position refuted in the previous chapter. If they appear *as* properties located in a given place, then we encounter again the regress that defeats the new attempt at reduction.

APPEARING VS. SENSE DATA

If we accept appearing as ultimately reducible to neither epistemic nor nonepistemic physical terms, then we are left with the choice between sense data (or appearances as mental objects) and appearings as mental processes, or perhaps as processes relating the mental to the physical. I have so far used the act-object-adjective and process-adverb terminologies interchangeably in describing ways objects appear or apparent properties. Again, in my view, little rides epistemically on the choice, since in either case perceptual beliefs will be validated through appeal to beliefs about appearings, and some of the latter beliefs will be validated immediately. Difficulties beset either account of the ontology, but in the end I find the adverbial, or appearing, view of apparent properties, along with the direct realist account of the perception of physical objects that appear, preferable.

The standard objections to sense data vary in my view from inconsequential to decisive. The epistemic objection that, once we posit sense data as immediate or direct objects of perception, we have no reason to believe in the existence or properties of physical objects, can be avoided or refuted. It can be avoided if mental objects are equated with images and hallucinations, and the physical object-appearing analysis is applied to ordinary perception. Here it will have to be admitted that the two types of experience can be phenomenologically indistinguishable at the time they occur, but this does not prevent us from holding them ontologically distinct. (Indeed the materialist distinguishes these contexts ontologically also, although in different terms.) The more thoroughgoing believer in sense data as direct objects of ordinary perception can counter the objection by pointing out that it is based on a narrow view of induction. We need not compare sense data with physical objects and their properties in order to infer to the nature of the latter from knowledge of the former. We would have more or less the same reasons for inferring to the best causal explanations for sense data as for inferring to the best explanations for ways we are appeared to.

Objections or puzzles regarding the nature of sense data themselves are somewhat more damaging. First there are the standard problems regarding individuation and duration: for example, whether eye movements that alter the visual array create new sets of sense data or cause changes in persisting data. We seem perfectly free to choose either answer. The defender of sense data can reply that physical objects too have vague boundaries (think of subtracting a molecule at a time from the chair on which you are sitting), and that we exercise choice, for example, in individuating parts of physical objects (how many parts does the chair have?). But the degree of choice or mere stipulation in the case of individuating not only parts of mental objects but the objects themselves in itself raises the question whether we are referring to genuine objects or only to processes in which various qualities appear. A more serious problem here is the one regarding indeterminate properties. The idea that an object can have such properties, for example, spots or stripes but no particular number of them, is puzzling. But if such properties of sense data are to be fully determinate, then they will not capture the ways objects appear, since, for example, objects can appear spotted without appearing to have a determinate number of spots (more precisely, in the nonconceptual sense of 'appear', objects can appear spotted without appearing determinately spotted in regard to number). If fully determinate, then, sense data cannot fulfill their function of capturing the ways things appear; they cannot serve as loci for apparent properties.

The greatest difficulties with sense data relate to the multiplication of objects perceived. It is highly counterintuitive to claim that we perceive *only* mental and not ordinary physical objects, that such things as tables and chairs cannot be perceived but must be inferred to exist. Aside from intuition, which perhaps should count for little in epistemology, the best explanation for the nature of our perceptual experience is that it is caused in a certain way by objects with certain kinds of properties. The sense data theorist who is also a realist will appeal to this explanation to justify his realism. But the causal relation in question is precisely the relation of perceiving physical objects. Thus, one who accepts this form of induction and also sense data as objects of normal perception must hold that both sense data and ordinary physical objects are normally perceived, perhaps the latter by means of the former. But this alternative proves to be little better.

While it does not strictly follow from the fact that we always perceive sense data that we never perceive ordinary physical objects also, it is difficult to accept that when I look directly at an object, say my typewriter, against a dark background, here the dark wood of my desk, I see two radically different kinds of objects, one mental and the other physical, and that the former resembles the latter in certain respects but not in others. When I look at such an object, the phenomenology is that of perceiving one object. I can understand that this object may not have all those properties that it appears to have, but not that those properties it only appears to have really qualify an ontologically distinct object simultaneously perceived and phenomenologically indistinguishable from the typewriter I see.

If this second object is located in physical space where it appears to be (assuming it appears to be anywhere), then there must be two different objects with identical boundaries in the same place at the same time, one of which can be perceived only by me. In fact there must be, in addition to the physical object, as many objects as subjects seeing that one physical object, and perhaps many more if those subjects move while they are perceiving it. Once we recognize that at least one sense datum object is required for each of those subjects at different distances and angles from the physical object, this alternative becomes not merely implausible but seemingly inconceivable. The problem is that, if each sense datum has the shape it appears to have, as it must if there is not to be a regress of apparent properties, then we cannot conceive how objects of all these different shapes could occupy precisely the same position in physical space. Even considering only one subject, if his angle of vision is such as to overcome the operation of shape constancy, so that the physical object appears a shape different from its physical shape, then the sense datum cannot occupy the same space at the same angle to the perceiver as the physical object, for only an object with the shape of the latter would appear the shape of the former at that angle and distance.[6] If, to avoid this objection, we say that the sense datum object is not located in physical space where it appears, then we must admit that it has a new property that is only apparent and does not really qualify it. This alternative again generates a regress in the attempt to capture apparent properties.

Not only spatial properties but other relational qualities that sense data are supposed to have or lack give rise to equal difficulties. Consider causal powers. Mental causes remain explanatorily superfluous for accounts of cognition and behavior. At least, sense data play no obviously required causal roles. As loci for apparent properties, they are to serve as grounds and evidence for ordinary perceptual beliefs. But the fulfillment of this role requires phenomenological accessibility, immediate validation of some beliefs that refer to them, and perhaps causal antecedents in common with the perceptual beliefs they help to validate. They need not be causes of such beliefs. Even if sense data do enter into causal explanations for perceptual beliefs, it is clear that they do not cause these beliefs in the ways that physical objects do, for example, via media such as transmitted light in the case of vision. But this makes it problematic how we can be said to *see* sense data at all, since our concept of seeing includes some specification of such a causal chain.[7] (Unlike previous objections to sense data, this one applies to hallucinations and images as well as to ordinary perceptual contexts. Since the previous objections do not, the identification of hallucinations and images as mental objects is less implausible than the thesis that we perceive sense data normally. The claim that we see hallucinations may still be metaphysically uneconomical and must involve an extended sense of 'see'.)

Objections to the adverbial, or appearing, ontology can be raised as well and must be weighed against materialist and sense data accounts of apparent qualities. Here I believe the objections can be met more successfully. There is, first, the awkwardness of the appearing terminology, which can become so cumbersome as to threaten intelligibility. 'I am appeared to pale bluely and squarely inside(ly?) dark redly and circlely' is far more difficult to understand than 'I see a pale blue image inside a dark red circle'. And matters can become worse with increasing complexity in the visual array to be described, requiring adverbial modifiers of adverbial modifiers of. . . . This awkwardness does not in itself, however, signal a similar loss in metaphysical perspicuity. Compare 'He danced a slow and methodical variation of a waltz'. This sentence defies smooth translation into process-adverbial terms, in which 'slowly' and 'methodically' would have to modify 'waltzily'. Despite our inability so to translate into ordinary English, it is clear in this case that the noun-adjective locution misleads as a guide to the ontology of the situation. The same may be true in the case of describing the perception of apparent qualities. Our inability to understand or even formulate adverbial translations does not prove the act-object language metaphysically accurate. In general, that certain concepts seem indispensable for us does not prove that they are instantiated. Even if we find it not only easier but necessary to categorize experience in terms of mental objects and their properties when we describe it in certain contexts, this practical necessity does not establish the existence of mental objects as opposed to ways of appearing. (The same counterargument applies against certain arguments for realism at a later stage.)

A second argument against the appearing ontology is that it fails to provide sufficient structure to distinguish what can be distinguished within perceptual experience and to bring out resemblances among experiences and between apparent and real properties. The structure within experience is said to be determined by distinct objects with sets of discrete properties. Eliminate those objects and that order disappears, according to this objection. While appearing as a process normally relates subjects to physical objects, this relation to physical objects cannot be assumed to provide in itself the required structure, for two reasons. First, according to the appearing ontology there are no objects present in the cases of hallucinations and images; yet such experiences may be phenomenologically indistinguishable from normal experiences, and hence display completely analogous structures. Second, in the epistemological reconstruction, we appeal to the order within appearances to validate beliefs about physical objects and their properties. While this move remains legitimate despite the conceptual priority of beliefs about objects and their relations, it might not be so if there were no order in experience except that provided by its objects. That we must conceive of relations first in objective terms does not matter; but if we cannot then conceive of there being independent structure within experience itself, our reconstruction is in jeopardy. The argument here is that such structure must be provided by mental, if not physical, objects. If so, then the appearing ontology is inadequate.

In the absence of objects perceived, being appeared to at a

time is held to be a single process ascribed to a subject as a whole. One difficulty that arises for a proper description of the structure within such an experience has been called the "many property problem." The problem is, for example, to differentiate between, on one hand, seeing a red, square image and a green, round one, and, on the other hand, seeing a green, square image and a red, round one. Clearly it will not do to say in the first case that the subject is appeared to redly and squarely and greenly and roundly, since this will be true in the second case as well. If we link the adverbs into two single-place modifiers, red-squarely and green-roundly, then we lose the similarity between red, square images and red, round ones, since we no longer have red as a separable component of each. Yet these resemblances should also be expressible. (Intuitively, according to the appearing ontology, red, square images should resemble red, round ones in the way that slow tangoes resemble slow waltzes. It seems that the appearing analysis either loses distinctions expressible within the object ontology or loses similarities that can also be captured by the alternative framework.)[8]

There are two ways in which this objection can be answered, two ways in which both the differences and similarities within experience can be captured by an appearing or process ontology. The first involves appeal to distinct but simultaneous acts of sensing, processes of appearing, or events of being appeared to. In the example mentioned, one such process would be qualified by redly and squarely and the other by greenly and roundly.[9] Clearly it does make sense to talk of different processes occurring within a person at the same time, or of different events happening to him. Our metaphysics might become somewhat bloated here, since we would require as many simultaneous perceptual events as we have mental objects or parts of objects on the alternative account. But the appearing metaphysics would remain no less economical than that which posits mental objects. The second, a leaner and perhaps more intuitive way for an appearing ontology to capture the differences and similarities within experience, is by appeal to apparent spatial properties. It is true that if all appearings without objects qualify subjects alone, then there are no real spatial distinctions within them. But there are nevertheless apparent spatial properties that qualify the ways of appearing, for example redly and squarely to the left of greenly and roundly. Awkwardness and complexity of expression in more complex examples again constitute no bar to this interpretation of the structure within visual experience. The interpretation again preserves all inferences based on resemblances and differences among ways of appearing.

Both interpretations make clear that resemblances and distinctions among ways of appearing parallel exactly those ascribable to mental or physical objects. It might still be argued that the appearing ontology fails to capture the resemblance between a red image, for example, and a red physical object. In the mental object framework both types of entity can be similar in having the same property. I believe this seeming simplicity loses its attraction, however, in those cases in which it becomes implausible to ascribe such properties to physical objects as intrinsic properties, as it does (I shall argue) in the case of colors. In these contexts we have to say either that an object's being red, for example, consists in its causing red appearances or appearings, or that red does not qualify physical objects at all, only the ways they appear or the appearances they cause. Thus either red physical objects are not similar to red images at all, since there are strictly no red objects, or the similarity lies in the subject's being appeared to in similar ways when seeing a red object and "seeing" a red image. In either case the same property does not really qualify the two types of objects and therefore there is no advantage to the mental object analysis. Still, it seems that both objects and images can be square, and that when they are, there are two types of objects with the same shape. Since the appearing analysis denies that images are objects, it must analyze the similarity here in terms of the subject's being appeared to in the same way in the two contexts (this being further explained by appeal to similar brain states as immediate causes). While this analysis may be slightly less intuitive in itself, it is more consistent with the analysis of similarity in the case of color, an offsetting advantage.

The final objection to the appearing account is that it is false to the phenomenology of perceptual consciousness, specifically to its object-directed or intentional character.[10] Perception always seems to be directed outward at some sort of object or field, whether physical or not; yet the appearing ontology would deny objects to certain types of perception, or at least to (quasi-)perceptual consciousness in certain contexts. This objection does not seem to apply to the case of ordinary perception of physical objects. In that context the object-directedness of perceptual consciousness can be captured by the physical objects themselves, toward which attention is actually directed. Indeed I have argued that the appearing terminology is far more expressive of the phenomenology of ordinary perception than is the alternative sense datum framework, since we seem ordinarily to perceive physical objects and only physical objects. When it comes to hallucinations and images, the defender of the appearing account must say that the similarity between these and genuine perceptions (a high percentage of these pathological experiences are *not* similar to ordinary perceptions) lies in the extent to which there seem to be objects present in the former contexts even though there are no objects there. Phenomenological similarity, when it exists, need not reflect ontological likeness if it can be explained in another way, as it can here by appeal to structurally similar brain states. (The latter explanation of the similarity between veridical and hallucinatory experience fails only when apparent properties are eliminated altogether, as in the materialist account. Then the question remains as to how we know that the brain states that occur in ordinary perception are like those for images prior to neurological investigation in each case.)

If the main goal is fidelity to the phenomenology of experience, then we should accept a metaphysically mixed account, with mental objects present as images and hallucinations but absent from ordinary perception. If we prefer ontological economy (given the ability to accommodate the phenomena), then we shall eliminate mental objects altogether. In choosing between these two alternatives, we can note again the lack of differences relevant to epistemology. The two are identical when it comes to ordinary perception, the main subject of concern. Both distinguish ordinary perception from hallucination in regard to their objects, and both must provide epistemically accessible grounds for doing so. In addition to its economy, the second alternative has advantages if we take causal powers to be partly definitive of objects. We noted earlier the difficulty in believing that we perceive sense data when we cannot specify or even conceive of causal chains linking these supposed perceptual objects to perceivers. Not only objects of perception but objects generally are conceived as loci of causal forces. Mental objects cannot be conceived that way, another reason for preferring the appearing framework.

APPEARING AND CAUSAL CHAINS IN PERCEPTION

We noted above that the way something appears need not be causally efficacious in producing perceptual beliefs about it in order to function as a ground or reason for those beliefs. The explanatory link between appearing and perceptual belief can be secured through common causes for both. One might wonder why, if physical causes in the brain bring about both the way of appearing and the perceptual belief, these causes do not screen out the way of appearing from the explanation for the perceptual belief. They would, of course, eliminate it from the causal explanation, but not from that relevant to the epistemic evaluation of the belief. Ways of appearing remain relevant to the evaluation of the beliefs, even if they are not causally efficacious, for three reasons.

First, in close possible worlds in which the physical causal mechanism for perceptual beliefs, the hardware in the brain, is different, the beliefs still vary with differences in appearances. This is so because, whatever the physical hardware that evolves in other creatures capable of experiencing and forming beliefs on the basis of experience, it would have to be such as to enable the creatures to apply concepts from experience consistently. Given this evolutionary necessity, the probability that particular perceptual beliefs will be held is tied more closely to ways things appear than to the specific physical causal chains that have evolved, even though the physical chains may cause both the beliefs and ways of appearing. We saw in Part I that explanatory factors are preferred according to their effects on probabilities in close possible worlds. Second, ways of appearing are accessible in contexts of evaluation, while internal physical causes are not. Third, and related to this second point, to validate perceptual beliefs by appeal to the ways of appearing that are mentioned in their explanations leads directly to perceptual foundations, to beliefs about ways things appear. The validation of the latter beliefs immediately establishes this type of explanation for perceptual beliefs as true. The functional description of physical causes in the brain for such beliefs, however, forms part of neurophysiological theory. Explanations of this sort are epistemically far more sophisticated, emerging much later in the epistemological reconstruction.

Normally such epistemic priority as I have identified for ways of appearing might not signify explanatory preferability, since I argued earlier that explanations need not be known at all in order to be best. But here we are concerned with explanations best for the purposes of epistemic evaluation. Relative to this purpose, epistemic priority amounts to explanatory priority. Furthermore, this priority of appearance in the order of explanation comes into play when the two types of explanation conflict. If physical explanations for perceptual beliefs conflicted with appeals to how the objects of such beliefs appear to their subjects, such conflicts would lead us to alter the functional descriptions of events in the brain from which we reconstruct the physical causal chains.

I shall expand on the reasons for this priority in the next chapter. Here we are concerned both with the possibility of knowledge of appearances despite the likely absence of direct causal relations between them and beliefs about them, and with the relevance of appearances to explanations for perceptual beliefs despite their not causing such beliefs. I claimed above that we could not see sense data because sense data do not cause our experience in the way necessary for us to see. But while a direct causal relation is necessary for seeing, no such relation is required for knowing, the requisite connection there being explanatory. Thus we can base perceptual beliefs on ways things appear without appearances causing beliefs about perceived objective properties, and we can know about appearances without their causing beliefs about them.

We must now consider in more detail the claim of immediate validation for foundational beliefs about ways of appearing. The foundational character of these beliefs will be defended again in the next section, and the stability of these foundations in the following.

7

KNOWLEDGE OF APPEARING

FOUNDATIONALISM VS. COHERENTISM

The theory of knowledge presented here is foundationalist, but more weakly so than traditional versions, falling somewhere between those and strictly coherentist theories. Stronger foundationalisms would endorse all the following theses: (1) there are immediately justified (validated) beliefs, beliefs justified without appeal to evidence; (2) the validation of all other beliefs must terminate in one or more immediately validated beliefs (beliefs cannot be supported solely by other beliefs, unless the latter are foundational); and (3) foundational beliefs are infallible, incorrigible, or self-evident. The usual opposing, coherentist view is characterized by the following counterclaims: (1) there are no immediately justified empirical beliefs and (2) all beliefs must be validated by appeal to beliefs as evidence.

Foundationalists have had the worse of the argument in attempting to defend the claim of infallibility for empirical beliefs and in maintaining that every empirical belief must be traced back to experiential foundations for validation. Coherentists, as I argued in an earlier chapter, cannot show that coherence within a belief system guarantees truth (unless they redefine truth as coherence itself, an alternative to be attacked in the next chapter). I shall in this section defend my earlier contention that foundational beliefs about ways things appear can be self-validated without being infallible, incorrigible, or self-evident. I shall not maintain that the validation of every other empirical belief can be traced directly back to such foundations. This requirement is superfluous for avoiding the principle objection to coherentism. Once a broad enough set of foundational beliefs is fixed in place, it becomes far less plausible to hold that many alternative and incompatible belief systems display equal coherence with that set, or that they explain these foundational beliefs equally satisfactorily.

Clear instances of factual beliefs that cannot be traced back directly to foundations for validation are beliefs in the soundness of epistemic principles themselves, for example the inductive principle of inference to the best explanation. Rational acceptance of this principle depends on the belief that such inference tends to preserve truth. Within the realist framework we cannot grant this belief special status: it is simply a matter of fact whether inductive inference of this form is reliable or tends to preserve truth. The belief stands then as a counterexample to the demand for validation by direct route to foundational beliefs about appearances. In a later section I shall explicate the justification of this principle, having previously argued on the basis of it for a realist interpretation of experience and science, by appealing to the fact that best explanations must continuously adapt to inputs from the world. The principle then at least iterates, in that it becomes more explanatorily coherent to believe that it tends to be truth preserving. While the argument from adaptation is grounded at various points in beliefs about the nature of experience, there is no straightforward route from the inferential principle to any foundational beliefs that justify it. Indeed the (immediate) justification of foundational beliefs itself presupposes the principle (I shall argue). It is therefore more reasonable to say that the principle is justified in terms of the system of beliefs that results from utilizing it, an essentially coherentist claim. In arguing earlier that the demonstration of empirical knowledge requires appeal to foundations, I was not attacking the coherentist idea that mutual support among beliefs can be justificatory, only the claim that it is always so. Ungrounded circles may be vicious, but coherence with grounding at some points is a mark of truth.

I have admitted that our primary principle of justification is neither immediately justified nor traceable back to immediately justified beliefs. Beliefs that satisfy the principle can nevertheless be immediately justified. Immediate validation remains possible first because the principle does not serve as evidence for foundational beliefs. Appeal to evidence would nullify a claim of immediate validation; but validation by use of an inductive principle, although ultimately presupposing the reliability of that principle, normally does not appeal to it as evidence. Evidence for p consists in facts that render p more probable or that p renders more probable. Neither relation normally holds between a belief and a principle used in its justification. In order to show justification, even for immediately justified beliefs, we must appeal to other beliefs, including perhaps belief in those justificatory principles we use. But certain of our beliefs can be immediately justified without our being immediately justified in believing that those beliefs are immediately justified. Appeal to other beliefs in demonstrating immediate justification shows only that immediate justification does not iterate in this way.

While the use of a justificatory principle that is itself validated only on the basis of coherence may be benign when establishing foundational beliefs, it does show, together with those beliefs, that knowledge exemplifies neither the simple web structure of coherentism nor the pyramid (inverted pyramid?) structure of strong foundationalism. Both these architectural models represent philosophical simplifications of a structure that is, not surprisingly, more irregular and complex. Immediate or self-justified beliefs play a major role in the validation of perceptual beliefs about objects, but not that of foundations sufficient in themselves for the justification of all other beliefs. Foundationalism and coherentism as usually stated do not exhaust the possibilities, since the former typically holds that every justified belief must derive its justification linearly from immediately justified beliefs, and the latter typically holds that all beliefs are justified only in relation to other beliefs as evidence. These are both extreme positions, between which there is much room for alternative theories of knowledge, like the one advocated here.

INFALLIBILITY

Traditional or strong foundationalism fails not only because the stock of immediately justified empirical beliefs, being limited to those about appearances, is too small to support the whole of empirical knowledge directly, but also because the class of infallible beliefs about experience, if not empty, is useless for grounding knowledge. Before arguing this point, we should distinguish more carefully between immediately justified or self-validating beliefs, infallible or incorrigible beliefs, and self-evident propositions.[1] Working backwards through this list, a self-evident proposition would be one known to be true without any evidence for its truth. We need not pause to consider whether there are such propositions, since it is evident that those of the form 'I am appeared to F-ly', those previously indicated as the contents of foundational beliefs, do not satisfy this criterion. 'I am appeared to redly', for example, is not only not self-evident for me but most often false, i.e., whenever I am not appeared to redly. Even if we build in a specification of the time of utterance, I require evidence in order to know when it is true, one type of evidence being my belief that I am so appeared to. That the content of such a belief is not self-evident does not damage our program. It is not required that the proposition expressing the content of a belief be self-evident in order for the belief to be self-validating.

Proceeding through the list of traditional foundational categories, the term 'incorrigible', meaning uncorrectable, would be as pejorative in epistemological use as in criminological, were it not invariably linked with the notion of infallibility in the former context. An incorrigible but not infallible belief is to be avoided, whether in the foundations or elsewhere. We may therefore skip to infallibility. A belief that p is infallible when its being held entails p. There is one way of interpreting beliefs about appearances so as to make them appear to be infallible. Interpretations of beliefs of the form 'I am appeared to F-ly' differ according to how we take the terms replacing F to refer to or pick out the phenomenal properties in question. We might claim that these terms are used purely demonstratively, their references being secured ostensively in relation to present sensations. Here the ways of appearing are treated as unique phenomena, as particulars incapable of recurrence, not as properties that might be reinstantiated. The use of the appearing terms here approximates to that of proper names of demonstratives, serving only to focus attention on the single sensation or phenomenal state. At this level of pure demonstrative use error seems impossible: the term introduced becomes meaningful only by succeeding in referring; and the truth of the belief expressed, if it is a belief, is presupposed by its being held, by its expression's being meaningful.[2]

The qualification in the last sentence—"if it is a belief"—is serious, however. I am first of all not certain that such use of predicate terms as names not for reinstantiable properties such as colors but for unique phenomenal states (without reinstantiable properties?) is intelligible. I am willing to grant for the sake of argument that it is, first because the concession turns out to be inconsequential, and second because I shall argue later for an account of reference that allows sophisticated language users broad control over the reference of their terms via specification of certain associated descriptions. Here it seems that a subject might specify a description of a certain phenomenal property by location in his visual field, if not with the implication that the property cannot be reinstantiated, at least without the contrary implication that it was instantiated previously or could be again. If he is willing to specify the apparent property so narrowly and shift predication so readily with each change in phenomenal state, then error, that is, inconsistent application of the predicates, appears impossible.

The concession is inconsequential first because, even if the purely demonstrative use of the predicate term is intelligible, it remains questionable whether the resulting sentence expresses a genuine belief. 'I am appeared to F-ly' becomes 'I am appeared to thusly', its meaning approximating to that of 'I name this appearance "F." ' While a sentence containing a name in the predicate position, for example, 'He is named Tom', can express a belief, an act of dubbing or giving a name, whether to a person or, in this unusual context, to an appearnce, does not seem to express a belief. Second, even if such strange cognitive states were to count as momentary beliefs, they could be of no use in a system of knowledge. Certainly they could not function as foundations. Without concepts capable of reapplication, there could be no beliefs regarding the order among sequences of appearances, no beliefs about appearances that would ultimately warrant belief in objects, even objects of the phenomenalist variety.

Thus the notion of infallibility is an epistemic dead end. The appeal to this notion lands us in a dilemma: if, on one hand, infallibility in beliefs about appearances is attainable at all, it is so only at the price of an impoverishment of content so severe as to render the beliefs epistemically useless. If, on the other hand, the beliefs are of the natural sort, if they express recognitions of properties via reinstantiable concepts, then they are liable to misrecognition, inconsistent application of the concepts, or error. Any time a concept is reapplied, it seems that it can be applied wrongly, if memory of the correct application fails. The fallibility of belief here is simply the fallibility of memory. While ascription of a reinstantiable property via a previously used concept need not be explicitly comparative, memory of the correct use is required for correct application. First-person ascription of properties to appearances may not always allow for independent verification, but the absence of such tests does not imply the absence of error.

A strong foundationalist might still reply that even reapplicable concepts or predicate terms can be applied to appearances infallibly. There are two remaining alternatives that differ at least in intent from pure demonstrative use. First it might be said that the term replacing F in 'I am appeared to F-ly' refers to whatever (most salient) property qualifies both the present way of appearing and those paradigms originally picked out by this term. Presumably there will be some similarities among these episodes, some properties in common in relation to which the belief is true. According to the second alternative, the term refers to a property now attended to and conceptualized originally from some paradigms, but not necessarily ones now remembered. Here there might be some earlier appearances to fill the role of paradigms. The problem in both cases concerns the status of the concepts applied and hence, once more, the usefulness and genuineness of the beliefs expressed.

In fact a dilemma similar to that faced in the case of pure demonstrative uses arises again in relation to these alternatives. Regarding the second alternative, there is little difference from the earlier case of pure demonstrative use of the predicate terms. Here as well the property is picked out demonstratively and held to have been instantiated on unspecified other occasions. Once more no true recognition is registered, no knowledge that could serve in the validation of less cautions claims. The first alternative, which specifies the paradigms more explicitly, but not the common property, shares the same sterile fate. A subject has a concept only when he can apply it consistently to instances. At a sophisticated level the required consistency can be achieved via an associated description, so that one can refer to whatever property or properties are common to a present object or appearance and those previous ones to which a term was applied, if one so intends. But the ways of appearing so weakly specified as they are in the first alternative will not capture an order within experience, knowledge of which could ground inference to the nature of physical objects. Predicates used in this way are once more not projectable, not generalizable to predictive inferences, and hence are of little or no use. Once more specification of the apparent properties such as to render their ascription infallible also renders them epistemically irrelevant. A predicate specified only to pick out whatever similarities obtain between some present appearance and some previous ones, without having any particular similarity or more specific property intended, cannot be used to express an epistemically foundational belief, if the latter is to enter into the justification of beliefs about the nature of objects. Infallibility in empirical belief is again purchased at the exorbitant price of all usable content.

Foundational beliefs must then be expressed in terms that can express beliefs about objective properties as well, if the former are to justify the latter. The application of such terms is always fallible, although certain sources of error in objective beliefs do not affect beliefs about appearnces. specifically, physical objects can appear other than they are, while appearances cannot. Subjective and environmental factors that cause objects to appear other than they are alter their appearnces; they do not cause the appearances to appear other than they are. The former is tautological, the negation of latter unintelligible. Appearances can appear *to be* other than they are (simply another way of saying that beliefs about appearances are fallible), but they cannot appear other than they are.

The facts that objects' appearing other than they are is most often the reason why they appear to be other than they are and that this source of error does not affect appearances themselves have led some philosophers to distinguish sharply between errors in the two domains, often calling errors regarding appearances "merely" verbal or conceptual. The term "merely" often misleads here. An error regarding the nature of appearance is merely verbal only if the subject applies a predicate consistently in his own idiolect but incompatibly with normal public use of that term. Most errors regarding appearances are not of this type but rather result from failure to attend with sufficient care to the ways the objects appear or from failure to remember a previously applied term. The characterization of such errors as conceptual is nevertheless accurate, since they involve a misapplication of concepts that is not explained by correct application at some more basic level, as is the case when objects appear other than they are. But conceptual errors of this sort are no less real and no less empirical than errors regarding physical properties. They are empirical or factual because the belief that I am appeared to F-ly involves an implicit belief that it is correct to apply 'F' to the present way I am appeared to (which, in the case of reapplication, implies that 'F' was applied in this way previously). They are equally or more serious or real than errors regarding physical properties because, in the case of the false beliefs about appearances, the errors may involve misunderstanding of how the concepts generally are to be applied, rather than simply misapplication in a single instance.

IMMEDIATE VALIDATION OF FALLIBLE BELIEFS

If infallibility is unattainable in foundational beliefs, it might nevertheless be argued to be required, so that antifoundationalists might regard the admission of fallibility as fatal to the foundationalist's program. There are several possible arguments to be considered here. All related to the fact that, if a belief is fallible, then its truth is only probable. One might hold first that, if the truth of a belief is (only) probable, then it must be probable only in relation to some other beliefs or propositions, hence not basic. The premise is in one sense correct, but the conclusion does not follow. That a proposition is probable relative to others does not mean that the latter necessarily function as evidence for the former. It is the absence of relevant evidence for first-person beliefs about appearances that renders them basic. The only first-person evidence for the way something appears is a belief that it appears that way. Its appearing that way is made probable also by a host of physical factors, but the latter are not usable evidence for the former; rather, the converse is true. The relevant principle in this case is that, if q best explains p, i.e., accounts for its probability, and p is antecedently accepted, then p constitutes evidence for q. Regarding beliefs about appearances, they are explained by the appearances alone. As explained in chapter 4, given the truth of such a belief, that is, the fact about how the subject is appeared to, the probability of the belief's being held is far greater; and in the epistemic context no other facts enter prominently into this explanation or signficantly raise the probability of the belief's being held. Thus, although such a belief is only probably true (albeit this probability is normally very high), its being held is the only evidence for its truth, and so this initial objection to the foundationalist on these grounds fails.

But fallibility may still seem a problem for the foundationalist. If beliefs are fallible, then under certain conditions they are false. But then it seems that one can be justified in such beliefs only when there are reasons to believe that these conditions do not obtain. The beliefs then would not be immediately justified but justified only in relation to these reasons. When unfavorable conditions for the formation of fallible beliefs obtain, one will generally be mistaken; so how could one be justified in such beliefs, how can these beliefs be validated, without sufficient assurance that these conditions do not obtain? If the principle of inference to the best explanation provides validation (as I assume here and shall argue in a later section), then the question is misdirected to the case under consideration. If someone asks why I believe that I am appeared to redly, for example, the best explanation normally is simply that I am so appeared to. The truth of this belief about an appearance requires only that I apply the predicate term consistently. The fact that I can form a coherent belief of this sort at all indicates that I am capable of the requisite conceptual stability. If I am attentive and careful, I can assume proper application of my concept. This does not entail that I cannot make a mistake. Various conditions—insanity, drug-induced pathology, total inebriation, etc.—could destroy my ability to conceptualize apparent properties consistently. But these conditions, which might lead to false belief, which would cause instability in the application of phenomenal concepts, probably also would prevent such beliefs from forming at all, so that the possession of a particular belief of this sort is evidence for its own truth.

A further relevant point here is that I cannot gather evidence for the requisite capacity without presupposing the very capacity I am trying to establish. In fact the ability required to sort and interpret the supposed evidence not only presupposes but is far more sophisticated than a mere capacity to apply concepts consistently to properties as they appear. Thus, while there are defeating conditions for foundational beliefs, one cannot and need not rule them out in advance by gathering evidence. Such beliefs are either unjustified or self-justified. To imagine that they are generally false, hence unjustified, is to imagine a far more complex explanation for their possession than the explanation that appeals to their truth alone, to the consistency in conceptualization in which their truth consists, that is, to their self-explanation. This second objection to fallibilistic foundationalism then fails too.

A third, related objection holds that, if foundational beliefs are merely probable, if the validation of beliefs about physical properties rests on large conjunctions of such beliefs about appearances, and if the beliefs are independent of one another, then the probability of these conjunctions (if large enough), hence of the perceptual and theoretical beliefs that rest on them, will be low. Validation of the latter beliefs by appeal to the former will then fail. We might attempt to answer this objection by arguing either that foundational beliefs regarding related appearances are not independent of one another (so that their probabilities are not to be merely multiplied) or that conjunctions of them need not be very large for purposes of validation. If either disjunct is true, then, given high enough probabilities for the individual beliefs about appearances, the probabilities of the conjunctions can remain sufficiently high as well.[3]

But these answers, while not entirely incorrect, mislead somewhat. The problem lies in the implications that larger sets of independent propositions render justification or validation weaker, when the opposite is the case. The more numerous are the independent accepted propositions or facts that receive the same explanation, the stronger is the reason for accepting the explanation as real or true. Inference to the best explanation is greatly strengthened when a common explanation is provided for what otherwise appears disparate or independent. The systematizing and simplifying effect of explanation, welcome from the point of view of understanding, is greater in this case because of the elimination of what would otherwise be gratuitous coincidence. For the fact that the same explanation can be provided for seemingly independent phenomena would have to be accepted as gratuitous coincidence were the explanation not interpreted as true or real.[4]

I shall return to this point later in the chapter on realism. Here, in light of it, the better response to the latest objection regarding probabilities is to note that one false belief about an appearance, which would render false any conjunction of such beliefs, does not necessarily defeat the validation of a perceptual or theoretical belief that appeals to the entire set of foundational beliefs in question. In other words, we need not conjoin sets of foundational beliefs when appealing to them in the validation of other empirical beliefs. We do not base the probabilities of other beliefs on probabilities of conjunctions of foundational beliefs. Rather, we seek explanations for the facts about ways things appear, these facts themselves being accepted as explanations for beliefs about appearances. If some of the latter explanations are wrong, if some of the appearances are other than we take them to be, corrections most often will not affect the appeal to physical properties in the explanation of the entire set of appearances, given that the errors are few and the set in question large. Such errors regarding appearances result from subjective factors and rarely from changes in the external arrays. Thus the deeper explanations can remain intact despite isolated errors in the foundation beliefs, as long as the latter are generally true. We have seen that we are justified in believing most foundational beliefs true, in believing that we are capable of the conceptual consistency in which their truth consists. The objection regarding probabilities of conjunctions then becomes irrelevant to our account of fallible foundational beliefs.

A final objection along these lines accepts that foundational beliefs have to be only mostly true in order to serve as foundations but claims that this status requires that it be analytic that they are mostly true.[5] This objection resembles the first in this set, but on a metalevel, since it claims that, if it were only an empirical fact that most foundational beliefs are true, then this fact would have to be established by appeal to evidence, evidence regarding the general reliability of perceivers or conceptualizers, for example. Our present critic can then proceed to attack either the general notion of analyticity or its application to the statment that most foundational beliefs are true. I see no way to defend such an application and would not want to rest any claims on this dubious notion. But I have argued that we are justified in believing most foundational beliefs true because of the preferability of that explanation that appeals to their truth over explanations that would hold them systematically false, that would posit general inconsistency in the application of predicates to ways of appearing. This reason for believing these beliefs generally true is not evidence for their truth, evidence that I have argued we cannot have, but the reason why they can be immediately validated.

BELIEFS ABOUT APPEARANCES AS INDISPENSABLE

Our central thesis in this section has been that a belief about an appearance is the sole first-person evidence for its own truth, since the best explanation for a subject's having such a belief appeals only to his being appeared to as he takes himself to be appeared to. Several aspects of this central claim remain to be clarified, limited, and defended. First, although a belief about an appearance must be acknowledged before it can count as the sole first-person evidence for the nature of the appearance, we need not worry here about the justification for the claim that there is such a belief. We are interested in the validations of our empirical beliefs given their existence, not in our justification for believing we have such beliefs. It is not part of my thesis that beliefs about beliefs are generally self-explanatory in the same way that many beliefs about appearances are. The psychological category of belief is more complex than that of appearance. Beliefs have multiple behavioral criteria. Persons may be self-deceptive regarding their beliefs, and such delusions may be revealed by their actions. Delusion may be difficult to imagine, however, in the case of a belief that one has a certain belief about an appearance. But further debate on this level is immaterial, since the immediate validation of beliefs about appearances does not depend on first validating that such beliefs exist.

This is certainly not to say that beliefs about appearances are dispensable in the process of validating other empirical beliefs. We cannot ignore the evidential status of these beliefs and validate perceptual judgments directly in terms of appearances in themselves or in terms of the conditions in which such beliefs arise. Regarding the former alternative, it was argued in the previous chapter that appearing in itself is nonepistemic, that it need not involve conceptualization or belief. But, while such nonepistemic appearing plays a role as a source of empirical concepts, until conceptualized it cannot enter into the validation of beliefs. Not only is there no immediate knowledge in the sense of knowledge unmediated by concepts but we cannot appeal to any nonepistemic contact between subject and object in demonstrating the possession of knowledge. Of course, *after* we have validated our foundational beliefs, we can then say that other empirical beliefs are justified not simply in relation to these beliefs but in relation to actual appearances or experience itself. But the appeal to experience is not basic in the epistemological framework.

The same objection applies to the idea that perceptual beliefs could be immediately jutified in terms of the conditions in which they arise. Appeal to these conditions comes one step later in the epistemological reconstruction than appeal to experience. Furthermore, justification of perceptual beliefs by appeal to nonepistemic conditions would not be foundational in the sense in which epistemologists require foundations. If we are to hold perceptual beliefs justified not in relation to belief about appearances but directly in relation to the conditions in which they arise, we would still have to demonstrate justification, that is, validate these beliefs. We would have to show why beliefs arising in these conditions are generally true, and in this case such demonstration would amount to providing evidence for their truth. The provision of such evidence, if by way of explanation, will lead us back to beliefs about appearances. In any event the notion of immediate justification in terms of objective conditions will not provide us with foundational validation. We seek immediate validation, the demonstration of knowledge without appeal to to other beliefs as evidence, and only self-explanatory beliefs can provide such foundations.

CONFLICTING EXPLANATIONS OF BELIEFS ABOUT APPEARANCES

Immediate validation requires not only that appeal to the truth of beliefs about appearances (to the consistent application of phenomenal predicates to the facts about ways things appear) be explanatory or account in itself for the probabilities of the beliefs' being held but also that this be the best among possible competing explanations in the epistemic context. This explanation must be preferable in this context to possible future physical or neurophysiological explanations of these beliefs, for example. Let us grant for the sake of argument that there are discoverable psychophysical laws (although this is certainly a philosophically controversial concession).[6] If there are such laws, they presumably must be higher-order, not directly relating types of physical brain states with beliefs having certain contents, for example, but obtaining between tendencies to produce brain states with certain structual relations to others and tendencies to form beliefs with relations to other cognitive states such as to form coherent or rational systems. We may even grant that, on the basis of knowledge of such laws, future neuropsychologists might justifiably override the explanation that a subject is appeared to in a certain way when he reports a belief with that content. What I deny is that they could override whole classes of such reports on the basis of their psychophysical theory.

Could scientists decide, for example that subjects are generally mistaken when they report being appeared to redly? In the previous chapter I noted one reason why the explanation of such beliefs in terms of their truth takes precedence over explanations in terms of physical hardware. That reason appealed to the natural selection of hardware sufficient for consistent application of concepts in relation to experience. Given this evolutionary requirement, the satisfaction of which is itself sufficient for rendering most beliefs about appearances true, the truth of such beliefs is more closely tied to their being held across close possible worlds than are those particular neurological causes that operate within us to produce them. There is another reason for this priority as well, having to do with the derivation of those psychophysical laws that would ground the casual theory whose explanations might pose our problem.

The second reason why the conclusion that first-person reports on experiences are generally mistaken could not be acceptable is that it would indicate faulty grounds for the assumption of the laws on which it would be based. Functional descriptions of neurological states as beliefs or causal antecedents to beliefs would rest upon prior determination of psychophysical laws linking structures in the brain to coherent systems of cognitive states, systems rendering particular states within them rational or rationally explicable. The discovery of these laws then in turn depends on finding higher-order correlations between structural relations among brain states and relations among beliefs and other psychological states, which relations render the psychological states coherent. (These correlations themselves would be explained in terms of the natural selection of neurophysiological types with tendencies to instantiate or mirror such coherent patterns of relations.) The charge of systematic errors regarding properties of appearances, in contrast, would impute instability to the application of simple concepts or predicates such as to undermine that minimal attribution of rationality necessary for any assignment of beliefs at all to the subjects in question. (We noted earlier that conceptual ability sufficient for forming coherent beliefs about appearances suffices also for making such beliefs generally true.) Thus the development of a theory that might appear capable of overriding beliefs about appearances, assuming as it would a minimal coherence in the psychological states of its subjects, could not result in the assignment of systematic falsity to these beliefs, for which only a minimal stability in application of concepts suffices for truth.

There may be contexts, I shall argue later, in which we would be justified in assigning systematic falsity to the beliefs of some class of subjects regarding independent objects and their properties. Conditions could be such as to result in systematic illusion, so that these subjects rationally arrive at globally false perceptual beliefs on the basis of their sensory evidence. But in order for them to arrive at a coherent set of expressible beliefs at all, such that we would be prompted to ascribe beliefs and other psychological states to them, such unfortunate subjects would need the capacity to conceptualize properties consistently from their perceptual experiences. Thus, if they were further able to conceptualize appearances as appearances and assign basic properties to them, we would have to count such assignments coherent or consistent and the beliefs expressing them mostly true. Our psychophysical theory for these subjects would be built upon the prior ascription of a coherent system of cognitive states to them. This system, it has been argued, presupposes conceptual ability sufficient to make most beliefs about appearances true. This is the reason why any conflict between explanation of beliefs about appearances by appeal to their truth and explanation by appeal to the neurological causes of these beliefs would indicate only incorrect stipulation of the psychophysical laws on which the causal theory was based.

8
LIMITATIONS AND COUNTERARGUMENTS

NATURALLY SALIENT PROPERTIES

The major limitation on the scope of our thesis regarding the validation of beliefs about appearances by appeal to self-explanation is its restriction to beliefs utilizing a certain class of concepts of predicates, beliefs about only certain apparent qualities. The thesis does not apply to all reports of appearances, some of which are not self-explanatory. My belief that I am appeared to C-sharply, for example, might not be best explained by the fact that I am so appeared to. Even if I am generally reliable in such judgments and correct in this one, the explanation for my present belief is not simply its truth but the fact that I have been successfully trained to make such judgments. On this score judgments regarding appearances in the class of tones differ little from judgments of actual tones. I could be correct in believing that a note appears as C-sharp to me when it is really B-flat, if I consistently apply the term 'C-sharp' but happen to off in my judgment of this tone by a note and a half, perhaps because it is played on a piccolo and tones in the higher octaves sound more sharp to me. But, barring such unusual cases, it seems no easier to judge correctly the apparent tone of a sound than the actual tone. Indeed, considerable training is required before musical sounds appear to be any tones in particular.

If this were true of judgments regarding appearances generally, then the beliefs they express would not be self-explanatory. Our thesis then rests upon the existence of a class of naturally salient properties, concepts formed in relation to them, and predicates with which to express these concepts. Given such concepts, it will not be necessary for explaining beliefs that apply them to appeal to training in their conventional use. The history of conceptual development that rendered such beliefs possible for particular subjects will be relevant to the explanations of their beliefs only insofar as it enabled their concepts to be applied consistently. Such application, I have held, equates with truth in this domain. In my own case I do not appeal to that development as evidence that my present beliefs about appearances are true. Rather, I can assume from the fact that I have such beliefs that I also have the concepts requisite for forming them and have therefore undergone the necessary development in my distant path. This order of validation explains why the sophistication of the concept of appearance itself does not affect the epistemically foundational character of beliefs about appearances. My having learned the concept of appearance at some point in my childhood is irrelevant to the explanation for my present belief that the ink on this page appears black to me. If someone were to ask why I believe it appears black to me, the only answer seems to be that it does.

In this respect the status of the concept of appearing is less crucial to the explanations for particular beliefs about appearances than are the concepts of the phenomenal properties in question. Doubtless the prototypes for such beliefs refer to properties as they appear or merely their ways of appearing. What is crucial is whether the concepts involved form parts of a conventional system whose acquisition is the result of social training. As we saw in the case of judging tones, if the explanation for a belief about an appearance must appeal to the fact that the subject has been successfully trained to respond in terms of certain conventional categories, then the belief is not self-explanatory. If reports about ways things appear are to be self-explanatory, they must therefore refer to properties that are not only phenomenally accessible but also natural targets for perceptual consciousness. The truth of such reports must not result from successful programming in the application of concepts of these properties but must rather be sufficient in itself to explain the beliefs expressed, hence inferable from the possession.

That the requirement for naturally salient properties and

basic concepts and predicates developed in relation to them is benign is evident from the fact that it can be demonstrated independently of the epistemologist's enterprise. The existence of such properties and the ability to conceptualize or generalize to later instances from early perceptions of them is the foundation of the capacity to learn, hence to survive. From the infinite set of similarities that could be noted among any sets of objects or environmental situations, subjects (including animal subjects) must focus on certain properties in order to define those generalization classes on which all learning depends. The characteristics in question must define classes for purposes of identification useful to the ends of behavior. When an animal sees or feels fire for the first time, for example, it would be logically possible for it to note any of an infinite set of properties—grue-type properties,[1] that of being a non-raven, that of having at least one molecule, etc. Of course it must instead note such characteristics as heat, brightness, color, etc., in order to generalize to other instances of fire so as to avoid them.[2] Even were the animal capable of endless surveys, this focus could not result from neutral observations of similarities among sets of perceived fires, no matter how large and varied those sets. Selection must rather be natural or inborn. This is not to posit innate concepts, only tendencies to conceptualize or generalize in certain directions from perceptual encounters.

Humans are no different in the dependence of all their inductive capacities upon such tendencies. These capacities cannot themselves be all acquired or learned through selective reward or reinforcement, since rewards themselves must be recognized as such by the organism. In addition they must be recognized as rewards for having made particular inductions rather than others from previously experienced situations, particular inductions from another set of possibilities. Inductive errors can of course occur and be corrected, but their correction again depends both on tendencies to correct in particular directions rather than others and on recognition of negative reinforcements for prior generalizations. The natural selection of certain properties as salient, as bases for inductive generalizations, can be explained initially with the biological theory of natural selection. We presumably select green-type rather than grue-type properties for conceptualization, for example, because objective properties correlate with the former rather than the latter, so that only the former provide behaviorally useful bases for predictions.[3] (The objective properties in question are not colors but those that cause color appearances.)

Human language builds not only on projections of naturally salient properties but on the construction by the prelinguistic child, given his native inductive capacities and developing behavior patterns, of a framework of representation for a world of relatively constant, individuated objects. The perceptual object constancies of color, size, and shape apparently develop during this period; identifying properties come to be perceived as relatively constant through changing conditions of perception. This occurs as the infant comes to distinguish objects from his own momentary responses to them, as the same objects come to figure in different behavior patterns, and as the latter relate them to other objects in the same patterns. The process is virtually complete before verbal learning intervenes, and it provides a universal perceptual and conceptual framework presupposed in the acquisition of language.[4]

This conceptualized perceptual framework does not constitute the full basis for language acquisition, however. There is yet another cognitive layer to consider. Mapped onto concepts of objects and their salient properties—concepts based on natural inductive tendencies—are prelinguistic representations utilized in thought prior to conventional language use. I denied in an earlier section that perception involves literal inferences, thereby undercutting a major argument for positing a "language of thought" underlying the use of conventional language.[5] While the brain is so structured that it generates perceptual experience and beliefs from physical sensory inputs as if it were constructing hypotheses from data, as if it were inferring to the best explanans (distal stimulus) for the physical proximal stimulus, it is epistemically pernicious to view this process as one of genuine inference from epistemic data. Real inferential reasoning requires a subject who reasons; the use of language requires a subject to interpret the symbols or representational elements; and the brain is not such a subject. Nor are its physical "data" epistemically basic, that is, data in the epistemologist's context. But while an unconscious language of thought known only to the brain is to me unintelligible, there is no doubt that conscious thought by genuine subjects occurs on a large scale prior to the acquisition of conventional language, and that the latter builds also upon the former.

Representation is required for a broad range of intelligent behavior and problem solving at the animal level and in the prelinguistic infant. At least, representational thought enters into the only plausible explanations for such behavior, in which subjects must not only conceptualize perceived situations but envisage as yet unrealized possibilities and absent situations. Examples of such behavior abound. A dog remembers where his bone is and returns to the spot to protect it at the approach of a rival. Such behavior does not reduce to the manifestation of mere practical knowledge, knowledge how to retrace his previous path, since he knows how to return to the spot from many different locations. This seems to require some sort of cognitive map, imagistic representation if not propositional knowledge, called into use when the animal represents the possible threat to his possession. Yet less controversial in its interpretation is the behavior of the infant who wants his parents to hand him the rattle out of reach, or that of the older infant attempting to insert shaped blocks into holes of matching shapes. The latter proceeds at first by trial and error, but at a later stage seems undoubtedly guided by representational imagery. Finally, and perhaps least contentious in its suggestion of prelinguistic representation, is the fully intelligent behavior of the congenitally deaf prior to their learning a conventional language. Such examples are not isolated but typical of highly intelligent behavior prior to language, behavior that seemingly must be guided by thought freed from the immediate perceptual context and therefore requiring some form of representation.

The representational elements in question, not being conventional, are not learned through social training but developed from perceptual encounters in behavior. The process unfolds as behavior becomes directed beyond the immediate perceptual context to absent objects, objects previously distinguished from different behavioral patterns involving them. The reference of such representations is not determined by their place in some mapping imposed on an uninterpreted symbolic system but is rather a natural extension of the causal relations by which perceptual experiences are said to be *of* certain objects. We find a progression of protoreferential and referential relations from percept, to perceptual concept, to nonlinguistic representation, to early language proper, and to more sophisticated language use. Perceptual experiences, we have seen, are of those objects to which they stand in certain causal relations. In relation to such experience, subjects come to conceptualize or classify perceived and then unperceived objects into types, the objects being included in the extensions of these concepts if they have certain properties in virtue of which they are classified. Concepts, we noted previously, are ascribed to subjects as recognitional capacities: a subject has a concept of an object when he can recognize it as being of a certain kind and a concept of a property when he recognizes objects instantiating that property. Predicates, whether linguistic or nonlinguistic representations, express concepts; that is, they apply to objects if the objects fall under those concepts. Natural predicates, in expressing perceptual concepts, refer to certain naturally salient properties and apply to objects instantiating those properties if they serve to focus perceptual (recognitional) attention on those objects or properties in their presence, or if they stand in for conceptualized perceptions of them in various cognitive operations leading to behavior in their absence.

Thus the primordial reference relation of nonlinguistic representional elements to objects and their properties is determined neither by the resemblance of these elements (even if imagistic) to their referents nor by their structural place within a symbolic system. It is determined rather by their having causal effects on mental operations and behavior similar to those ensuing upon perceptual recognition of the objects in virtue of their naturally salient properties. We may surmise that the reference of early verbal representations is also fixed by the psychological or functional roles of the representations—their standing in for particular perceptual experiences as direct stimuli to behavior or in cognitive operations that mediate between stimuli and responses—and by the causal histories of the perceptions for which they come to substitute. Such representations come to refer to objective situations via the direct causal relations between perceptions and objects and the functional roles that the symbols inherit from the corresponding perceptions. The referential relation is not reducible to a direct causal relation to objects with salient properties but derives both from the surrogate functional role of the representations and from the causal origins of the perceptions from which they arise. This dual origin of linguistic references is foreshadowed phylogenetically by prehuman signals such as danger cries or mating calls. These vocalizations focus perceptual attention or stand in for perceived affective situations, although without specific reference to or description of isolated elements in those situations.[6]

Like their phylogenetic precursors, the child's initial verbal responses do not seem intended to pick out single objects or particular reinstantiable properties of them but relate to affective or behaviorally relevant aspects of objects or situations in virtue of certain of their salient properties. Such responses function more or less like mass terms in referring to types of objects that exist scattered in space and time. Even at this level, however, the verbal symbol does not capture or refer to all features of the perceptual experience that it accompanies or represents, only those elements conceptualized in virtue of their prominent properties. Linguistic training in the use of conventional terms builds both upon the objectification of experience alluded to earlier and upon this origin of reference in preconventional representation.

While reference to specific properties as ways of appearing is a long way conceptually from these first primitive referential relations, it has two points of relevance to our project notable here. First, if reference derives from a complex but natural relation between predicates and certain perceptually salient properties or ways of appearing, rather than from social indoctrination into a conventional symbolic system, and if we can come to refer explicitly to some of these same ways of appearing as such at a conceptually sophisticated level, then explanations for beliefs about these appearances need not appeal to the symbol user's success at having mastered the system, only to the truth of the beliefs in question, that is, to his consistency in classifying the present instantiation of the phenomenal property. Our earlier argument regarding foundations remains intact, its scope only somewhat reduced, as mentioned at the beginning of this chapter.

Our second point prefaces the discussion of realism and reference in the next part of the book. It concerns the determinateness and scrutability of reference of the predicates under discussion, given those relations to perceptual experience that ground these predicates. As we shall see, several recent anti-realist arguments rest upon a supposed leeway in the assignment of referents to terms and beliefs, a leeway to assign referents so as to maximize the truth of ascribed beliefs and avoid skeptical possibilities implicit in the realist view of objects as independent (in their intrinsic properties) of our conceptual schemes and theories. The realist must show how determinate references to such objects is possible, and the initial premise can begin to be established here. Primitive predicates, we noted, refer to those naturally salient properties causally related to the perceptions which use of the predicates focused or for which they substitute. Such reference is fixed for the subject himself by the prominence of those properties that appear prominently to him. From the third-person point of view, we can pick out those properties (definitive of objects prominent in the visual field) to which the child refers by seeking the best explanation for his verbal behavior, given the naturally salient properties that he confronts. And we can infer to the latter properties given the similarities between his visual system and environment and ours.

There is, as noted above, a certain metaphysical ambiguity in the early use of predicate terms as one-word sentences. Such terms do not serve to identify particular discrete objects; nor is reference to an object's properties distinguished from reference to its surfaces, for example, at this level. But such ambiguities are resolved by later explicit categorization in developed language use. The important thing at this level is the focus on certain properties rather than others and the scrutability of such focus, not the lack of conceptualization of properties as properties or of the objects instantiating them as discrete objects so describable. Just as a subject can have an object appear to him without conceptualizing the episode as an appearance, so he can refer to the way it appears without conceiving of his referent as such. A more problematic source of inscrutability than the lack of specific metaphysical categorization of the referents of primitive predicates is the possibility of permutations of the terms such that they refer to different sets of phenomenal properties. But while many such permutations would be compatible with the meager evidence of early verbal behavior alone, they would not fit those explanations for the behavior that appeal to the way the subject perceives or is appeared to in the context. His behavior is one clue to the proper assignment of referents for his beliefs and utterances, but the guiding factor is our inference to those properties represented as salient within his perceptual experience, assumed to be tolerably similar to our own on grounds of explanatory fit with our many other similarities.

More developed reference is complicated in many ways relevant to our later discussion. Singular or subject terms become distinguished from general terms or predicates, and these from connectives and operators. Indoctrination into the use of a conventional language system allows for a linguistic division of labor and social determination of a speaker's referents. Speaker's reference, that to which speakers refer on particular occasions, comes to be distinct from the reference or extensions of terms in the language they use. Theoretical terms are introduced and can be differentiated from observational terms, however vague and shifting the boundaries. All these complicaitons allow for more precise specification of objects and their properties at the same time as they make more contentious the claim of a uniquely best determination of reference for given utterances, ascribed propositional attitudes such as beliefs, or theories. The hope is that reference can be foundationally grounded in much the way I have claimed knowledge to be anchored to a set of foundational beliefs. Indeed I am suggesting that certain primitive predicates function in both capacities. Just as it becomes more difficult to envisage equally coherent but incompatible belief systems once a sizable stock of foundational beliefs is fixed with which others must cohere, so once certain predicates become attached to certain instantiations of perceptually salient properties as paradigm instances of the natural concepts they express, and once these predicates are projected in the normal ways, it becomes more difficult to imagine permutations of terms and referents that would generate equally good explanations for verbal behavior.

I have suggested here the primacy of speaker's reference over of terms within a conventional language, the primacy of predicate reference over that of names or genuine singular terms, and the more obvious priority of certain perceptual concepts over theoretical ones. The reference of predicate terms in conventional language builds upon primitive reference to naturally salient properties and is abstracted from speakers' reference to those and then other properties. In the next chapter I shall outline a descriptive theory of reference for singular and natural kind terms that presupposes the primacy of predicate reference suggested there. Once our predicate terms are fixed, we can pick out those real singular entities and kinds that satisfy certain privileged descriptions associated with the names and kind terms in use. Having so fixed subject terms as well, we can then proceed from reference to observables to talk of unobservables, given suitable connections between them. If reference to theoretical entities and properties is to be fixed by prior reference to observables, such determination must result from the multifarious connections among the two types of terms— for example, the fact that some theoretical terms are introduced via analogical models or by appeal to explanatory causal relations to observable phenomena.

The full argument awaits the next part. First we must tie the remaining loose strands from the argument regarding foundations.

PRIVATE LANGUAGE

I have claimed that primitive reference to naturally salient properties is determinate or fixed. Some philosophers of Wittgensteinian persuasion may still wonder how such reference could be fixed. Earlier I claimed that the truth of a foundational belief that I am appeared to in a certain way lies only in my consistent use of the term for the phenomenal property in question, that such use can be inferred in the best explanation for my having such a belief, and that this use need not conform to conventions governing terms in public languages, although the acquisition of the latter depends on prior abilities to conceptualize consistently from perceptual experience. These claims glaringly contradict the conclusion of Wittgenstein's notorious "private language argument," and so they must be defended against plausible readings of his influential reasoning. Those familiar with his *Philosophical Investigations* and its vast secondary literature will appreciate the need to refer to various readings of the argument. These seem to fall into two classes, a narrower and broader interpretation of Wittgenstein's point and its premises.

The narrower reading focuses on sections 243–65 of the *Investigations*. There Wittgenstein denies that a property term can acquire meaning (or have its reference fixed) ostensively in relation to a private experience alone. One cannot focus on a property within one's experience and fix the reference of a predicate term by intending it to apply to reinstantiations of that property in the future. The crux of the argument appears to be the implicit claim that meaning and reference depend on the ability to follow rules for the consistent use of terms. We assume that fixing the reference of a term consists in adopting and adhering to a rule that determines in advance just that to which the term will be correctly applied in the future. But in the case of the private definition there can be not genuine distinction between actually following such a rule and only seeming to oneself to be following it. Whatever future appearance seems to one to fit the initial intention to apply the term *will* fit it. More precisely, there will be no distinction between fitting the intention and not fitting it, since nothing in the original act can rule out a later application of the term as incorrect. Without any distinction between consistent and inconsistent use, between following a rule that determines proper application or reference and breaking the rule, the notion of consistent application and hence of fixed reference is inapplicable itself.

Wittgenstein dismisses the reply that the distinction lies in the difference between, on one hand, remembering the original focused property and projection of the term intended in the original act of fixing reference and, on the other, misremembering those features present in that original situation. Personal memory cannot be the criterion of correct use here according to him, since once more no real distinction can be drawn between remembering and misremembering. The latter claim seems to commit a verificationist fallacy of confusing correct memory or application of a rule with knowledge that one remembers or applies the rule correctly. It seems that one could misremember without realizing it and that one could remember correctly without being able to verify that one does so. Hence there could be a genuine distinction between remembering and misremembering even though one might be unable to verify that one remembers in this context. An opponent of the narrowly construed argument might claim that only memory, and not verification of memory, is necessary for consistent use or fixed reference of terms referring to appearances.

But Wittgenstein's point may not rest on this confusion, since he may be claiming that only knowledge of correct memory, and not simply memory itself, could save the reference of terms in a private language. A language user does not know the meaning or reference of a term if he does not know when it is being correctly applied; and he cannot know this on the basis of memory alone, it can be claimed, if there is no way for him to check the correctness of his memory. Knowledge of correct application or consistent use requires knowledge that one's memory is correct, not just correct memory. Even accepting our own earlier analysis of knowledge, a Wittgensteinian might claim that the explanation for a present belief about a private appearance or experience that appeals to veridical memory is no more plausible than that which appeals to a seemingly genuine but mistaken memory.

Despite acquittal from the charge of a verificationist fallacy, under this first interpretation the private language argument remains unconvincing. In raising skeptical doubts about memory as a criterion of correct recognition of sensory states or appearances and of correct application of terms that express this recognition to such states, the argument appears to throw out the baby with the bathwater. If the intended contrast on this score between private terms referring to appearances and use of terms in a public language dissolves under scrutiny, then the argument leads to an unintended general skepticism regarding rules of language, consistent use of terms, and fixed reference. The problem is that one must resort in the end to personal memory or private recognition in any attempt at verification, including verification of one's proper use of public or conventional terms against use of these terms by others. To check any memories against those of others, one must interpret the noises they make in accordance with personal memory of the meaning and use of their terms. Predictions can be made on this basis and coherence among memories achieved, but the same is true in the case of a private language. Thus the claim that one could be generally mistaken without knowing it in regard to appearances is in the same boat with a general skepticism about conceptual consistency and the reliability of memory from which there may be no sure return. It seems that the avoidance of such skepticism requires an assumption of general consistency in the application of one's concepts, whether to public or private objects and episodes. One must assume some knowledge on the basis of personal memory not verifiable independently of personal memory.

This reduction of the narrow interpretation of the argument brings us to the broader interpretation, enunciated most fully and recently by Kripke.[7] Here we accept as an initial premise a general skepticism regarding the adoption of rules of language as we conceived it above. The problem in fixing the reference of terms lies not in the fallibility of memory or in lack of checks on memory in the single-person case but in the idea that this fixing can be accomplished by means of intentions to apply terms in certain ways based on past applications. The question is how such intentions can rule out any further applications of the terms as inconsistent or incorrect. This question is directed at applications to publicly perceptible objects as well as to private appearings, to green grass as well as green images, although Wittgenstein thinks that we can ultimately make some sense of the demand for consistency in regard to the former but not the latter (except perhaps derivatively from application of terms to properties in the public domain).

The narrower interpretation of the argument centered on the possibility of checks that a language user is following rules created by intentions to project predicates in certain ways from initial paradigm cases. In this narrowly construed attack on private language Wittgenstein seemed to be claiming that such checks are possible only in the public domain. But under the broader interpretation his claim is rather that such intentions to project use of predicates must be empty. Here his key example relates not to private language but to understanding a function or rule that determines the proper sequence of numbers in a series.[8] A subject thinks he understands the rule when he comes to intend to go on producing the numbers in a certain way. But whatever he does later on he will interpret as in accord with his earlier intention, and the latter will be interpreted as directing the later practice. Thus again we cannot distinguish between his following the supposed rule and his only seeming to follow it, as long as we restrict attention to the individual subject and his intentional states.

I have phrased the skeptical thrust of the broader argument as directed against the determination of the proper use or reference of terms by intentions to project applications from paradigm cases. Kripke rather tends to raise the question whether it makes sense to speak of a person's meaning one thing rather than another by use of a term such that future use must conform to this meaning. Wittgenstein himself speaks skeptically of both meaning[9] and intention,[10] but most often questions the idea of grasping a formula or rule at a given time such that proper practice in the future must be governed by one's fixed interpretation of the rule. However one phrases the skeptical question, it challenges us to make sense of the demand for consistency with earlier applications of terms, where the criteria for consistent use are determined in advance in relation to those earlier uses or states of the subject at those times. We may think of the point at which a person creates or grasps a linguistic rule or comes to mean something in particular by the use of a term as that point at which he forms the intention that is to govern future use. According to the present interpretation of the Wittgensteinian argument, an act of so intending can do nothing more than focus attention again on the paradigm instantiations; it cannot determine what future objects or episodes are to be properly included in the extension of the term in question. Furthermore, however long one has applied a term, there remains this problem of underdetermination of further use. The problem does not lie in memory: correct memory simply repeats the focus on the paradigm cases. Remembering cannot, any more than the original intention that is remembered, determine that broader class for which the paradigm case was to be paradigmatic.

Suppose, for example, that in the future I begin to apply the term 'green' to the sky on a clear day, to sapphires, etc. Would such application be inconsistent with my previous use and intention to apply the term, or would it rather indicate that I had intended to use it to mean grue rather than green? Implicit in Wittgenstein's attack on the commonsense notion of following a rule is the claim that there can be no answer to this question when it is restricted to my use alone, since nothing in my prior state could rule out an interpretation of it as an intention to mean grue. When we come to compare my use with that of others on the other hand, then we can say that my use is inconsistent or that I am not properly following the rule that governs the use of the term 'green'. These criticisms of my use reduce to the obvious point that my use is inconsistent with that of others, that they are not inclined to accept it, that I depart from the rule that captures the regularity or agreement in common social use of the term.

According to the broad interpretation of the argument, it is this contrast between my inconsistency with the regular social practice and the lack of any specifiable inconsistency in my own use considered by itself that explains the impossibility of a private language. In the private language, or in any person's language use considered in isolation from that of others, we can make no sense of inconsistent or incorrect usage (hence no sense of correct usage either), while each member of a community of language users can be inconsistent with the others. Since ascription of language use requires a distinction between correct and incorrect understanding and application of terms, since one's use of genuine language can always be normatively evaluated in this way, there can be no private language.

Kripke rejects as a reply to this argument a dispositional account of meaning or reference according to which an intention fixes the reference of a term for a subject by creating a disposition in him to apply the term in certain fixed ways in the future. In appealing to such an account we could not make sense of a subject's being disposed to make errors in applying the term in certain contexts. Nor could we say that fixing the reference distinguishes proper from improper future use or justifies particular applications of the term. None of this could make sense because whatever the subject was disposed to do would be by definition correct. And whatever he does or would do in however distant a future would be what he was (in some sense) disposed to do in those conditions. Once more the intention would fail to create a distinction between correct and incorrect use; it would fail to create or constitute a genuine (normative) rule of language. In the absence of a notion of inconsistency for a single subject, we still could not speak of his use as consistent or correct.

Whatever its wider implications for an account of language and truth, it is clear that this interpretation of the argument against private language is equally damaging to any Cartesian-empiricist program of beginning a reconstruction of knowledge from beliefs about one's own experiences. More specifically, this broader interpretation, applicable over the whole range of an individual's use of language as considered in itself, is as negative in its implication for my position as its narrower and more easily dismissable counterpart. In holding that the truth of a foundational belief consists in application of the term referring to the phenomenal property consistent with prior application, but not necessarily with conventional use of the term, I must be able to make some sense of this notion of consistency in light of the Wittgensteinian challenge. Otherwise I cannot maintain that the truth of a belief about an appearance, the fact that one is appeared to in a certain way, best explains in itself the belief that one is so appeared to. For the truth of such a belief alone to explain its being held, reference to the phenomenal property must be natural rather than trained, and such reference must be immediately inferred to be correct. That the first of these requirements is met was argued in the previous section; here we must address the second by making sense of correct reference (in contrast to incorrect reference).

In answering the private language argument we can first

dispute Kripke's dismissal of the dispositional account of meaning or consistent use. We can say that consistent application of terms referring to naturally salient phenomenal properties means application that is consistent with the subject's natural inclinations to conceptualize those properties or project the terms on the basis of perceptual encounters. Kripke's objection, following Wittgenstein, to the relevance of dispositions is that they cannot generate a distinction between correct and incorrect applications of terms. But here we *can* derive a notion of error or inconsistency. We need not say that, however a subject applies a term on a particular occasion, he must have been disposed to apply it that way from the beginning. If any way that he applies a term must be consistent with his fixed disposition to apply it, then the dispositional account fails to generate the crucial distinction. But appeal to naturally salient properties again solves the problem of moving from reference on particular occasions (which I argued in the previous section to be fixed by the functional role of the representation and the causal history of the percept for which it stands) to consistent or correct use and fixed extensions for predicate terms. A subject may be naturally disposed to conceptualize a property and hence project a representation or term in a certain way, and yet, because of interfering factors or simply faulty memory of the naturally salient property to which the term was first applied, he may apply the term in a way inconsistent with his original disposition, that is, wrongly. (We earlier dismissed skepticism regarding the distinction between remembering and misremembering, once we agreed that there was something to remember, i.e., a genuine use and projection of the term.) Thus in the individual case there can be both a disposition that defines correct usage of a term and explicable departures from it or errors in particular applications of the term.

Suppose again that I begin to apply my private term for green to blue things. We questioned whether this shows that I am inconsistent and misapply the term through inattentiveness or forgetfulness, or rather shows that my original intention or disposition was to project a private term for grue. Recall that for Wittgenstein there can be no answer to this question, hence no genuine question. But the question can in fact be answered by inferring to the best explanation for my earlier practice. If we assume that green is a naturally salient property (an assumption compatible with vagueness at the boundaries), then my intention would have been to project a predicate referring to green if to a perceptible property. I will naturally perceive an object as green but not as grue, although I can come to conceive of the object as grue. Thus if I begin to apply the term that I previously applied to grass and emeralds to the sky and sapphires, then my new application will be inconsistent with the old. Either I will have changed the meaning of the term or I will hold false beliefs. In regard to beliefs about appearances, inconsistency would indicate false belief if it did not persist as a new and consistent usage. An isolated aberrant application of a predicate signals a false belief as the best explanation of the aberrant use. Persistence, however, indicates a new disposition to use the term in a fixed way to refer to a different property. In either case we can make sense at this level of both inconsistency and incorrectness, and hence, by contrast, of both consistency and truth.

The Wittgensteinian or Goodmanian might question my appeal to naturally salient properties in this context. He might wonder again what in my present state when I look at grass constitutes my perceiving green rather than grue. But this objection only raises again the question whether there are naturally salient properties, and I argued previously that there must be such properties if language learning, indeed if any inductive generalization, is to be possible. A different question is how I know that green is the naturally salient property that I perceive, rather than, say, grue. One might think that my realist belief that the grass would be green even if I were not perceiving it provides the answer. But it is unlikely that I would have such beliefs for all grue-like properties (and in any case I myself do not believe so for green). In regard to green as a way of appearing, the answer is rather that appearing greenly but not appearing gruely enters into the best explanation for my believing that I am appeared to greenly.

This answer assumes that green is a naturally salient property, however, and we need not assume so. The point is that there must be some properties that are naturally salient and hence that are naturally perceived as those properties rather than as their grue-like counterparts. Given such properties, subjects will have natural dispositions to fix the extensions of terms that pick out objects instantiating them. Given such dispositions, as well as explicable departures from them, the private language argument can be answered. Its full answer requires a more complete theory of reference, to be provided below, that maintains the determinateness of this initial stock of predicates. It requires also further demonstration of the normative force of natural salience, demonstration of its link to truth in the realist's sense via an argument from natural selection, again to be provided in the next chapter. Here we have considered only the question of consistency in applying predicates to appearances.

Before leaving Wittgenstein's argument, we might note briefly but more explicitly those philosophically radical implications that we have at least for the moment sidestepped. If ascription of language use depends on making sense of linguistic practice in normative terms, and if, as Wittgenstein holds, we can understand the normative dimension only in terms of agreement or lack of agreement of particular individuals with others in the linguistic community, then we can make no sense of representational systems outside the context of social conventions and no sense of truth and falsity outside the contexts of social agreement. It follows from the argument that, while a linguistic community can correct the application of a predicate by an individual, i.e., can ascribe false belief, misunderstanding, or idiosyncratic use to him, as members of a community we cannot conceive of the entire group's being mistaken in its beliefs or even of its shifting the meaning or use of its terms. One might think that the criterion for meaning change is satisfied when a later group disallows applications of predicates allowable in the earlier community. But this will not do. If our descendants begin to apply 'green' to the sky, for example, they may come to disallow its application to green things (things now thought to be green). But they, as we, will be applying the term to grue things. 'Green' can therefore be interpreted as meaning grue throughout the entire time span, as not having changed its meaning. The point is of course general. Anything to which a community applies a term can be interpreted as falling under the proper meaning of the term or original common intention so to apply it, so that all common or agreed usage becomes correct usage, expressing true beliefs. On this view, predicates expand, as it were, to encompass all new objects to which they are applied.

Wittgenstein's objections to private language therefore seem to hold of the community's language as a whole. If so, then the argument seems to be self-refuting at the higher level at which language is undeniably learned and used. Wittgenstein escapes contradiction, however, by giving up the notion of truth or consistency to which a community's practice must conform. The private language argument itself implies the reduction of truth to warranted assertibility. With this reduction goes the loss of the world as a set of objects possessing properties independently of our sets of beliefs, theories, or language games. If truth reduces to agreement, as it must if a community cannot err in its application of predicates, then we cannot conceive of agreed applications of terms being incorrect or aberrant. But then the properties of objects are all relative to our agreed ascriptions of them, and we must abandon our realist beliefs.

Nor, if we accept the private language argument, can we ascribe either representation or belief prior to the acquisition of conventional language. Beliefs involve ascriptions of reinstantiable properties via representational elements whose references are fixed to those properties. But according to Wittgenstein, this fixing is impossible outside the context of the relation of individual to social convention. His argument then makes far more difficult, if not impossible, both an account of prelinguistic intelligence and a conception of how conventional language could have developed as a social institution or be acquired by individuals. How could conventional connections between symbols and objects and their properties have been established if subjects could not think of the objects without utilizing the conventionally connected symbols? How can we account for the adaptable, highly intelligent behavior of certain animals and prelinguistic humans without ascribing representation and belief to them? How can we say, as we do, that the meaning of a conventional term has changed over the ages, or that an entire community held a false belief (prior to our disagreeing with them), if meaning and truth reduce to agreement in use and warranted assertibility? The private language argument forces all these seemingly unanswerable questions upon us.

We have avoided the antirealist implications of this argument for now by providing an account of inconsistency and incorrect use of basic or natural predicates. In making sense of both consistency and inconsistency in the representations of an individual prior to or independent of his acquisition and use of conventional language, we can make sense in the same terms of a community's being inconsistent or mistaken in its application of predicates. For a community will tend to project predicates onto naturally salient properties just as an individual will. Once we have a stock of natural or basic predicates, others can be generated from them by processes of combining, narrowing, extending, and analogy, and then taught and learned through training. Reference to observable and then unobservable objects can then be fixed via description (an account of which will be provided in the next chapter). Given reference to objects in the realist's sense, consistency in the application of predicates is only a necessary, not a sufficient, condition for true belief. But since it remains necessary, it was necessary here to account for its possibility.

REPLACEABILITY

We now have a stock of self-explanatory foundational beliefs that ascribe naturally salient phenomenal properties as ways of appearing. I argued previously that the self-explanation of these beliefs, explanation that appeals only to the facts believed, competes favorably with conceivably conflicting explanations that appeal to the physical causes of these beliefs in the brain and environmental stimuli. There were three reasons for this priority in explanation. First, the causal explanations themselves must be validated or shown to be true, and part of the process of validation appeals to beliefs about appearances, beliefs themselves immediately validated. Second, given the requirements of cognitive evolution, beliefs about appearances will be true in possible worlds in which the physical causes vary (hence the probability of their being held will be more closely linked to their truth than to their specific physical causes). And third, conflicts between self-explanation and neurophysiological explanation would indicate only faulty inference to the psychophysical laws that ground the latter.

In this final part of the chapter I shall consider again the opposing contention, the thesis that purely physical explanations will prevail, if not at the present time, then in the long run. According to the view we shall now consider, such explanations could come to prevail by default, when in the future those predicates by which we currently pick out phenomenal or observational properties come to be replaced by the terms of physical science. The replaceability in principle of terms referring to both mental states and commonsense observational properties by terms of (future) physical theory has been argued by such philosophers as Sellars, Rorty, Feyerabend, and most recently Churchland, the latter two actually advocating that we begin the process of replacement.[11]

The thesis of replaceability can be linked with that of scientific realism. The scientific realist will hold that physical science provides not only the greatest explanatory coherence but also the most accurate description of physical reality. If our goal is accurate description of the environment and the facilitation of superior explanation and predictive power, and if we could be trained to respond to simulation directly in terms from the framework of the currently best microtheory, then such training would seem to best realize this goal. Replacement is inferred to be possible from the premise that perceivers are causal indicators of far more accurate information than they currently report. According to replacement advocates, they could report directly by vision on wavelengths of light and on reflective, absorptive, and radiative properties of surface molecular aggregates, and by taste and smell on the chemical composition of objects. The argument for replacement is that such reports would reflect a true rather than a false theory. At least they would reflect a theory more likely to be true, if we accept, as the scientific realist does, that theories with more explanatory and predictive power are more likely to be true.

Implicit in this comparison is the claim that phenomenal and observational language (terms referring to appearances and to ways we perceive objects to be) itself constitutes or reflects a theory of mental states and physical reality. It is the supposed breakdown of the observational-theoretical distinction that lends credence to the replaceability thesis. Advocates of replacement view the language of appearing itself as theoretical in several different senses. First, our ascriptions of properties to objects directly on the basis of perception constitute a (naive) theory of physical reality, although such ascriptions are not inferred from any set of data as premises. They constitute a theory in that they form a more or less coherent and mutually supportive set in terms of which we explain and predict various perceived interactions among objects. Furthermore, while the organization of the perceptual field into objects may be fixed in the Kantian sense of being a permanent structure of our sensibility, we learn to ascribe properties to those objects directly on the basis of perception by socialization into a particular cultural worldview. We are trained to acquire the observational concepts we use. Phenomenal descriptions of appearances borrow all their terms from such ascriptions of properties directly to objects; hence they reflect the naive realist, culturally evolved theory from which they are derived. Second, rather than ascriptions of properties to objects being inferred from appearances or beliefs about appearances as data, the latter presuppose the former and are inferable originally from them. We come to ascribe mental states or ways subjects are appeared to by inferring to explanations for their naive and sometimes mistaken perceptual beliefs, although we later acquire the ability to report directly on appearances in response to stimulation. Third, and perhaps most important for the thesis of replaceability, the significance of phenomenal concepts derives from their roles in systems of related concepts and beliefs in which they function, rather than from their associations with isolated repeatable features of sense experience.

Churchland provides an argument to the effect that the meanings of terms referring to phenomenal properties are stipulated not in relation to particular sensations that prompt their use but by reference to related terms and sentences accepted by the subject as true (entering into his theory of the world).[12] The argu-

ment appeals to fictitious beings who see gradations of temperature in objects visually: hot things appear white to them and cold
things black, with all gradations of gray between. In translating
their perceptual reports in such cases it seems clear that we
should take them to be expressing beliefs about perceived temperatures rather than colors. Otherwise, we will have them saying things like 'Snow is black'. Of course the converse is also true
of their translations, if they are not to have us believing that snow
is hot and that people tend to wear hotter clothing in warmer
climates. The proper translations show that we are to interpret
observational and phenomenal concepts, our own as well as
those of alien cultures, in terms of the systems of implicative
relations they form with other concepts in some theoretical set.
The meanings of terms used to report observations, whether of
appearances or of reality, are given not by ostension of those
phenomenal properties whose appearances occasion their use
but by indicating the types of descriptive, explanatory, and predictive sentences and theories in which they function. So
Churchland concludes from his science fiction example.

It is because appearing language is supposed to be theoretical
in these senses that it is deemed replaceable by the terms of a
better theory, that of present and future science. But while
some of the more familiar claims associated with the attack on a
sharp observational-theoretical distinction, for example, the
claim that sensation in itself is nonconceptual and nonepistemic, or that a subject's beliefs can affect the ways things appear to him, are not damaging to our foundationalist position,
the replaceability thesis, with its Sellarsian view of concept formation and holistic theory of meaning and reference for appearing terms, cannot be accepted. First there is the obvious
point that, if reports about how things appear can be replaced
by an entirely different set of basic observation reports, then
reports of how things appear are not stable as foundations for
empirical knowledge. Our epistemological position would be
secure only for the time being. If I am right about the
epistemologist's need for immediately justified foundations,
then our presumed gain qua scientists from the coming change
in vocabulary would be our loss qua philosophers. Second, if
one cannot grasp the meaning or reference of a phenomenal

term until one has mastered a set of terms as related in a whole theory, and if one must be trained or socially indoctrinated to view the world through the medium of such a theory, then beliefs about appearances cannot be self-explanatory.

The latter thesis indicates why we cannot accommodate the replaceability thesis by extending the class of foundational beliefs to include reports of appearances in the new vocabulary. I have previously admitted that certain beliefs about ways of being appeared to are not self-explanatory. Our previous example was that of being appeared to C-sharply. Here the explanation for my true belief that I am so appeared to must appeal to my having mastered a complex system for classifying tones. Although the concept of C-sharp can be applied in relation to a single sensation, it cannot be fully grasped until one appreciates the entire tonal scheme into which this particular tone fits. And of course only training enables one to acquire the set of skills involved in picking out tones. What is true in this respect of judging C-sharps will undoubtedly be true of perceptual judgments in the framework of a microtheory as well, including judgments in those terms of how things appear. Because this is so, a new set of foundational beliefs cannot be generated in such new terms. And because, according to Sellars and others, the same holistic theory of concept learning and belief formation applies even to perceptual and appearing judgments in the realm of common sense, the latter are both replaceable and incapable of immediate justification. Thus the antifoundationalist thrust of the replaceability thesis runs as deep as its own conceptual foundations.

Previous sections of this chapter presented a very different picture of early concept development. In criticizing the replaceability thesis we shall briefly review and expand upon the reasons for the implausibility of its underlying theory of learning. Preliminarily we might try some more superficial and obvious probes at its more explicit claims. One might first argue that the new vocabulary would lack some of the descriptive power of the old. The scientific framework might be superior in explanatory coherence and for describing objects in the sense of ascribing intrinsic or nonrelational properties to them. But everyday purposes often call rather for identifying objects relative to others in the vicinity, relating them to present (nonscientific) projects, noting their aesthetic qualities, and so on. All this may be more easily accomplished by noting those properties relational to us that we currently report in the broad categories of phenomenal terms.

The antifoundationalist argument is not refuted, however, by showing that Churchland is pragmatically off base or overly zealous in suggesting that children be taught scientific rather than current phenomenal terms. The initial question is rather whether such replacement is possible for reports of appearances. Its possibility does not require reduction or translation of the old observation vocabulary into the new. Shared entailments are not necessary, as some enemies of materialism have claimed.[13] This requirement assumes a base of descriptive content that must be captured by the vocabulary of the new framework, but the advocate of replacement denies that assumption. If that which is explanatorily most coherent describes best as well, then there is no reason for a superior theory to preserve the content of the inferior older framework. Indeed, if there were such extensional equivalence between the frameworks, then the gain foreseen from replacement would be illusory. Furthermore, *if* replacement were possible, then presumably the new language would remain rich enough for everyday purposes of identifying objects. For aesthetic evaluation, an aesthetic vocabulary, like a moral vocabulary, would survive alongside the scientific.

But the question remains whether replacement is indeed possible. Let us be more precise about the lack of extensional equivalence between the old vocabulary and the new. Consider first color reports. In fact we could not report wavelengths of light reflected from object surfaces simply by observing the objects and the ways they appear. The reason is that perceptions of a particular color can result from a large disjunction of different waves. The crucial factor is the ratio in which the cones are stimulated. And this is not the only reason for the lack of one-to-one matchup between molecular configurations on surfaces, wavelengths reflected, and perceived colors. The latter depend also upon the state of adaptation of the subject's visual system, his set and attention, the colors of surrounding areas, and other purely subjective factors. Thus, if we at-

tempted to report on wavelengths, or even apparent wavelengths, in everyday contexts directly by observation, the best
we could do would be to begin a lengthy disjunctive statement
or estimate rough probabilities. Nor can we report on mean
kinetic energy in the surface molecules of objects from felt temperature. Also relevant to the felt temperature are the temperature of our skin and the conductivity of the material in question. The best we could do here would be to infer an estimate of
the physical property from the felt temperature plus visual identification of the material in question and knowledge of its con-
ductive properties.

The seemingly obvious point underlying this initial objection to the replaceability thesis is that the physical properties
of light waves and movements of molecules, as opposed to
colors and felt temperatures, do not appear to humans. If we
maintain that they do appear, it seems that we must admit that
they appear only *as* colors and felt temperatures. The intrinsic
physical properties, it seems, must be inferred from the relational properties that constitute how the physical phenomena
appear to us. This necessity does not seem to be a matter of
cultural convention or linguistic training but rather seems to
derive from the evolution and present structure of our sensory
systems. We simply do not have spectrometer or electron-
microscope eyes or thermometer skin. It is because only certain properties are phenomenally accessible to us, given the
sensory systems and types of mental states that we have, that
common languages of different cultures are remarkably uniform in the kinds of properties directly reportable within
them. Acquisition of the ability to be aware of radically different properties on the phenomenal level would seem to require
not simply different cultural indoctrination, but the acquisition
of different sensory systems. While we could train our children to report noninferentially in terms that we use only on
the basis of inference, it seems that they still would not be
reporting on what appears to them in the new terms.

This objection, though in the end sound, remains superficial,
since the replacement advocate would reject the claim that phenomenal statements report what immediately appears. This
claim again assumes a theory-neutral base of descriptive con-

tent that can be captured by such appearing statements. One way to reject it is to accept a reductionist account of perceiving. Here observation reports express not what appears but only reliable beliefs acquired noninferentially in response to stimulation. Such reports are distinguished not by content but by their causal connection to stimulus patterns and by the fact that they can be made quickly and reliably in that causal context. According to this criterion it is clear that what is observational for the scientist, for example, that there are thirty-five milliamperes of current in the wire, would not be so for the layman unarmed with the background theory. The ability to acquire beliefs of this sort expressed in particular terms is always itself an acquired skill on this view. Reports of appearances here simply express more tentative beliefs in the same terms. Although more easily justified because less bold in their commitments, such beliefs represent a yet more sophisticated skill. Rather than reporting immediate data, appearing statements express noninferential but culturally relative beliefs in slightly more subtle form.

I criticized this epistemic account of perception at length in a previous chapter. The main objections to it were its inability to provide an account of perceptual and intellectual development early in life and its failure to account for the rationality of various perceptual reports. Recalling the first objection, the rich developmental process in the first year of life, culminating in the extraction of perceptual invariants and constancies that enable the infant to perceive relatively permanent objects with stable qualities in spatial relations, becomes unintelligible if we deny perception prior to the acquisition of beliefs or concepts. For it is through interaction with the perceived environment that these early perceptual concepts develop. We cannot understand how objects could come to be recognized unless they were first perceived or discriminated. The equation of perception with acquisition of belief therefore makes little sense in this context. Regarding the second objection, I claimed that we cannot appreciate the rationality of either deviant or ordinary perceptual beliefs if we rob the subject of those reasons to which he appeals in defending those beliefs. He typically appeals when challenged to the ways things appear to him, not to the physical causes of his beliefs in his brain or to more tentative beliefs. The latter appeal would be redundant rather than justificatory. In robbing subjects of the reasons for their perceptual beliefs, we also deprive the epistemologist of the grounds for his system of empirical knowledge.

The advocate of replacement need not be a reductionist or eliminative materialist, however. He can accept appearing as irreducible if he views it as a product of a process of conceptualization rather than as data for that process. The main underlying thesis is that the association of an observation term with some feature of a sensation is not only less important for determining its meaning than the relations of the term to others in a conceptual system; it is also a product of the subject's indoctrination into the system or theory. Despite allowing the irreducibility of appearing, the answer to our objection remains that phenomenal predicates cannot categorize what immediately appears, since nothing immediately appears. What does appear is what comes to be reported by use of observation predicates, rather than the converse. Hence it cannot be objected to the replaceability thesis that scientific properties do not currently appear. They can come to appear to subjects suitably trained. This change would not then require altered sensory systems, only altered abilities to attend to properties of objects in the perceptual environment.

The deeper reply to the replaceability thesis thus takes us back to its underlying theory of learning and its relation to experience. The claim that the ways things appear is a product of socialization into a theory, while plausible in relation to certain *alterations* in appearances, lacks any plausibility whatsoever in relation to more primitive and natural ways that human subjects are appeared to. We can be trained to notice properties we had not noticed before, so that these properties appear to us for the first time as a result of this training. We also constantly reinterpret the objective properties that manifest these appearances in light of newly acquired theoretical beliefs. But such training is possible only because subjects are able to find new phenomena or reinterpret previously encountered properties by learning their relations to other, already conceptualized appearances or observations. Before one acquires even initial perceptual concepts, one must have perceptual experience. It is clear that one cannot be trained to be conscious or aware *ex nihilo*. When a subject is perceptually aware, he is always aware of something's appearing in some way, although he may not yet conceptualize (be able to recognize) the phenomenal qualities that appear. Thus there must be appearances prior to theory and prior to training in the terms of a theory.

The ability to learn any system of categorization depends, I argued, not only on prior experience without concepts but on natural ways of conceptualizing perception and projecting properties that appear. These necessary conditions apply to the learning of language as well, so that linguistic programming cannot explain all ways things appear. Before one can learn or respond to language, one must learn to discriminate and identify the phonemes, and the account of such learning must not presuppose what it is trying to explain. These concepts of the different sound patterns must then be mapped onto the previously developed perceptual scheme of objects and their properties—a complex representational scheme virtually complete before language learning, presupposed in linguistic training, intervenes.

Perhaps the proponent of replaceability need not claim that nothing appears prior to socialization, nor even that all perceptual concepts are culture- or theory-relative, only that primitive appearances and concepts may be so transformed by later imposition of a culture's dominant theories as to retain none of their original content. If the acquisition of our present commonsense stock of predicates by which we pick out perceived properties marked a transition from more primitive ways of conceptualizing that are lost forever to us in this process, then the appeal to naturally salient properties would be epistemically empty, irrelevant to the defense of foundational beliefs, and the prediction of further replacement by the terms of another, more sophisticated theory would regain plausibility. Thus it must be counterargued not only that certain phenomenal properties are naturally salient and certain predicates naturally projected but also that the former continue to appear as possible targets of belief after the acquisition of naive and sophisticated theories of physical reality.

The latter claim is also easily defended. If naturally salient properties are those biologically selected on the basis of relevance to successful behavior—for example, those qualities that enable us to discriminate and recognize middle-sized objects in the immediate perceptual environment—then those same properties should continue to be prominent as referents for commonsense predicates, rather than disappearing in the process of acquiring that vocabulary. The truth of this prediction is evidenced in several ways, first by the relative uniformity of certain basic phenomenal terms, for colors and shapes for example, across languages and throughout written history. Psychological evidence attests also to the minimal effect of verbal training on certain ways of appearing. Certainly the thesis that language functions as a mediating cue that renders originally indistinguishable stimuli distinctive has been entertained and tested by psychologists. It currently finds little favor, even among those whose experiments are restricted to older children and adults.[14] The effect of verbal knowledge is minimal in the perception of illusions, movement, and causal connections, cases in which the distinction clearly emerges between the manner of appearing and the interpretation in physical terms of the physical property that appears, given suitable background theory. One may know that two lines are equal in length, but they may continue to appear unequal; one may know that discrete dots are being flashed on a screen, but they may appear as a single dot moving across the screen; etc. In the first case the two lines appear unequal, but to one with suitable background theory they may also appear *to be* equal. The latter fact does not alter the former, which is the primary perceptual phenomenon. The minimal effect of linguistic programming has been shown more directly as well. The availability of more numerous discriminating terms in particular languages, color terms for example, does not appreciably enhance abilities of their users to discriminate. The Whorfian hypothesis, suggested by Sellars's account of the acquisition of concepts as determining ways of appearing, does not hold up. Discriminability does not appear to be linked to codability, the ability to represent phenomena symbolically, although coding may facilitate memory in certain cases.[15] Finally, common sense itself and the everyday examples it affords attest to the immunity of certain ways of appearing from changes in theoretical beliefs (although appearance can be affected by expectation, especially in ambiguous perceptual situations). Certain appearances will not change with changes in the relations among terms used to report them. When we learn new relations among color terms, for example, that they are mutually exclusive, or new facts about the color red, for example, that it will appear when various wavelengths of light are mixed, fire engines do not thereby appear different in color.

Common sense may very well commit us to a naive realist view of objects and their intrinsic properties. In so doing it may prove to be a mistaken theory, committed to a mistaken explanation of how things appear, although not recognized or normally formulated as such. The mistakes are readily demonstrated. Because of the radical relativity of color perception, for example, different shades are ascribed to the same parts of the same objects in similar conditions by different observers. Such ascription remains undetected in everyday contexts because of the vagueness and broadness of our everyday color terms. But this commonsense practice contradicts the equally common notion that uniformly colored surfaces have single determinate shades. The abandonment of this theory need not lead us to abandon its basic phenomenal terms, however. We would be forced to do so only if the meanings of such terms were a function of all the beliefs they were used to express. If that were the case with meanings generally, then every theory, indeed every thesis, would be incommensurable (unable to be translated or compared) with every other. Such radical holism is therefore no more plausible for meaning than for concept acquisition. If there is rather a fixed reference for phenomenal terms uncommitted to a theoretical interpretation of the properties to which they refer, then the claim that beliefs about appearances can stand alone as self-justified remains viable.

At this point our main hurdle to accepting such a notion is Churchland's argument regarding the translation of alien perceptual reports. His conclusion in the case described—that we should translate the alien visual reports as statements about temperature—seemed to show that the meanings and referents of phenomenal terms are indeed functions of implicative relations within a theory, that it is impossible to isolate core senses that fix reference by association with repeatable phenomenal properties as they appear. The answer to this argument is that there are no simple and accurate translations of the reports in question. Certainly the alien reports will not correlate exactly with our *felt temperatures*, with what is reported in our phenomenal reports, since, as pointed out, those reports depend not only on the kinetic energy in molecular aggregates on surfaces but on other features of the materials in question and on the states of our tactile nervous systems. I do not mean to invoke the bogeyman of incommensurability. I mean only that, if we intended to be accurate in translating, we would have to tell the full story about how one major determinant of our felt temperature, the one that physical scientists refer to as "temperature," appears to these beings visually. And, in saying that it appears *as colors* rather than *as felt temperatures* we are using these phenomenal terms in their core, theoretically uncommitted senses. Thus our understanding of the story illustrates rather than disproves the need for theory-neutral core referents for phenomenal terms.

Beliefs utilizing phenomenal terms to refer to ways things appear can then remain indifferent to changes in our metaphysical commitments that occur with changes in science. Whatever qualities we ultimately ascribe to objects, this ascription need not lead us to abandon our description of the ways they appear to unaided perception. Foundationalism of the sort described here need not be seen as a threat to scientific realism or as an ally to instrumentalism, as a foundationalism that sought to preserve commonsense ontological commitments would be. I shall argue in the next chapter that we must indeed be committed to the most coherent explanatory theory. But this theory must include in its account explanations of why things appear as they do.

While foundationalism of the sort defended here leads directly (through the use of its justifying principle) to a defense of scientific realism, exclusive attention to the practice of science from the internal viewpoint can be misleading for the epistemologist seeking an epistemic (validating) reconstruction. For the concept of data that is of immediate relevance to the practicing physical scientist is far from that intended in traditional epistemology, Cartesian or otherwise. According to the traditional epistemologist, data for the scientist would lie near the frontier of theoretical interpretation. Such data do change radically with major changes in theory. Scientists report test results and measurements in theoretical terms and in relation to instruments inscrutable to those untrained in the current background theory. Given that reports of measurements by our instruments change, that such reporting parameters as mass, motion, acceleration, and temperature have shifted in their fundamental significance, it seems to some philosophers that we should change our view of the measurements of human perceptual systems as measuring instruments. Hence the replaceability thesis.

I have agreed that our interpretation of those intrinsic physical properties that appear to us should alter with changes in theory, and that we could perhaps make noninferential reports of such properties, although they would not be perceptually or epistemically fundamental. The epistemologist's story must begin long before the scientist's data, however, if it is to grasp the structure of knowledge and the rationale of its development. Indeed, recognition of fixed foundations in appearances, instead of threatening scientific realism, as naive realist foundations would, is necessary to its adequate philosophical defense. Although not of immediate relevance to the scientist, such recognition is necessary to the broader characterization of the scientific enterprise, in relation to which we pledge ultimate allegiance to some distant descendant of current theory. We cannot characterize this future theory simply in terms of its explanatory coherence. As the standard objection to coherentism points out, there may be many stories and myths of equal internal coherence. In this context as well, there must be a fixed base with which the rest of the theory must cohere as explanation, if it is to be scientific.

There are two possible replies to this final point. One is to take the fixed base with which future science must cohere as present and past scientific theory. Future science must explain the degree of success of earlier theories (without necessarily incorporating their laws or observation categories). It is the convergence of theories in this sense that is to justify the realist's faith. The other response is to view the causal connection with sensory stimulation as a guarantee of a link with physical reality, rather than fidelity to appearance or experience. Probably both these ideas underlie some materialists' claim that it is the "self-correcting" nature of science, rather than its base in experience, that distinguishes it from myth.

But to say that science self-corrects is to refer to its attempts to incorporate anomalies instead of ignoring them; and it is difficult to see how anomalies, data outside the grasp of a current theory, arise at all if experience is fully molded by the categories of that theory. The appeals to convergence—i.e., to progressive expansion and alteration of theories—and to causal links to stimulation do not succeed in distinguishing science from myth. Sets of myths too can converge on unified explanations, and they arise via some causal connections with stimulation (as do all human response). Unless there is some other characteristic of past science that distinguishes it, there is no virtue to convergence and nothing in it to encourage the realist. Instrumental success is relative to purpose and purpose to theory, as the foes of foundationalism point out. Attempts at distinction by further specifying the causal connection to stimulation also seem hopeless. It seems that we must include in the broad specification of the scientific enterprise explanations and predictions of ways things appear. If we distinguish between certain appearances and their physical interpretations, holding that the interpretations but not these appearances themselves shift with theory changes, then the rationality of our commitment to science as descriptive of reality becomes secure. Indeed, as I shall now attempt to show, the same model of rational justification secures the foundations as well as the most coherent explanatory theory.

PART III
REALISM

9

THE INFERENCE TO PHYSICAL REALITY

In my view the validation of belief in a realm of objects independent of our perceptual experience and conceptual schemes requires an inductive inference from the nature of that experience to its probable causes. Other philosophers have held that various features of the epistemic relation between experience and its objects renders such an inference invalid or impossible. They have pointed out that our concepts of appearances are parasitic on concepts of objective properties, that we cannot formulate an independent order within experience from which we could infer to objects as its explanation, that such an explanation would not admit of subsequent corroboration either directly or by testing of novel predictions, that we therefore lack independent epistemic access to *either* term of the relation between experience and objects, that our very criteria for knowledge presuppose knowledge of objects and their properties, and finally that the formulation of the realist's thesis presupposes its own validation. While invalidating an inductive inference from experience to physical objects, these points are meant to show that the connection is epistemically stronger and more certain, that the existence of objects and our knowledge of them is entailed or conceptually necessitated by our beliefs about our experiences.

A PRIORI ARGUMENTS

Before filling out the inductive defense of physical realism, I shall canvass more closely the various a priori arguments to show why they do not and cannot succeed. The main problem with such arguments lies in the contradiction between the realist's thesis that real objects transcend all experiences of them, in contemporary terms that truth transcends justification, and the a priorist's claim that statements about experience conceptually imply the existence and properties of real objects. Any argument that defends a conceptual rather than contingent relation between appearance and physical reality loses the independence of objects from conceptual and perceptual schemes that is the hallmark of a full-blooded realism. What is implicit a priori in our empirical concepts cannot at the same time remain indifferent to changes in those concepts. But properties of real physical objects do not depend on the concepts we have of them. Any Kantian or transcendental deduction of the objective realm therefore must either remain wholly idealist or leave the thing-in-itself untouched, as Kant himself was so careful to do.

I conceded earlier the conceptual sophistication in the notion of an appearance, but claimed that the lateness of its acquisition is irrelevant to the order of epistemic justification. We may grant that this relative lateness is a matter of necessity: we can learn to restrict ascriptions of properties to appearances only when we learn that certain conditions are unfavorable for perceiving or when we learn of subjective contributions to the ways things are perceived. Unfavorable conditions must be contrasted with favorable, and the concept of the subjective emerges only by contrast with the objective environment. These concessions are compatible with the claim that knowledge of objects must be validated by appeal to the ways they appear, that our only evidence for objective properties is sensory evidence. It is also compatible with recognition of the possibility, once subjective contributions to perception are recognized, that they may so infect the process of perceiving that all we take to be the case empirically in regard to nonrelational objective properties only appears so. The intelligibility of such global skepticism is, I shall argue, a correlate of the realist's thesis of the independence of objects from the data in experience by which we know them. Such skepticism remains intelligible despite this first point regarding conceptual priority.

We may grant also that not only our concepts and terms but perception itself reflects a realist attitude. Perceptually prominent properties tend to be those that aid in the identification and recognition of physical objects. As Gestalt psychologists showed many years ago, the appearance of the perceptual field is organized so as to accentuate object boundaries. The perceptual constancies of size, shape, and color serve object recognition. Experiments reveal that even non-objects, for example discrete dots flashed on a screen, are perceived as single objects moving across the screen. The behavioral value of such selection, hence its evolutionary explanation, is obvious. If we are to react successfully to objects, we must perceive them as such, often on the basis of fleeting and incomplete cues; hence the illusions of objects in highly abnormal environments. Even prior to concept formation, then, perceptual consciousness appears to be committed to the existence of objects arranged in physical space. But, as in the case of concepts, such perceptual ontological commitment cannot demonstrate its own validity. The fact that appearances are perceived almost always as appearances of objects is compatible, for example, with the Berkeleyan thesis that objects reduce to collections of (objectlike) appearances. Objects in the realist's sense, on the other hand, whether or not perceived as stable wholes, retain their properties irrespective of the ways we perceive and conceive them. We are interested here in the epistemic warrant for our naive realist attitudes, and we cannot validate such attitudes merely by noting that we have them.

A point related to those regarding attitudinal priorities, but one seemingly more inimical to the order of inductive validation I propose, derives from Sellars. He argues that the supposed inference to physical objects cannot be of the ordinary scientific kind, a common inference to the best explanation, since here there is no independently formulable data from which to infer, that is, there is nothing to explain.[1] Presumably it is the order within the sequence of experiences or appearances that is explained by appeal to relatively constant physical objects as their (partial) causes. But we cannot capture this order except in terms that refer to objects themselves in physical space. The problem is not simply that our linguistic terms for many appearances, terms that help us to classify them, are borrowed from the language of physical objects, for example chairlike, doglike, etc. This borrowing only reflects again the conceptual and perceptual priorities in ascribing properties to objects noted above.

His point here may rather be that the full structure within experience, all the predictable regularities in sequences of experiences that are supposed to form our data, can be captured only through the use of hypotheticals and counterfactuals that presuppose the conclusion of the supposed explanatory inference. Having just seen the chair in my office, I can predict that if I return there I will see a chairlike appearance, and that if I had been there earlier I would have been appeared to in that chairlike way. The antecedents of such expressions make essential reference to locations and movements in physical space. I know what experiences I have had and will have and would have had in other circumstances only by knowing my location and that of other physical bodies in space and time. There is then no independent knowledge of the supposed data, no knowledge of an orderly sequence of experiences from which the existence of objects only contingently related could then be inferred. The conclusion seems to follow that any inductive argument from the order within experience must beg the question by assuming what it is trying to infer.

Once more, however, this argument implicitly confuses epistemic with conceptual priority. As earlier arguments, all it demonstrates is the necessity for realist language for describing and classifying appearances. It does not show that such language refers to objects beyond these ways of appearing. That certain concepts are required for us does not show that they are instantiated in the ways we take them to be. (I take it that we do naively intend to refer to objects whose real properties remain indifferent to our percepts and concepts. How we can so refer or even intend to refer is another question to be addressed later.) Pragmatic necessity within a conceptual scheme does not equate with truth, at least for the realist. We need not in fact *know* of objects in order to believe we are appeared to as we are. We need only to conceive objects as stable wholes (not necessarily as independent, although we do conceive them that way) in order to conceptualize appearances. That such concepts must be used in the premises of the inductive argument does not beg the question of knowledge of their real objects.

Once we do justify belief in an objective world to which experience must adapt if behavior is to be successful, *then* it might be argued that the pragmatic necessity of a concept indicates its probable instantiation or approximate truth to its object. It would then be unexplained cosmic coincidence if the only way we could make sense of the world had nothing to do with its real structure. But it is clear that the latter argument, no matter how fleshed out, is inductive, an inference to the explanation with fewest unexplained and unexplainable remainders, requiring further justification of the inductive principle of inference. The existence of the concepts in question and their necessity for us remains a psychological fact that enters as a premise into this argument. That such concepts are indispensable for the formulation of other premises in the argument is not reason to infer a priori to their truth or instantiation. Our ordinary concepts and language commit us not only to realism but to dualism as well. In both cases further argument is required beyond noting those naive metaphysical theories built into our ordinary linguistic practice.[2]

The inability to remove physical parameters from our specifications of orderly sequences of appearances is one reason for the failure of the program earlier in this century to translate physical object statements into sense data statements. The view known as analytical phenomenalism holds that statements about objects must reduce to statements about their perceivable properties, to the ways they appear. But they will appear only under certain physical conditions, reference to which cannot be eliminated by further sense data statements. In addition to physical conditions, physical location must be irreducibly specified as well, since only physical location distinguishes qualitatively identical but distinct objects. Analytic phenomenalism is defeated also by the very psychological facts that partially motivated the introduction of sense data in the first place. The phenomena of perceptual relativity, the fact that objects (according to our best theories and experimental data) can appear in different ways due to purely subjective factors, implies lack of entailments in either direction between objective properties and the ways they appear. At most we could expect probabilistic correlations, connections far too weak to equate with translations or equivalences of meaning. Finally, if meanings involve intensions and not simply references, it is clear that the meanings of object statements cannot reduce to those of sense data or appearing statements. Aside from the fact that we intend to refer to objects in the realist's sense and not simply to our own experiences, there is the obvious point that, even if we could remove reference to physical parameters from the hypotheticals and counterfactuals that translate physical object statements and replace such reference with enormously complex strings of sense data statements, we do not intend such strings as part of the meanings of our object statements.[3] We cannot mean that of which we cannot conceive.

The multiple failures of translation, however, are simply irrelevant to the realist's thesis. (I mention them because they have been widely thought to be relevant a priori.) Such failure shows again only that we intend to refer to objects beyond experience. The success of the translational enterprise, if we can imagine the success of a project doomed from the start, would show only that we do not so intend. The former does not show that we succeed in so referring (the realist's thesis); and the latter would not show in itself that we could not somehow succeed in spite of ourselves. That our concepts of objects do not reduce to concepts of appearances cannot establish that there must be objects beyond appearances, except in the idealist's sense of objects.[4] Thus any argument that trades only on the priority, indispensability, or irreducibility of object concepts must remain insufficient for the realist's task.

Another reason for taking the leap from sensory evidence to physical objects to be a priori rather than inductive derives from Roderick Chisholm, although, as in the case of Sellars's argument, it may be inspired by Kant, the father of the transcendental argument. Chisholm holds that epistemic principles themselves must be a priori, although not analytic, propositions. Our justification for accepting the principles can derive only from our beliefs about them or about examples that fall under them. He has in mind not our principle of inference to the best explanation but more specific epistemic rules linking sensory evidence to objects, such as the claim that when a subject takes himself to perceiving something F, it is reasonable for him to believe that he is perceiving something F.[5] (Chisholm takes our inductive principle to be useless here, since he holds that explanations require independent support in order to be accepted as best.[6] I shall argue that, at least in certain cases, the fact that an explanans appears to explain best a body of data is in itself a reason for accepting it as true.)

Analogies with moral principles support this view of epistemic rules. Consider the specific principle that acts of charity are prima facie right. This is not analytic, rightness not being included in the meaning of 'charity', but it is not derived from empirical evidence either. One can decide prior to perceiving acts of charity, and certainly without perceiving a property of rightness inherent in such acts, that they tend to be right, although this recognition will not follow an analysis of meanings. We might take the rule to be implicit in our moral practice, but we must also admit that one's judgments on such matters need not accord with the dominant practice in order to be correct. An individual's judgment may be more consistent with other accepted principles and judgments than is the dominant practice or consensus on the specific moral issue.

Several further analogies between moral and epistemic principles appear to support a similar analysis of the latter, such as the analysis offered by Chisholm. First, epistemic principles may be said to be normative or evaluative. As do moral principles, they involve the application of standards. When we evaluate a brief or claim as knowledge, we grant it a positive status and place a higher value on it. Given this analogy and the recognition of moral principles as nonempirically derived, one is tempted to think of evaluations in general as lying beyond the realm of empirical or straightforward inductive validation (even if supervenient on empirical properties). Second, just as we design our moral principles to accord with our specific moral judgments, so when we set out to establish criteria for knowledge, we must be guided by our confident acceptance of certain claims to know. As argued in Part I, an analysis of knowledge and its criteria that in itself implies skepticism where we most confidently take ourselves to know will be dismissed as too stringent. This suggests that coherence between principles and judgments, expressing overall consistency in evaluation, is the goal of epistemology as it is the goal of normative ethics. If coherence or consistency in evaluation is our sole goal, then our principles are grounded only in the specific judgments they imply. They need not preserve truth in the sense of correspondence to external fact, and they therefore require no independent validation themselves. If we take the analogy to ethics seriously, then there can be no problem linking internal coherence to truth, as there is not in ethics, where truth reduces to consistency with accepted judgments that themselves have survived critical scrutiny.

But precisely because of the plausibility of this characterization of moral truth, the analogy with ethics begs the question against realist construals of empirical knowledge. Specific moral judgments on the base level appear to differ from empirical judgments in a crucial respect. While the best explanation for a moral judgment would not appeal to an independent moral property of rightness or goodness as partial cause for the judgment (nor do such properties enter explanatory chains linked to such judgments), it is the realist's contention that independent objects and their properties do enter explanatory chains for judgments about such properties and about ways of appearing.[7] This difference, if real, requires a different status for epistemic principles as well. If inference to the best explanation justifies belief in objects to which empirical judgments must adapt or correspond, then epistemic principles (including that one) must generate and preserve truth in this sense, and the epistemologist must try to show that his principles do just that. It is true, as noted earlier, that in evaluating a belief as knowledge we thereby grant it a positive status; that is, we make a normative judgment. But the value we thereby place on the belief is conditional on our valuing knowledge or truth itself, either for its own sake or for its pragmatic worth in the realization of other goals or projects. Epistemic appraisals therefore represent less pure judgments of value than do moral appraisals.

It does not suffice then to produce a set of epistemic rules that cohere with our intuitive judgments about what we know. Rules stating what it is reasonable for a person to believe, given his coherent set of foundational beliefs and epistemic intuitions, may take one a priori, without the aid of an inductive inference, from reasonable belief in sensory evidence (or in what one takes oneself to be perceiving) to reasonable belief in objective properties. But if the realist is right, we must aim here not simply at reasonableness or internal coherence but also at empirical truth. Such leaps from appearances to objects will preserve truth, I maintain, only if they link the objective properties in question via explanatory chains to established ways of appearing or to beliefs about appearances, and only if inference to the best explanation itself tends to preserve truth.

Suppose, for example, that the true explanation for what we take ourselves to perceive appealed to the chicaneries of an evil demon or to superscientists who program perceptual experiences into our brains directly. Then the reasonableness of our perceptual beliefs would remain irrelevant to their status vis-à-vis knowledge. The only way to rule out such explanations, I shall argue, is by application of the usual criteria for best explanations. We can rule them out as intuitively implausible (intuitions can count here if we can show that explanations that seem best to us are likely to be true), because they leave further natural questions about the nature and motivations of the superbeings unanswerable, etc. If such explanations (and other alternatives) do not appear best, and if we can provide inductive support for the principle of inference to the best explanation, then we can establish the realist position on inductive grounds. It cannot be established a priori if such alternative explanations for perceptual beliefs cannot themselves be ruled out a priori, as I shall argue they cannot.

Thus, if the realist is right about the existence of objects and properties independent of beliefs that make them true or false, then epistemic principles without inductive support can be of no ultimate use. But if inference to the best explanation itself can be validated or warranted, then I believe the realist position can be established on that ground (the argument will be provided in the next section). And once we do accept an independent physical world to which human projects must adapt, then I

believe we can provide inductive support for the proposition
that explanations that appear best in the long run tend to be
approximately true. In providing such support we utilize the
principle that we seek to establish. Hume's point remains well
taken. But it does not follow that the entire enterprise is trivial-
ized, since the support for the principle might still have been
lacking. While we cannot escape a broad circle (or spiral at
different levels) of coherence as our criterion of truth, we can
avoid the narrow circle of a priori epistemic principles and
coherence only with our naive intuitions. The argument in support of epistemic principles must then be more complex than
the methodology of normative ethics, where the only goal is
"reflective equilibrium" or consistency. It is true that we must
begin with confident intuitions in deriving criteria for both
rightness and knowledge. But, while in the former case we cannot make sense of a perfectly coherent system of judgments and
principles that is entirely false (except from the point of view of
some other developed moral system), this possibility is intelligible when the aim is true description of a subject-independent
reality. For this reason Chisholm's analogy breaks down, and
epistemic principles, as well as specific claims to empirical knowledge beyond sensory experience, require inductive support.

Before presenting that inductive argument, we may consider
one final, more recent and ingenious a priori argument for
realism from Colin McGinn.[8] His argument depends upon the
semantic characterization of the realist's thesis. I have been
claiming that realism requires objects independent of our perceptual and conceptual schemes. One way of unpacking this
elusive notion of independence is in terms of the contrast between truth on the one hand and justification, warranted
assertibility, or verification conditions on the other. Those conditions that provide socially accepted warrant, even in the long
run, for making statements in the domain taken to be real cannot guarantee the truth of such statements. This characterization, due mainly to Michael Dummett,[9] captures the connections between realism and skepticism that were also noted
above. If truth conditions are to transcend justification conditions, then skepticism, even global skepticism, must be intelligible (at the same time it must be false if our realist concepts are

instantiated). It must be possible (but not actually the case) that all those statements about objects in a real domain that are reasonable or justified for us may at the same time be false, even those of maximal coherence within a maximally corroborated theory at the Peircean end of inquiry.

McGinn's argument trades on the fact that the justification conditions for physical object statements consist in certain experiences, the having of which makes it proper to assert such statements, while the justification conditions for statements about experiences consist in certain types of physical behavior, the perception of which warrants the ascription of various mental states. Thus for the physical realist, the truth of physical object statements transcends that of experiential statements, while for the mental realist, the truth of experiential statements transcends that of physical object (or event) statements. It seems to follow that realism in regard to the mental requires realism regarding the physical, and conversely. The realist's thesis regarding either realm cannot even be stated without appeal to the other. If objects or events in the warranting domain are not real, then they will not serve their warranting function. There will be nothing from which the objects or events taken to be real, that is independent, can be independent. Since one must presumably regard either the mental or the physical as real, it seems that one must in fact be a realist in regard to both realms. At least if his thesis is to be stated in semantic terms, it seems on a priori grounds that the realist must be thoroughgoing. And the semantic statement of the thesis may be the only way to make clear the otherwise obscure notion of independence at the heart of the thesis.

One might nevertheless attack McGinn (and Dummett) by questioning the semantic interpretation. On closer consideration it becomes clear first that the semantic requirement is only necessary, not sufficient, for the truth of realism traditionally construed. Truth conditions of physical object statements must not only transcend justification conditions; the former must also be satisfied, at least sometimes. But even when truth conditions for physical object statements do transcend warranting conditions in experience and are at the same time satisfied, and even if we have good grounds for the latter claim, it might still be claimed that realism fails to be established.[10] It could be, for example, that such truth conditions consist in experiences beyond all those that humans ever have, perhaps experiences of a deity, as Berkeley's metaphysical theory suggests. This objection is partially handled by the realist's requiring that truth conditions for physical object statements transcend even ideal experiential warrant, that such statements be possibly false even when all compossible experiences have been had at the ideal end of inquiry. Of course we must talk of all possible experiences for humans, not those by definition veridical, as a deity's might be. Experiences of a god defined to be omniscient might be materially sufficient to establish the truth of physical object statements (but would the god know what it is to experience an illusion?) This would not refute the realist's thesis if the veridicality of these experiences lay not in their coherence but in their match with physical object statements not entailed by statements of all possible human experiences. I shall argue that we can understand the notion of physical conditions independent of all possible human experiences. To understand this notion we must be able only to conceive of all such experiences together as fallible. That their veridicality then consists not in correspondence to physical objects but in coherence with divine experiences whose veridicality lies only in *their* coherence can be ruled out on inductive grounds, since the Berkeleyan explanation for the order within our experiences is not as good as that which appeals to physical objects (a claim to be defended in subsequent sections). Barring the possibility of divine, but not human, experiential coherence as truth conditions for physical object statements, the semantic statement of the realist's thesis, suitably strengthened as above, does capture a necessary condition for its truth, and best captures as well the notion of independence at its heart.

The first real problem with McGinn's argument lies rather with the premise that warranting conditions for statements about experience consist only in observations of physical behavior. I have assumed the more traditional first-person point of view as the foundation for an epistemological reconstruction. Here the initial question is whether appearances or experiences are as we believe them to be, which I answered by providing an analysis of an inductive version of immediate validation. A further inference of the same form takes us from appearances to physical objects and their properties, and an explanatory inference yet later in the story to the experiences of others. (By now, having distinguished several times between conceptual and epistemic priority, we should be immune to the objection that the concepts of one's own mental states develops only in relation to the concept of other subjects of mental states.) Thus, according to this Cartesian-Lockean program, the issues of realism for experiences and physical objects are not symmetrical and mutually dependent. In my own case it is obvious that I do not employ behavioral criteria in order to judge appearances. The question of their real nature or properties arises only in relation to my beliefs about them and their independence from those beliefs. In order to accept (my) experiences as real, I therefore need not be a realist a priori in regard to the realm of the physical.

Suppose, however, that we do require appeal to the experiences of others as well in order even to raise the question regarding the existence of physical objects beyond experiences and, as seems uncontroversial, we also appeal to physical behavior to warrant belief in mental states of others distinct from that behavior. Would such mutual warrant establish a priori the existence of two independent metaphysical realms? Couldn't it still turn out that what appears to be physical behavior reduces to appearances of such behavior or, as is thought more likely by many, that what appear to be mental states logically independent of the physical realm reduce to (second-order or functional) complex patterns of physical states? Our suspicion of the claim that such reductions are impossible derive from our recognition of the standard weakness of transcendental and other a priori arguments for realism: the idea that the existence of the real could follow from features of our concepts or from conceptual dependencies alone. McGinn's argument, as earlier ones of this type, appeals in its premises only to certain conceptual requirements for us, in this case requirements for stating the realist's thesis in a certain way. The standard objection, still valid here if the realist is in fact right, is that such premises cannot by themselves demonstrate that the concepts in question are instantiated in the real world.

What McGinn's argument shows, if he is right about the warranting relations among statements referring to the domains of the mental and the physical, is that the issue of realism regarding one of these realms will not arise for us unless we presuppose objects or events in the other realm. And if we presuppose objects or events of either type to be independently real (in the sense of independence indicated), then we will be presupposing those of the other realm as well. But the fact that the issue would not arise for us as it does, that we would not conceive it as we do, if we did not assume realism for both realms, does not show that this assumption is correct for either. No matter how we conceive the issue, it could still be that only experiences, or only physical phenomena, exist. If we did not possess both concepts, we would not conceive of their objects existing independently from anything else, since we would not conceive of anything from which they were independent. The issue of the irreducibility of appearances, for example, arises only once we take physical phenomena to be real, even though we can establish properties of appearances before conceiving them as independent from or irreducible to the physical. Our concept of the real develops in contrast with our notion of the apparent, and our realist concept of truth in contrast with justification or warrant. But that we must conceive of justification conditions for statements as real or independent shows neither that such conditions exist independently from anything else nor even that they exist at all.

Thus, even if McGinn is right about the symmetries in conceptions of justification conditions, his argument fails to establish realism of either sort for the same reasons that other a priori arguments for realism must fail. Often when such arguments try to show what we must know in order to pose the issue, they in fact seem to aim at showing only what we must believe. Often they show not what we must believe, but only what we must conceive of. Even if they do show what we must believe or presuppose, nothing of significance follows. It follows from the fact that we must believe p in order to pose an issue as we do that we are justified in believing p, only if we are justified in posing the issue as we do and are justified in believing what we must believe in order to pose it that way. Even if we are justified in believing that *p*, the realist's point is precisely that justification cannot guarantee the truth of propositions referring to the real. The only thing of significance that follows from the definition of realism, therefore, is that a priori arguments cannot establish the truth of the thesis.

THE INDUCTIVE INFERENCE

A brief reminder of the main argument of the previous part of the book will introduce our inductive argument here. The defense of empirical foundations, the validation of beliefs about appearances, depended there on an inference to the best explanation. In my view that inference provides the only satisfactory answer to skeptical challenges, challenges intelligible even at the foundational level. Skeptical alternatives similar to those often raised against the rationality of belief in the world of physical objects could have been raised on the prior level, that of appearances, as well. It is conceivable, for example, that an all-powerful, malicious demon changes our applications of phenomenal terms constantly without our noticing this instability, so that our beliefs about how we are appeared to are generally false. The intelligibility of this hypothesis follows from the fallibility of our phenomenal beliefs, argued for at length in Part II. The skeptical hypothesis is empirically equivalent to that which appeals to the truth of these beliefs in explaining their being held. The beliefs in question remain the same whatever their correct explanation. Thus we see already at this level that, if any of our empirical beliefs are to be validated, we must have inductive grounds other than accuracy in predictions of data for preferring certain explanations or theories to others. Explanatory coherence must make some theories preferable without entailing their truth.

We previously compared explanations for beliefs about appearances that appeal to their truth with those that appeal to the physical causes of these beliefs, arguing that their truth is more closely tied to the probability of the beliefs being held across close possible worlds. It is clear that other grounds on which we generally prefer certain explanations to others rule out skeptical alternatives as preferable. Appeal to a demon who causes us to form false beliefs about appearances by confusing our applications of phenomenal terms is highly counterintuitive and leaves many questions that naturally arise regarding more precise causal antecedents, the nature, origin, and motives of this being, and so on, unanswered and seemingly unanswerable. Accepting such beliefs as true, on the other hand, leads to explanatory chains that encompass our deepest empirical theories, as I shall proceed to argue. Thus grounds of explanatory depth and fruitfulness lead us to prefer explanations that appeal to the truth of beliefs about appearances over skeptical alternatives.

The inductive validation of belief in physical objects shares the same structure and forms a continuous sequence with the establishment of the empirical foundations. This structure should not be confused with a pragmatic or instrumental justification of the nonskeptical theses.[11] I am not saying merely that *if* we seek deeper explanations, of *if* we want to be scientific in the way we infer, then we ought to accept these theses. Such hypotheticals can be countered by others, for example, 'if we want to be innovative and imaginative, then we ought to accept the demon hypothesis'. My argument for realism in regard to physical objects is thoroughly epistemic rather than pragmatic. The only epistemic reason for belief is probable truth. The argument therefore has two steps. First, if beliefs about appearances are to be accepted as generally true, then belief in physical objects can be validated as well, since application of the same principle of inference is involved at both levels. Of course the grounds for these two types of belief are not the same. Application of the principle of inference to the best explanation shows beliefs about appearances but not beliefs about physical objects to be immediately validated. But once we accept propositions regarding sequences of appearances on the basis of beliefs about appearances alone,[12] we must accept propositions about physical objects according to the same principle. At least we must accept them if appeal to physical objects can be shown to explain such sequences better than alternatives. This demonstration is therefore the first step in the argument. The second step, which is common not only to both these levels but to the justification of scientific realism at deeper levels of explanatory theory, will await discussion of the latter topic. That step will consist in the defense of the principle of explanatory inference itself as generally truth preserving.

In arguing that appeal to physical objects provides the best explanation for sequences of appearances, I shall not claim that only such appeal can explain particular appearances or sequences of them, that these could not be explained in any other way. We could explain particular appearances without ever leaving the level of sensory experience by appealing to lawlike connections among experiences themselves or to objects in the Berkeleyan sense of classes of appearances. (That this sense does not capture the meanings of our ordinary object statements is again immaterial.) One can induce to such lawlike regularities from experiencing particular sequences that would be more probable given these laws, and then note this probability relation by way of explaining particular appearances or sequences of them. Such explanations fit Carl Hempel's nomological-deductive or probabilistic models. (We might not obtain universal laws at this level or even uniform probabilities. All generalizations might include ceteris paribus clauses. But rough generalizations can suffice for explanations too.) We may grant that appeal to such generalizations is genuinely explanatory according to our partial analysis of explanation in Part I. Of course making even rough generalizations explicit at this level would be enormously complex and perhaps, as we granted earlier, impossible without the use of object language. The actual referents of the object terms, however, can be taken to reduce metaphysically to Berkeleyan objects.

It might be protested that certain phenomena, even on the sensory level, can be explained only within a realist framework. One example might be that of systematic illusion, the perceptual enhancement, beyond objective cues, of contrasts and focused elements in the perceptual field.[13] Such distortion by accentuation of objective properties can be explained in terms of the adaptive advantages of faster discrimination and identification times for focused elements made possible in this way. This example might seem difficult for the nonrealist because

intuitively it seems difficult to think of systematic or pervasive
illusion itself, as well as its evolutionary explanation, except in
realist terms. The former seems difficult because phenom-
enalists interpret illusion as anomalous experience that fails to
cohere. But when illusion is pervasive, lack of coherence may
seem unintelligible. However, when we realize that systematic
illusion is discovered in relation to a standard of measurement
by (apparent) instruments against which it *is* anomalous, the
problem dissolves. Regarding the naturalist or evolutionary
mode of explanation, while some philosophers have associated
this with the concept of realism,[14] I see no direct logical connection here either. Although it is natural to construe adaptation as
adaptation to environments of real objects, recalcitrant experiences might do as well. All we require to explain change or
development as evolutionary are constraints with which we
must cope, but such constraints could derive from within experience rather than from without. Later, an argument from adaptation will enter indirectly into the justification of realism by
helping to justify the principle of inference in terms of which
the realist position is established. But the connection between
this style of argument and the realist's thesis is more subtle than
that of entailed assumption.

Let us then accept that the same range of particular experiential phenomena can be explained within a nonrealist metaphysics. There remain other inductive grounds for preferring the
realist to the empirically equivalent nonrealist views, most
prominent among them here being explanatory depth. Appeal
to objects in the physical realist's sense explains more deeply in
two ways. First, particular appearances, explainable in both
ways, are given deeper and more satisfying explanations in realist terms. While appeal to generalization on the same metaphysical level can be genuinely explanatory—we can explain why a
particular emerald is green by noting that all emeralds are
green—our desire to know *why* things are as they are or appear
as they do is more deeply satisfied when we are given a causal
explanation. Thus, if we are provided with a theory of color
vision and light transmission, we have a deeper and more satisfying explanation of why this emerald appears green than if we
are simply told that all emeralds appear so. (Of course we might

not be interested in understanding the former, but we would still admit that it is a deeper explanation.) In the former case we understand why this particular gem appears as it does or why we are appeared to in such a way in conditions we describe as seeing an emerald, while in the latter case we simply remove the anomalous nature of the experience by fitting it into a system of experienced regularities. If depth of explanation counts as part of explanatory coherence—and it is certainly a criterion we use in evaluating explanations—then the realist metaphysics is justified on grounds of coherence.

We may tie in this appeal to explanatory depth with our analysis (in Part I) of explanation in terms of probabilistic connections across close possible worlds. The physical explanation of why an appearance is as it is screens off the appeal to regularities within experience because of an asymmetry in these connections. In close worlds in which the physical causes of a green appearance are present but in which there have never been appearances of green before, hence no regularities into which to incorporate this one, the green appearance still follows. But where other elements of the experienced regularities are present, for example emerald shapes, immediately prior experiences as of mining emeralds, etc., but some of the physical causes, for example (unexperienced) neurophysiological conditions or lighting conditions, are absent, the green appearance will not follow. Hence the latter is more closely tied to the physical causes than to the prior sequences of appearances into which it fits. This is predictable from the fact that these sequences themselves are explained by appeal to the (prior operation of) the physical causes. (The reason why all phenomena explainable in realist terms are also—more weakly—explainable in phenomenalist terms is that we in fact only infer to particular causes on the basis of already experienced sequences of appearances, sequences from which we might at the same time infer to regularities among other possible similar experiences.)

The second, closely related sense in which realist explanations are deeper relates to experiential regularities or laws in terms of which the nonrealist explains particular appearances or sequences of appearances. Such regularities include those within single sense modalities, those that relate appearances from one modality to those of another, those that relate ways things appear to unaided perception with the apparent results of measurements and, finally, comparisons among various types of (apparent) measurements. Taking an example from the first class, when I walk around my desk, I can predict or explain my visual experiences by appealing to some combination of the laws of optics and the operation of shape and color constancies. Such laws themselves may be taken to capture and express only previously observed experiential regularities and inductive projections from them. But, as mentioned in the previous paragraph, regularities themselves, the ultimate explanatory level for the (nontheological) phenomenalist, are explained for the realist by appeal to the ways that light reflected from the surfaces of the object affects the visual system. Breakdowns or anomalies in the normal regularities are in turn explained by unusual environmental conditions or malfunctions in the visual system, anomalies that generate regularities at another level. Here the gain in explanatory depth is even clearer than that noted in the previous paragraph: what is ultimate for the nonrealist is itself explained in realist terms. It is not that the realist's terms are necessary for expressing the regularities in question. We noted earlier that their pragmatic necessity does not establish the reality of their referents. Here the existence of objective referents is established if deeper explanations seem better (across a broad range of interests) and if seemingly better explanations tend to be approximately true.

When we turn to the other classes of experiential regularities, the inductive argument becomes yet stronger. Here we must explain not only the regularities among appearances within particular sensory modalities or among measurements but also the fact that these sets of regularities coordinate with other sets across modalities or modes of apprehension. These coordinations are not a matter of conventional stipulation; nor do they result from associations of observed correlations. Why, for example, does my estimate of the shape of my desk on the basis of vision agree quite closely with my estimate based upon touch or with the results of measurement? I do not begin with three or more concepts of length derived from these different sources and then join them by association or convention. Rather there is one concept instantiated by properties ascribable on the bases of these different criteria. This fact strongly suggests by way of explanation a single set of objective properties of real objects apprehended in these different ways.[15] In fact there is no other explanation remotely plausible, and none even possible without moving to metaphysical levels beyond appearances. That is one reason why the so-called primary qualities, those perceivable by more than one sense and subject to quantified measurements, have seemed to many philosophers more real than qualities, such as color, that appear to only one sense. Denying the physical reality of the former leaves unexplained the remarkable degree of agreement across different criteria for ascribing these qualities. A nonrealist might appeal to the structure of the mind in attempting to explain such agreement, but it is hard to see how the details of this explanation could be filled out without appeal to the neurophysiological structure of the brain and its reception of physical stimuli from objects. Again the comparative depth of the potential physical explanation and fruitfulness of the realist assumption is obvious.

In general, when such striking correlations among appearances or observed phenomena are noted, such that the probability of certain observations seems to vary strongly with that of others, this not only signals that the former set might be explained in terms of the latter but also cries out for explanation itself. The covariance of probabilities indicates to us that the phenomena in question are not independent of one another. This dependence relation is naturally interpreted as some type of causal connection, whether direct or consisting in a common-cause or causal chain for both sets of phenomena.[16] To specify the causal connection is to explain the phenomena in realist terms. (The nonrealist notion of cause, which itself reduces to that of regularity, would not explain the correlation but merely reiterate it.) To fail to specify the connection further is to deny the dependency, to reduce it to a coincidence, or to elevate it to an ultimate law beyond further comprehension, except perhaps in terms of its relations with other regularities in experience. Pointing out the latter relations does not produce understanding in the way that the specification of a causal mechanism does.

It is true that the quest for explanations must end somewhere in appeal to ultimate regularities, whether of the deterministic or merely statistical kind. There will therefore always be counterexamples to the demand for explanations of these seeming dependency relations. But where such explanations can be provided, either by appeal to entities in the same metaphysical category as the phenomena in question (as when we explain a set of connected physical clues by reconstructing a crime), or by appeal to entities on a more "theoretical" level (as when we explain appearances by appeal to physical objects or explain observable physical reactions by appeal to unobservables), then our understanding benefits from interpreting the referents of the explanans realistically. If the satisfaction of our understanding indicates a probable finding of truth (still to be argued), then realism for the realm in question is established. Here the correlations in judgments based on appearances can be provided with a common-cause explanation in terms of physical objects.

In the following chapter we will note a familiar criterion of strong scientific theories: when such theories generate novel predictions that are later verified, or when they explain a broad range of diverse physical facts or observations, they are regarded as more likely to be true. A key premise for accepting this norm is similar to that used in the argument above: either it is incomprehensible why the same theory should explain seemingly unconnected phenomena (when it was not specifically designed to explain all of them), or the theory is approximately true (which would explain its success), or its success remains to be explained by some later yet more comprehensible theory. In one sense this argument is almost the converse of the previous one. In the first argument, seemingly connected phenomena must have their connection determined as real; in the second, only appeal to real entities or true laws could explain seemingly unconnected observed physical reactions. But both utilize the criterion of explanatory depth in noting the realist's ability to explain what otherwise are ultimate or incomprehensible regularities or more superficial explanatory connections. There is also a deeper connection in practice, in that theories are often corroborated by a combination of these developments. Phenomena previously unconnected in our understanding come to be seen as correlated through application of the explanatory framework of the theories.

There are other obvious differences between the levels of belief in physical objects and in scientific theories, in that belief in physical objects is not inferred or consciously formulated to explain appearances and in that physical objects, at least those that enter into initial explanations for appearances, are observable. But the epistemic validation of beliefs on both levels, like that for foundations, requires application of the same principle. That belief in physical objects is not consciously theoretical but perfectly natural for us can enter as a premise into an argument for physical realism, if another acceptable premise is that our brains (or minds) are adapted to the environment as it is. The fact that such belief is automatic or natural is linked to the fact that appeal to physical objects explains experiences most intuitively. The truth of the former premise does not show that inductive validation of such beliefs is superfluous or that skeptical challenge is unintelligible here. This step in the epistemic reconstruction forms a continuous sequence with the earlier and later steps, a feature of this account that will give added strength to the position of the scientific realist. If the only satisfactory answer to the skeptic at each stage of this challenge depends upon an inductive inference of the same form as that at each other stage in the argument, and if the earlier steps provide the only premises for the later ones, then, if the earlier steps are acceptable, so are the later ones. Middle-sized physical objects provide only an epistemic bridge from appearances to the theoretical entities or processes of scientific theory, and belief in some of the naively assumed properties of the former may be the most vulnerable when the later picture emerges.

Thus far in this chapter I have argued that appeal to physical objects explains particular appearances more deeply than does appeal to regularities within the realm of appearance and that the former also explains the regularities themselves that are ultimate or inexplicable for the nonrealist. There are skeptical and nonskeptical alternatives to the framework of physical objects on the level deeper than that of appearances as well; for example, the Berkeleyan thesis that God causes the regularities within our experience or the skeptic's evil demon or superscientist who programs our experiences exactly as if they were caused by physical objects. I shall argue later against the semantic antirealist that these alternative explanations are perfectly intelligible and possible. That they are not inductively best or equal to the appeal to physical objects is clear on grounds previously noted. If God caused all the lawlike regularities in our experience without creating physical objects, then, as Descartes pointed out, he would be a deceiver. At least his motives would be far from clear, as unclear as the mechanisms by which he worked this enormous deception. The same obscurities as to motives and mechanisms, that is, as to any attempt to carry the purported explanations to deeper levels and make them more explicit and detailed, infect the superbeings of the skeptic's imagination. Not only do we not know why or how they produce the sequences of appearances for us that they do; we also have no idea why they make it seem to us as if there are physical objects. The latter question, natural here, does not arise given the initial explanation of appearances that we all naturally accept, and accepting the explanation as true leads to deeper and more satisfying theories to explain physical interactions. Certainly whatever psychology and programming apparatus one could dream up for the superbeings could not be as rich or testable as the theories of physical science and neurophysiology. The inductive verdict here is abundantly clear despite the fact that all the alternatives on this level are empirically equivalent, that accepting physical objects as real in itself leads to no novel predictions regarding appearances.

There is no need to belabor this stage of the argument further. Realism in regard to physical objects, the mere claim that there really are such things and that they do not reduce to classes of appearance or experience, has long been uncontroversial. What is important for the later argument is how the position is best established and how thoroughgoing it must be. Regarding the former, I have pointed out that application of the same principle justifies acceptance of foundational beliefs, physical objects, and theoretical entities and processes. This indicates that there may be no good reason, once one accepts beliefs on any of these levels, to withhold beliefs on the others. (The skeptic may still muster special arguments, to be answered later, against scientific realism and against reference to fully independent physical objects.) A second point about the method of validation, the appeal to grounds of (explanatory) coherence, is that it utilizes the very criterion of justification for belief usually accepted by the nonrealist. Broader and deeper explanations increase inductive coherence within a set of beliefs, so that the defender of a coherence theory of justification or truth would have to accept realism on his own grounds if the above argument is correct. If realism then implies a correspondence rather than coherence view of truth, then the nonrealist notion of truth would lead to a contradiction.

The latter premise appears correct as well. Coherence among beliefs referring to physical objects can entail their truth only if all properties of such objects are possessed relative to our way of perceiving and conceiving them. Only if our conceptual scheme determines the ways objects are can its deployment in maximally coherent theories logically entail the truth of these theories. But the existence of objects that causally explain our experiences seems to imply that they must have some nonrelational properties, that they must be some way in themselves independent of whether or how we relate to them. How can there be real objects that have no properties in themselves? Physical objects could causally influence experience and belief through input in the form of stimuli even if we had no access to the nature of their intrinsic properties. But if we have no grounds for believing that we have such access, we must still admit that there must be some such properties. (How we come to conceive and refer to them is a later topic.) The realist who despairs of providing these grounds is therefore left with Kantian unknowable things-in-themselves. The alternatives reduce to skepticism or the demonstration of knowledge in a thoroughgoing realist sense of correspondence of belief to independent reality. (The latter demand does not equate, however, with a demand for a single true or best theory, since there may still be alternative true descriptions of the same real properties—for example, alternative ways of classifying determinate shades of color under broader color terms.)

Despite the stringency of this requirement, the realist need not despair, since the inference to objects as best explaining sequences of appearances is at the same time an inference to objects with certain properties. Only appeal to those properties explains why things appear as they do. Deeper theories will alter our view of best explanations and of those properties that really exist in the physical universe. But at each stage inductive inference will appeal to certain properties and relations among them as explanatory. If such inference tends in the long run to preserve truth, that is, to produce beliefs that correspond to the real, then the thoroughgoing realist demand for knowledge not only of physical objects or processes but of their intrinsic or independent properties can be satisfied. The notion of objects without such properties is vacuous, but the argument that establishes the existence of physical objects infers to certain of their real properties as well.

Why must we infer to independent properties? Since we encounter objects only through their causal relations to our sensory systems, in initially explaining appearances we might appeal only to properties of those relations, or to distal physical stimuli as the physical terms in the relations. Our initial inference might not take us to supposed independent properties of objects as explanatory. (The notion of a stimulus is more sophisticated than that of an object with intrinsic properties, but that is again irrelevant to the order of epistemic validation.) When we seek deeper explanations, however, we will ask why objects stimulate our senses as they do, and this question is answerable only by attributing properties to the objects themselves (or to the objects in relation to environmental conditions such as light). It remains true that we must conceive of such properties by means of our conceptual capacities and categories. But recognition of this truism does not force us to admit the impossibility of truth in the realist sense. In answering the skeptic we must argue only that our concepts can capture or correspond to real properties. This is the same as arguing that our inductive capacities and the principles they generate tend to produce true beliefs, an epistemological obligation I have already acknowledged.

The principle of inductive inference remains to be defended later. But we have seen that, if even the foundations can be validated, then physical realism can be as well. Finally we can point out in the same vein that the phenomenalist too requires inductive inferences to explain appearances as best he can in terms of experiential regularities. He must use at least a form of enumerative induction to infer to the regularities themselves. Gilbert Harman has argued that enumerative induction is itself justified only by inference to the best explanation.[17] According to him we can infer from all observed A's that are B's that all A's are B's because the latter explains the former. I am not sure that the explanatory inference provides the basis for all enumerative induction. When we infer not to all members of a class but only to the next one we are likely to observe, the latter inference seems more secure or less risky than the former, and therefore perhaps more secure than the explanatory inference as well. It would be difficult then to construe the explanatory inference as the ultimate ground of the more secure enumerative induction, as it might have been if we deduced the latter from the universal enumerative claim inferred as explanatory. We might avoid this objection to Harman's thesis by inducing from the observed cases to a lengthy disjunction of possible classes as explanatory and then infer to the single next case from that disjunction. That too may seem a roundabout way to make the latter inference. I argued earlier, however, that we must infer to some lawlike connection among the data in order to project an observable regularity; hence an explanatory inference may be required after all.

Whatever the relations among these inferences, since the universal enumerative inference, the one at which the phenomenalist aims in seeking laws among appearances, is no more secure than the explanatory induction, the phenomenalist is on no more secure ground than the realist in his attempt to explain appearances. While less bold metaphysically, he is no less bold inductively. But if the realist's principle of inference is at least as secure as the phenomenalist's, then so is the metaphysical position established through its application. Again we see in a different way that there is no sound reason for accepting the foundations but not what explains them best as true or real.

10

SCIENTIFIC REALISM AND
UNOBSERVABLES

Scientific realism is often defined as the theses that the theoretical terms of science refer, that its laws are approximately true, and that scientific progress is a matter of discovery, not pure invention.[1] Filled out with the proper theories of reference and truth, and somewhat hedged, this definition would suffice. Without these amendments it does not. Given only the truth of the definiens, the reference in question might reduce to reference to appearances or to observable physical interactions, the approximate truth of laws reduce to coherence within the theories or to pragmatic success in predicting observable reactions, and the discoveries reduce to findings of new observable regularities. Later I shall suggest a criterion of reference that could supplement this initial definition. Anticipating this criterion, we may modify the characterization of scientific realism to state that certain central theoretical predicates are instantiated by unobservables, or that certain privileged theoretical descriptions are satisfied by such entities or processes. This characterization captures the idea that there are unobservable entities or events independent of our theories to which the theories refer, the idea at the heart of the realist's interpretation of science. I am more interested here in the reality of unobservable entities and processes than in the truth of laws as stated in particular scientific theories. As several authors have recently pointed out, laws expressed in the mathematical formalisms of various physical theories often apply directly only to highly idealized models.[2] The scientist's method of inferring to the best explanation is often indirect. He will seek first to capture a body of phenomena by appeal to an idealized model governed exactly by the

216

equations of his theory, but only structurally analogous in certain ways to those entities assumed to be causally responsible for the phenomena in question. The laws of the theory, while not directly applicable to the phenomena, nevertheless generate accurate predictions on the level of observables by providing analogues of phenomenological laws—which describe the observable regularities—when appropriate corrections are made. Thus approximation by analogy runs in both directions: from the idealized model to the theorized entities and processes that are inferred to cause the phenomena, and from the laws applicable to the model to observable regularities.

Prediction requires only this capturing of the observable regularities in the idealized forms of the theoretical models. Deeper explanation, on the other hand, requires specification of those (causal) factors that best account for the probabilities of the phenomena in question across possible worlds. Theoretical laws, while perhaps not applicable directly even to unobservables when real factors outside the scope of the laws are discounted, play a role in such explanations also. Their role is that of suggesting those causal factors, prominent by analogy in the models as well, that do account for the observed regularities. In the case of physical theories these factors are properties of microentities and the forces acting on them. Thus reliance on inference to the best (deepest) explanation requires realism in regard to laws only insofar as these are taken to specify real causal factors. The realist's thesis concerns the reality of these factors and of the theoretical entities that instantiate them.

The argument for the rationality of belief in this thesis closely parallels that for the validation of belief in physical objects. Again I shall consider, preliminarily, some popular recent arguments that I take to be unconvincing or irrelevant, and then fill out what appears to be the proper inductive inference to unobservables.

As in the previous chapter, on physical realism, we can note here first that the dispensability or indispensability of theoretical terms purporting to refer to unobservables in the statements of theories is irrelevant to the realist's theses. First, a nonrealist can accept that theoretical terms cannot be translated into terms referring to observables. He can take theories to assert the existence of unobservables while refusing to accept them as literally true (only as successfully predicting the phenomena). But second, a realist can accept without qualm the much-discussed implication of Craig's theorem, namely that, given any set of scientific theorems with both theoretical and observable terms there will be another set with only observation terms having the same observable consequences. Aside from the formal proof of this theorem,[3] the philosophical implication regarding conservation of predictive power under transcription is perfectly intuitive. The predictive power of a thesis consists in its enabling us to infer certain observations on the basis of having made or being able to produce others, that is, in its establishing connections among observable phenomena. Once such connections have been established, we would expect that in principle we could appeal to them alone for purposes of prediction (although deeper explanations might screen out these probabilistic relations across possible worlds). Whether theoretical terms are required for predictive purposes in the initial formulation or actual use of a theory, as opposed to its final formal statement or use in principle, is in itself also irrelevant to the realist's claims. The point was made earlier: that certain concepts are necessary for us when we formulate our beliefs or theories does not establish their instantiation or ontological commitment in the realist's sense to their referents.

One might think that if transcriptionism failed, or rather failed to provide formulations useful for discovery or actual prediction, then the instrumentalist would be on even weaker ground than the phenomenalist regarding observable physical objects. This is because observable objects can be interpreted metaphysically as classes of experience, and we can understand why appeal to objects in that sense might be explanatory and predictive. But no similar interpretation seems available for theoretical entities, if the latter are not observable or experienced. The instrumentalist would have to admit not only that experienced regularities are ultimate or inexplicable but also the fact, inexplicable in his view, that the discovery and specification in practice of these regularities requires reference to things that do not exist at all, not even as observables. (The possibility mentioned above that reference to theoretical entities reduces to reference to observables is less plausible than its counterpart in relation to physical objects and experiences, given the theory of reference to be specified below, since no key descriptions of theoretical entities would be satisfied by observables, while certain identifying properties of objects might also be properties of ways they appear.)

THE SUCCESS OF SCIENCE

This argument brings us to inductive justifications for scientific realism. The argument here is not from the indispensability of theoretical concepts or terms in the formulation of our beliefs to the conclusion that such concepts must have instances, but rather from the role that such concepts play in the discovery of observable regularities and subsequent prediction of and control over experience to the explanation that such concepts must correspond to the real. The success of appeal to theoretical entities and processes in enabling us to predict phenomena on the observable level is explained by the fact that such unobservables causally account for the phenomena in question. Only real entities or processes can enter causal chains.

Despite the recent popularity of the realist argument based on the model of inference to the best explanation that seeks to explain the success of science by appeal to the reality of theoretical entities, I do not believe that the strongest argument is precisely this one. At least it is not unless success includes explanatory depth and not simply predictive power and the ability to incorporate observable data into sets of regularities. If theories develop and new ones emerge in order to accommodate predictive anomalies, then we should expect improvement in predictive power. If the regularities captured on the observable level are themselves real, and if new theories broaden our grasp of them by incorporating previous anomalies, then this process of theory design will itself explain scientific success. According to the nonrealist it is this capacity of self-correction in light of recalcitrant experience or observation that explains the success of science, not the fit between theory and unobservable reality.

Sometimes new theories predict or explain data for which they were not specifically designed, and sometimes constants from new equations turn up later in domains seemingly far removed from the original context of explanation: Planck's constant is an example. Such unexpected corroboration may seem more difficult for the nonrealist to accommodate. It might seem that only the reality of the theoretical entities or theoretical properties of unobservable processes could explain why they seem to have unexpected effects. But even in such cases the nonrealist can argue that such occurrences indicate only the reality of the observable regularities captured by the theory, that these are more widespread or pervasive than perhaps originally thought, and that the idealized model of the theory is well designed to capture them. This explanation presupposes the reality of the observable regularities themselves. The more thoroughgoing nonrealist need not accept them; or, rather, he can view them as the product of the structure that our minds impose upon the world as encountered in experience.

One might find little ground for choice among these competing alternatives, taken in themselves as explanations for the success of science. Given only this single fact to explain, and given that each alternative accounts for the probable success of the enterprise, it seems that we must look elsewhere for a decisive argument for realism. Realists have argued that only the assumption of their thesis can explain the goal of scientific development against which success or progress is measured, that goal being the convergence of theories to a unified description of physical reality. In light of this ideal, scientists consider the existence of equally serviceable but incompatible theories as an impetus to develop a single, more comprehensive theory that will explain the predictive success of the prior contenders. Realism is considered the ground of this goal or normative ideal, since the notion of correspondence to a single reality is incompatible with the possibility of two contradictory theories' both being true (although they might have equal instrumental value). Realism also allegedly explains why scientists test new, more embracing theories by subjecting them to precisely those conditions in which the effects of their posited unobservables would be most apparent (one way or the other): only a realist causal interpretation of such effects seems to explain the rationality of this method.

But once more the nonrealist can reply. First, the relation

between realism and the ideal of unification or convergence among scientific theories is not as strong as suggested. An argument from nonconvergence as a premise to nonrealism would be plausible, although the argument requires dismissing skepticism as an alternative conclusion. I will consider that argument in chapter 12. The argument from realism to convergence is equally complex, requiring a particular view of reality as itself relatively simple and unified, and of our process of inquiry as adaptive to that reality in such a way as to generate an accurate representation of it. Other views of reality and of our place within it that qualify as realist give little reason to affirm that scientific theories will converge to a single ideal. More important here, we can derive both the normative principle and the supposed fact of convergence from nonrealist premises as well. One encompassing theory has greater coherence than two incompatible theories, when the latter taken together represent the current state of knowledge. Thus the goal of coherence in itself generates the normative ideal. Considerations of fruitfulness and predictive power also often argue for attempts to combine originally disparate theoretical domains, so that theory may be extended to capture new realms of phenomena, for example, those studied by biochemists. The ideal of convergence can be accommodated in terms of the goal of coherence, or in terms of unity of purpose or practice or of the structure of the mind, rather than by appeal to the unity of an independent world.

Second, regarding the method of testing theories by attempting to falsify causal inferences from the assumption of real unobservables as specified by the theories,[4] the nonrealist may respond as he did when challenged by the unpredicted predictive success of some theories. If the best way to discover or capture regularities in observable phenomena is to seek to extend or incorporate theories or devise new ones that posit unobservables to model the generation of such regularities, then the best way to test for the latter is to test the implications of the models. Nonrealists of course have their reasons for shunning the realist physical analogues of these models—for example, skepticism regarding the truth-preserving character of those criteria by which we infer to the causal factors suggested by the models, or doubt stemming from reflection on the diversity of models in the history of science or on the possibility of empirically equivalent but theoretically incompatible models. I shall attempt to answer some of these doubts later. Given them, the nonrealist recognizes the heuristic value of inferring to theoretical models and testing for observable regularities by reference to them, but continues to regard them as simply inductive bridges between previously known relations among phenomena and future discoveries of broader regularities. The nonrealist explanation for the heuristic value of such models at any stage of inquiry appeals to their relation to earlier successful models and to their ability to extend those regularities from which they are originally inferred. The explanation for success in the method is that the only successful models, those that capture a broad range of empirical phenomena and are fruitful or suggestive of further extensions, survive. Given the three-level picture of typical scientific theories suggested above (observable regularities, idealized model to which mathematical formalism applies, and physical-causal analogue of the model), the nonrealist will argue that the middle level does all the theoretical work, the realist's physical analogue being excess metaphysical baggage. This explanation does constitute a rival account of successful scientific practice and progress.

EXPLANATION BY APPEAL TO UNOBSERVABLES

We have just seen that the realist's best card does not lie in the explanation of the predictive power or progress of scientific theories. What the realist explains better or more deeply is not the success of science but those very phenomena that science itself seeks to explain. (It must also be shown below that inference to the best explanation itself tends to deliver truth.) There are several related arguments here, all closely connected to our earlier argument for physical realism.

There it was pointed out that the explanatory inference to physical objects by which belief at that level is validated is at the same time an inference to certain (kinds of) properties of those objects as best explaining ways of appearing. But the achievement of some sophistication in the collection of scientific data and design of theory brings the realization that these observable properties initially posited in such explanations may not enter into the best explanation for the appearances in question. The best explanation for colors as ways of appearing, for example, does not ascribe such observable properties directly to objects themselves. It rather appeals to external conditions such as the absorption and reflection of light of various wavelengths determined by the molecular configurations on object surfaces; that is, it appeals directly to unobservable properties of objects and their physical environment. The latter explanation draws upon theory validated in many other domains and, together with neurophysiological research on the visual receptors, accounts very precisely for perceived colors. The former, naive picture leads to contradiction, to the ascription of incompatible determinate shades to the same surface parts on the basis of how they appear to different perceivers under similar conditions. There can be little doubt which explanation is preferable.

Our first argument for scientific realism, then, is that if appeal to objects itself is validated only via explanatory inference, if that appeal must refer to certain perceptible properties in order to be explanatory, and if certain appearances can be explained satisfactorily (causally) not by those initially posited properties but only by direct appeal to unobservable properties, then scientific realism has the same positive epistemic support as physical realism generally (although more problems or skeptical challenges remain to be answered in relation to the former). This claim can be further substantiated by noting again that inference to physical objects is preferred on epistemic grounds to alternatives such as appeals to superbeings because of the depth and fruitfulness of the physical theories to which the former but not the latter lead. But these theories sometimes involve direct reference to unobservables, so that the justification for physical realism once more turns out to support scientific realism equally. (Both equally presuppose that explanations that lead to deeper understanding are more likely to be true.)

This first argument appealed to identity in content in the validation of physical and scientific realism: physical objects with unobserved properties best explain appearances. A second parallels the form of the argument for the preferability of physical realism over phenomenalism. This is the argument that regularities that are ultimate for the nonrealist can be explained by the realist, who therefore provides a view of reality more satisfacting to our understanding. Before turning to this argument, something more should be said about the regularities of which I have been speaking at the level of experience and observable physical phenomena. Others have pointed out that there are no strict lawlike regularities at either of these levels, only approximations to these or statistical correlations.[5] Appeal to the microlevel is then to explain why macroscopic objects behave or experiences occur with the degree of regularity they exhibit. If it is assumed that entities at the microlevel do, in contrast, obey strict laws, this premise may itself enter into an argument for a realist interpretation of such entities. Additional premises might include the claim that strict lawlike interactions are more simple or better understood and some inference from simplicity or comprehensibility to probable reality. But even if these last two premises could be appropriately fleshed out, the first assumption regarding reactions among microentities remains extremely problematic. I refer not simply to the irreducibly statistical nature or uncertainties associated with determinations of such properties as position and momentum in quantum theory but also to the fact mentioned earlier that laws at this level, like those at the macrolevel, determine trajectories only in idealized circumstances, in the absence of disturbing forces or other laws, some of which resist simple combination.[6]

Given this difficulty, the argument from simplicity of laws to the existence of entities that satisfy them fails. The fact that theoretical laws often apply directly only to idealized models not only defeats this argument for realism, it also figures prominently in a recent antirealist argument. Nancy Cartwright argues from this fact to the literal falsity of scientific laws. Given their falsity and the fact that such laws nevertheless figure in explanations (albeit not in the direct way claimed by the covering-law model of explanation), she concludes that inference to the best explanation is not sound, that we cannot in general infer to the truth of preferable explanans.[7] But if such laws function in deepest explanations, as I indicated above, by indirectly specifying causal factors that combine in complex (and perhaps currently unspecifiable) ways to produce observable effects, then her argument is answerable. In utilizing these laws to infer to deepest explanations, explanations that indicate why things occur as they do or with the probabilities they have, we infer to the entities, forces, and processes that directly enter such explanations. We need not infer to the truth of laws that we take to govern only idealized interactions in order to utilize such laws in inferring to the best explanation to produce true beliefs about the referents of such inference. We need establish only that such inference beyond observables is warranted.

Let us then return to the level of observables, where nonstrict regularities and probabilistic connections themselves cry out for explanation. Everyone agrees, despite old and new riddles concerning induction generally, that inference to the best explanation, with its implicit realist attitude toward the referents of the explanans, is proper and often required when it remains on the level of observables. Here it may be bolstered by other principles, for example analogy or enumerative induction, as when we infer from certain tracks to the past presence of a cat, knowing also that such inferences have been verified in the past in similar situations. The principle used here may be related also to the law of increasing entropy, to the idea that certain kinds of order derive, if not from intelligent design, at least only from other sources of order or orderly processes.[8] As pointed out previously, such explanatory inferences are strengthened further when otherwise unconnected phenomena (or seemingly related phenomena whose real connection remains to be determined or inferred) receive a common explanation, as when the inference to the cat explains not only tracks but the unraveled ball of yarn, overturned saucer, etc. In such cases explanatory inferences explain not only the separate phenomena, each of which provides separate additional support, but also the connection among them. This is accomplished by finding single continuous causal processes or types of process underlying their occurrences.

Controversy arises only over whether the method of inference should be extended to realist appeals to unobservables, when observable causal processes cannot themselves account for observed correlations or for otherwise disparate phenomena that are made parts of unified pictures by such inferences. The realist emphasizes the continuity of method in the everyday and scientific contexts. Granted that some phenomena without explanation require none, why should this be true of all phenomena that cannot be explained by appeal to other observables, when many such occurrences can be explained by reference to unobservable causal or probabilistically connected processes? It would appear more coherent to assume that such explanations, especially when they account for otherwise unaccountable connections or correlations among observable phenomena, point to real unobservable as well as observable processes. Granted also that we cannot support explanatory inferences to unobservables by enumerative induction or analogy to other cases in which direct verification later followed. But indirect verification by appeal to positive outcomes of further causal predictions can strengthen such inferences, and the principle of seeking explanations for order in other orderly processes also applies. Once more the latter principle must be counterexemplified at some points, but is the proper line always drawn where direct observability of plausible explanans ceases? Can that somewhat fuzzy distinction (between observable and unobservable objects) bear the weight of all our ontological commitments?

Before returning directly to that question, we may consider a proper nonrealist response to the assumption noted above that some observable phenomena can be explained only by reference to unobservables, which then must be interpreted realistically in order to be included in true explanans, i.e., in order to be understood as causing or accounting for the probability of the observable phenomena. We should rather admit, according to the nonrealist, both in the spirit of Craig's theorem and in line with our argument in the previous section, that particular observable phenomena in principle can be explained by appeal only to observables. If theoretical terms can be eliminated in principle while preserving the observable consequences of a theory, then the regularities so expressed and captured will account for the probability of those consequences in terms of the observable antecedents. Despite this point, the two arguments regarding explanatory depth applied at the prior level have equal relevance here.

First, not only appearances but particular physical phenomena receive deeper explanations by appeal to theoretical entities and processes. Often only such appeal explains why such phenomena occur, providing a more satisfying explanation than the pure Humean or Hempelian fitting of the macroevents into observable regularities. Indeed in many cases, to eschew the deeper explanation is to leave the phenomena in question totally mysterious, although not unexpected. Are we to say that the radio begins to play when we turn the switch because radios always react that way (or always react that way after certain observable actions are performed at studios and in the walls of homes), avoiding all reference to electric current and electromagnetic waves? If we do not take the latter reference literally or realistically, then it fails to explain in a way different from the former explanans; that is, it fails to explain why the radio works. Avoidance of skepticism in light of reflection on changes in scientific theory or on the problematic features of quantum theory (both to be discussed) seems less difficult than refusing to believe that the radio works because it runs on electric current and receives waves of various frequencies. (If one argues that electric current is observable because we can observe its effects, then so are subatomic particles observable, and the distinctness of the nonrealist's position disappears.)

We may link the preferability of the deeper explanation to our earlier accounts of explanans that screen out others. The account appealed to strengths of connections across possible worlds. In the radio case we must compare connections between radio waves, electric currents, and radio receptions on the one hand and observable actions in studios and in the building of homes (that we take to be the broadcasting of waves and wiring for currents) and radio receptions on the other. In worlds in which waves are emitted and current runs through radios, they will receive the signals even if humans did not perform the observable actions that we take to result normally in the observable events. In worlds in which those actions are performed but the waves are not emitted or the current is not on, we do not believe that the radios will play. It is clear from this mental experiment that we take the appeal to the unobservables to provide the stronger explanation of the phenomenon in question.

Second, the argument is only strengthened when we turn to regularities on the observable level, ultimate for the nonrealist but explainable within a realist framework. Are we to say that certain chemicals combine readily while others remain relatively inert without appealing to atomic theory, which explains why these reactions occur as they do? Such theory of course is validated in many other domains as well, explaining not only the periodic table of elements and therefore all chemical compounds but such diverse regularities as spectral lines, gas pressures, Brownian motion, fission and fusion reactions, electroplating, etc. The validation extends even to measurement of unobservables themselves, corroborated by the values of other present unobservables that correlate with methods of measurement and underlying theories thereof elsewhere. At a relatively sophisticated stage of theory and experiment, as in the case of particle physics, the two mesh, such that theories of the workings of experimental apparatuses, themselves requiring a realist interpretation, support theories that predict experimental outcomes. Regarding the former theories, realist interpretations are required to explain how we can seemingly use certain unobservable particles to produce desired experimental effects. (Ian Hacking, who has recently emphasized this justification for realism, seems to think it differs in kind from ordinary inference to the best explanation.[9] I disagree, since in my view we can validate beliefs that we actually use such unobservable means to experimental ends only by so inferring.)

As argued earlier, the inference is stronger when, as in the case of atomic theory, otherwise disparate observable phenomena, one for which the theory was not originally designed, are linked and provided with a common explanation. The nonrealist explanation for such occurrences appeals to the reality of the observable regularities captured by the theory and to the fact that such regularities may extend to unexpected domains. We earlier allowed this explanation as an alternative account of the increasing predictive success of scientific theory as it develops. But in the present context we can see the preferability of the realist framework. First, where the connections are made by the theory itself, they may not be clearly manifest on the level of observables. There may be no observable resemblances between blackbody radiation, Brownian motion, X-ray diffraction by crystals, and electroplating of metals, yet all can be used to compute an Avogadro number (the number of molecules in one mole of a substance).[10] The same point can be made in regard to Planck's constant and such phenomena as the photo-electric effect, spectral lines, specific heats of solids, and chemical reactions explained by the contemporary theory of the atom. The agreement of theory with the outcome of these different measurements provides strong corroboration for the theories and links these diverse phenomena. The linkage in each case is not a matter of some observable regularity extending into unexpected domains (unless the regularity is held to be that of measurements differing by constant amounts, the measurements themselves being comprehensible only as measurements of unobservable properties). Second, in cases where new and unexpected observable regularities are discovered on the basis of theoretical development, the truth of the theory in question explains why such unexpected regularities exist, a fact that must otherwise remain unexplained. If we are justified in seeking to provide explanations where otherwise there are none (or none equally plausible), then it seems we must accept the realist framework in this context. And the antecedent must be true if our more basic empirical beliefs are validated against alternatives in the only way I have argued they can be: by appeal to the principle of inference to the best explanation.

The nonrealist at this point can respond in either of two ways. He can question once more our principle of inference as it extends to theoretical levels, or he can argue that we can explain by appeal to unobservables without interpreting the latter realistically. This last response reduces, however, to ones already considered. We have noted that best explanations must be true. Assuming a correspondence notion of truth (to be further defended), this implies that the unobservable entities to which such explanations appeal must be real. If they are not real, then they cannot cause or otherwise account for the probability of the observable phenomena, unless the explanations reduce to appeals to broader observable regularities under which those to be explained are subsumed. But then the former must be further subsumed or explained within a realist framework, which in any case provides the deeper explanations of why the regularities are there to be found. Thus the nonrealist must fall back to the illegitimacy of inferring to unobservables and remain content to leave observable regularities unexplained.

OBSERVABLE, UNOBSERVABLE, AND SUPERNATURAL

We may summarize the reasons against placing such heavy metaphysical weight as partial realists require on the distinction between observables and unobservables. In my view the distinction between certain types of properties that appear and those that do not is relatively stable and central to the foundationalist theory of appearing outlined in the previous part of the book. This is not to say that certain predicates or properties are purely observational or that an exclusive distinction between observational and theoretical can be drawn in relation to properties. Rather, I made the weaker claims that certain predicates that refer to observables cannot be replaced by theoretical predicates, that only some properties appear (although they may be instantiated on the theoretical level as well), and that some of these properties are naturally salient and predicates picking them out naturally projectable.

In regard to entities, I argued that our interpretation of those objects that (manifest properties that) appear is not fixed but rather subject to constant reinterpretation with the development of physical theory and technology. From the side of technology there is the obvious blurring of the observable/unobservable distinction by the many instruments that enhance our powers of perception. Entities formerly unobservable become observable when new instruments are invented (according to our best theories of the way those instruments work). Such enlarging of our perceptual powers makes it clear to us also that, had our sense organs been different, had they incorporated biologically the *modi operandi* of the mechanical aids, then we would have perceived different types of entities. This understanding, which itself broadens our point of view, is central to realism in several ways. Not only does it raise the possibility of skeptical doubts regarding our naive perceptual criteria for assigning properties to objects but it also points up the arbitrariness or anthropomorphism of the observable-unobservable distinction as applied to objects.

The distinction becomes even blurrier when we try to maintain it by distinguishing between seeing objects and seeing only their effects. We saw above that the nonrealist must distinguish between observing entities and observing what appear to be the effects of supposed entities to keep his position from disintegrating when he admits that we can observe subatomic particles in cloud chambers. Certainly scientists do speak of observing such entities in cases in which the nonrealist must maintain that only (what realists call) their effects can be seen. But it is doubtful that this distinction itself can be made sharp. Ordinary seeing is seeing objects by means of their effects on our sensory system. Granted that we ordinarily see the objects and not their effects; granted also that seeing effects, for example tracks, can often be distinguished from seeing the objects that cause them, for example cats; in laboratory contexts where complex instruments are used, precisely the contexts that interest us here, it can become problematic to differentiate seeing entities by means of the instruments from seeing (what realists call) their effects on the instruments. Of course a distinction that is fuzzy at the edges can still be a distinction. The point here is not simply that the category of observables is fuzzy; it is that the category is too arbitrary or contingent upon our present powers of observation to bear the metaphysical weight placed upon it by the partial realist.

An equally telling point concerns the source of the distinction. Presumably we differentiate the classes in question on empirical grounds. But then it is science itself that both differentiates most precisely and at the same time explains the distinction. If we look to physical theory for the grounds and explanation of the distinction, then we find reference to unobservables in both.[11] Things appear visually that absorb and reflect light in certain ways, both the light and the structures of surfaces that reflect and absorb it being unobservable. That we must appeal to unobservables in order to draw the distinction precisely again does not show in itself that both relata are real. The point is rather that the grounds on which we draw the distinction provide no reason for attaching metaphysical weight to it, for taking it to be a distinction between the real and the unreal.

Quite the contrary. The realist interpretation of unobservables is the perfectly natural one, given the meanings (and lack of translatability) of theoretical terms. That it is natural places the burden of proof on those who deny it (given the justification of epistemic principles to be provided). In the following two chapters I shall consider those reflections on contemporary and historical theories that attempt to meet this burden. Rather, they reveal that, while contemporary science becomes difficult to interpret realistically at a certain level, the difficulty at worst indicating that certain realms of the real will remain beyond our grasp indefinitely (although we can predict some of their effects quite accurately), this limit is not reached immediately as we infer from observable entities to (normally) unobservable ones. Reflection on scientific method and epistemic validation reveals a continuity in this transition that argues strongly against such an immediate limit. Beliefs regarding observables are also underdetermined by their empirical evidence, at least in the sense that there exist empirically equivalent explanations, alternatives that account for the same sequences of appearances. Throughout the epistemic reconstruction, we must therefore rely on inductive criteria for preferable explanations other than the criterion of saving the phenomena. The rationality of our ontological commitments at every level thus depends ultimately on the defensibility of these criteria and on our using them to infer to the best available explanations for data validated at the prior level. Given that the justification of scientific realism employs the method used in inferring to theories and testing them, a method continuous with less sophisticated rational inquiry, rather than relying on particular features of past or current theories, that justification should survive problems in interpreting the theories.

Before testing that survivability in more detail, we may conclude this section by reconsidering the surviving general methodological point of the nonrealist, the claim that the demand for explanations must end somewhere. We must accept some unexplained regularities or posited uniformities (such as the assumption that free particles travel in geodesic trajectories). The truth of this claim might appear incompatible with the methodology that I take to warrant realism. If the demand to provide deeper explanations wherever possible were genuine, then we would have to infer indefinitely to deeper underlying causes, rather than resting content at any point with unexplained regularities. In the end, science might have to return to theology, since, when we run out of physical laws or statistical correlations and particles, there always remain divine intentions to explain regularities at a level yet deeper. The threat of this reduction of the realist's principle of inference obligates her to provide some principled reasons for breaking the process of inference at certain points beyond observables but short of supernaturals.

She might try pointing to the predictive barrenness of the appeal to divine intention. We certainly could expect no new discoveries or extensions of theory to new domains on the basis of such explanatory hypotheses. But of course sole appeal to this criterion of legitimate inference plays into the nonrealist's hand. Exclusive reliance on it would signal that predictive power is what really counts, that there is no epistemic value to deeper explanation in itself absent predictive fruitfulness, and therefore no reason to take deeper explanations in general to be more likely true. Relying only on this criterion we would then suspend judgment or ontological commitment when faced with empirically equivalent theories, exactly what the nonrealist recommends. We must then find other grounds for differentiating legitimate explanatory inferences. Fortunately, several other standard criteria for evaluating explanations disqualify appeals to the supernatural despite their seeming theoretical depth.

First, such appeal does not really deepen our understanding of the explananda (presumably regularities at the subatomic level), since we have no conception of the mechanism or the precise link between the supposed divine intention and their effects. This, coupled with the lack of predictive power, renders the appeal epistemically sterile. Not only would our understanding not be deepened by such an explanation, not only would no natural questions be answered, but many more would arise without possibility of answer. If we halt the process of inference at sets of statistical regularities and conservation laws of interactions among elementary particles (for example, exchanges that would explain the four force fields, were such exchanges corroborated and understood), then we are left with brute regularities but also with no reason for thinking that they should be any different or must be provided with further explanations. Such base-level physical explanations and the interactions to which they would appeal would be continuous with earlier appeals to atomic theory, chemical reactions, interactions among observable physical objects, etc. If we infer beyond all these physical explanations to supernatural intentions, we derive an immediate and ultimate discontinuity and raise all the unanswerable theological questions—for example, those regarding the discrepancy between the actual design of the universe and the inferred attributes of the deity. (If it is pointed out that appeal to human intentions and other mental states generates a similar discontinuity, the answer is that such appeal is genuinely explanatory and that the inference is both at a different level and, if the arguments of Part II are correct, unavoidable.)

We need not rehearse further the myriad theological perplexities in order to recognize perfectly respectable reasons for applying our principle of explanatory inference only within the realm of science as ordinarily construed. We continue to maintain a realist attitude toward the referents of those explanations shown to be best among competitors as long as doing so accounts for the probabilities of the explananda in ways that deepen our understanding of why they occur as they do, and as long as doing so does not raise naturally pressing but in principle unanswerable questions. We may return then from this brief flirtation with the gods to the only slightly more mundane world of contemporary physics.

11
RELATIVITY AND QUANTUM MECHANICS

Obvious limitations of space and (one hopes, not so obvious limitations of) knowledge will restrict my discussion of these theories. I shall not aim at even the most popular level of exposition of their contents. Our only interest here lies in the problems they create or seem to create for the realist interpretation of science defended in the previous chapter. While the defense rested upon the method and goal of explanatory inference rather than upon specific results at particular times, the problem created for it is serious if the dominant theories of the present century defy all attempts at realist interpretation. Borrowing freely from analyses of others, I want to assess briefly the extent, if any, to which these theories present that problem and how the realist might respond to it. I shall not attend to all the metaphysical issues associated with the theories. For example, I will not assess the reality of space, time, or space-time (or oppose reductionist, relational accounts). Our epistemological orientation generates an interest in the kinds of things we can know, but I shall restrict that interest to the problem of theoretical entities and the possibility of a realistic interpretation of science and physical theory generally.

RELATIVITY

The most obvious way in which the theories of special and general relativity might be thought to threaten not only scientific but physical realism itself concerns their implications for our view of the so-called primary qualities, traditionally thought to be real, intrinsic properties of objects themselves. Such qualities include extension in space (or shape), duration, and mass. The implications in question are slightly indirect but quite clear. According to special relativity it makes no sense to ask for the objective spatial interval between two points or for the temporal interval between two events (such as the events of taking measurements at the endpoints of an object's sides).

If we measure units of time by uniform motion, for example, round-trips of light pulses, and our clock is moving, then each pulse will have to travel a longer distance at the same speed per unit of time measured. Each unit of time will therefore take longer relative to a stationary clock; i.e., moving clocks slow down. Since distance is a function of time for moving objects, it follows from the relativity of time that lengths are also relative; moving objects shorten in the direction of their movement. But in the context of special relativity, in the absence of accelerating frames, which ones we consider moving and which stationary is purely arbitrary. The relations are therefore symmetrical: each observer, considering himself at rest and others moving, will consider the clocks of the others slow and the lengths of their objects shortened relative to objects at rest (relative to him). We therefore cannot speak of length (hence of shape) or duration except relative to the choice of a frame. Hence such properties can no longer be considered intrinsic properties of objects themselves. Intrinsic mass may go by the board as well in relativity theory in order to conserve momentum, although transforming mass is not the only way of doing so.[1] Despite the fact that none of this will be apparent except at speeds well beyond those normally observed, the relativity of the traditional primary qualities must alter our view of their nature.

If secondary qualities are at all relative to our perceptions of them, qualifying only ways things appear (as I shall argue further below), and if, given Einstein's theories, primary qualities are relative too, then what becomes of the intrinsic or real properties of physical objects? The question is ill formed, trading on an ambiguity in the use of the term 'relative'. While the relativity of properties to our ways of perceiving them, such that they are not instantiated unless we are perceiving them, is damaging to a characterization of them as real or objective, relativity in Einstein's sense does not have the same implication, for two reasons. First, within an inertial frame of reference, lengths and times are objective relations. While they are relative to the specification of a frame as at rest, they are not relative to human observation or measurement. We can therefore think of them as objective tertiary rather than binary relations. The primary qualities of objects remain independent of consciousness, since within frames they are what they are whether or not we observe or measure them.

Second, if relativity to frame remains bothersome for the realist, as well it might given the symmetry of relations between frames and the arbitrary nature of the specification of one as the rest frame, then he can still appeal within the theory to an objective property invariant across inertial frames. This property, the spatiotemporal interval, is neither spatial nor temporal but instead a space-time property involving a relation between the square of space separation and the square of time separation between two points (or events). The invariant interval may not seem to have much physical significance for us, since we cannot visualize it (except in geometrical diagrams) and we tend to think of physical properties in visual terms. We can nevertheless recognize that intrinsic physical properties may not be visualizable. Our visual systems have evolved for use in our environment of low velocities, where they can estimate stable macroscopic properties fairly accurately. This explanation for what we can visualize does not equate visualizability with real or physically intrinsic properties. We can therefore accept that the latter may be neither spatial nor temporal but spatiotemporal. (The explanation for the agreement of our senses in regard to primary qualities, mentioned in chapter 9, now appeals not to the reality of those properties but to a common cause for ways of appearing in real spatiotemporal properties.)

Thus the theories of relativity in themselves pose no threat to realism in the philosophy of science, although they do alter our view of what is real, giving us spatiotemporal properties and mass-energy rather than what we ordinarily conceive as their separate components. More serious threats might be seen to arise from conventionalist claims associated with the theories. There are genuine conventional elements; we can rephrase our earlier brief description into terms that make this clear. It is a matter of choice or convention which frame we take to be at rest, and also how we split the spatiotemporal interval into spatial and temporal components (although obviously the sets are constrained by the fixed relation between these components). But we have seen that such room for choice does not damage the realist view. Further conventionalist claims, some attributed to Einstein and others associated with his theories by philosophers, would be far more damaging if sustained. In measuring spatial and temporal relations within a chosen frame of reference and in measuring the curvature of space-time in general theory, certain assumptions regarding the synchronization of clocks and congruence of measuring rods at a distance and regarding paths of free particles or light rays have been held to be conventional, such that different choices generate empirically equivalent theories.[2]

Only local synchronization and congruence are directly observable. If, as in Newtonian theory, there were no limit to the speed at which signals could be sent from one place to another, then simultaneity could be established nonrelativistically and clocks could be synchronized at a distance. If signals could be speeded up indefinitely, then the last event to occur at point B before a signal could reach B from point A would be simultaneous with the sending of the signal from A. If distant clocks, say of the light pulse type, could be synchronized observationally, then they could be used to establish the congruence of distant measuring rods. But the constant limit c implies that these relations are nonobservational even within chosen reference frames. Einstein himself appears to have viewed the one-way velocity of light, as opposed to the round-trip velocity that is locally measurable, as a matter of stipulation.[3] Then it is also conventional, even within a reference frame, that we count the event of a light signal's reaching B from A as simultaneous with the event at A that occurs half-way between the sending of the signal from A and its being received back at A.

If we must also stipulate the rigidity of measuring rods (equivalent to congruence at a distance), as it seems we must if the light clocks that might be used to measure them in different places cannot be verified to run at constant speed, then all lengths become conventional and not simply relative to inertial frames. Since the uniform contraction or expansion of rods upon transport would follow from a universal force affecting them all equally, it seems that we are free to choose among empirically equivalent sets of geometries together with physics (metrics plus force fields). We can maintain a Euclidean (Minkowski) geometry for space-time in light of observation, for example, if we posit forces that affect the lengths of measuring rods, speed of clocks, and paths of light rays.

These conventionalist claims have been associated with Einstein's theories both because of his comment regarding the one-way speed of light and because the limit to the velocity of electromagnetic signals, central to the theories, makes comparison of times and lengths at a distance nonobservational, hence not directly verifiable. Such claims are more damaging to a realist interpretation of the quantifiable properties of ordinary objects than is the relativity of separate spatial and temporal intervals to reference frames. In the latter case, invariant spatiotemporal properties remain. In the former, all physical dimensions become dependent on our choices (beyond the conventional use of terms to refer to dimensions), hence not real in themselves. If these claims are sustained, then we are faced with empirically equivalent theories among which we are perfectly free to choose. We would then lack grounds for belief in the reality of properties as determined by any one of those theories. Such radical underdetermination of theory by evidence therefore must be refuted by the realist.

An initial reply might be that these alternative geometries and physics, which differ in offsetting postulation of forces and choice of metrics, are not simply empirically equivalent, but also alternate descriptions of the same reality, that is, physically equivalent. The realist can countenance different descriptions that use different categories or systems of classification and that are true descriptions of the same real domain. A simple example (if colors were real) would be that of color schemes using terms that divide the spectrum at different points and thus generate different true ascriptions of color. But that reply is not satisfactory for relativity theory. Two descriptions, one of which ascribes force fields at certain space-time points and the other of which does not, cannot be physically equivalent (hence both cannot be true), if one is a realist about forces. Even a defender of scientific realism who equates the gravitational field with the degree of space-time curvature in a region will not be a non-realist regarding force fields in the way necessary for holding these alternative theories to be physically equivalent.

Hans Reichenbach, an early and influential advocate of the conventionality thesis, simply equated forces with geometrical deformations (of measuring rods, rays of light, and so on).[4] But this reduction fails to capture the meaning or preserve the reference of the term 'force' as it is incorporated from usage outside the theories of relativity. For the realist, the meanings of such theoretical terms are not exhausted by their observational consequences. They typically refer to real unobservables, although they are most often introduced in terms of relations (for example, causal relations) to observable phenomena, relations themselves learned observationally but then conceived by analogy to exist among unobservables as well. Such will be the interpretation here, since the nonrealist reduction of forces to their geometrical effect fails to accord with the assignment of other real properties to force fields by contemporary theories. Being a nonrealist in regard to forces would have repercussions for one's view of such properties as mass and energy.[5] (One could speak of undetectable, systematic deformations without equating these with the presence of force fields. But this still would not result in physically equivalent theories, since 'deformation' too has its reference fixed outside this theoretical context.)

If the realist then accepts the reality of force fields and deformations but admits the empirical equivalence of different combinations of geometries and postulated forces, then he must find grounds for believing one among these alternative theories in order to accept space-time dimensions as determined by that theory as real. But this is simply the problem that we have encountered several times before of choosing from among empirically equivalent explanations for the same phenomena those that are preferable on other inductive grounds. As noted earlier, such choices must be made at every level in validating empirical beliefs. The explanation for beliefs about appearances that appeals to their truth was preferred to explanations that count them generally false; the explanation for appearances that appeals to physical objects was preferred over those that appeal to superprogrammers; the explanation for physical interactions that appeals to physical unobservables was preferred to both nonrealist and supernatural explanations. In these prior cases the grounds for rational choice included explanatory depth and fruitfulness (utility) and the avoidance of unanswerable questions. Such grounds for preferring some empirically equivalent explanations to others must be indicative of approximate truth if any of our empirical beliefs are to be validated. Similar and related grounds apply to the present context of choice among alternative geometries and postulations of forces. Thus, while recognizing that the theories of relativity themselves may be amended or replaced in the distant future, we certainly have epistemically sound reasons now to prefer their standard formulations to alternatives.

Advocates of the conventionality thesis typically recognize only predictive power or the ability to capture the observable phenomena as an epistemic ground for choosing among theories (other grounds are held to be merely heuristic). Empirically equivalent theories therefore all have equal claim to belief or equal probability of being true. While, in their view, there may be good reasons for working with one of the empirically equivalent versions rather than another—one version might be easily understood and usable for generating predictions and another totally unwieldy, for example—these reasons are not, for conventionalists, indicative of (nonconventional) truth, nor are they reasons for belief. But if we recognize such inductive grounds as reasons for belief, then relativity theories again present no special problems for the realist. Thus far I have argued that appeal to such grounds is necessary for avoiding skepticism at every level. If correct, this argument refutes the partial realist, who reserves his skepticism for scientific theories or for empirically equivalent theories.[6]

I find no reason to take observationality or the ability to predict observable phenomena as marks of truth but not other standard grounds for preferring certain explanations over others. In addition to earlier arguments against placing metaphysical weight on the observable-unobservable distinction, we have noted that we must often amend what we believe on the basis of observation in light of theory. We have seen as well that the same inductive criteria to which we appeal in justifying choices among theories also guide choices of explanatory hypotheses on the level of observation, for example, inferences to the prior presence of a cat or to the culprit in a crime. One could, with sufficient ingenuity, imagine alternative, more complex, and counterintuitive, but empirically equivalent explanations for the evidence in all such cases. That the usual inferences can sometimes be directly verified later provides, if anything, further inductive support for the criteria ordinarily used in the absence of immediate verification of the explanans.

No one disputes that many of these standard criteria apply to the choice among empirically equivalent geometries and physics. Although the one-way velocity of light and rigidity (absent differential forces) or distant congruence of measuring rods cannot be directly verified observationally, certain hypotheses about them are more natural, more coherent with other validated beliefs, and more fruitful than others. The Michelson-Morley experiment is taken to demonstrate that the round-trip velocity of light is independent of the direction in which the signal is sent.[7] To assume that one-way velocity nevertheless varies undetectably with direction would thus already introduce a perplexing discontinuity. One explanation for just this discontinuity might be simply that we have chosen a weird metric and that *all* velocities are relative to such a choice. If there were no other systematic changes in physics associated with different metrics, that answer might be acceptable, although I would argue that we would then have a case in which we simply associate different symbols with various dimensions, that is, a case of intertranslatable, physically equivalent theories. The many other changes required by different metrics block the latter response for the realist but also render the conventionalist thesis much broader than might be thought from consideration of this one phenomenon. As the conventionalist thesis expands, it becomes easier to argue against it. So long as the thesis is restricted to geometry, we can argue that unless we are willing to greatly expand our conventionalism, we cannot find a good reason for taking geometry to be conventional. This argument parallels the broader theme of this part of the book, to wit, that unless we are willing to be nonrealists across the board, even when it comes to the truth of foundational reports, we cannot be nonrealists in regard to the theoretical.

As noted, the assumption that the one-way velocity of light varies with direction affects other areas of dispute as well—for example, the synchronization of distant clocks and the congruence of distant rods within a chosen frame. In the case of clocks, abnormal hypotheses would have to introduce inexplicable discontinuities when the limit of transport velocity of the clocks approaches zero. Indeed all velocities would have to vary in mysterious ways with direction within frames: when A passed B at velocity v, B would not pass A at velocity $-v$. In regard to measuring rods (themselves measurable by light signals), deforming forces, if posited to explain expansions and contractions, would have to affect all materials equally, and this would create a discontinuity with the effects of accepted force fields. Inexplicable changes in energy would have to be postulated as well to preserve coherence with other parts of physical theory. Not only do all these discontinuities raise unanswerable demands for explanation but the many interconnections among theoretical components and standard assumptions regarding measuring devices such as light pulses or rods would render theories that result from unnatural assumptions unusable. Standard Lorentz transformations would not be preserved intact under unnatural hypotheses; hence, laws of physics would not look the same across apparent inertial frames.

Thus the issue here does appear to reduce to the epistemic significance of the usual inductive criteria, and the conventionalist theses reduce to the denial that these criteria indicate truth.[8] If my earlier arguments are correct, then conventionalism, to be consistent, would have to be much less localized than the discussion of space-time relativity alone indicates. In fact, at every stage of skeptical challenge, the conventionalist's proper response would have to consist in a stipulation. (Reichenbach was more consistent than his successors in this regard. See note 2 for this chapter.) But the idea that it is merely conventional, a matter of stipulation, whether ordinary objects exist unperceived, for example, does not respond satisfactorily to skeptical challenge. Beyond such counterintuitive characterizations of

particular hypotheses regarding unobserved entities, stipulation, if it is to substitute thoroughly for explanatory induction
in answering the skeptic, would wreak havoc on our ordinary
notion of truth. That notion, whether of the coherence or correspondence variety, does not include so much room for truth by
choice.

The conventionalist might reply that the case of geometry is
distinct in that our inductive criteria pull in opposite directions
here; that is, he might make the Kantian claim that Euclidean
space is more natural or simple for us, and that those complicated hypotheses regarding measuring devices are necessary to
preserve the Euclidean nature of space in light of observations
that appear to support the general theory of relativity. But this
claim is off the mark. In the context of relativity, we cannot
speak of Euclidean space at all, only of Minkowski space-time.
Comparisons of Minkowski space-time with three-dimensional
Euclidean space and of the latter with two-dimensional Euclidean space may be valuable in teaching the theories of relativity,
but they become philosophically misleading in the objection just
raised. The heuristic value of these comparisons is that they
make the difference between flat and curved plane spaces
visualizable from our three-dimensional vantage point. But we
can visualize neither alternative spaces in three dimensions nor,
as we noted earlier, space-time, whether curved or not. These
must be conceptualized in terms of observations we would make
within them and assumptions regarding the paths of free particles or rays. It is then questionable whether Minkowski space-
time is simpler or more natural for us to conceive than Reiman-
nian. If it is, then its naturalness derives from a projection of
measurements over distances normally accessible to us. That
these measurements systematically change at far greater distances naturally suggests either curvature in space-time or
forces that deflect light and other particles from geodesic trajectories. The latter forces, as we have seen, are the more problematic to conceive. Thus there is no division of inductive criteria
regarding the general theory of relativity. (I leave aside the
relative complexity of the mathematical formulations, since in
any case we are speaking now of the properties of space-time

itself, a metaphysical issue tangential to our general concern with scientific realism.)

I shall return to this central problem of empirically equivalent theories in a more general way in chapter 12.

QUANTUM PHYSICS

As we turn from relativity, which I have held to pose no major problem for the realist, to quantum mechanics, the picture changes. The problem here is the lack of a coherent physical model with which to interpret the mathematical formalisms. The theory utilizes different models in applying its equations in different contexts. Some of these are recognized to be purely fictional, such as oscillator models of the atom. But there is no single causal model, or more precisely no single, coherent physical analogue for the various models of the theory, from which we could infer to the nature of the subatomic realm. While the realist can allow different idealized or analogical models to be used in deriving predictions or developing new formalisms, he requires at least the possibility of a coherent account in terms of the causal (not necessarily deterministic) properties of theoretical entities. The latter is lacking in quantum theory.

From the very beginning, the introduction of the quantum hypothesis into atomic theory created physical anomalies. In the Bohr atom, electrons could occupy discrete orbits and could jump from one to another when emitting or absorbing integral amounts of radiation, but they could not occupy the regions between these fixed orbits. This discontinuity in space-time trajectories already violates our concept of a physical particle and its possible world-lines. Bohr's initial combination of a classical model for the orbital paths and quantum jumps for the transitions prohibits any notion of a causal process or mechanism for the latter. Hence, gaps are introduced in the physical model of the atom, making a realist interpretation problematic.

With Schrödinger's development of the wave equation there was initially some hope of eliminating these gaps or discontinuous processes. Both he and De Broglie sought to interpret the wave equations of the formalism in straightforward physical terms.[9] Quantum jumps between orbits of electrons were to be eliminated in favor of standing waves, with the concept of frequency replacing that of integral energy amounts, and the concept of wave packets, interpreted realistically, replacing that of particles. (In De Broglie's model, the wave was to guide the path of the still-existing particle.) But the problems facing such interpretations have proven insuperable for the majority of physicists. These include the fact that the wave function is complex rather than real in all its values; that, for an n-particle system, it must be located in $3n$ dimensional space rather than real space; that the wave packet disperses or spreads in space while free electrons and other microentities seem to retain particle properties in certain experimental contexts; and, related to the previous point but yet more mysterious, that the wave packet collapses to a narrow locus upon measurement. Regarding the latter notorious feature of the use of the function, if interpreted in realist physical terms, it seems to reintroduce the problematic discontinuous process at the heart of quantum theory that the wave model was to eliminate. The collapse cannot be viewed as a continuous causal interaction between the measuring device and the microsystem since, for one thing, measurements can be taken (or inferred) for particular elements of a system without physically disturbing those elements. Thus once again seemingly nonlocal or discontinuous processes without conceivable mechanisms of interaction infect attempts at a realist interpretation or physical model.

Because of these problems, other interpretations soon followed. Quantum mechanics provides an unusual case in the history of physics, in which a mathematical formalism (or several equivalent ones), capturing a broad range of empirical data, generated a series of competing physical interpretations. This history indicates in itself the problems involved in developing a coherent physical model for the theory. Following the model of physical waves, the Born interpretation in terms of probabilities and related frequency interpretations, including Einstein's, appeared to hold out the best hope for the realist (although Born did not design his interpretation with that aim, and it was incorporated into the nonrealist Copenhagen interpretation). According to Born, the wave function simply states probabilities of outcomes for possible measurements; more precisely, the square of the function gives the probabilities for particular measurements' having particular results. Electrons can retain their corpuscular character rather than being literally spread in space. The wave function only defines the chances of finding them at various precise positions. This interpretation overcomes the problems of the physical wave mode. The complexity of the function is overcome by taking the squares of its values. The spread of the wave packet in configuration space becomes unproblematic, representing only our knowledge of the physical situation and not that situation itself. Similarly the collapse of the wave packet represents the change in our knowledge brought about by a measurement. According to the statistical or frequency interpretation, the wave function represents a set of similarly prepared physical systems rather than a single system, and its reduction signals the selection from among these of one system for measurement (again, a change in our knowledge of the situation).

Both of these interpretations might appear to reopen the door for a realist interpretation of the systems represented, although an admission of ignorance (the introduction of hidden variables) regarding precise states of individual systems prior to new measurements would have to accompany such an interpretation. Even so, both old and more recent data block the realist from embracing this view of the wave function and so from thinking that the complete physical picture can simply be added in the future to the currently incomplete but nevertheless unproblematic probabilistic theory. What we do know about single systems does not mesh well with the view of them as particles with determinate trajectories of which we are only at present ignorant. First, certain experimental contexts reveal genuine wavelike behavior of entities such as electrons. They exhibit diffraction by gratings and interference that cannot be explained in terms of particle trajectories and therefore suggest again the physical reality of waves. Second, the wave function itself generates probabilities (superpositions of states) incompatible with the assumption that the systems have all the properties measured prior to the measurements' being made. Third, while the realist view of these interpretations requires that some sophisticated hidden-variable theory be true of single systems with determinate physical properties, all such theories, if they preserve the assumption of local or continuous causal processes, seem to run afoul of recent experiments modeled after the Einstein-Podolsky-Rosen examples and the Bell inequality (to be briefly described below).

The wave-particle duality, if ineliminable, itself blocks a coherent physical model of the entire domain of quantum mechanics. Particles and waves have incompatible properties. Particles move in definite space-time trajectories and collide with obstacles at points or narrow loci; waves propagate in particular configurations (with particular frequencies and lengths) but without precise loci or trajectories, interfere, and may be diffracted. Yet the data on such entities as electrons and photons has long suggested both models. Both electrons and photons exhibit interference after passing through diffraction gratings, which is inexplicable by appeal to particles or ray optics. In the case of electrons, conceived from the beginning as particles with determinate mass and charge, wavelength can be computed from momentum in agreement with calculations from interference bands. On the other hand, light, long conceived in terms of waves, behaves as particles in such phenomena as the photoelectric effect, the Stern-Gerlach effect, and Compton scattering. The photoelectric effect—the emission of electrons from illuminated metals—can be explained only by appeal to photons and quanta of energy.

Perhaps the most puzzling contexts of all are the double-slit experiments, in which both wave and particle behavior is manifest in the same experimental apparatus (although relative to different measurements). When both slits are open, an interference pattern emerges on the plate behind the slits, which is inexplicable on the thesis that each electron goes through one slit or the other. If a measurement is taken at a slit, electrons do register there, but the pattern on the plate changes. If one slit is closed, electrons will pass through the other without exhibiting interference; but if both are open, single electrons emitted slowly will show the interference pattern, apparently being affected by the opening at the distant slit (nonlocal causality). When the electrons are viewed as waves, they collapse instantaneously upon measurement at a slit or at the plate. The attempt to combine the wave and particle models, for example by De Broglie's idea of waves guiding the trajectories of particles or by wavelike particle trajectories, is defeated both by the interference at slow emission rates and by the indeterminateness at a time of such properties as momentum and position, definitive of corpuscularity.

Some authors have linked the Heisenberg indeterminacies to the wave-particle duality, on such grounds as that a particle's wavelength can be computed from its momentum, so that a particle with a given momentum must be spread like a wave rather than precisely located. But it seems best to consider indeterminacies, especially those associated with other noncommuting variables, as additional headaches for the realist. If the uncertainties are ultimate within the theory, they prevent interpretation in terms of a realist physical analogue, not because nature cannot tolerate irreducible probabilities but because our concept of a particle cannot tolerate the absence of those properties that define determinate and continuous space-time trajectories. The problem cannot be overcome by viewing the uncertainties as limits to our knowledge caused by uncorrectable disturbances in measurement. This view of their origin would be realist, since the properties would have to exist beforehand in order to be disturbed. It does not work, however, for at least three reasons. First, as noted earlier, one can measure (infer a value) without physically disturbing the element measured. Second, ascribing complementary properties simultaneously violates well-established ascriptions of energy values.[10] Third, superpositions of states appear incoherent if complementary properties are to be determinate at all times.

Given both the wave-particle duality and the indeterminacies, microentities have, to put it crudely, both too many (incompatible) and too few (defining) properties to fit a single, coherent physical model. And the properties they appear to lack seem to be acquired in a totally mysterious way upon observation. It is not surprising then that the dominant Copenhagen interpretation should have been strongly antirealist in its implications. This interpretation accepts indeterminacy as ineliminable and accepts the necessity of ascribing both wave and particle properties to the same systems in different contexts. The wave function gives only probabilities, its eigenvalues corresponding to results of possible measurements. The central principle of complementarity replaces incompatible ascriptions of properties by ascriptions only under certain measurements. Incompatible properties cannot be simultaneously measured. Each experiment or observation is therefore conceived as constitutive of the observed phenomena, as making the properties of the system determinate, but not in the realist causal sense of physically affecting preexisting determinate properties. The antirealist thrust is clear from both the absence of determinate properties prior to measurement and their acquisition upon measurement.

Bohr himself resisted characterization as an idealist. He viewed the complementarity principle only as a limit to the extension of classical concepts to the quantum domain. Perhaps he is better characterized as a kind of Kantian realist, in that he held the microentities we observe to be real, although knowable only as they appear to observation. Some supporters of the Copenhagen interpretation also likened the relativity of properties to measurements to the relativity of Einstein's theories. Just as we cannot speak of distance, velocity, or simultaneity until we choose a frame of reference and a way of synchronizing clocks, so on Bohr's interpretation we cannot speak of position or velocity without specifying some experimental procedure to measure them. But Einstein was no Kantian, and he is said to have been properly scornful of this facile comparison. As noted above, the theories of relativity retain invariants independent of the observer's point of view or observations: events themselves in space-time, spatiotemporal intervals between them, and continuous causal processes relating them. The Copenhagen interpretation, on the other hand, is much closer to Kant in its dissoluble mixture of the subjective (observation) and objective. But Kantianism is realist only if it acknowledges ultimate skeptical elements, only if it recognizes unknowable things-in-themselves, which Bohr never did.

There are further problems with retaining any semblance of a realist view under the Copenhagen interpretation. Foremost is the fact that the theory so interpreted fails to render measurement or observation itself comprehensible, as a coherent relativism should. We have seen that measurement cannot be interpreted in physical-causal terms, since values can be determined, as in the Einstein-Podolsky-Rosen contexts, without local causal process or effect. Nor can the relativity in question be understood in Kantian terms as a relation between human perceptual or conceptual categories and their objects. Cases such as that of Schrödinger's cat show that the wave packet must sometimes be interpreted as collapsing prior to human observation.[11] In this thought experiment, a microprocess has a certain quantum probability of interacting with a macrosystem (Geiger counter) that, if triggered, will electrocute a cat. Clearly the status of the cat as alive or dead does not await human observation for its resolution. The wave packet must collapse upon interaction with the macrophysical system. This suggests again a physical, causal account of the measurement process. But, coupled with the prior point, the case seems to rule out any coherent picture of measurement. This makes it yet more difficult to view the theory and its orthodox interpretation in any but the most instrumental terms, as a merely formal device for predicting outcomes of measurements themselves interpreted classically.

Thus there seems to be no coherent realist model, no single physical analogue, of the quantum theory as it was developed. Yet the enormous success of the theory requires reemphasis if the realist is to confront the problem honestly. With the Pauli exclusion principle, the theory accounts for the assumptions of the Bohr model, which in turn account for chemical properties and reactions. Also predicted are such phenomena as alpha decay, the photoelectric effect, specific heats, and scattering and spectroscopic phenomena. If we are to be realists about atoms, we must also admit that quantum theory is at present the only theory of the atom. The problem created for scientific realism therefore looms large, although some physicists might question that concession. They might argue, as Bohr himself did, that the problem derives from the attempt to extend uncritically and without limit concepts from classical physics into the quantum domain. While such concepts provide visual metaphors there, we should not expect reality at that level to be exhaustively characterized in those terms.

I have granted that visualizability is no necessary criterion of the real in every domain, our powers of vision and visual imagination having evolved as a means of adaptation to our environment of relatively close, midsize objects. Nevertheless, the challenge posed by quantum theory for the realist argument from scientific methodology cannot be dismissed so easily. The problem is neither the lack of visualizability nor a nostalgia for or insistence on classical notions but rather the lack of any alternative concepts with which to frame a coherent physical model for the theory. While the concept of relativistic space-time with Lorentz transformations could replace the Newtonian concept of absolute space and time with Gallilean transformations, in quantum mechanics we have nothing but the classical concepts of particle, wave, and field with which to conceptualize the more recently discovered domains. The contents of these concepts are determined by classical physics from analogies with observable objects and waves, and certain properties remain critical for their application. The latter fact does not imply that either the properties or the concepts are instantiated. Nor does it mean that these concepts cannot change so as to alter those properties that warrant their application. But in quantum physics, our failure to frame a coherent physical model with the seemingly requisite notions of particle and wave has not suggested alterations in those notions or new ones to replace them.

It is the apparent discontinuities in spatiotemporal processes that have prevented consistent application of concepts of the physical. Again, spatiotemporal continuity seems criterial for applying physical concepts, as it is central in the identification of physical entities. While the purely formal concepts of the quantum theory derive their meanings solely from their places within its statements, the lack of isomorphisms with sets of physical concepts, derived via analogies from observational contexts, blocks the derivation of a single model or physical analogue for it. This in turn renders a realist interpretation problematic. The mathematical formalism by which we predict observations seems to require a physical analogue to its models in order to be interpreted realistically. How then can the realist respond?

The simplest hope was for the stipulation of hidden variables that would facilitate the assignment of values to unmeasured properties to replace the mysterious collapse of the wave packet. But recent experiments modeled after the Einstein-Podolsky-Rosen thought experiment and the subsequent Bell inequalities seem to provide reason for rejecting that hope. The original Einstein-Podolsky-Rosen argument was designed to show that microproperties had to exist prior to measurement, that quantum theory is therefore incomplete. The argument appeals to two particles that interact and then separate, such that from the measurement of one, for example of its position or (in later adaptations) spin, one can infer the like value (in the case of spin, the opposite value) of the other. This inference can be made whichever of the two quantum incompatible properties one chooses to measure. Barring instantaneous action at a distance, the measurement actually made at one point cannot affect the properties of its (space-like separated) counterpart. The original authors concluded that the latter must have all the properties in question prior to the measurement of the former.[12]

In the ironic aftermath of the Einstein-Podolsky-Rosen article, Bell showed that in such contexts the realist hidden-variable interpretation results in different predictions from those of quantum mechanics. From the realist Einstein-Podolsky-Rosen assumption he derived certain inequality relations among sets of pairs of particles that differ from the wave function's probability assignments, since the derivation of the inequalities requires the assumption of determinate values where the quantum theory does not assign them.[13] Experiments measuring spin and polarization were then conducted and were found in the majority of cases not to support the predictions of the hidden-variable theory.[14] Thus a thought experiment originally designed to refute or show the incompleteness of quantum theory on the assumption of only local causal processes led to experiments that again seemed to demonstrate the violation either of the premise regarding causality or spatiotemporally continuous processes, or of the conclusion regarding determinate values. This dealt a severe blow to hidden-variable theories and hence once more to realist interpretations of the quantum formalisms.

Physicists and philosophers continue to seek ways to solve the problem of measurement in the context of quantum theory and to avoid the mysterious discontinuity in the transition from a single superposition of states to a series of eigenvalues. Representing the final stage of the measuring device as itself a superposition (if compatible with observation) brings it into the domain of the theory, but is of no help to the realist, given the difficulty of interpreting superpositions in physical terms, a difficulty highlighted by such cases as that of Schrödinger's cat.[15] I assume here that attempts by philosophers, for example Arthur Fine and Bas van Fraassen, to defend the possibility of local hidden variables against the Bell results do not succeed in a plausible way. The possibilities they invoke appear to me implausible in light of the probabilities borne out by the results and the conservation laws assumed, but a review of that literature lies beyond our scope here.[16] I shall rather explore other avenues of response for the realist.

Another attempt to avoid the instantaneous leaps of the theory that violate limitations on action at a distance so central to our concept of the physical involves the adoption of an alternative logic. The basic idea of this attempt is to avoid conjoining or alternating complementary descriptions. While there are different versions, some involving additional semantic values, a principal tactic is to give up the distributive laws. Nondistributivity follows from the derivation of the new logic from the Hilbert spaces of the quantum theory. From the fact that a particle has any of a number of possible positions and any of a number of possible values for momentum, it does not follow that it has a simultaneous position and momentum: $(P_1 \vee P_2 \vee \ldots \vee P_i) \cdot (M_1 \vee M_2 \vee \ldots \vee M_i) \not\Rightarrow (P_1 M_1 \vee \ldots \vee P_i M_i)$. Likewise, from the falsity of $(P_a M_1 \vee P_a M_2 \vee \ldots \vee P_a M_i)$, it does not follow that $P_a \cdot (M_1 \vee M_2 \vee \ldots \vee M_i)$ is false. If the antecedent of the first expression and the consequent of the second are both true, then a particle can have sufficient properties that measurement need not miraculously create them, even though the particle does not have incompatible properties simultaneously.[17] In this way, at least some of the physical anomalies of the quantum theory seem to be solved or avoided, making a realist model once more a coherent possibility.

Three objections to this ploy appear to me insuperable. At

least they appear insuperable if one reasons in the usual way. If one refuses to reason in the usual way, then no objections to one's position can ever be insuperable. One simply refuses to conjoin the objection with the position. Even when the position leads directly to a contradiction, normally considered the ultimate refutation, one simply disallows the contradictory conjunction or the logical laws needed to derive it. This possible generalization of the quantum logic ploy lies at the heart of the first two objections to it. First, one can reason to the adoption of quantum logic itself in the face of physical anomaly only by using ordinary logic in one's reasoning process. If quantum logic is to replace ordinary logic entirely, so as to be usable in the justification of its own adoption, then it must be shown to be sufficient for all ordinary deductive reasoning. To my knowledge this has never been shown.

The Quinean claim, underlying the quantum logic movement, that the correct application of a logic to the world is a broadly empirical matter, analogous to the application of a geometry, cannot be sustained universally. While Euclidean geometry could be abandoned completely in the derivation of the most plausible explanatory physical theory, the same is not true of classical logic. One cannot reason to the adoption of a logic without presupposing a logic in one's reasoning, and it seems likely that an examination of the connectives used in such a process will reveal them to be of the ordinary kind. We have models of possible worlds with non-Euclidean geometries (in which we can locate our physical universe). But the notion of a possible world in which ordinary logic fails is far more problematic, since logic determines the possibility of worlds.

It is true that one can sometimes use a certain structure in reasoning to a conclusion incompatible with that structure: we can sometimes throw away the ladders on which we cognitively climb. Such might be the case with naive realist ascriptions of physical properties that lead to deeper explanatory theories incompatible with them. A proponent of quantum logic might seek an analogy with that case as well as that of geometry. We are to begin with ordinary logic and then see how much of it has to be modified for the sake of physical theory. But in the case of logic, dispensing with the ladder threatens to remove the basis from many reasoning processes, including that presumed to justify the modifications. Dispensing with some of our naive realist beliefs, by contrast, leaves us with the foundations in appearances on which to establish the more sophisticated explanatory theories.

The limitation of nonclassical logic to the quantum domain gives it an ad hoc quality that adds force to the second objection. This is that choices of deviant logics that remove anomalies from theories by fiat, as it were, renders the theories to that extent immune from falsification by reducing their empirical contents. The impetus to seek new physical theories in light of anomalies is thereby reduced as well. If such a procedure were justified generally in science, let alone elsewhere, the results would be disastrous. It can be replied that the case of quantum physics is extraordinary, given both its degree of empirical success and the nature of the anomaly of discontinuity in physical processes and in action at a distance. But if we are speaking of centrality or degree of entrenchment, it is difficult to see how any principles could be or should be better entrenched than genuine logical laws, since their renunciation renders reasoning itself to that extent impossible.

Third and last, it is far from clear that the use of quantum logic removes all obstacles to a coherent physical interpretation of the theory. Michael Gardner has shown, for example, that prohibiting distribution is not a natural way to resolve the paradoxes of the double-slit experiment. In fact distributivity seems to hold unproblematically in that context. If A_1 represents a particle passing through the first slit, A_2 a particle passing through the second, and R a particle's striking a point on the plate, then $(A_1 \lor A_2) \cdot R = (A_1 \cdot R) \lor (A_2 \cdot R) = 0$.[18] More broadly, even if quantum logic expresses the physical anomalies of the theory, this would not increase our understanding of the physical domain to which the theory applies. We would still be left with indeterminate states when the determinateness of the properties in question seems definitive of the proper application of the only available physical concepts. The adoption of the alternative logic would simply embed this situation more deeply into our conceptual scheme. Rather than aiding in the development of an adequate physical model for the theory, this move would take us further from the fulfillment of that realist requirement.

The prospects appear bleak then for a realist interpretation of quantum theory as it stands. Does this alter the status of the argument for scientific realism? That argument was based on an inference to the best or deepest explanation, on taking the terms of such an explanans to refer. It was also argued that causal explanations, which explain why phenomena occur as they do or with the probabilities they have, are deeper than those which simply incorporate a particular phenomenon or local regularity into some broader set of regularities on the same level. The latter suffices for prediction, *if* some as-yet-unexplained lawlike connection is inferred from the broader regularity, but deeper explanation requires an unpacking of that connection, in causal terms if we are speaking of empirical knowledge and scientific explanation. The additional claim of the scientific realist that science tends to produce our deepest explanations must be distinguished from the grounds for taking a particular current theory to provide the best explanation possible for the data in its domain. The former claim is based straightforwardly on the method of scientific inference, which includes both the attempt to incorporate phenomena by analogy to idealized models governed by the mathematical equations of a theory and the attempt to relate those models to real physical analogues whose elements cause the phenomena. When the latter step cannot be completed, as in the case of quantum theory, this fact does not indicate that deepest explanations are not true or lack referring terms, only that the theory in question does not explain on the deepest level.

The failure to provide the deepest sort of explanation for a set of phenomena does not signal predictive incompleteness, so that we may grant that quantum theory is complete instrumentally without its providing a counterexample to the principle of inference to the best explanation. (Its probabilistic character may or may not be superceded when the quantum theory is replaced by a theory more amenable to realistic interpretation.) I did grant earlier both that atomic theory explains such phenomena as chemical reactions and also that quantum theory is *the* theory of the atom. Certainly there is a tension in that conjunction. Perhaps the most reasonable way to resolve it at present is to believe that causal processes involving factors isomorphic in certain ways to atoms and their parts underlie the various phenomena explained by atomic theory, but that quantum mechanics, while predicting localizations of causal influence, does not explain in that ultimately most satisfactory way causal properties of microprocesses.

What does not seem reasonable is to view the problems of interpreting the quantum formalism as forcing a restriction of ontological commitment to observables. (I use "observable" here, as earlier, not in the technical sense of the quantum theory itself but in the ordinary sense in which we observe only the macroscopic effects of processes in the quantum domain and never dimensions of those processes themselves. The more technical use would destroy the distinctness of the nonrealist position.) It does not seem reasonable to deny some knowledge of unobservable causal processes underlying such phenomena as chemical reactions and the workings of electric appliances. Perhaps even more suggestive of such processes is the more direct evidence provided by cloud chambers, bubble chambers, etc. The most subtle scientific antirealist can no more explain away our conviction that *something* unobservable causes those tracks than he can dismiss the unobserved but observable cat as the probable cause of the earlier mentioned tracks.

My basic strategy is to accept both the principle of inference to the truth of (what appears to be) the best (possible) explanation for accepted phenomena (referents of previously validated beliefs) and the claim that science in the long run tends to produce our best explanations for empirical phenomena. But I also accept that quantum theory does not explain deeply enough to warrant a fully realist claim to knowledge of its domain. There are various ways to make this compromise realist position somewhat more precise. That most respectful of the current theory and perhaps most common among realist physicists involves belief in certain properties of particles, such as mass, charge, and spin, but suspension of belief in such complementary properties as position and momentum. I previously noted that this has serious problems due to the centrality of concepts of these properties in our notion of physical particles. It might be replied again that the notion of precise, pointlike position, for example, is more an artifact of the idealized models of classical particle physics than a reasonable extrapolation from ordinarily observed positions.[19] Perhaps we might grant that positions have a degree of spread in space. On the other hand, this concession to the theory does not explain the change in its representation of the property (or other properties) upon measurement. Nor does it remove other difficulties in interpreting superpositions of states. A more radical move in the same spirit is to conceive microparticles as extraspatial (and perhaps extratemporal), only collections of such particles being conceived as acquiring spatiotemporal properties such as position and (relative) velocity. But this conception issues a large promissory note to reconstruct our notions of space and time in a way compatible with a general physical realism.

There are two remaining, highly speculative alternatives for the realist here. One is to assume that quantum physics will be replaced eventually by a theory more amenable to direct realist interpetation. Given the failure of hidden-variable theories to date, the alteration would seemingly have to be conceptually radical yet conservative of the breadth and precision of the present theory's instrumental success. Again the conjunction seems problematic. Indications from within the theory itself of the direction of some future conceptual revision are nebulous. On the one hand, superpositions seem to point away from the concept of independent particles. On the other, much of the success of atomic theory seems to rest on its atomicity. One can only point to such transitions as those from Ptolemy to Copernicus and from Newton to Einstein as precedents for then inconceivable and fundamental conceptual revisions that preserved and extended earlier instrumental successes. Not only philosophical perplexities of the quantum theory but its seeming incompatibility with basic assumptions underlying relativity perhaps foreshadows a further revolution. What is lacking at present are focused anomalies on the observational or experimental level (despite unexpected violations of parity) and any hint of an alternative or fundamentally different theory.

Hence the realist at present has no more than a vague hope in this direction.

The final possibility is that reality at this level will simply elude our complete grasp indefinitely. This possibility can be countenanced by a realist, as long as its acknowledgment derives from the extension of inductive inference to its proper limits rather than from a priori arguments on the relativity of all knowledge. Realism raises the threat of skepticism at every level, and perhaps renders it inevitable at a certain depth. Only the hubris of the idealist allows him to escape this threat, but without rendering his position more philosophically attractive. That not all aspects of reality should be transparent in principle reveals the obvious finitude of our brains and their limited evolutionary history. Perhaps the inconsistencies of the quantum theory do signal not merely the inadequacy of our observational and classical physical concepts for capturing all of physical reality but the ultimate limits of our quest for explanations. But at this relatively young stage of science, it is certainly too early to tell.

12
FURTHER PROBLEMS FOR SCIENTIFIC REALISM

SYNCHRONIC RELATIONS AMONG THEORIES

Before considering diachronic shifts among theories, we should return to an issue touched upon in the previous chapter's discussion of geometry—the problem of empirically equivalent theories competing at a single historical stage. If theories can have the same observational consequences, such that no experiment could ever distinguish them, and yet make different assertions about physical reality on the theoretical level, then in the absence of other (nonobservational) inductive grounds for choosing between them, realism leads directly to skepticism or suspension of belief. A standard argument against the realist is that he fuels the skeptic by positing genuine alternatives without rational ways to support belief in any of the competitors. It is true that realism raises the threat of skepticism by rendering it intelligible at deeper metaphysical levels. The question is whether this threat can be overcome in the face of empirically equivalent versions of the world at various depths of explanation, including the scientific.

Let us then look again at some seemingly incompatible but observationally identical theories. The underdetermination of theory by empirical evidence, at least in the weakest sense, follows directly from the fact that the relation of evidence to theory is inductive: no theory is strictly implied by any body of observation. It is easy to generate trivial examples. One can simply permute the predicates of two or more theoretical terms, say 'molecule' and 'electron', applying to the first term all those predicates that one previously applied to the second. The variations will then appear to make different claims, although obviously their observational consequences remain the same.[1] Somewhat more serious examples involve expanding single theoretical terms into multiple ones, such that the multiple terms together preserve the observational implications of the simpler theory. This is one way of looking at the postulation of different metrics with compensating force fields that we considered in the previous chapter.

Examples of term expansions indicate that the problem of empirically equivalent theories is generated, at least in part, by the Quine-Duhem thesis of theoretical holism, the thesis that theories are tested by observational evidence only as wholes. Another way of stating the thesis is to point out that anomalies leave choices as to which theorems to revise and which to hold constant. Different choices generate empirically equivalent theories with different theorems, i.e., physically different systems from the realist's point of view. In this way the thesis of holism leads directly to the problem of empirically equivalent but incompatible theories. If none of the alternative versions is preferable, then we cannot infer to the truth of any. If truth conditions are determinate only for combinations of theorems, then it may seem problematic as well to claim that theoretical terms refer determinately. The realist requires both determinate reference and the (approximate) truth of some physical model.

He has two responses. In some cases, as we have seen, he can claim that apparently different theories are not simply empirically but physically equivalent. Physically equivalent theories may be simply synonymous. Presumably this is true of the 'molecule'-'electron' variants. The permutation of predicates simply associates different noises with the same theoretical concepts, an instance of what Hilary Putnam has called trivial semantic conventionalism. Whereas the realist will want to agree with the nonrealist in the molecule-electron example that, despite appearances, the permuted variations remain physically equivalent, really say the same thing, I argued against this Reichenbachian interpretation of alternative geometries and physics in the previous chapter (I will consider that argument in a more general way below). In slightly more interesting cases we have not strictly synonymous theories but alternate true descriptions of the same physical domain. Here the requirement is weaker than term-by-term translation but stronger than the requirement of observational equivalence. "Intertranslatability" is satisfied if there is a common definitional extension of the two formulations. Two theories can be so extended if the terms of each can be defined in the terms of the other, such that, when these definitions are added to the respective theories, they come to say the same things. A simple illustration of the difference between strict synonymy of term-by-term translation and common definitional extension is provided by the example, mentioned in the last chapter, of schemes that divide the color spectrum in different but equally exhaustive ways. Here the terms of one scheme will not correspond to those of the other, but terms can be combined from one to translate those of the other. The extended schemes can then be used to say the same things not only in regard to apparent colors but also in theoretical claims, if any, regarding real colors.

A condition for physical equivalence possibly still weaker than intertranslatability of the sorts I have specified is the fit of apparently different theories with the same models. What really counts for the realist is not even the identity of idealized models governed by the theories' equations or theorems but the suggestion made by the identity that theories have the same physical analogues or causal explanations. For theories to be physically equivalent, causal explanations must be the same for all possible phenomena. Only identical models seem reliable in this regard; it is hard to imagine that different idealized models would suggest the same physical analogues and causal processes underlying all conceivable observational data. It is also true that theories must be translatable in at least a formal sense (ignoring external meanings) in order to fit all the same idealized models. However, if the realist pursues this line of response, he can dismiss the requirement that apparently different theories have all the same physical analogues, provided that one theory is really more basic or broad and contains the models or analogues of the others. Putnam's example of a physical geometry built up from points versus one with extended neighborhoods as basic units, may be of this sort, if the latter can be constructed from the former.[2]

We saw earlier, however, that he cannot always rely on this line of defense against examples of underdetermination and the claim that, in light of it, skepticism results from the attempt to interpret theories realistically. The idea that empirically equivalent theories are always equivalent *tout court* can be advanced only by the positivist, for whom theories are only instruments for predicting observations, and only observation statements admit of truth conditions in the correspondence sense. For the positivist there is no threat of skepticism from underdetermination, because there are no truth claims to be skeptical about. If all empirically equivalent theories have the same truth conditions, this can only be because their truth conditions are exhausted by the observations. Truth conditions become equated with verification conditions, exactly what the realist denies. In fact the many differences between realism and positivism, at least those central, logically related theses, can be made to fall out from the positivist claim that empirically equivalent theories always say the same things (only in different ways). The equation of truth conditions with observations implies that we cannot refer beyond the observational level, that the only inductive criterion or evidentiary relation is that of "saving the phenomena," and that the only way of explaining is to subsume (in however fancy a way) the phenomena under sets of observational regularities.

While the positivist philosophy of science offers a consistent set of views on reference, truth, evidence, and explanation, it does not mesh smoothly with its own implicit realism regarding observables.[3] How is it that we can refer beyond verification conditions in appearances when we make statements about observable objects? The equation of statements verifying theories with statements about independent observable objects ignores that the latter also have verification conditions that must be transcended in acts of reference. We noted in chapter 9 in a similar vein that the scientific instrumentalist, if he is to have a complete epistemology, must face the problem of underdetermination or empirically equivalent theories too, only at earlier stages in the reconstruction. Specifically, he must confront both explanations for appearances that compete with appeals to physical objects and the difficulties raised by Hume and Nelson Goodman for explanations of observables by incorporation into projected regularities. The fact that the epistemologist requires inferences to the truth of best explanans at the levels of appearances and observables weakens the positivist response to the problem of empirically equivalent theories in science. That response requires that the truth conditions for explanations lie solely in the phenomena to be explained.

The realist must steer a middle course between maintaining that all empirically equivalent theories are the same and the claim that there are many different ones with no sound inductive grounds for choosing among them. The former leads to instrumentalism, the latter to skepticism. He must specify when theories are physically equivalent and maintain that when they are not, inductive criteria for rational preference are generally available. He must show, finally, how reference beyond verification conditions is possible and how his inductive criteria link with truth. The latter two steps remain for later discussion. I have just indicated criteria for physical equivalence. Intertranslatability of either the stronger (term by term) or weaker (common definitional extension) sort will depend on the sources of meaning for the theoretical terms. In regard to the three parts of a typical physical theory—the mathematical formalism, the idealized models to which the formalism exactly applies, and the physical analogues that enter causal explanations—it would be simplest if the meanings of terms in the models were determined entirely by their places in the theory, while those of terms in the physical analogues derived entirely from external, ultimately observational contexts. This is not quite true, although not bad as an approximation. Especially in the mediating models, the semantic schemes may be complex. Terms such as 'molecule' and 'electron', for example, may be purely theoretical in themselves, but predicates applied to them, such as 'momentum', accrue meanings by analogy from many other contexts. Thus Quine's example generates synonymous alternatives only when *all* predicates applied to molecules in the one model are ascribed to electrons in the other. Otherwise the causal accounts suggested by the alternatives will be very different, and there will be no inductive grounds for believing the permuted version.

The central point is that translatability for the realist requires the preservation of meanings that accrue to theoretical terms and predicates from outside the context of the theories in question.[4] Semantic extension by analogy from nontheoretical to theoretical levels can be very important for interpreting both the mediating, idealized models and their real physical analogues. Even structurally isomorphic, empirically equivalent theories would not be physically equivalent if their borrowed predicates differed in sense. The false claim that the meaning of theoretical terms accrue solely from their places in their respective theories therefore gives a wrong idea of equivalence among theories. The thesis approximates to truth only for those parts of theory most removed from empirical content.

That empirical equivalence alone does not imply equivalence *tout court* is clear from structurally different mathematical theories with no observational (hence equivalent observational) consequences and no models in common.[5] That 'intertranslatability' in the technical sense of a mere structural mapping, together with empirical equivalence, does not suffice for physical equivalence is clear from cases like those of metrics plus forces (considered in the previous chapter), in which the combinations have identical observational consequences and perhaps can play the same roles in some simple theoretical contexts but give rise to different physical assertions, given the meanings of such terms as 'length' and 'force'.

The realist, then, will not generally claim physical equivalence for empirically equivalent theories. But whether he therefore has a serious problem depends again on how broad our inductive criteria are and whether they can be taken to indicate truth. The burden of proof lies not on the realist to show that in principle there cannot be observationally indistinguishable but distinct theories without inductive grounds for choosing between them. He can even accept limited cases of that sort and suspend judgment between those alternatives in the areas where they disagree. To counter the realist inference to the most plausible explanations, one must rather produce many real examples of the problematic kind, and these must involve ultimately developed theories, so that the realist cannot respond by simply suspending judgment in a narrow domain for the time being. If it is not feasible for him to show that some of the apparently incompatible versions are physically equivalent, then he must show that there are inductive grounds for choosing among them—that is, if there are many real cases.

We saw from the example of geometry some of the pitfalls for the nonrealist in specifying real examples from science. First, he may ignore some of the criteria according to which one explanatory inference is preferable to another. Second, he may deny that explanations that are better on these grounds have a greater chance of being true (a claim still to be defended). Third, he may ignore some of the evidence on the basis of which one can inter to a preferable explanation. I shall argue in the next part of the book that the latter is the case with antirealist claims regarding the indeterminacy of reference, claims based upon taking the totality of data for a theory of reference to consist in verbal responses (from which dispositions to future utterances are inferred) or in the totality of expressed beliefs ('theory' in the broadest sense) at a time. After we take all relevant evidence into account, consider all inductive grounds for preferring certain explanations to others, and infer on the basis of these to the approximate truth of explanations that appear ultimately best, there do not seem to be so many examples of full-scale underdetermination. We have just seen that Putnam's case of geometries of points and of extended neighborhoods may be dismissed. Another of his examples consists in the alternatives for classical physics of particles with action at a distance versus fields.[6] Classical physics is not a case of an explanatory theory that seems ultimately best (although it certainly once did). Ignoring that point, the claim that the choice between particles and fields is underdetermined would have to be greatly fleshed out to be convincing, given the possibility of intertranslation for some versions of the alternatives, the implausibility of notions of action at a distance without fields, the difficulties in more recent physics of making do with only particles, and the possibility for extensions of these versions of different observational consequences.

In real science one finds serious problems of theory choice only in what may be called transitional periods. In those periods, inductive criteria may seem for a time to pull in opposing directions, and individual scientists will align themselves with one or another among seriously competing theories according to the relative weights they personally assign to those different criteria. But such periods, as Thomas Kuhn points out,[7] are the exceptions, and eventually scientific opinion for the most part converges, at least temporarily, on preferred competitors. The Quine-Duhem thesis then ceases to trouble the scientist in practice, when he continues to test the preferred theories experimentally. Despite the revisability in principle of all parts of theory, those hypotheses actually tested are those that would be revised in inferring to a new explanatory account in the face of anomaly.[8] That many incompatible accounts remain tied in such periods on accepted inductive grounds is precisely what the antirealist has failed to show.

We must still face other arguments, however, deriving from examinations of those transitions between theories that we have just begun to consider.

THEORY CHANGES

The arguments in question derive from Kuhn, who (together with Paul Feyerabend, Norwood Hanson, and others) rewrote the history of the process of theory change. The standard view[9] had been that science progresses toward a unified and complete theory cumulatively, through the discovery of new laws and the reduction of older theories to newer, broader, or more basic ones. Reduction occurs when the laws of the older theory are deduced from those of the newer one via a set of bridge principles by which the entities and processes of the former are redescribed in the terms of the latter. The model for such change was the reduction of thermodynamics to classical mechanics. This process of reduction is equally amenable to realist or nonrealist interpretations. The realist views the process as one of redescribing real entities or systems at deeper metaphysical levels, the same systems being truly describable as gases or collections of molecules. If truth conditions for theoretical statements consist only in observations, however, then reductive definitions in effect simply incorporate sets of regularities into broader sets.

Kuhn rather takes as paradigms such transitions as that from Newton to Einstein. Here the conceptual shift is held to be so fundamental that the meanings of central terms alter, such that the referents of the older theory cannot be said to be redescribed in the terms of the newer, and the laws of the former are shown to be inapplicable rather than deduced intact. The waning and waxing theories in such transitions, rather than being either compatible *or* mutually inconsistent, are incommensurable, in that scientists lack a theory-neutral observation language to which to retreat in comparing these referentially distinct systems. Such theories help to define ontologies and worldviews as parts of "paradigms" or "disciplinary matrices" in which practicing scientists operate. Kuhn's terms are meant to indicate the all-encompassing nature of different models of scientific practice, including theories in the usual narrower sense, experimental procedures, (theory-laden) data to be explained, problems to be solved, etc.

This account gives rise to antirealist arguments of two sorts. Both again seek to link realism with an inevitable skepticism. The first does so by drawing a skeptical inference from reflection on the historical sequence of incommensurable theories. If (1) there is no theory-free observation, if (2) theories specify different ontologies with different principles of individuation for picking out what is real, if (3) there is no convergence or preservation of reference and truth across theories, and if (4) there is nevertheless an independent world with structures of individuation that theories attempt to describe, then it seems gratuitous to believe that our present theory has succeeded in specifying what is real, where earlier theories failed. The ability of a theory to solve more puzzles, when these are defined simply in its own terms, does not seem to indicate a superior or more nearly correct ontology. Furthermore, if reflection on past transitions fails to reveal a convergence toward the present ontology (Kuhn claims that the ontology of contemporary science is closer to that of Aristotle in some respects than to that of Newton),[10] this weakens yet more the grounds for belief in the success of our current paradigms in picking out the real. The Kuhnian rather infers inductively to similar transitions in the future. In light of this projection, he renounces realism in order to avoid skepticism. Accepting a view of truth as warranted assertibility relative to overall theories at given times, he assumes a more tolerant attitude and says that, relative to their information and classificatory schemes, our ancestors' theories (as well as our own) embody truth. A nonrealist alternative is to continue to interpret the meanings of theoretical concepts in terms of truth conditions but commit only to their success on the observational level.

The second sort of argument concentrates on the reasons why scientists accept the theories they do. If theories are incommensurable and there is no requirement to capture a set of theory-neutral data, then there cannot exist a fixed and objective algorithm for deciding among competitor theories. Each of two competitors can be preferable on grounds that it itself establishes for handling problems it defines in relation to its own set of data. While Kuhn acknowledges the usual inductive criteria for preference (scope, accuracy, simplicity, etc.), he argues that scientists can give them different weights and even understand and apply them differently. Sociologists of science following Kuhn have emphasized economic and professional reasons for supporting particular lines of research rather than others. I have been assuming not only that inferences to the best explanations tend to preserve truth but that science tends to produce such explanations in the long run. I have argued also for a continuity in explanatory accounts of knowledge beginning in foundations in ordinary ways of appearing. The second argument here attacks both assumptions by viewing scientists as wedded to certain modes of explanation, ways of interpreting data, and even ways of perceiving for essentially nonepistemic reasons.

Let us answer this second skeptical argument first. Kuhn's own point is that the criteria usually cited for theory choice, while accurate as abstract summaries of scientists' reasonings, represent merely subjective values, therefore differ in application and weight, and therefore can give rise to different choices without the possibility of evaluation by appeal to considerations beyond these criteria. Problems addressed and standards for evaluating solutions differ across scientific communities despite our ability to sort those standards into broad categories. The situation here according to Kuhn resembles that in ethics, where we can isolate shared sets of values or right-making characteristics but should not expect such agreement to generate universal judgments on concrete moral issues. This conception of science, however, suggests widespread instantiation of the problem dismissed earlier in this section, namely, the situation of many incompatible theories' being taken as serious competitors at a given time. (For the moment I am setting aside the claim that competitor theories are more often incommensurable than incompatible; it will be answered below.) Kuhn's own view of normal science creates an internal tension by contradicting the expectation of widespread instantiation. Normally the community of scientists seeks to extend theories upon which there is broad agreement. In revolutionary periods (such as the twenty years or so following 1905), when there are serious competitors in the field, there is generally insufficient evidence to settle the inductive grounds for preference.

Kuhnian sociologists of science would not see normal periods as indicative of the ascendancy of theories that are objectively better or more nearly true. As mentioned, they emphasize sociological and ideological explanations for such temporary consensus. These explanations may appeal to the broader political or sociointellectual climate—for example, the climate in pre-war Germany as conducive to the attack on deterministic causality in quantum physics—or to more personal professional motives of scientists, their support of theories that apply their expertise or further their careers. The questionable assumption here is that such explanations must compete with those that appeal to epistemic grounds for the ascendancy of various theories. In well-designed, well-functioning institutions, personal professional motives will tend to favor positions defensible on grounds that further the basic goals of the institutions. In science there is first of all the aim of predictive accuracy; this is connected with technological goals; and these in turn are linked to both political and professional motivations. The predictive aim is better satisfied by theories offering explanations that are superior on inductive grounds. (Both explanation and prediction rely on knowledge of probability relations. While best explanations are not necessary for predictions, which may express knowledge only of regularities and not of mechanisms, best explanations generally screen off weaker probability relations and are therefore predictively superior.) These connections ex-

plain why sociological explanations should not generally compete, at least in the long run, with those that cite the epistemic
or inductive preferability of ascendant theories. To see inductively superior theories as triumphing over competitors in the
long run is not to deny that scientists will tend to support such
theories for professional reasons.

The broader emphasis on science as a social endeavor is of
course a healthy offshoot of Kuhn's approach. I began my validating reconstruction of knowledge with beliefs about ways of
appearing as immediately justified. Traditionally this approach
marked an antisocial and even solipsistic view of the knowing
subject. But it need not be so. We can and should acknowledge
social influences on both ways of appearing and, more important, upon inferences to best explanations. I shall later view the
ways things appear as results of the evolutionary history of the
species. They are partially results of cultural heritage as well,
and often so in science, where theory instructs experimenters
how to look for and interpret results. Inferences to explanatory
theories themselves are more obvious social products, even
when, as in the case of Einstein, they are the highly original
products of relatively isolated geniuses. The point here is simply that social, professional, and institutional influences con-
duce to epistemic goals when the latter figure prominently
among institutional aims and when methodology therefore
maximizes the role of environmental input in the selection of
theories.

Normal science seems to show that differences in interpreting and weighing inductive criteria are not perpetuated without
concrete resolution. We do not normally find a spectacle of
fundamental conflicts at the level of basic theory (although disputes over philosophical interpretations may seem perpetual).
The complete answer to the claim that the grounds usually cited
for theory preference nevertheless represent values of scientific
communities lacking in deeper epistemic support awaits the
defense of the principle of inference to the (seeming) best explanation as tending to preserve truth. The belief that *only* sociological explanations can be offered for theory choices derives
from a despair of rational justification, from the claim that each
theory determines its own standards for evaluation. Kuhn

rather admits common standards, but holds that they are understood and applied differently. Normal science and a defense of commensurability refute this claim. Nevertheless, even strong convergence of theories would not in itself justify the inductive criteria that scientists use. Additional defense of the broad principle will be offered below.

If there are grounds for taking the best explanations to be true (and seemingly best explanations to be approximately true), then these will justify those more specific criteria according to which we rank explanatory systems. We need not search, as many philosophers do, for more direct links between the specific criteria (such as simplicity) taken separately and truth-preserving inferences. The deeper epistemic significance of the specific criteria lies simply in the fact that rational inquirers (or human brains) take them to indicate better explanations. The fundamental question concerns the relation of the truth- or explanation-seeker to the epistemic environment, or, in more naturalistic terms, of the brain to its physical environment. We do not evaluate the brain as an inferential machine by evaluating the separate inductive criteria it utilizes. Rather we justify those criteria by noting their use in inferential reasoning processes that we have reason to believe sound. For this reason I have not concentrated on analysis of the separate parameters of inference to the best explanation. Such analysis is more germane to explication than epistemological defense.

Similarly, I shall not explore the various formal algorithms proposed by confirmation theorists for the justification of specific scientific hypotheses. The reasoning of scientists that most interests us here is best characterized as falling between the confirmation of hypotheses by use of algorithms obeying the probability calculus or the various adaptations of Bayes's theorem on the one hand, and the essentially nonrational, Kuhnian commitment to whole disciplinary matrices on the other. Our probabilistic interpretation of inference to the best explanation captures some central features of the Bayesian approach: for example, the claims that degree of confirmation of a hypothesis is proportional to the likelihood of the hypothesis (the probability of the evidence given the hypothesis) and inversely proportional to the prior probability of the evidence.[11] These ideas are captured by our demand that the explanans raise the probability of its explanandum and by our acknowledgment that explanations are strengthened when otherwise independent data (whose prior joint probabilities are therefore lower) receive a common explanation. In addition, some analogue of the assignment of initial probabilities to hypotheses in the Bayesian model is required to distinguish among possible explanatory accounts all of which entail or would equally raise the probability of the explanandum. Here, on the one hand, we choose the account that seems most likely or plausible on other grounds. These grounds might include enumerative induction from other, similar data receiving a like explanation or, when the inference is more novel, weaker analogies from observable phenomena. On the other hand (and opposed to the Bayesian formula), we do not always select the alternative that is initially most plausible, since we also prefer broader accounts more likely to be fruitful in extending to other explananda. Especially in the Kuhnian context, the inferences that most interest us are those of great and original theoreticians, when they infer to new explanatory schemes fundamentally different from and often broader than earlier theories. (While initial probability is increased when a broader set of already accepted phenomena is explained, it is decreased by a broader set of potential falsifiers in untested consequences.) Formal methods for confirming hypotheses already in the field seem somewhat inapplicable in such circumstances. Yet we want to say that revolutionary inferences, when they appear to lead to best overall accounts, have a reasonable chance of being approximately true.

At this point in the argument the main hurdle to this claim is the skeptical inference from Kuhn's historical thesis, our first antirealist argument. Here the problem is incommensurability, evidenced by radical and nonconvergent shifts in ontology. Incommensurability, if genuine, makes it gratuitous to assume that our present (or particular future) theories succeed in picking out the real when earlier ones failed to do so. Should we not infer that molecules and atoms will go the way of caloric, phlogiston, absolute location, and the luminiferous ether? Other critics have noted that the thesis of incommensurability derives in large part from an assumed theory of meaning and its seeming implications for a view of reference. Kuhn's assumption is that the meanings of theoretical terms are determined by the theorems in which they function, by the theoretical beliefs that they are used to express.[12] This holistic, descriptive cluster theory of meaning opposes the positivist view according to which theoretical terms are (partially or fully) defined through analytic postulates that connect them to observation terms, whose meanings in turn are given by direct connection to experience. The attack on analyticity and on the theory-observation distinction led Kuhn and other critics of positivism to the assumptions that all terms of a theory share a common semantic characterization and that all parts of a theory in which they appear determine their meanings in common. These assumptions, together with the premise that meaning determines reference, imply that major changes in theoretical beliefs will shift the meanings of terms enough that referents picked out, if any, will be different also. From this the skeptical inference follows inductively.

I began to criticize this notion of meaning earlier. It is easy to heap additional abuse upon it. First, in the present context, the thesis of incommensurability to which it leads differs from the views of most practicing scientists, who take rival theories to be incompatible rather than incomparable.[13] Given a possible lack of philosophical sophistication on their part, this criticism might not be telling, except against those who urge philosophers of science to take the attitudes and practices of scientists more seriously. Second, and more to the point, the Kuhnian view of meaning lands its proponents in a dilemma. If we restrict the variables determining theoretical meaning to the theorems of the particular theory in question, then we reintroduce a radical distinction between its theoretical terms and the ordinary terms we apply in testing it and in expressing our other beliefs. Such semantic isolation of theories leaves us with no clue how to interpret their resulting abstract formalisms. If we are charitable and interpret them so as to maximize apparent truth, then all theories come out true (since all have models, even if the models are unintended when externally derived meanings are taken into account), and science becomes nonempirical. If we instead recognize that the meanings of theoretical terms connect to ordinary language through webs of analogy, then we see that the holistic theory of meaning leads to the absurd conclusion that any two different belief systems must be incommensurable (or, on a slightly weaker theory, that any two systems involving beliefs in different regularities or laws must be incommensurable). Disagreement becomes impossible on any level.

Making the notion of meaning precise has proved an elusive task since Quine's attack on synonymy and analyticity. It is clear, however, that the implicit view of reference is what counts for Kuhn's incommensurability thesis. (Inscrutability of reference will be considered later.) I began to develop an alternative view of reference in the previous chapter and will complete a brief sketch of it in subsequent chapters. Its main motivation is to demonstrate the possibility of reference to independent objects. For the more modest purpose of preserving reference across change in theory, one need only minimize the relativity of reference to particular beliefs. The Kuhnian holistic descriptive criterion, at one extreme, makes relativity nearly complete. More moderate views allow for greater possibilities of common reference across different beliefs and for false beliefs about referents. At the other extreme is the causal theory,[14] according to which a term type becomes connected to a referent by an introducing act and continues to refer to the same or like entities via causal chains from the introducing act to later uses. Beliefs about a referent are irrelevant to its status as referent if the right causal connections obtain. The theory therefore may seem ideal for arguing, against the incommensurability thesis, that earlier scientists were in many cases referring to the same theoretical entities referred to by current scientists, while holding false beliefs about them. If reference is retained while the content of theories improves, then we can preserve notions of progress or convergence and deny the radical shifts in ontology that lead to the strong skeptical inference.

The causal theory too, however, faces insuperable objections. In the present context the problem is precisely the extreme to which it goes in opposing the holistic descriptive account. While the latter fails to allow for retention of reference across change in belief, the former locks reference into contexts of introducing acts. Literal reliance on events introducing terms would render reference inscrutable to those lacking information about the events, and it would fail to allow for any change in reference later. As Fine points out, when interpreting theory changes we want sometimes to say that our scientific ancestors referred to the same theoretical entities that we do, sometimes that they failed to refer completely, and sometimes that they referred to different entities. The latter two options may apply to different uses of the same terms, for example 'phlogiston', which sometimes referred to oxygen or hydrogen, sometimes to nothing. Fine concludes that in many cases there is no answer to the question of reference: we can tell different stories about referents of older theories while still comparing them to newer ones.[15] I prefer a criterion that makes reference determinate while leaving all the options for interpretation of theories available. We want to allow for wrong theorems about real unobservables in both past and present theories and allow as well for improvements in ontology. These aims can be accomplished by means of a descriptive theory that singles out certain privileged descriptions, generally with low content (in my account, those descriptions from which users of terms would not retreat in the face of possible error), as determining reference. This criterion will match the causal theory in application when central descriptions specify certain effects of the intended referent, otherwise not.

Alternative criteria of reference avoid the skeptical inference regarding current physical ontology by eliminating the premise that the theoretical beliefs of earlier scientists always failed to refer. In those cases in which we continue to say that there was such failure, we can simply note the progress in the transition to recent theories in order to block the inference that the latter fail to refer as well. But we must be able to specify the nature of this progress and why it indicates superior ontology. And to the extent that we judge earlier theories false even when they refer, we must be concerned to block a weaker skeptical inference that present theories, while they also refer, are equally false. Reference across theory change does not guarantee covergence of successive theories upon the truth. How strong a claim to convergence or progress need the realist make? How strong a claim can he make in behalf of current theory in light of Kuhnian reflections on the history of science? Such reflections do require a degree of modesty, much as did our consideration of interpretive problems in quantum theory, although neither necessitates abandoning the realist conclusion of our earlier argument.

Modesty is manifest in our recognition that the seemingly best available explanatory account will not be ultimately best. This recognition warrants a retreat from a claim of truth to belief in approximate truth in inferring to seemingly best explanatory accounts, even above the level of quantum theory. This retreat might have seriously affected our realist interpretation of the referents of such accounts if we had argued that that interpretation is necessary to explain their success. The standard realist argument that only the truth of a theory can explain its success is seriously compromised by the retreat to approximate truth. Since approximate truth is literal falsity, it does not follow from the fact that truth explains predictive success that approximate truth does also.[16] We need not struggle with this problem, since the standard argument was not our argument.[17] I rather sought to establish the necessity of inference to the best explanation for avoiding skepticism at every level and the superiority of explanations—for both appearances and observable interactions—that appeal to real unobservables. At these levels, as at the level of quantum mechanics, we first infer to the seeming best explanation and then hedge our bet to belief in approximate truth. This shift does not negate the earlier inference. (Even if the standard argument for realism were sound, mine would be the more fundamental. One who is not convinced that inference to the best explanation leads to true, approximately true, or at least referring accounts would not accept realism on the ground that it explains the success of science best.)[18]

While the shift to approximate truth is not damaging to the proper argument for the realist, he does owe some account both of approximate truth itself and of the improvement of theories in regard to it. The latter blocks the weaker skeptical inference from the falsity of earlier theories. The notion of approximate truth should not be analyzed, as in the recent British tradition, in terms of the number of true propositions in the statement of a theory.[19] A theory may contain no true statements yet still be approximately true. In fact, if we take the statement of a theory to consist in its interpreted mathematical formalism, then, as we have acknowledged, the laws so stated will be true only of idealized models. Indeed the last claim may be too strong in application—scientists may be content to use simplifications or approximations to more exact laws that would govern their constructed models. Even apart from Kuhnian considerations, then, reflection on the synchronic structure of theories reveals approximations at several levels. Laws may be only approximately true even of idealized models; the models will only approximate the behavior of empirical systems on the one hand and the unobservable causal processes of which they are analogues on the other. It is the realist's retreat to approximate modeling of unobservables that now concerns us.

To say that a theory is approximately true is to say that the causal processes suggested by its models approximate to those involving real unobservable entities.[20] Terms entering descriptions of such processes (which terms are not part of the formal statement of the theory) either refer to or specify (ideal) entities structurally similar to real ones. Predicates pick out instantiated properties or properties similar to those instantiated in the relevant domain, or within a certain margin of error for quantitative predicates. This is all, of course, very loose, but suffices to indicate for our purposes a notion of progress or convergence sufficient to block a fully pessimistic induction from the falsity of previous theories. It is clear that this notion of approximate truth does not require later theories to retain either the precise causal mechanisms or the precise laws (as limiting cases in specified boundary conditions) of earlier ones. In fact progress requires that models governed by laws more closely approximating observable regularities suggest different causal processes than earlier models suggest. Both this measurable progress on the observable level and the ability of later theories to explain earlier theories' degree of success on that level indicate to the realist that the later theories more closely approximate to the truth in the sense specified.

Progress on the observable level includes the explanation of an increasing range of independent phenomena. As I argued earlier, increased breadth indicates that newer explanations are superior to the older in the areas in which they overlap, and hence that newer explanations are more likely to be (approximately) true. Often the additional explananda include the degree of success (and failure) of the superceded theory. A later and superior theory is not required to provide such an explanation, but one will be forthcoming if the physical analogue of the newer theory approximately obeys the laws of the older one. I am not arguing that the approximate truth of a later theory explains the theory's own success *or* that of its predecessors in an obviously better way than do explanations of success that lack a realist interpretation. The explanation by appeal to approximate truth is seen to be better only after the theory is recognized to be approximately true. A theory is held to be (approximately) true because doing so allows a deeper explanation of all the physical phenomena explained, not because instrumental success cannot be explained by appeal to the method of constructing and developing theories *as if* they were true.

Not only the coreferentiality of earlier and later theories, then, but also the notion of degrees of similarity of approximation to truth allows us to avoid skeptical inferences from the failures of reference (in some cases) and falsity of earlier theories. As long as later theories can be argued to be, in their physical analogues, closer approximations to truth than earlier ones, the inference is blocked. Aberrations from linear progress on the theoretical level can also be recognized by the realist and more easily accommodated when he can explain their observational successes and failures. Sometimes aberrations can be seen to result also from attempts to explain what later appears to need no explanation, for example, constant relative motion. Theories can disagree over what constitutes an explanatory problem and in that sense determine their own standards. In such cases, however, where the theories overlap in their physical domains, there will be other disagreements and therefore other bases for comparison. Similarly, new theories can lead their proponents to seek new and different observational data or appearances and in that trivial sense alter the data (obviously without completely determining ways of appearing). The data for two theories need not appear the same in order for the theories to be comparable. It is sufficient either that we take some of the same entities to appear in the two theoretical contexts or, at least, that we understand and can explain what did appear to scientists under the grip of the earlier theory. We can then explain both sets of appearances better by means of our superior theory. Hence we have greater reason for believing the new theory true, greater reason for believing it approximately true when considering it more modestly or soberly in light of history, and therefore greater reason for believing it closer to the truth (in the sense indicated) than its predecessors.

This concludes our brief consideration of historical relations among theories. It has given us no more reason to abandon or override the argument for scientific realism than did our consideration of currently dominant theories and current possible alternatives to them. In both cases we should retreat from claims to truth to a notion of approximate truth, but no further.

SECONDARY QUALITIES (COLORS)

I have been arguing that we should accept as real those entities and processes that enter into best explanations for ways things appear. The obverse also holds for the realist. We should not accept as real properties or entities to which such explanations do not refer. I noted in the section on relativity that current theory alters our view of the so-called primary qualities, showing in many cases that they are relational rather than intrinsic as we naively think. The extent of this tranformation from naive realism to the scientific view has occasionally been exaggerated by philosophers. The claim, for example, that physics reveals objects to be neither solid nor stable is false, since these concepts remain well defined for and true of macroscopic objects. Furthermore, as I argued above, while such properties as length or extension in space may be relative to a space-time framework, they are not relative to human observation or consciousness. In addition, other space-time properties remain invariant across frames, and so intrinsic relatives of the traditional primary qualities remain.

Since Galileo and Locke, realist interpretations of the secondary qualities have been the more controversial. Many distinctions between the two classes of properties have been drawn, for example that ascription of the secondary but not of the primary qualities is relative to single sense modalities. As noted above, this provides a stronger initial sense for ascribing primary qualities to objects, since otherwise independent appearances thereby receive common explanations. This ascription is modified, we have seen, by deeper theory and ultimately defended only via some theory relating sensory systems to their environment. The central point here, however, is that, while relatives of initially ascribed primary qualities enter seemingly ultimate explanations for both physical interactions and ways of appearing (along with such new and only weakly analogous properties as spin and charm), appeal to secondary qualities as they appear is totally absent at the microlevel. Since in the (inductive) realist's view the only justification for ascribing properties as real lies in inference to the best explanation, the status of secondary qualities becomes problematic. Realist philosophers have responded in several different ways. I shall concentrate on the case of colors, as is usual, since these, unlike sounds and tastes, are perceived and initially ascribed as properties of objects themselves. (I shall have something to say by analogy about other secondary qualities.) After considering alternatives, I shall defend the most radical view, denying that any objects are literally colored.

Physical science itself, if interpreted realistically, seems to leave us with the option of viewing colors as emergent properties of objects, which are in turn regarded as collections of microparticles. There is certainly no inconsistency in ascribing properties to collections but not to their individual parts (or the converse, as with charm and spin). Although we do not refer to colors by name in causally explaining physical interactions, perhaps we can reduce colors to or identify them with causally efficacious physical properties of collections of entities. The identification introduces a sharp metaphysical distinction between real and apparent colors, but that is not implausible for physical properties. Of the two most popular positions identifying real colors with physical properties, the first was Locke's, according to which secondary qualities are powers objects have, in virtue of their primary qualities (microstructures), to cause certain sensations in us (to appear in certain ways). The second position more directly identifies the qualities with the physical bases of their appearances—either wavelengths of light or the molecular configurations on surfaces that absorb and reflect light of various wavelengths. More precisely, the property of having a particular color is light's property of having a certain wavelength or a surface's property of having a particular molecular configuration.

An initial difficulty for the Lockean view is that we see colors, but it seems strange to say that we see hidden powers in objects. We shall not be ultimately guided by ease or strangeness of expression, however (as we were not in the debate between sense data and appearing). The more serious difficulty involves specifying which sensations or appearances determine the correct ascriptions of particular real colors. A specific color, on this view, is a power to appear in a certain way in certain conditions, but which way and when? The only noncircular mode of specification requires a class of normal perceivers and a set of normal conditions. The color red, for example, is the power to appear in such conditions to these perceivers in a way they call red. The problem is that the class of normal perceivers and conditions cannot be specified for determinate shades. Since this difficulty applies as well (somewhat less directly) to the remaining alternative for realistically interpreting colors, and since this alternative finds more current favor, we may evaluate it first.

The identification of colors with particular wavelengths of light falls to the objection that we see colors but not light reflected from objects. Seeing light (as opposed to sources of light) is not simply awkward to conceive; if we saw the light that reaches our eyes, we could see nothing else. Seeing molecular configurations is not similarly impossible, if we see them not *as* molecular configurations but as colors. Hence the phenomenological objections to this identification are not decisive (although at least one, to be mentioned in a moment, should give us pause). Phenomenologically it does not seem that we can discriminate molecular structures: they may act on us by selectively reflecting light but, since discrimination is necessary for perceiving, it does not follow from these effects that we see their microcauses. Nevertheless, if objects are collections of molecules and we see objects, then we see collections of molecules. Seeing x is a transparent context, although seeing x as y is not. Hence it is possible that we see molecular configurations and discriminate them as well, although we can see them only as colors and not as microstructures. Seeing a color does not seem to be like seeing a pattern of molecules, but again this objection is handled in the same way. It is also true that we must infer to molecular structure but know of colors noninferentially, by directly seeing them; but once more this could be because we see the structures only as colors. Finally, according to Wilfrid Sellars and Bruce Aune,[21] perceived color is continuous or homogeneous, in that all subregions of a colored expanse must be colored, while molecular structures are gappy. This objection too is inconsequential if the homogeneity characterizes only the appearance of the color and not the property itself.

While the above objections may seem to lack force, there is another that brings out better the phenomenological difficulty in identifying color with its physical bases. This is that perceived color properties and the corresponding predicates lack sharp boundaries, while physical properties are determinate and distinct. The realist, I shall argue later, can allow for vagueness in our concepts and predicates, and also in ways things appear. However, the idea that real physical objects can be vague or indeterminate seems to be incoherent, although I can offer no defense of this intuition except to say that the attribution of vagueness to things as opposed to concepts and appearances is a category mistake. In regard to perceived colors, the continuous nature of the spectrum makes it possible to arrange patches, from red to orange, for example, so that adjacent patches cannot be discriminated. Patches then seem to be both the same as and different from their neighbors; less mysteriously, the ways they appear are vague, as are the predicates that we apply to them. Perhaps we can still identify the colors with their physical bases and claim that they only appear vaguely, being fully determinate in themselves. But then we lose the observability of color properties: colors are not as they appear. It should have been clear from the earlier objections also that the physical identification renders colors partly unobservable—if the property of being colored is the property of having a certain surface microstructure, then we can perceive the property only as it appears and not as it is. But colors seem to be paradigmatic of fully observable properties. To say that the color blue (as opposed to a blue object) appears other than it is may be unintelligible to the layman unarmed with this strange metaphysical theory. The nonobservability of colors under the physical interpretation should be at the heart of the phenomenological objection.

The really decisive objection to the view we have been considering, however, is that molecular configurations are not correlated one-to-one with specific shades of seen color (even ignoring the vagueness problem). Nor is there any nonarbitrary way to restrict the class of discriminable shades so as to achieve the necessary correlation. The physical variables that affect how colors appear are sufficiently multifarious, extending well outside particular objects perceived, to make the identification of colors with them highly implausible. First, mixtures of various wavelengths are indistinguishable in regard to colors seen. Specific shades have to be identified with large disjunctions of reflecting surfaces. Second, in addition to light reflected from particular areas, perceived colors vary with light reflected from surrounding areas and with previous stimuli, accentuating simultaneous and successive contrasts. (Contrast and boundary accentuation serves general adaptive purposes in perception.) Thus, for the purposes of correlation, "normal conditions" for perceiving particular shades would have to be those of "aperture perception," that is, perception of uniform patches in isolation, a situation that almost never occurs. Third, even reflection from an object in relation to others fails to determine perceived color. Rather, the crucial variable in color perception appears to be the way that surfaces modify (not simply reflect) available light in relation to other surfaces in the display.[22] The physical basis for colors is too complex and spread out to be identified with the colors of particular surfaces.

When we take not simply external physical but also internal physiological or psychological variables into account, the prospects for identifying colors with physical bases become, in my view, hopeless. Viewing a particular colored surface over time tends to reduce its perceived saturation and increase that of subsequently perceived complementary shades, because of the adaptive states of the neurons. For this reason, small patches appear brighter than large ones. Even such factors as expectation and attitude can affect what colors are perceived. A leaflike shape may be perceived as green when a similarly reflecting patch of another shape is seen as gray. A standard text on color states: "Any given object or medium may have many different appearances even under exactly the same physical conditions depending on the attitude, experience, and subtle perceptual factors of a given observer."[23] Color constancy, the operation of which causes objects to vary less in apparent color than one would predict from their reflected light, might seem to reintroduce a closer correlation between color and physical properties of the objects themselves, but it actually introduces further variation. This is because it varies with such factors as the surrounding objects and the age of the perceiving subject.

Given the number of discriminable shades (eight to ten million) and the number of variables that affect those colors perceived on identical surfaces, it becomes clear that the agreement among subjects on the use of color terms results largely from the breadth of those terms, the number of discriminable shades falling under each of them. In fact, precise matching tests reveal that subjects have different matching functions, hence that they see different specific shades on the same surfaces in the same external physical conditions.[24] Furthermore, the abilities of normal subjects to discriminate colors differ considerably: no particular subjects are best over the whole range. Given this fact, the assumption that colors are in any sense observable properties becomes inconsistent with the claim that objects themselves have determinate shades of color. We cannot strictly identify observed colors with any factors in the physical array, either inside or outside particular objects observed. Varying abilities to discriminate block the identification of a class of normal perceivers who perceive the shades to be reduced to physical properties. Nor can normal conditions be those optimal for discriminating. Some discriminations are made better under ultraviolet light, yet we do not identify colors seen in those conditions as real. Nor, finally, are normal perceivers and conditions average or usual ones, since, as noted, average perceivers see different colors in usual conditions.

The color response *in the normal observer* can be affected by: energy variations in the color stimulus, spatial and temporal relationships within the stimulus field, the areas of the retina stimulated, the state of the observer's visual mechanism, and the observer's mental attitude. (Italics mine.)[25]

This inability to single out nonarbitrarily either a class of normal observers or a set of normal conditions of perception clearly defeats the Lockean analysis, according to which an object of a determinate shade is one which causes normal perceivers to see that shade in normal conditions, and its color is the power to have that effect. But it also nullifies the only way in which the more direct identification of perceived colors with their external physical bases could be explicated. The distinction between real and apparent colors allows only the former to be so identified. This avoids some seeming counterexamples. But if real colors can sometimes be observed, then we must be able to specify when they are observed, and this requires reference to normal observers. Our inability to pick out in any nonarbitrary or noncircular way the set of such observers, such that they all perceive the same colors in the same environmental conditions, thus defeats all nonskeptical, physicalist analyses of color.

The alternative is to hold that colors are simply ways of appearing. I answered several possible objections to this conclusion earlier, in the chapter on appearing. That properties analyzed adverbially are harder to express was held to be no objection to the metaphysics. Language, especially that used to refer to observable properties, evolves to serve everyday purposes of identification, not to reveal in its grammar a true metaphysics. I shall later deal more fully with the claim that it is built into the meanings or uses of color terms that objects must instantiate color properties. One argument behind the claim (in barest form) is that, since we learn color terms in relation to public paradigms, and since justified or correct use of such terms applies them to such paradigmatic objects, it is inconsistent, in violation of rules of language, to deny that these objects are colored. The argument, as I shall reply, misconstrues the necessary conditions for communication and language learning. Shared ways of appearing suffice. Realism in regard to any set of entities or properties is an open question to be settled inductively. The inductive grounds lead us to accept as real entities and properties that enter deepest explanations for ways of appearing. Colors are not among the real properties, although they are prominent among the ways of appearing themselves.

13

THE PRINCIPLE OF INFERENCE

OTHER PRINCIPLES AND STRATEGIES

Before providing positive support for our central principle of inference, we may note its avoidance of some notorious problems for other inductive principles. As noted early in the third chapter, simple probabilistic rules of acceptance, which call upon us to accept any hypothesis to which a probability greater than some n $(n > \frac{1}{2})$ is assigned, fall prey to the lottery paradox, while the principle of inference to the best explanation does not.[1] I do not infer that my ticket will not win as an explanation for the large number of tickets; nor does the large number of tickets *best* explain my not winning. While the large number of tickets raises the probability of my not winning, this relation is screened out by that obtaining between the drawing of another ticket and my not winning. Thus, for our principle, there is no problematic explanatory chain leading to the conclusion that no ticket will win and hence to inconsistency.

We may again contrast the principle under its probabilistic interpretation with Bayesian rules for confirming (assigning higher probabilities to) hypotheses as well. In chapter 12, I noted the parallels between the demand that an explanans raise the probability of its explanandum and the Bayesian proportionality of degree of confirmation to the probability of the evidence given the hypothesis, and between the strengthening of inference to the best explanation by diversity among the data explained and the Bayesian inverse proportionality of degree of confirmation to prior probability of the evidence. I also noted there that the role of antecedent probabilities in the Bayesian scheme is sometimes inappropriate in inferring to best explanatory accounts. Sometimes we prefer broader theories with lower antecedent probabilities. There is also a problem in the very idea of confirming scientific laws as true, if laws as stated apply only to idealized models and if we retreat to a claim of only approximate truth even for the causal analogues of theories.

Beyond these differences in application, the so-called paradoxes of confirmation fail to affect our inductive principle. The presence of a white shoe confirms Hempel's hypothesis that all ravens are black, given that hypotheses should be confirmed by verification of their logical consequences.[2] But the raven hypothesis certainly does not best explain the presence of the white shoe, if it raises the probability of the shoe's being white (or of the white thing's being a shoe) at all. Similarly, the observation of particular emeralds confirms Goodman's grue hypothesis, but the thesis that all emeralds are grue (green if observed and blue otherwise) does not explain best for us our observations of the color of emeralds. What seems best to us by way of explanation here (ignoring inferences to deeper levels of scientific theory) involves naturally salient properties and, hence, projectable predicates. Thus inferring to the (apparently) best explanation will not be affected by Goodmanian alternatives. The principle of inference rules them out as serious skeptical possibilities. Finally, Mary Hesse's paradox of transitivity for confirmation is avoided.[3] If f confirms h and h implies g, then f should confirm g, given that we want observation of instances of a hypothesis to confirm the prediction of future instances as well as the hypothesis itself. But then if h is equivalent to the conjunction of f and g, and f therefore confirms h, then it will confirm g as well. This means that any observation sentence will confirm any other one with which it can be conjoined. The paradox is not a problem for the principle of inference to the best explanation, since h will not generally explain f if h is equivalent to f and g. The probability of f will not be significantly raised by h if f is fully accounted for in other terms.

Many philosophers seem to think that in order to justify inference to the best explanation as generally truth preserving one would have to demonstrate connections between truth and the other criteria used in evaluating explanations, for example, simplicity. It is argued, for instance, that since we have no reason to believe that the world is really simple rather than complex, and since we nevertheless prefer explanations that are simpler and choose them on pragmatic grounds, we should distinguish such grounds from criteria for truth. The same might be said of other grounds for better explanations—fruitfulness, comprehensibility, economy, conservatism or analogy, etc. One may wonder why any of these, taken in themselves, should be indicative of truth. I have no new or more obviously epistemic criteria to add to the usual list; the task of fully specifying and analyzing actual criteria used is one for cognitive psychologists. Whether we do have grounds for thinking the world simple or relatively uniform (Hume's problem of induction)—grounds that would support conservatism or analogy in inductive inference as well—will be considered briefly later. But, as we have argued, there is no need to find separate links between these explanatory criteria and truth. Nor need we be able to provide formal analyses of such elusive notions as that of simplicity. The significance of such criteria derives from their use in inductive inference, while the justification for such inference, as we shall see, makes no appeal to the separate criteria.

We may also, as argued earlier, rule out intuitionist, a priori, and nonespistemic or merely pragmatic justifications of the inductive principle. First, it is not sufficient that our inductive epistemic principle captures our more specific intuitions regarding knowledge. Such "reflective equilibrium" or internal coherence among epistemic beliefs does not suffice for truth (although it might suffice as a criterion of moral truth within a system of values) unless it can be shown to indicate correspondence between empirical beliefs and independent reality. We have seen that use of our principle of inference requires a realist interpretation of inferred explanans, hence a correspondence notion of truth. While the validation of the principle must appeal ultimately to coherence among the total set of beliefs generated through its use together with other inductive principles, that set must be far broader and more clearly connected to its objects than the set of intuitions regarding knowledge claims. There is nothing within the latter set alone to rule out systematic error. Given realism, there will be possible worlds in which there is such wholesale error, and we must have some reason for believing our world not to be among them. That reason must lie outside the realm of epistemic intuitions themselves.

Similarly, it will not do to define rationality in terms of the use of accepted inductive principles and then to argue that their use must therefore (tautologically) be rational or justified. As realists we must again link this notion of rationality with that of truth, and it is only in that linkage that its real justification lies. Nor will it suffice simply to recall our earlier argument that best explanations must be true. If that claim is correct, and we if do actually infer to best explanations, then such inference transmits truth from premises to conclusions. What actually accounts for the occurrence (or probability of 1) of an actual event must itself be actual. But given that best explanations must be true, the problem in validating the inductive principle is to show that seemingly best explanations approximate to genuinely best accounts and hence to truth. There is again no guarantee that our actual inductive practices, no matter how laudatorily described, lead to truth.

Finally, we cannot rest content with "vindication" of our epistemic principle in terms of its usefulness for our purposes (other than truth seeking). Vindication cannot substitute for validation, the demonstration of a likely connection with truth. If our purpose or goal is that of providing explanations or doing science, then the vindication is trivial. If we have some broader goal, such as coping successfully with or reshaping our environments to meet material and social needs, then a demonstration that use of the inductive principle furthers that goal does not respond to skeptical challenge unless (approximate) truth is shown to be (probably) necessary for that success. But then we are back to validation. It is clear that the justification of basic or first epistemic principles must be either nonepistemic or circular (less pejoratively, the justification must appeal to mutual support or coherence of some sort among the various principles and the beliefs derived from their use). While nonepistemic vindication is insufficient for our purposes, I hope to show that mutual support can provide some reason to view our principles as truth preserving.

Although purposes other than truth seeking cannot suffice

in themselves to justify induction, the truth-preserving character of inference to the best explanation is not ruled out by the relativity of explanans to explanatory purposes noted in the first chapter. As we pointed out there, which factors are made part of explanans proper and which are relegated to background or field conditions can vary. Nevertheless—despite variations in best explanations with context—those best in any context must cite factors that help to account for the occurrence of their explananda. Hence, while pragmatic factors that affect the preferability of certain explanations cannot suffice to validate the principle of inference, neither do they block epistemic validation.

The normative argument of this book thus far has established the need for our inductive principle at every epistemic level of validation of empirical beliefs. The only alternative to acceptance of the principle, then, is skepticism of the most radical sort, which denies to us not only theoretical knowledge but knowledge expressed in everyday perceptual beliefs and even knowledge of how things appear. It might be objected, however, that knowledge of such matters would not be defeated absent the principle in question, but only the epistemologist's ability to reconstruct or demonstrate it. There is a difference, I maintained earlier, between the layman's and epistemologist's points of view, in that the layman may have knowledge without being able to demonstrate it or justify his beliefs. I also maintained that we (or our brains) do not explanatorily infer perceptual beliefs from ways of appearing (or from physical stimuli), although the epistemologist validates these beliefs via such inferences. Nevertheless, universal skepticism regarding empirical knowledge remains the rational alternative to acceptance of the inductive principle. While we may have knowledge without being able to demonstrate it, if we cannot demonstrate it then we have no good reason to deny skepticism. Without any good reason for believing that we have empirical knowledge at any level, skeptical agnosticism would seem the most rational stance. At least it would seem most rational for the epistemologist or the reflective inquirer whose beliefs have been challenged. (A seemingly stronger skepticism, skeptical atheism, would not really be stronger; indeed it would not be consistent, since it would claim that we know at least that we lack certain other knowledge.)

We may therefore view the inductive principle as a presupposition of all rational empirical inquiry. If its use does not lead to truth, then its failure implies that the world is not a place amenable to rational truth seeking by humans at all. It can then be considered a basic assumption of human rational inquiry. If, as truth seekers, we are to allow any assumptions, then one necessary to the very enterprise itself would seem the most innocuous. To say that we may assume this principle if we may assume anything and that this assumption is required to begin the process of inquiry if any assumption is required is a form of vindication for the principle. But it is a form of vindication closer than any other to epistemic justification. For our goal here is truth itself, and we must accept the principle in question in order to have any reasonable or reasoned chance at arriving at truth. At least we must accept it in order to have any reason for believing that we do arrive at empirical truth. Vindication even of this form remains a less than wholly satisfactory reply to the skeptic. It gives us no ultimate ground on which to stand epistemically. We can do somewhat better. Additional support for the principle can be derived from other inductive principles insofar as their joint use results in a coherent and plausible belief system, from iterative use of the principle itself at different levels, and from the content of beliefs derived through its use.

INDUCTIVE VALIDATION OF THE PRINCIPLE

Support for our principle is provided both by commonsense or instinctive commitments on the observational level and by principles of reasoning by analogy and by enumerative induction. We have noted that obvious fact that inferences to best explanations can be verified when the explanans refer to observables. We have also linked explanation to prediction that can be observationally verified both directly and indirectly. While best or deepest explanation is not necessary for prediction, which may express only observable regularities (themselves only weakly explanatory), deeper explanations, involving stronger probabilistic connections, often screen out superficial regularities. For example, doctors may be able to predict later symptoms of a disease from earlier ones without understanding the pathological condition that best explains them. But knowledge of that condition will screen out the more superficial connections for purposes of prediction as well, in that some of the symptoms may vary while the overall course of the disease does not. It is also true that some highly explanatory theories may be only weakly predictive. A prime example is Darwin's theory, which will be relevant to our later discussion. Although certain general predictions regarding the comings and goings of species issue from the theory, more detailed and specific ones would require more detailed knowledge of relevant initial conditions available, if at all, only in retrospect. Such examples, however, do not negate the connection, involving appeal to common probabilistic relations, between explanatory and predictive inferences.

That connection is relevant here because we take the connection between successful prediction and truth to be quite direct. From the commonsense viewpoint, predictions are successful when and only when they come true. This thesis for the most part survives deeper epistemic criticism, although verification by observation requires that the perceptual beliefs be validated via inferences to best explanations in the epistemologist's reconstruction. Despite that requirement, and despite the fact that our instinctive beliefs and attitudes in regard to certain types of properties require correction at deeper levels of theory, there remains a relation of mutual support between explanatory inference and observation. The relation is sustained partly through the connection with prediction and its verification.

We have seen that use of the principle of inference is extended from observational to nonobservational levels through a process of analogical reasoning. Analogy enters the extension in several ways. First, the unobservable realm is envisaged to be sufficiently analogous to the observable to allow the construction of explanatory models. These models are held to be similar to observable causal mechanisms and, if ideal, to real unobservable causes. Second, as we have seen, we may utilize an analogy between cases in which best explanations can be directly verified and cases in which only indirect testing is possible. Enumerative induction, closely related but perhaps not entirely reducible to reasoning by analogy and inference to the best explanation, operates in the extension of the latter to new domains beyond direct verification as well, along with principles of entropy and uniformity derived from the use of all three inductive principles (best explanation, analogy, and enumerative induction) applied to observational cases. We discover that orderly processes or regularities require explanations that appeal to deeper probabilistic connections, and we infer that these uniformities will extend into as yet unobserved or unobservable realms so as to allow for truthful inference to the best explanation there.

The principle of inference to the best explanation supports the other inductive principles as well as being supported by them. It supports enumerative induction, for example, both in specific contexts, in which regularities deeper than those observed are inferred to explain those observed, and in regard to its general reliability, since the best explanation for the many regularities displayed in nature appeals to nature's general lawlike character. Similarly, we may infer deeper explanations for extensions of observed analogies. The joint use of these inductive principles thus results in a coherent set of beliefs in which each source of empirical knowledge supports the others. The separate principles also seem necessary if they are jointly sufficient for any empirical knowledge at all. This of course does not guarantee the right sort of connection to the world for any of them but begins to indicate that criteria of coherence are better satisfied by the belief in the generally truth-preserving character of them all.

For the principle of inference to the best explanation in itself, yet stronger support stems from its iterative use in deriving further beliefs or theories from beliefs or theories derived from the principle's initial application. Here appeal to the models of evolution and adaptation to a selecting and resisting environment becomes relevant. Once we infer to independent objects as entering best explanations for appearances, selection by this environment is seen to operate at several levels and in several ways. We may claim that the pattern of inference itself must have been literally selected in the course of biological evolution, both because an analogue of the pattern (as I will explain below) operates at the perceptual level, where the organism must acquire information about its environment in order to survive, and because genuine explanatory inference at deeper levels enhances chances for the survival of the species as well. Furthermore, particular explanations or theories are selected by the environment, not in the literal, biological sense but in the extended sense in which exact predictions and delicate measuring operations must adapt to environmental inputs in testing for and eliminating alternatives.

It can be denied that natural selection is relevant to scientific inference in these ways, for example, on the ground that scientific theories were of no use in those primitive settings in which biological selection took place. Abilities with primitive weapons may have served purposes of preservation, but obviously neither advanced technology nor pure theory served any such purpose. In fact, in the more contemporary setting in which they function, technology, as an offshoot of pure theory, appears to threaten survival as much as enhance its chances. It may be pointed out also that, where selection has operated, for example, in relation to the evolution of sensory organs, the result is not taken to be pure revelation of truth about the physical environment. Things generally do not appear as they are, colors being a primary example, as emphasized above. In fact, the evolutionary point of view seems incompatible with a naive realism for perceptual beliefs, since the sensory organs of primitive species and of the most sophisticated (not necessarily humans) are alike products of selection through interaction with natural environments. Speaking not simply of survival but of other biologically conditioned general aims such as happiness makes matters only worse, since we know of wildly untrue myths that have served these aims as well as or better than seemingly true theories. Thus both the claim that natural selection has relevance for the pattern of inference captured by our principle and the thesis that selection, if relevant, connects it to truth can be contested and stand in need of further defense.

The defense of the former claim—that of the influence of selection—appeals again, in greater detail, to the continuity between perception and inferential forms of intelligence, to the survival value of explanatory inference itself in its general operation, and to the extended sense in which even sophisticated theoretical inferences are subject to environmental selection. Regarding the first point, while I denied in chapter 6 both that perception involves literal inferences from ways of appearing and that the brain literally infers from physical stimuli, I noted that perceptual beliefs arise *as if* inferred from stimuli whose contents do not entail those of the beliefs. We may therefore think of an analogue of explanatory inference as wired into our perceptual apparatus as a product of evolutionary selection. We also saw, in chapter 1, an analogue of explanatory inference in prediction as a form of probabilistic reasoning, a form with obvious evolutionary value. Both analogies express cognitive continuities that should lead us to expect survival value for the general form of reasoning captured in our principle of inference. In fact, we have claimed that explanations themselves are often most predictive on the observable level when they screen out more superficial regularities. This feature of explanations suggests that the pattern of inference itself may have been selected. Survival value may be found at deeper levels of inference too. Explanatory theories may primarily serve the purpose of simply satisfying our curiosity to know, but that drive and the hypothetical forms of reasoning that express it greatly enhance the capability of the species to cope with different and changing environments. First, such reasoning allows surrogate experience to develop in thought and so helps the reasoners to avoid many life-threatening encounters. Second, while sophisticated modern technologies may threaten the continuation of the species, there can be no doubt that the technological product of explanatory theory in the broadest scheme of things has reshaped a variety of environments in a way that best explains the present dominance of the species.

It is plausible then to view the pattern of reasoning captured by our principle of inference as a literal outcome of natural selection. We are still a large step from the validation of the principle's later products. Specific theories are not biologically selected. Nevertheless, we can claim that literal selection of the general pattern of reasoning is relevant at all levels if we can show that the selection of cognitive processes depended generally on the processes' truth-producing or truth-preserving character and if there is no reason to suspect a discontinuity in this respect between directly verifiable and theoretical inferences. Additionally, in an extended sense, environmental pressures (in the form of experimental results) select theories. This process of selection is real, despite the influence of theory itself on the design and interpretation of experiment. And despite the merely analogous relation of such selection to biological selection, they are equally relevant to the defense of the principle and of its products as true, if probable truth is selected in the same way in both cases. It remains then for us to show how selection of the nonbiological sort operates upon genuine theory, how this contrived environmental selection is analogous to natural selection, and why environmental constraints of both sorts lead to approximate truth.

In regard to theory acceptance and rejection, it can be denied that experimental testing is sufficiently analogous to render even the metaphor of selection appropriate. Disanalogies abound. On the environmental side, the environment that is to select among competing theories is often specifically designed to do so. An experiment may be designed to test specific parts of theories while other parts are presupposed in the interpretation of the operation of the apparatus itself. Such environments are often highly artificial, created so that regularities observable in the experimental conditions approximate to laws governing ideal models of the theories under test. On the side of theory, we find not random variation, as among biological species, but intelligent design, and preservation in the face of environmental adversity (anomaly) until an even more intelligently designed theory emerges. In combination, these features can suggest the Kuhnian model in which theories and associated experimental procedures together determine a set of problems for practicing scientists and the order of standards by which solutions are to be appraised.

These disanalogies, however, do not override the similarities between the two types of selection or objective constraint that suggest similar relations between the cognitive products of these selective processes and the goal of true description. First, the relation of theory to experiment is not always as described above. Sometimes, for example, an "environmental niche" in the form of a well-defined set of experimental data exists prior to a plausi-

ble theory that fits it.[4] Perhaps also the intelligent design of
theory to fit data as explananda often masks an earlier process of
"random variation" or trial and error (in action, thought, or
subconscious brain processes) upon which it builds.[5]

Second, and more important, even when experiment and
theory are as described above, the disanalogies with processes
of natural selection need not override analogies relevant to the
emergence of accurate representation. Even when experiments
are designed specifically to confirm or complete (by filling in
values for constants) accepted theories or to test competing alternatives, and even when their outcomes are interpreted with
concepts from the theories themselves, the outcomes may nevertheless express selection by objective constraints. The effect of
these constraints becomes more obvious when the results of
differently designed experimental procedures converge in a
common best explanation. The very fact that theories of different apparatuses and procedures mesh with a common theory of
unobservable processes, and the fact that alternatives to the
latter are less likely to mesh as well as it does the broader the
diversity among the procedures, attest to the efficacy of the
experiments in selecting among possible competing alternatives. Actual random variations are not required for selection to
operate in a way that justifies the claim of objective constraints.
Despite this possible disanalogy with natural selection and another deriving from the artificiality of experimental contexts, it
remains true that theories must adapt to environmental input
in the form of experimental outcome, in precisely the sense in
which variations, although not random, are eliminated by failure to fit an objective, although not natural, environment. Just
as the relativity of explanation to explanatory purpose does not
imply a lack of objectivity from the side of theory, given that all
factors cited as explanatory must contribute to the probabilities
of explananda, so the interaction between design of theory and
design and interpretation of experiment does not imply a lack
of objective pressure from the side of testing, given that fit is
never an automatic product of that interaction.

If we accept this dual relevance of selection, both natural and
contrived, to the principle of inference, the central question
becomes whether the fact of such control by the environment

indicates a tendency toward truth in what is selected. In beginning to answer this second question, let us look again at the most basic levels at which inference to the best explanation, or something analogous to it, operates. Both negative and positive arguments regarding the relevance of selection to truth derive from the continuities between perceptual and inferential forms of intelligence. In noting that things do not appear perceptually as they are (or at least that we do not take them to be as they appear perceptually when we infer to deeper explanatory accounts), in regard to colors, for example, one can generalize to question any connection between truth and selection or usefulness for behavior. If the only objective constraint is that of natural selection, and if this process fails to generate true belief at the perceptual level, where the historical process of control is most plausible, why should we believe that truth-preserving mechanisms are selected at levels of inference further removed from the course of natural evolution?

The question underestimates both the influence of selection for patterns of reasoning themselves and the connection between selection and truth at the perceptual level. While ways of appearing may be deceptive in regard to the objectivity of certain kinds of properties, it still seems that modes of perception must reveal much (truthful) information about the environment, for example, regarding object boundaries and locations, in order to be useful and hence to be selected. Even systematically deceptive appearances are taken to correlate approximately with differences in objective properties. Consider, for example, our taking objects to be (or to appear) green rather than grue. Presumably the former predicate is natural for us because projecting perceived color properties in this way has been selected. Presumably it has been selected because it has been more useful over time, and has been more useful because it is more closely correlated with objective properties. One may wonder how selection could work in such cases. If we define 'grue', as is sometimes done, as 'green before the year 2,000 and blue afterward', then the predicates would have generated the same expectations in the era when natural selection took place. But there are a series of related definitions for similar predicates such that, over time, they correlate less well with objective properties than do natural predicates. (These claims rest on inferences to the best explanation, but I am arguing here only for the iteration of the principle in relation to its products.)

Thus there appears to be some connection between selection and approximately truthful information at the perceptual level. When we infer to deeper explanatory levels, we take ourselves to be correcting for purely subjective contributions to the contents of perceptual beliefs. We infer to the objective causes of such beliefs, that is, the physical world. It is true that the only constraint is that of environmental input, both in the historical process of biological selection and at the sensory nerve endings. But at the deeper, objective level we may add to the selection of the pattern of reasoning itself the much finer adaptations in behavior required to accommodate inputs in the form of precise measurements and to reshape the environment with advanced technology. While explanatory inferences and predictions from everyday observations are more directly confirmed or disconfirmed and, hence, more directly controlled by objective encounters, deeper ones tend to be more exact and in that way more sensitive to correction by controlled environmental input. Given this additional objective control operating on the products of explanatory inferences as the inferences are extended to new explanans, as well as the idea of correction operative on the deeper levels, we have more rather than less reason for taking the products of conscious explanatory inferences, as opposed to naive perceptual commitments, to be true. There is an additional layer of coherence on the deeper level as well, in that our theories of measuring instruments cohere with our taking the explanations confirmed by measurements to be true. Our theories of sensory systems, on the other hand, do not cohere with a naive realist view of all qualities that appear to them.

I admitted above that a rival explanation for the success of explanatory inferences in science is possible. The rival states that such inferences are designed to capture regularities on the observable level, which regularities, if real and sufficiently broad, will continue to confirm the inferences even if their conclusions are not true (truly descriptive) and their referents not real. There is no account of the general success of the inferential pattern to rival that which appeals to the pattern's truth-preserving tendency. The lack of plausible alternatives is clear when we attempt to explain successful behavior, either animal or human, from a commonsense, third-person point of view. Any explanation that bases successful action on total misconception or lack of relevant information requires many more premises, normally having little plausibility. Precisely because of the lack of rival explanations, the principle is self-supporting when used to infer to directly confirmable explanatory accounts (at least those not overridden by later and deeper accounts). In addition to noting the possibility of an alternative explanation for the success of science, I argued that we have no reason to expect the (shifting) line of physical observability to mark epistemic discontinuities. Given those arguments and the fact that the rival explanation for scientific progress was found to be, all things considered (after the independent inference to unobservable causes), less plausible than the realist's explanation, we again have ample reason for generalizing the connection between objective pressure and truth found at the level of observation or perception.

One may still wonder how the environment could select for truth at any level, as opposed to empirical adequacy or predictiveness on the level of experience. Psychological processes and theories that are behaviorally successful should be selected, but we know that there will be incompatible theories (and perhaps processes as well) that will have equal observational and hence behavioral consequences. How could the environment select from among these? When it comes to theories, we choose those that appear simpler and otherwise more plausible. These criteria are to be linked to truth via the selection of psychological processes that determine what seems to us simpler and more plausible. But might not different processes generate behavioral success, such that what appears simpler to one person appears more complex or incomprehensible to others? Once more, how could the environment choose from among these? The real question, however, is whether a cognitive or perceptual process would be likely to be useful if it did not yield information about the environment that selects it on that basis. An explanation of selection that posits behavioral success in an environment whose nature entirely escapes us, without positing the causal mechanisms underlying behavioral success, must also elude our grasp completely. (Again, I am arguing only for the iteration of the principle in relation to an objective environment to which we infer by using it.)

I shall conclude this chapter with some comments on the structure of the argument presented here, but a brief review of its main steps might be in order first. After arguing that other accepted sources of knowledge and principles of inductive inference support and are supported by the principle of inference to the best explanation, I argued that the principle receives additional support through iteration in relation to its early products. Specifically, once we infer to an independent, objective realm as part of the best explanation for sequences of appearances, we recognize that both the pattern of reasoning and particular theories or explanatory inferences must be seen as products of selection. The inference pattern is plausibly viewed as having been naturally selected for its usefulness on all levels. On the level of observables, the tendency toward truth provides the only plausible explanation for that usefulness. While a rival explanation for the success of science is possible, it is more plausible to accept an explanation analogous to that on the level of observables; that is, it is more plausible to extend the relation between selection of best explanations and truth to deeper levels of explanation as well, given the greater degree of control by environmental input there and the correction for initially dominant subjective factors in later theoretical inferences.

It is obvious that the justification offered here for the principle of inference to the best explanation is coherentist (more pejoratively, circular). We have recognized the unavoidability of appeal to coherence, including explanatory coherence, as the fundamental criterion of justification. This appeal is inevitable both because we cannot escape our beliefs to compare them with reality and because ultimately basic epistemic principles cannot be validated by appeal to more basic principles. But mutual support among such principles and between them and their products is not necessarily viciously circular. Regarding our inability to escape the circle of beliefs, coherence becomes problematic as a criterion of truth only when it remains unconnected to foundational empirical beliefs that ground it to objective reality. In our reconstruction the criterion of explanatory coherence provides such grounding when applied to certain beliefs about appearances. Regarding the ultimacy of first principles, many philosophers have noted that the justification of deductive principles is analogous in this respect. We can demonstrate that deduction preserves truth given the ways we define the connectives and operators, but the demonstration requires deduction at every step. I argued earlier that deductive principles as we know and use them may be indispensable to reasoning of any significant complexity. But I made a similar claim as to the indispensability of our inductive principle for empirical knowledge.

Regarding circularity in general, questions are begged and validations rendered useless when full statements of premises explicitly contain the conclusions they are intended to support. That is not the case here. While the principle to be validated and others of equal status were used in the justificatory argument, that argument contained no premises stating the principles in question. One may wonder where the difference lies between presupposing (the validity of) a principle by using it and explicitly stating it in the premises of the argument. The difference is that use of a principle in its own validation does not necessarily trivialize the procedure, whereas genuinely question-begging arguments are trivial and of no interest. The validation here is not trivial or question-begging because the use of the principle did not make the desired result automatic. The conclusion that use of the principle tends to preserve truth was not foregone. In fact, we saw in an earlier chapter that it becomes problematic at a certain depth to continue taking seemingly best explanations to be true. Our skepticism was limited there to some very late products of the principle, for example, quantum theory. But it would certainly have been possible, had similar problems emerged early and often, to impugn the reliability of the principle by appeal to its own use. Hence the circularity of our validation does not trivialize the mode of argument, as it would if the conclusion were present in a full statement of the premises.

The main problem, once coherence among principles and

their products is established, is to link the criterion of coherence with the notion of truth as correspondence. We have seen that our application of the coherence criterion generates a requirement for correspondence, in that explanatory coherence (depth) increases by an inference to realism, which in turn, by implying the logical insufficiency of coherence itself, implies a correspondence notion of truth. But I have argued here that the use of a coherence criterion also establishes the required link between explanatory inference and truth. If my premises are correct, then the coherentist can reject neither the correspondence notion of truth nor the validation of the principle of inference. We can note once more that the real contest is between the radical skeptic and the more optimistic realist. As in ethics, the skeptic who refuses to accept any premises or principles cannot be reasoned out of his position. In our case, however, we have been able to show not only that our principle is indispensable in providing reasons for believing that we have any empirical knowledge at all but also that it is more reasonable (coherent) to believe that there are overriding reasons of this sort.

PART IV
REFERENCE

14
CRITERIA

The normative argument of this book thus far has presupposed that we can refer to independent objects whose real properties are only contingently related to the ways they appear. It remains to sharpen up the notion of independence contained in the realist's thesis and to fill in an account of reference that will justify what has been assumed until now. In light of various arguments by semantic antirealists, the very intelligibility of the realist's position must be defended. I argued earlier that a priori arguments in defense of this position fail. But semantic antirealists maintain that reference requires conceptual, a priori, or necessary links between conditions taken to warrant the ascription of properties to objects and conditions in which those ascriptions are true. Some take these connections to fall short of entailment: meanings of empirical statements are only partially specified in terms of warranting or justification conditions. Others take truth to reduce completely to warranted assertibility or justification. In either case objective properties lose the independence from our concepts and experiences (warranting conditions) that the realist thesis demands. The possibility of global skepticism (the thesis that our most warranted theories could contain wholesale falsity), which I have claimed to be entailed by realism, is lost. The skeptic's thesis becomes not simply false but unintelligible, in violation of rules of language.

In this chapter I shall criticize the Wittgensteinian notion of criteria as involving necessary or a priori connections short of entailment. In the next chapter I will turn to some arguments that attempt to reduce the notion of truth entirely to that of warranted assertibility.

CRITERIA AND LEARNING LANGUAGE

The term 'criteria' was used earlier to refer to necessary conditions for the proper application of concepts. This use is compatible with the claim that such conditions, when not simply consisting in the presence of the object or property in question, i.e., in truth conditions, are inductive indicators of that presence. In the post-Wittgensteinian literature the term has had a different sense. It has been used in antiskeptical arguments to indicate noninductive or necessary evidence, or a priori, conceptual, or semantic links between apparent and real properties, observable and unobservable properties, or between properties and the objects to which they are ascribed.[1] Criterial properties, in these arguments, constitute noninductive evidence short of entailment. While their ascriptions do not entail statements of the presence of that for which they are criteria, it is supposed to be a necessary truth that normally the two are linked. This connection is knowable a priori and is a matter of meaning or linguistic rule. Such is held to be the connection between appearing yellow under white light and being yellow; between being yellow, ovate, waxy skinned, acidic tasting, grown on trees, and being a lemon; and between moaning, writhing, clutching parts of one's body and being in pain. The skeptic who admits the presence of such criteria but questions the presence of their criterial relata, not simply in specific instances but in general, violates rules of language and therefore fails to be intelligible. His position could not possibly be correct. But the intelligibility and possible truth of global skepticism is entitled by the realist's thesis that objects and their properties remain independent from our experiences and concepts. He must therefore reject widespread appeal to criterial connections in the strong sense of 'criteria' indicated.

Beyond avoiding such appeal, I shall argue that the notion of evidence short of entailment, which is nevertheless necessarily evidence, itself cannot be instantiated. Furthermore, the relations between appearance and reality and between properties and objects that instantiate them are not known a priori but, as I have mentioned, inferred inductively. (Epistemic validation of beliefs in these relations rests on inductive inference.) Let us first examine criteriologists' arguments to the conclusion that such relations must be known a priori, not inductively. These arguments trade on the slogan 'meaning is use' and on a certain view of how reference is learned and understanding of terms achieved.

The crucial feature of criteria that is supposed to entail their peculiar evidential status is that only on the basis of them can one pick out or identify that for which they are criteria. Since we can pick out real objects and properties only on the basis of their criteria—those immediately accessible conditions in which we teach people how to apply terms to them—the application of terms or concepts must be correct when and only when such criterial conditions obtain. One understands a term or concept when one can apply it correctly, when one can distinguish things or properties to which it correctly applies from those to which it does not. Meaning is what one understands when one understands how to use a term. Hence the meanings of terms are specified in terms of those criteria according to which they are correctly applied. In this account, meaning determines reference. Reference is secured, therefore, only via knowledge of criterial conditions. A term referring to real properties or objects therefore refers to whichever ones are present when their criterial conditions obtain. We identify properties and objects only by experiencing those conditions that constitute criteria for their presence, for the proper application of terms or concepts to them.

The account states further that when warranting conditions for statements fall short of truth conditions, which is the case when we refer to real properties and objects observed (if at all) only in virtue of our experiencing their criterial conditions, then it is impossible to state nontrivial conditions which entail that the properties or objects are present and to know when such conditions obtain. Regarding the relation of apparent to real properties, it is held, for example, that objects which appear yellow in normal conditions are yellow. But it is clear that such an object would not be yellow if the physical basis for its color appearance changed whenever it was not being perceived. Similarly, a lemon is a yellow, waxy-skinned fruit, but such a fruit is not a lemon if it has large purple seeds and sprouts into a pine tree when planted. Obviously it is not possible to list all bizarre exceptions in advance, so correct entailments cannot be achieved by that method. While for some terms, for example those referring to appearances, meanings are stipulated in terms of conditions that entail correct application, and for some statements, for example those specifying certain ways things appear, meanings are stipulated directly in terms of truth conditions, the meanings of terms and statements referring to the real must be given in terms of conditions that guarantee not truth but justified application—that is, in terms of criteria.

Since the satisfaction of criteria does not entail truth, the account continues, we cannot say that statements of criterial conditions exhaust meanings. We cannot mean by saying that something is F only that the criteria for being F are satisfied, when it is possible that they be satisfied when the thing is not F. If we say that something is F, we cannot mean that it is probably F but may not be (why not just say that?). A standard criterion of correct translation is preservation of truth. If a sentence in English can be true when one in French is false, one cannot be a translation of the other. Yet the lack of entailment implies that a statement affirming the satisfaction of criteria may be true when a statement affirming the presence of the property or object for which they are criteria is not. Therefore the meaning of the statement that something is F cannot be exhausted by saying that the criteria for being F are satisfied. The full meaning of such statements can be stipulated, if at all, only by stating the conditions under which the statements are true.

The conclusion for the criteriologist, however, is not that meanings must be stated in terms of truth conditions, but rather that they cannot be fully specified in a nontrivial or noncircular way. The best we can do in teaching meanings and uses of terms referring to the real is to point out or describe criterial conditions in which the terms are properly ascribed. But there remains a conceptual or necessary connection between the experienceable criteria and the properties and objects whose presence they indicate. According to the criteriologist, the alternative to recognizing such connections is skepticism. To establish a merely contingent connection between appearance and reality or between objects and their properties would require an independent way to pick out or identify the real objects. But this is precisely what we lack. The skeptic cannot possibly be right, however, since we must in fact refer to whatever stands in the proper semantic relation to those criterial conditions that govern the use of the term in question. The semantic relation is specified as follows: *necessarily* that which satisfies the criteria for being F *normally* is F. This relation is learned by learning the linguistic rule governing the use of the term that refers to F. Since it is necessary that whatever satisfies the criteria for being F normally is F, it is also necessarily true that satisfying the criteria constitutes evidence for being F. The semantic relation implies a noncontingent epistemic relation.

It is supposed then to be a necessary, conceptual truth that what appears yellow in normal conditions is yellow. If something appears yellow but is not, then conditions are not normal. Being yellow *is* just appearing that way normally. This is not simply a matter of fact but a matter of meaning. (Contrast the discussion of colors in chapter 12.) Similarly, a lemon simply *is* a yellow, ovate, waxy-skinned fruit. This is part of what we mean by 'lemon', despite possible bizarre exceptions. The term 'real' no longer signifies independence from our conceptual scheme. Rather, it becomes a term of contrast with 'merely apparent', where mere appearance indicates abnormal conditions. The relativity of the real to the normal conditions in which we apply our concepts and to what we experience in those conditions may be an unhappy consequence for the realist. But according to the semantic epistemology outlined here, it is a correlate of the only way we can learn to refer with our terms and pick out properties and objects with our concepts. The positive corollary is that the skeptic is provided with a short and decisive answer.

NECESSARY AND A PRIORI EVIDENCE

We may begin our criticism of the semantics of criteria by considering more closely to the notion of necessary evidence. Can F necessarily be evidence for G when there is no relation of entailment between them (between statements ascribing them)? We have noted that the satisfaction of criteria indicates the presence of that for which they are criteria only in the context of certain other regularities or in the absence of defeating conditions. Something that appears yellow in normal conditions is yellow, but not if it would appear blue if perceived when not being perceived (and not, as argued earlier, if it would appear different shades to normal perceivers in the same external conditions). A yellow, ovate fruit is a lemon, but not if it would sprout a pine tree if planted. Belief in real objects or properties of certain kinds therefore implies commitment to a nonenumerable list of counterfactuals. The criteriologist claims that the truth of all such defeating counterfactuals entails abnormal conditions, so that it remains a necessary truth that criteria normally determine true ascription of real properties. Can this claim be maintained?

The question is how it can be necessarily true that such conditions are abnormal; for if it is only contingently true, then the idea of necessary evidence collapses. It cannot be necessarily true that F is evidence for G unless it is necessarily true that F normally indicates G. It cannot be necessarily true that F normally indicates G unless F normally indicates G in all possible worlds. If we think of possible objects in all possible worlds, it seems that appearing yellow in daylight is just as much evidence of the changeable object mentioned above as it is evidence of yellow objects. A world in which yellow, waxy-skinned fruits had purple seeds and sprouted pine trees would be a world in which our criteria for lemons normally indicate things quite different.[2] That which is necessarily true is true in all possible worlds. But it is not true that conditions normal in our world are normal in all possible worlds. It is therefore clearly false to say that conditions normal in our world are necessarily normal. But then what is abnormal in our world is not necessarily abnormal. For criteria to be satisfied in the absence of that for which they are criterial in our world does not necessarily signify abnormality. Hence, criteria are not necessarily evidence (although in fact they are evidence, i.e., inductive evidence).[3]

Given any noncircular stipulation of normal conditions, it cannot be necessary that such conditions are or remain normal. But suppose we simply define normal conditions as those in which criteria connect to their real properties or objects. If we simply legislate normal conditions as those in which criteria for an object indicate its presence rather than the presence of one of the other strange objects we can imagine, then we might get a necessary truth, but not a very interesting or serviceable one. For it will not then be necessary that normal conditions as so defined normally, usually, or for that matter ever obtain. Not only could we not know a priori that normal conditions normally obtain if normal conditions are defined as those in which things and properties appear as they are; we would in fact require criteria by which to identify such objective conditions. The epistemic problem would shift from that of finding out when real properties and objects are present to that of finding out when conditions for observing them are normal. This is the same problem in a different guise. The regress in regard to the need for experienceable criteria would be vicious. The criteriologist then cannot define normal conditions both as those normally obtaining in our world and as those in which criteria are always evidence for their objects. Yet he needs both for his concept of necessary evidence.

There are, it is true, related senses of both 'normal' and 'real' in which the real is relative to those conditions viewed as normal. This is a pragmatic sense of 'real' according to which we identify things for everyday purposes in terms of their real colors, shapes, sizes, etc. What is important for everyday purposes of identification is that the properties in question be relatively stable. By contrast, 'merely apparent' qualities are too variable to be usable for identifying things to others. In this context normal conditions themselves vary according to usefulness. Normal conditions for identifying colors—daylight or white light—often obtain. Those for identifying shapes—viewpoints perpendicular to surfaces—rarely occur. They are considered normal because no more usually occupied viewpoints reveal more stable properties and because at those angles seen shapes most closely approximate to felt and measured shapes. With size, normal conditions are a matter of approximating to a relation to a conventional standard, once more a matter of convenience. In none of these cases do normal conditions necessarily reveal metaphysically privileged or independent properties. The sense of 'real' that is relative to some definition of normal conditions is purely pragmatic and apt to mislead the metaphysician or epistemologist if he assumes a deeper significance for it.[4]

In like manner we can relativize ascriptions of properties to the satisfaction of experienced criteria only if we recognize such properties to be relational. For any way F that x appears in conditions K, we can assign a property G to x which causes it to appear or is its disposition to appear that way in those conditions. We can then leave further description of that property unspecified. But if we are after true description of real objects, there will remain a seemingly intelligible question as to the nonrelational or independent properties these objects have. For the realist, the notion of an object with no properties apart from its relations to human subjects is empty. But we cannot simply adopt linguistic conventions for assigning real properties to objects. We cannot simply decide that certain experiences will count as evidence for them. We must rather show why those experiences render the instantiation of such properties as we describe probable. Our linguistic conventions regarding justification must be governed by what we take to be real connections rather than the converse. As such they are always subject to question and revision.

Having dismissed the notion of necessary evidence for real properties, we must still address the argument that, where criterial conditions constitute the only type of evidence for certain properties or objects, indeed constitute the only means of identifying properties and objects observable (if at all) only in virtue of experiencing such conditions, the connection between criteria and the properties and objects identified by means of them cannot be merely contingent. If one understands the meaning of a term when one knows how to use it properly, and if proper use is governed only by the criteria according to which it is applied, then it may seem again that the connection between criteria and that for which they are criteria must be a matter of meaning. If, as realists, we continue to think of meaning in terms of truth conditions, it still seems that, if we are to be able to distinguish correct from incorrect usage of language, we must be able to tell when such conditions obtain. But we can tell only on the basis of criteria. How then can ascription of properties on this basis be generally mistaken?

If people call things F on the basis of certain criteria, then it seems it can be known a priori that some things that satisfy the criteria are F. This will not be necessarily true, since the world could have been such that all things satisfying the criteria also had other qualities that disqualified them from being F, as in the worlds imagined above. Nevertheless, it can be claimed still to be a rule of language in our world that things which satisfy the criteria are F, a rule of language subject to change if conditions drastically alter. The argument now admits that rules of language operate only within given empirical contexts, but holds that, where they do operate, one can acquire knowledge on the basis of them that it would be gratuitous if not nonsensical for a skeptic to question. Despite the counterargument above, then, the criteriologist may still have an effective weapon against the skeptic. Although the criterial relation does not amount to necessity, nevertheless a connection in virtue of a linguistic rule, which can be known without examining particular objects, may be sufficient for his armchair refutation of skepticism.

We may evaluate this remaining argument first in relation to objects for which certain properties are supposed to be criterial, and then in relation to real properties for which certain appearances are taken as criterial. We may grant that lemons, for example, are what most people call lemons. That is, it makes no sense to say that 'lemon' does not properly apply to lemons, at least in our world. If we call things lemons on the basis of such properties as being yellow, ovate, etc., then it seems to make no sense to deny that lemons have such properties. But the question remains for the skeptic and the realist whether it *is* on the basis of such real properties that lemons are identified. In fact we will apply the term 'lemon' to whatever *appears* yellow, etc., to us, but that does not give us a priori knowledge that things which really are yellow (if such there be) are what we call lemons (are lemons), or that what we call lemons really are yellow. As long as there exists some shared basis of agreement on when to apply the term, we can achieve consistent application. But this shared basis can consist in common ways of appearing rather than in the common apprehension of real properties.

If we call things lemons on the basis of how they appear, then perhaps we can know simply by knowing our language that lemons (if there are such objects) appear yellow, ovate, etc. But this is not knowledge of necessary truths, since lemons might have appeared differently. Nor is it knowledge required for the ability to refer to lemons. Children lack concepts of appearing and hence knowledge of appearances (although they ascribe properties according to how things appear to them), but they have no trouble referring to things like lemons. Finally, such knowledge does not generate a priori knowledge of real properties. It is useless as a weapon against Cartesian skepticism, which remains fully intelligible. Thus what can be known a priori about objects lacks other relations to them that criterial properties are supposed to bear.

What, however, of the argument that real properties themselves are assigned only on the basis of common ways of appearing? If the connection here can be known a priori, then the points of the previous two paragraphs are nullified. While it is true that we ascribe properties to objects when they appear to us in certain ways in everyday contexts, it is not true that such properties can be defined or analyzed (even partially) in terms of their appearances. For many properties there is not even the temptation to do so. The property of squareness (and other shapes), for example, is not whatever property appears square to us in normal conditions. It rather has an objective, structural definition. Here it is clearly a contingent matter whether objects with that objective structure appear square to us. It is a matter of how our sense organs receive such information from the environment. We see from such cases that the fact that our only evidence for ascribing such properties to objects derives from sense experience does not imply that the relation between appearance and reality must be noncontingent or a matter of convention.

We also see that, while we must be able to conceive or state truth conditions for statements in order to analyze meanings in terms of such conditions, we need not be able to do so in terms of experiences that verify the truth of those statements. This is clear from other examples as well. The atheist may count as perfectly intelligible talk of a deity and know which properties such a being would have without being willing to count any conceivable experi-

ences as confirming divine presence or existence, the instantiation of those properties. At worst he could dismiss all such
experiences as hallucinatory. His understanding of religious discourse consists in his knowing what would make such discourse
true, not in his willingness to countenance confirming experiences, even those taken to be criterial by believers.

The case of squareness shows that, even where there is only
one kind of evidence for the presence of a particular kind of
property, this does not mean that our concept or term for the
property must be defined, wholly or partly, in terms of such
evidential conditions. There is an ambiguity in the notion of
'picking out' or 'identifying' in the criteriologist's argument. We
can identify, that is, have a concept of, a property by knowing
how it is or would be instantiated (truth conditions), without
specifying such conditions in terms of possible experiences (warranting conditions). The case of religious discourse shows that
we can identify, that is, define, objects in terms of properties
that we never take to be experienced or instantiated, nor even
conceivably experienced. The case of lemons shows that we can
identify, that is, refer to, everyday objects on the basis of how
they appear, rather than by experiencing their real properties.
Neither identification in the sense of conception or definition
nor identification in the sense of reference, then, requires
knowledge of real properties as they are instantiated. (A positive account of reference will follow in chapter 16.)

There is also an ambiguity, in the criteriologist's argument, in
the notion of 'correct application' of terms or concepts. Application that is correct for everyday purposes or that accords with
conditions in which terms are taught and learned can be questioned in metaphysical or epistemological contexts, when it is a
matter of ascribing properties taken to be nonrelational or independent of our experiences. Of some such properties, those
considered simple or undefinable by earlier philosophers, we
would lack concepts if we did not experience instantiations. We
might not have had the concept of yellowness, for example, if
we had not experienced it. Furthermore, we are taught to apply
the term 'yellow' directly to objects when we do experience
yellowness. Later we are taught to restrict that application to
certain conditions in which things appear yellow. None of these

facts entails that those things to which we are taught to apply the term really are yellow, as opposed to merely appearing yellow. I have argued that common appearances suffice for such teaching and learning. In fact, as the possibility of spectrum inversion shows, even common appearances are not required: structurally similar or covariant appearances would suffice. Application that is correct in such conditions for everyday purposes of identification or public reference is not necessarily correct in ascribing real properties. In the case of secondary qualities such as colors, there is some temptation to define these in terms of how they normally appear. But we have seen that the attempt to identify colors with real physical properties that cause particular ways of appearing in normal conditions fails on empirical grounds.

The philosopher may then sensibly question whether objects really have the properties they appear to have in normal conditions and whether there really are objects with properties as they appear to him. In raising such questions he does not reveal a misunderstanding of property or object terms, as would a two-year-old if he were to question whether 'yellow' properly applies to lemons. The skeptical philosopher raises the question in a different sense, and the criteriologist offers no adequate reply in assimilating the two cases.

As for skepticism's being the only alternative to criteriology, the earlier inductive argument of this book represents a rejection of that claim. We can "identify," that is, refer to, real objects on the basis of how they appear without "identifying," that is, defining, their real properties in terms of appearances. We can then link appearances with real properties inductively. In that way we show connections among our concepts to be based on real connections in the world, rather than relying on the shaky distinction between meaning and belief in refuting the skeptic.

15
SEMANTIC ANTIREALISM

The argument regarding criteria, set out in the previous chapter, exploited the differences, granted by the criteriologist, between justification and truth conditions and between apparent and real properties and objects. Given the realist's notions of the latter, there could be neither necessary nor a priori connections between the apparent or the immediately accessible and the real. Semantic antirealists challenge the legitimacy of the distinction between justification or warranted assertibility and truth, or the legitimacy of the realist's appeal to truth. They typically question how reference could be made to objects whose real properties transcend conditions that warrant us in ascribing them. I shall discuss the arguments of two semantic antirealists, Dummett and Putnam, in this chapter and suggest a positive account of reference in the next.

MEANING AND TRUTH

Earlier I stated that Dummett's definition of realism is acceptable as a partial account, as stating a necessary condition for the truth of the realist's thesis. Throughout the long history of the realism-idealism debate, the realist has encountered notorious difficulty in specifying clearly the notion of independence involved in his claim that the world is independent of our perceptions and concepts. Dummett has suggested a way of specifying this notion that interprets realism as a semantic and epistemological, as much as a metaphysical, thesis.[1] For him the realist's claim is precisely that meaning must be defined in terms of truth conditions and that truth must be contrasted with verification or warranted assertibility. The realist takes his assertions to state that their truth conditions are satisfied, whether or not we are in a position to tell that they are. We know the meaning of an assertion when we know what would make it true, not simply what counts as evidence for its truth. The independence in question is the irreducibility of truth to warrant, coupled with the analysis of meaning in terms of truth conditions.

Dummett's account of realism is only partial, because he has stated only a necessary condition for its truth. That meaning is analyzed in terms of truth conditions (rather than conditions of warranted assertibility) entails that we intend our terms to refer to a determinately structured, independent reality, that we assert the existence of such states of affairs. It does not show that these states of affairs obtain or that our realist concepts are instantiated. But while not sufficient for the truth of realism, the truth conditions analysis of meaning and the contrast between truth and assertibility are necessary for the intelligibility of the realist's thesis.

In assessing that thesis we should avoid equating Dummett's acceptable (partial) formulation with another that he sometimes claims to be equivalent. For him the truth conditions analysis equates with the principle of bivalence, the idea that each statement is determinately true or false. Several paths lead to this equation, the clearest through the conception of a realist theory of meaning along Tarskian or Davidsonian lines. A Tarskian theory of truth entails all sentences of the form 'S is true iff p', where S names the sentence that replaces p or when p translates the sentence named by S. An example of such a sentence is ' "Snow is white" is true iff snow is white'. If a theory of this form is to serve as the realist's complete theory of meaning, it seems that he must accept the principle of bivalence. Otherwise, the designated sentence in the Tarskian schema might fail to be true (making everything to the left of the biconditional false) when the sentence on the right is not false. The equivalence will then fail.

Bivalence might also seem on intuitive grounds to be a requirement for the realist. The crucial cases for his position appear to be those in which there is no overriding evidence for a statement or class of statements, or those in which statements are conceived as possibly false despite the balance of evidence as projected indefinitely into the future. Here he claims that such statements can be true or false independently of the evidence. Lack of evidence does not imply lack of truth or falsity, and positive evidence does not rule out falsity. Concentrating on the realist's claims in regard to such cases can easily lead one to generalize to the principle of bivalence, to the claim that all statements are determinately true or false (whatever the evidence for them might be).

Despite such considerations, bivalence is neither necessary nor sufficient for realism, semantic or otherwise. Regarding sufficiency, consider phenomenalism as a form of antirealism regarding physical objects. The truth values of statements about objects are not logically independent of statements of their total evidence on this view, but the principle of bivalence may be satisfied. The phenomenalist translates physical object statements into subjunctive conditionals referring to possible experiences. If such conditionals are provided only when supported by sensory evidence, and if the evidence is taken to entail the truth of the translated statements, then the principle of bivalence will be satisfied.

The point is more easily made in relation to other domains of discourse. In the philosophy of law, for example, Ronald Dworkin has argued that every question of law has a determinate answer: every statement of the form 'It is the law that p' is determinately true or false (or, at least, according to him the possibility of bivalence's failing is so remote as to be safely ignored).[2] But truth here, of course, is of the coherence variety. A statement of law is true if it is more consistent with the body of established law than is its negation (not if it corresponds to some independent reality). One might well adopt a similar position with regard to moral judgments and the data base of settled (and suitably criticized) moral convictions. In both cases bivalence can hold while the hallmarks of realism—the distinction between truth and warranted assertability, the notion of correspondence, the conceivable falsity of a universally endorsed, maximally consistent theory—are absent. The ethicist who accepts the concept of moral truth just suggested can certainly imagine that both her particular judgments and her entire normative theory are wrong. Perhaps the reflective equilibrium achieved by her theory expresses coherence among a set of judgments all of which result from mere prejudice or malicious social programming. What she cannot imagine is that a suitably corrected and convergent ethical theory at the Peircean end of moral inquiry could be false. Here is where the contrast with realism, despite satisfaction of bivalence, lies.[3]

Thus the principle of bivalence is not sufficient for even a partial characterization of realism. Regarding the necessity of the principle for the realist, bivalence can fail for reasons relating to portions of our language and more deeply to our perceptual and conceptual abilities, rather than to any lack of independence or determinateness in the world. The realist's position, as characterized by the criteria mentioned in the previous paragraph, is not threatened by vagueness in our terms or concepts, although vagueness renders problematic the assignment of truth values to certain statements. Realism entails belief in a determinate reality but not in a fully determinate language with no "open concepts." As others have pointed out, the vagueness of many predicates is no accident or oversight to be remedied by simple stipulative adjustment. It typically characterizes, for example, not only observational predicates like color terms but ordinary kind terms as well. Citing Willard Quine's latest version of the sorites paradox,[4] if we imagine subtracting one molecule at a time from the surfaces of a table, we will be unable to draw a precise line at which 'x is a table' is no longer true of the object. Thus bivalence is problematic for a range of cases. Here it is clear that the problem lies not in any lack of determinateness in the realist's world. The world may be completely determinate in every space-time region and yet fail to determine 'x is a table' as true or false, because the concept of a table cannot be sharpened to the same degree.

The realist should then avoid appeal to the principle of bivalence. But the analysis of meaning in terms of truth and the contrast between truth and verification or warranted assertibility remain necessary for the description of his position. We saw in the discussion of criteria that realism in this semantic sense must be thoroughgoing in order to have any plausibility. We cannot be realists about truth but not meaning. We cannot analyze meanings as given by justification conditions and then continue to contrast justification with truth. Doing so leads to the absurd result that to assert that x is F is to assert that x is probably F but may not be. Since these assertions are not equivalent, if meaning is to be given by justification conditions, then truth must reduce to warranted assertibility as well. If we accept the antecedent but not the consequent, we must also renounce in all but strictly observational contexts the equivalence between 'It is true that p' and 'p', since the latter would assert only justification conditions and the former truth. Although we saw that this equivalence may be defeated by vagueness, it should not break down in all situations beyond direct verification.

The realist denies both the reduction of truth to and the stipulation of meaning in terms of warranted assertibility. Semantic antirealists, including Dummett, question the legitimacy of the realist's central distinction. For Dummett the realist's main problem is to show how the realist notion of truth can enter into explanation of linguistic practice. The demand is reasonable given the supposed links betweeen meaning, understanding, and truth. To provide a theory of meaning is to show what a language user knows when he understands sentences in the language. If that knowledge is knowledge of the conditions under which the sentences are true, it must still be manifest in their use. For understanding must be taught, acquired, and judged in the context of public communication. Meaning, and truth as its explanans, cannot escape all manifestation in practice, or we could never know whether others understand us.

Dummett suggests three related arguments against the realist's concepts of meaning and truth. All three rely on the following claims: (1) that meaning is what a language user knows when he understands a statement, (2) that a theory of meaning must provide an account of such understanding, and (3) that linguistic understanding and the knowledge that underlies it must be manifest in practice. He questions the compatibility of the realist's analysis of understanding, i.e., knowledge of meaning, as knowledge of evidence-transcendent truth conditions with the thrust of these three claims.

His first argument derives more specifically from considerations regarding language acquisition. He points out that we learn to use sentences correctly by being taught to make assertions with them in conditions taken to establish or evidence the truth of those assertions.[5] If understanding is what is acquired through this training process, then it becomes problematic how we could understand what it is for an assertion to be true independently of knowing what evidential conditions count in its favor. How, by learning to apply terms in certain experienced conditions, do we come to understand them as referring to properties that transcend all possible experiences of them, such that the truth of such ascriptions is understood to be logically independent of the evidence for them?

Dummett's second argument derives from his demand that the realist provide an account of the knowledge of truth conditions that is to constitute the understanding of meaning. According to him, stating truth conditions in the form 'S is true iff p' cannot give us a grasp of the designated sentence's meaning, especially if the sentence replacing p is formed by disquotation. We must already understand the meaning of the latter sentence in order to grasp fully the sense of the Tarskian sentence that contains it.[6] The same question might be raised regarding knowledge of assertibility conditions, since we might want to represent such knowledge by suitably transformed Tarski-type sentences. But there are differences. First, nontrivial statements of assertibility conditions will be possible for a broader class of sentences than nontrivial statements of truth conditions will be possible for, since evidence for assertions is more often statable in terms other than those of the assertions themselves. Second, and more important, assertibility conditions can be taught and expressed directly by assertions in those actual conditions. This will not be possible for truth conditions in the differentiating cases.

Dummett's third, closely related argument expresses the demand that understanding—knowledge of truth conditions according to the realist—be manifest in use.[7] If the realist's notion of understanding as transcending knowledge of verification conditions is to be genuinely different from its verificationist counterpart, it must make some difference to the practice of language users. But if using sentences correctly is using them to make warranted assertions, it again becomes problematic how such use could justify ascription of understanding that transcends conditions of warrant.

Dummett himself suggests in several places that the notion of truth derives from a broader notion of linguistic correctness in certain contexts in which appeal to verification or warranted assertibility seems insufficient to determine correct use. In the formation of certain compounds, the assertibility of the components does not imply the assertibility of the whole sentences. These non-assertible—functional compounds require an auxiliary notion to account for their assertibility conditions. Dummett sometimes suggests that the notion of truth plays this role.[8] Robert Brandom has systematized the examples that support this line of argument. In general, he points out, whenever one clause of a compound expresses a state of the speaker and the other ascribes that state to him, the compound may not preserve assertibility.[9] As a simple case, consider 'I believe that p,' 'p', and 'If I believe that p, then p.' Sentences formed from the first two schemas will have the same assertibility conditions, but assertibility does not transfer to the compound. Here we require a stronger criterion for the second clause, and the notion of truth suggests itself. If p is true, and not simply assertible by this speaker, then the compound will be true.

Unfortunately the realist's conception of truth is not required here—a notion of warranted assertibility broader than that of verifiability by particular speakers at particular times will do. That the realist's conception is not necessary becomes clear when we compare again the context of ethics. Consider the same problem as it arises when p is a moral judgment. It does not follow from my believing that an action is right that it is right, although for me the assertibility of the components may be the same. This does not establish realism as a metaethical theory, however. We need only distinguish between the speaker's warrant at a given time and the warrant for the convergent and maximally coherent judgment of the community at the limit of moral development. Verification is distinct from warranted assertibility in the Peircean sense, since the latter may not be accessible to current speakers. But the realist's notion of truth must also be distinguished at the other end of the spectrum from Peircean assertibility. It transcends this broader nonrealist concept, since for the realist even convergent and maximally coherent theories can be false.

Thus, to account for the failure of the preservation of assertibility in compounds such as that mentioned above, the antirealist need only posit a linguistic division of labor in which first-person warrants for self-ascribing certain states override, while some form of collective warrant or criterion of coherence overrides in expressions of the contents of those states. Certain other contexts in which we contrast truth with justification can be accommodated in the same way by the antirealist, in terms of the contrast between narrower and broader conditions of warrant. Conceptual change often results from criticism of conditions of warrant, as the latter are supposed to generate truth. In the clearest cases we discover that verification procedures lead to conflicting judgments (as I have claimed in the case of color ascriptions). The demand to abandon some of these procedures or to order them so as to remove the inconsistencies appears to derive from the concept of a single transcendent truth at which we aim.[10] But once more it can derive instead from the goal of consistent and convergent theory itself. The distinction between narrower verification and ultimate collective warrant again allows one to avoid appeal to realist notions of truth and meaning.

Dummett's three questions remain to be answered: How is it possible to acquire understanding in the realist's sense? In what does such understanding consist? And how is such understanding manifest in practice? We may begin with the first. Dummett himself suggests, only to dismiss, the idea that we may acquire understanding beyond the ability to verify through imaginatively extending our grasp of verification procedures themselves by analogy. By imagining beings in more advantageous positions in space-time or with superior capacities for acquiring corroborating evidence, we come to understand what would make our unverifiable sentences true and hence in what their truth consists.[11] He dismisses this idea, however, on the ground that we could not manifest such imaginative grasp of meaning in use. Perhaps the point is that our use of sentences must continue to be governed by whatever actual justification procedures we have.

It is not necessary to continue the argument in this direction, since the realist need not extend by analogy his grasp of verification for each unverifiable sentence he may claim to understand. The demand first of all oversimplifies the way that understanding of sentences is built up from understanding of terms. Terms can be learned originally from their contributions to verifiable assertions, or from their functions in explanatory models grasped partly by analogy, or from combinations of other terms learned in these ways, or . . . They can be recombined into sentences and theories that, in Quine's terms, face the tribunal of experience only holistically (or at least in chunks).[12] Even broader theories face this tribunal not alone but in relation to competing alternatives. The latter point is important here, because a theory thought to be verified or justified by evidence at a given stage of inquiry can be replaced by a theory more explanatory of that evidence without the former's becoming thereby unintelligible. An outmoded theory may lack conceivable evidence or further justification, all conceivable evidence being reinterpreted in terms of the new theoretical vocabulary. But we may nevertheless understand the old theory, for example that of phlogiston, as did our predecessors for whom it was justified.

Examples abound within science and without, including theories once but no longer in competition with serious scientific candidates for best explanations. Religious explanations of empirical phenomena once may have competed as serious contenders; they may even have been justified by the evidence in relation to available alternatives. As I pointed out before, however, an atheist at present can refuse to accept any conceivable evidence as verifying the existence of a deity while intelligibly denying that existence. He can also deny the possibility of conclusive falsification while continuing to understand the assertion of existence. Evidence here would consist in observations best explained as divine manifestation, but in this case some theory of hallucination might be preferable as a last-resort alternative. Whether or not the latter would be explanatorily preferable, and whether or not the atheist is able to picture a creature better situated to gather verifying or falsifying evidence, his religious talk need not lack sense.

Thus the link between one's current uses of terms in single assertions and one's having learned their meanings in conditions directly verifying applications may be extremely indirect. In fact there may be no conditions to which the terms correctly apply, if their meanings derive from those of other terms. Predicates may link to verifying conditions through thick webs of analogy, explanation, and other inductive and deductive relations among them. Understanding theoretical predicates, for example, seems not to be an ability to recognize (observable) conditions in which the predicates apply but an ability to incorporate them into explanatory schemas and perhaps to grasp certain analogies to predicates applicable to observable models. A similar point applies to the demand that the realist notion of truth be manifest in practice. We cannot demand for each sentence that there be a difference in use between realist and nonrealist notions of understanding. It is sufficient that there be a difference in attitude toward theories or sets of belief as a whole, a difference that can show up in certain features of general practices such as assigning referents or judging the truth of theories in relation to their total evidence.

If it is not necessary to extend our notion of verification in terms of sentence-by-sentence analogies in order to derive realist concepts of understanding and truth, how are these concepts derived and distinguished from their nonrealist counterparts? It is through extending our primitive notion of *error*, not verification, that we arrive at the realist's conception of truth as independent of evidence. For the nonrealist error remains conceivable only in relation to experiences and beliefs taken to be veridical: fallibility entails corrigibility. For the realist the truth value of a mistaken but justified assertion does not change when it is shown to be false. It would have been false had the counterevidence never materialized, even if there could not have been counterevidence. The realist demands that the concept of falsification be extended to include first the possibility of error despite the weight of all conceivable evidence and then the possibility of global error, the possibility of wholesale falsity of our ultimately corroborated theories. Thus he is committed to the intelligibility of global skepticism, while the nonrealist must deny not only the force but the sense of the skeptic's pervasive doubts.[13]

THE POSSIBILITY OF SKEPTICISM

The argument about criteria suggested that our notion of objects to which we apply predicates is realist in the sense that error is possible despite the weight of all evidence—the first realist demand. I argued in the last chapter that terms used to identify properties and objects as belonging to natural kinds are truly applicable only if an unlistable number of counterfactuals is true in each case. (Our application of the term 'lemon', for example, is correct only if the fruit to which it is applied would not sprout into a pine tree when planted, etc.) Such identification may then turn out to be wrong despite any finite amount of evidence to the contrary, since no finite amount of evidence could eliminate all possible defeating counterfactuals. While the evidence might warrant application of a term indefinitely, truth seems to be a different matter, entailing as it does counterfactuals not conclusively ruled out by the evidence.

Regarding the possibility of global error—the second realist demand—pervasive skeptical doubts have traditionally been made seemingly intelligible to us with the aid of such creatures as evil demons and brains in vats. The stories about them illustrate fully coherent belief systems that are uniformly false in ascribing properties to nonexistent objects. The possibility that we may be deceived by a Cartesian demon or programmed by superscientists seems to show that our own beliefs, even when maximally coherent or verified, may themselves be systematically false.

There are several possible replies available to the nonrealist. All argue that appeal to such creatures fails to demonstrate the possibility of maximally coherent, false beliefs. To begin with the brains in vats, if these are programmed to have beliefs shared by the scientists who maintain them, their beliefs, at least those lacking in indexicals, could be deemed true or false of the objects to which both the scientists and they (perhaps through the beliefs of the scientists) refer, according to the usual coherence tests. If the scientists instead program wildly false but internally coherent and verified beliefs into the brains, then three further nonrealist replies can be offered. First, the beliefs of the brains might be deemed false in this situation because they fail to cohere with those of the scientists and other inhabitants of their shared world. Second, the nonrealist, if wary of this union of the world of the scientists with that of the brains, could hold that the propositional attitudes of the latter fail to refer and therefore lack truth value. This contention might be supported by a causal theory of reference and the claim that the brains lack the proper types of causal relations to real objects. Here the lack of entailment from coherence to truth lacks a realist ring, since it does not involve reference to an independent world of objects. Then too, under this interpretation, we might hesitate to call the attitudes in question beliefs at all. Finally, it could be held that the brains occupy their own worlds, those defined by their sets of beliefs. Within those worlds their beliefs could be held true when coherent or verified, true of the objects in those worlds as their beliefs define them, i.e., true of their phenomenal objects, which are the only objects for them.

This last reply seems available in the case of the demon as well. For the nonrealist our willingness to countenance the demon need not shake our faith in the truth of our maximally coherent sets of beliefs. Within our world, the world defined for us by those sets, such beliefs remain true of the objects they specify. We can imagine them false only by introducing new beliefs with which they fail to cohere, by imagining them falsified. If we were to accept belief in the demon, we would have to alter other beliefs in the prior system. But the suggestion that the demon might exist, although never to be countenanced by our beliefs or revealed in our experiences, and that he might render our beliefs globally false of their objects, can be dismissed as incoherent by the staunch nonrealist.

Returning to the brains in vats, there may appear to be a problem for the final nonrealist interpretation with certain of the brains' coherent beliefs, for example, the belief that objects continue to exist unperceived and perhaps even unconceived. But possibly such apparently realist beliefs could be given some Millian interpretation (in terms of possible phenomena or experiences) that would make them true also. Or they might be shown to be false in Dummett's fashion by being shown to be inconsistent with the brains' genuine understanding of object terms. The fact that these creatures can refer only to phenomenal objects according to the nonrealist response under consideration gives rise to another argument, by Putnam, to the effect that *we* could not be such creatures. That we can think we might possibly be real brains in vats shows that we are not, according to him. If we were, we could think of ourselves only as phenomenal brains. But surely we are not phenomenal brains in vats.[14]

The claim that brains in vats could not refer to real objects must rest either on a causal theory of reference (the claim that the brains lack the proper causal interactions with objects necessary for reference) or on a demand to assign referents so as to maximize truths within the set of beliefs simultaneously ascribed (many of the brains' beliefs are true of phenomenal, but not real, objects). I shall later suggest an account of reference that is neither causal nor necessarily truth maximizing in regard to beliefs ascribed. Before continuing the argument on the global level, however, we might do better to return to a more local illustration of the lack of entailment from verification or coherence to truth. In addition to making the general claim of unspecifiable counterfactuals implicit in property ascriptions, it might be helpful to find a specific possible belief that is conclusively verified, that remains forever consistent with others and immune from falsification, but that is false. Such a local illustration can motivate us further toward the realist and away from the antirealist interpetations of the global cases, both of which remain viable at this point in the argument.

Let us then add a new creature to the metaphysical zoo, or rather borrow one from recent literature in the philosophy of mind. Imagine a person P and his physical replica R, an atom-for-atom duplicate. Construct a story in which P dematerializes without a trace shortly after R materializes. R's seeming memories now match P's former genuine memories. Specifically, R remembers having had an unhappy childhood, which, of course, he never had. It appears, nevertheless, that his belief must meet all pragmatic and coherence tests of truth: it can be verified but not falsified. Complete evidence here will fail to entail truth. It appears to be the realist's notion of correspondence, or lack of it, that determines the falsity of R's belief.

An initial nonrealist response to this story might be to say that in it P simply becomes R, so that R's belief is true of his, i.e., P's childhood. This move can be blocked. If we are allowed to use material criteria of personal identity, we can point out that there has been no physical process of division in this story. If such criteria are rejected, we can point out that there need not be even deviant causal chains between P's childhood and his replica's belief. We can imagine that the replica just happened to materialize as a physical duplicate. The causal criterion of memory cannot be completely rejected, although the nonrealist will provide his own interpretation of causation to accommodate it. Whatever the proper specification of causal chains involved in memory might be, there clearly is a difference between a genuine memory and one that accidentally, though accurately, represents some past occurrence. The required connection is not present in our story, making R's belief false although consistent with all the evidence.

A second nonrealist reply might accept the falsity of R's belief but hold that it is its failure to cohere with our understanding of the situation that leads us to declare it false. This reply will not work either. Beliefs are true or false within possible worlds. R's belief is false in his world and not simply in relation to ours, although it is coherent with all true beliefs in his world. There is nevertheless reason to emphasize the special point of view from which we are considering this highly artificial case. In defining the possible world as we choose, we acquire special access to the correspondence relations between beliefs and facts within it. In our world we rather share the fate of our science fiction counterparts in lacking such direct access. But the question here concerns not the criterion we use for judging claims to truth but the relation between that criterion and truth itself.

A final nonrealist response might be to imagine the possibility, in the replica's world, of (future) verificationist tests that might show his belief to be false. Many such conceivable tests can be ruled out in the definition of the case, but perhaps not all. Ultimately it seems that the nonrealist simply can take whatever criterion of difference we apply in saying that R is distinct from P and imagine a possible test for that difference.[15] Since this test will express our notions of identity and nonidentity, any attempt to rule it out will render unintelligible the claim that R replaces P and therefore has false beliefs about his past. If our criterion is physical identity, for example, then we can imagine a molecule tracer that will show R's physical makeup to be discontinuous with P's. The falsity of R's belief about his childhood will then be held to derive from its lack of coherence with the outcome of this conceivable verificationist test.

In responding, the realist might first question whether a test merely possible in relation to a given world maintains the equation between truth and coherence in that world. The nonrealist can maintain his position in this way only by equating truth with the coherence of an ideal, rather than actual, set of beliefs. Second, it is questionable whether the conceived test would demonstrate the falsity of R's belief to inhabitants of his world. Given the unlikelihood of the story I have imagined in a world otherwise like ours, overall maximization of coherence in the face of such a test would call rather for dismissing its reliability. Even if an ideal theory in such a world would include a theory of the molecule tracer, it would seem less implausible to ascribe a malfunction to the machine than to believe in the simultaneous disappearance of P and the materialization by chance of an exact physical duplicate. Our temptation to place the latter belief in an ideal set for that world derives only from our correspondence notion of truth, which again does all the work.

Finally, the most plausible moves for the antirealist in reacting to the global myths are not available here. There appear to be no deviant causal chains that would render R's belief true, at least none that would preserve a remotely plausible assignment of referents to his and others' terms. Nor is there any lack of coherence between his beliefs and those of others in his society. Finally, and most important, the nonrealist cannot plausibly take R's beliefs to define a world for him within which they are true. We cannot assign phenomenal referents, since the reference of terms like 'childhood experience' will be fixed by other members of R's linguistic community, who use such terms to refer, and by his intention to use the term as others use it. His belief cannot be taken to refer to his imaginary experience, since there will be a distinction in his world, as in ours, between imaginary and genuine experiences and childhoods. We cannot then map the belief onto an object that would make it come out true, despite the belief's meeting all operational and verificationist tests. We cannot reassign the referent without altering so many other assignments as to render the resulting scheme totally implausible as a way of explaining verbal behavior.

In meeting all tests for truth in his world, the replica's belief becomes part of an "ideal theory" or set of beliefs in that world. It therefore seems that the local example of falsity despite verification implies the possible falsity of an ideal global theory as well. At least not all beliefs in an operationally and theoretically ideal set need be true, although it is a further step to assert the possibility of wholesale falsity. This step too follows naturally, however, once we relinquish the idea of an entailment from coherence to truth. Once this idea is given up, there can be no limit to the extent to which our ideally coherent theories might contain falsity. I admitted in Part II that we would not ascribe beliefs (hence reference) to subjects that we did not view as minimally rational. However, such minimal rationality in my view requires only consistent application of concepts or terms in relation to ways of appearing: true beliefs, if any, only on the phenomenal level. In practice, of course, we do for the most part ascribe truth to mundane perceptual beliefs as well in interpreting the behavior, including verbal behavior, of others. But such ascription does not entail its own correctness. Nor are we constrained to this practice if, for example, we have some reason to suspect wholesale falsity in the beliefs of certain subjects (perhaps we can see that they are brains in vats). In ascribing beliefs and referents, our aim is to explain both verbal and nonverbal behavior, not to maximize ascriptions of true beliefs.

In seeking to extend the replica case, even to its initial seeming implication of a possible false belief in an operationally and theoretically ideal system, we next encounter Putnam's main argument against realism and the intelligibility of skepticism that it entails. According to him the realist is committed both to the ideal of a single true theory of the world and to the possible falsity of a theory that is ideal from the point of view of any tests that we could apply.[16] Putnam's first criterion of realism is not one that I or other realists accept. In the discussion of empirically equivalent theories, I allowed for different systems of categorization of the same domains. And the phenomenon of inevitable vagueness discussed earlier in this chapter makes it clear that any theoretical scheme we might develop, if it is to serve its human purposes, will be coarse grained in relation to certain classes of determinate properties. That objects have such properties independent of their classification within such schemes therefore does not imply that some single scheme must be capable of picking out a single structure that the world has. Realism therefore does not require either that there be a single ideal theory or that this single ideal theory be possibly false. What is required, given the implication of the replica case noted above, is that any theory, suitably corrected so as to be ideal in the sense of meeting all conceivable tests, be possibly false. The realist notion of the world's independence is derived, I have maintained, from such an extension of the everyday concept of error.

Putnam denies that an operationally and theoretically ideal set of beliefs could contain any falsity. Consider a "complete" theory or set of beliefs (a possibility that I denied above) that satisfies all operational and aesthetic, coherentist and pragmatic constraints on theories judged to be true. We know from model theory that such a set of beliefs, considered as an uninterpreted calculus, has a model in the world. We can then simply choose such a model and map the terms of the theory onto it such that they stand in a (Tarskian) relation of correspondence to it. According to Putnam this relation may simply be taken as truth. We cannot make sense of the claim that the theory might be false, since this would amount to the claim that our mapping does not pick out the real intended objects as they are related according to the real meanings of our terms, that it is the wrong mapping. But why should not the interpretation that maps onto those objects (and properties) that make the theory come out true be the correct one? In fact, if it continues to satisfy all the above-mentioned constraints, then it must be the correct one, since we have no other constraints to which to appeal in assigning referents. Here it is not a matter of accepting an a priori constraint to assign referents so as to maximize truth in the set of beliefs being ascribed and interpreted, a requirement rejected above. It is rather that, given the satisfaction of all other legitimate constraints, we can have no reason not to believe the theory in question true and assign referents accordingly.

If there are several models onto which such a theory could be mapped so as to come out true, then Putnam's argument implies that there are no grounds for choosing among them; that is, it implies a lack of determinate reference. Indeed Putnam, in recent writings, supports Quine's thesis of referential inscrutability and counts it as an additional weapon against the realist, who in his view requires determinate reference in order to specify his one true theory. (While I have denied the requirement of one true theory, the realist does require determinate reference if his theory is to be of epistemological interest, if he is to demonstrate knowledge of real objects.) Putnam offers a proof of the possibility of alternative reference schemes such that the same sentences come out true in all.[17] If different subjects actually used such different schemes, this difference would never be detectable from their linguistic practice, since they would continue to assert, to assent to, and to dissent from exactly the same sentences.

Despite the abstract possibility of truth-preserving alternative assignments of referents, neither Quine nor Putnam has ever provided even remotely plausible examples of alternatives to commonsense assignments of terms to everyday objects and properties. I do not believe that any alternative assignment would preserve a plausible psychology for speakers. None seems capable of entering into best or most plausible explanations for verbal behavior in various perceptual contexts. If we include within the data ways objects naturally appear and seek to explain verbal behavior that originates from primitive reference to such naturally salient properties, as described in the previous chapter, then alternative possibilities that preserve only the same assignments of truth to whole sentences are ruled out. Reference to naturally salient perceptual properties anchors reference to other observable properties via relations, for example, combinatory or abstractive, of the latter to the former. Similarly, once reference to observable properties is rendered determinate, theoretical properties can be singled out via analogical and explanatory (causal) relations to them. Finally, reference to objects can be specified via appeal to certain properties or privileged descriptions. We will refer to whatever real objects satisfy our intended descriptions or instantiate intended properties to which reference was previously secured as described above. (One may wonder not how bizarre reference schemes could be explanatory but how any reference relation could be psychologically explanatory, given Putnam's claim that reference can be independent of all conceivable psychological states. His examples of such independence will be disputed below.)

The account will be fleshed out somewhat and a way of specifying the descriptions in question will be suggested in the next chapter. The point here is that, given a base of reference to naturally salient properties among ways of appearing, there is no reason to think that the possibility of preserving ascriptions of truth to whole sentences while reassigning referents makes real reference indeterminate or inscrutable. It has been argued elsewhere that Quine's example of exchanging reference to rabbit parts or stages for reference to rabbits fails to preserve (relations among terms arising from) perceptions of spatial and temporal relations among properties together with criteria implicit in verbal behavior that we employ for identity.[18] Putnam's example of exchanging reference to cherries on trees for reference to cats on mats, while it may preserve ascriptions of truth to uttered sentences, fails to mesh with any theory of perception at all.

Quine's austere behaviorism and antirealist position on intentional states, as well as his thesis of underdetermination of theory by evidence, generates the indeterminacy and inscrutability theses for interpretations of language use. Rejecting the psychology and questioning the major supposed examples of underdetermination of physical theory, as I did in a previous chapter, we need not be detained further by the abstract possibility of truth-preserving permutations of referents, at least until examples with equal explanatory plausibility are provided. This possibility becomes assimilated to the many other cases of inductive skepticism generated by empirically equivalent theories considered earlier. There is no reason to believe, in any of the cases considered, including this one, that an adequate data base and application of criteria for preferable explanations cannot overcome such skepticism.

It can be claimed that the case of reference differs from other cases of underdetermination in its degree of dependence on an ungrounded choice of a particular scheme. The choice itself cannot be made fully explicit but must be simply presupposed, at least at a certain level. The reason is that we can specify referents for a language only in terms of another (meta) language. If we say that 'gavagai' or 'rabbit' refers to rabbits, the reference of the term used in the metalanguage can also be questioned, or rather must be assumed if the specification is to succeed. In this sense reference may seem ultimately inscrutable, if scrutability requires complete verbal expression.

But the realist can still question whether the reference relation for his first-level language really depends on a metalanguage whose reference relation in turn cannot be expressed or specified. He can rather maintain that only its statement depends on language at the next level. If this is all that inscrutability amounts to, then the realist on reference has an answer similar to his response to a much older idealist ploy. The old idealist trick was to point out that we cannot conceive of unconceived objects. To conceive of objects is to conceive of them as conceived. Hence all objects we can conceive must be thought of as relative to our conceptual scheme. The obvious response is that only appeal to objects with real, that is, independent, properties explains appearances best. Likewise, the realist can argue that the real relation that makes reference determinate iterates when expressed in a metalanguage. Furthermore, only appeal to real objects, e.g., rabbits, not to terms in a metalanguage, best explains the verbal behavior of users of terms like 'gavagai'. Appearances are conceptualized as properties of rabbits, not rabbit stages, and so descriptions associated with the term 'rabbit' will be satisfied by rabbits, not rabbit stages, whatever the level of metalanguage we use.

The nonrealist might counter further that best explanations for verbal behavior remain relative both to the psychological organizations of different speakers and, once more, to those offering and accepting the explanations. We may grant both points. The first means that alternative equally explanatory reference schemes might be readily produced for alien beings with different neurophysiologies and psychologies, for whom different or no perceptual properties seem naturally salient. It does not affect the scrutability of reference by fellow human speakers. The second point is irrelevant here as well. That certain evaluations of some explanations vary with explanatory purposes affects neither explanations for appearances that single out certain kinds of objects and properties (as opposed to neural states, for example, which might be preferred explanans in other contexts) nor explanations for verbal behavior that assign referents in line with those prior explanations on the perceptual level.

A final move for the nonrealist in this exchange would be to claim that perceptual salience itself is a totally subjective phenomenon and that we therefore have no reason to think that reference anchored in this phenomenon latches onto anything real or objective. But our previous argument that realism provides the deepest explanation for ways of appearing, together with the appeal to natural selection as an explanation for salience, showed otherwise.

It might appear, then, that Putnam's model-theoretic argument against realism and the possible falsity of an ideal theory, implying as it does indeterminacy of reference in relation to those models that allow us to count the theory true, can be dismissed simply by rejecting the skeptical thesis for reference. Indeed, other critics have attacked the argument for failing to take account of the way that language is embedded in the structures of perceptual contexts and the behavioral patterns they call forth.[19] Determinacy of reference is damaging to Putnam's argument if, as it is natural to suppose from his statement of it, different models can satisfy the operational and theoretical constraints imposed on his ideal theory. It then seems that the fault lies with the assignment of referents with an eye only toward preserving ascriptions of truth to whole sentences within an initially uninterpreted formal calculus. It is easily objected that we do not in fact assign referents in this way, in abstraction from context, in interpreting one another's speech. But this may misinterpret Putnam.

Suppose we grant that a plausible psychology would narrow

the acceptable models to one. This may itself be the result of adhering to Putnam's operational and theoretical constraints. His point then becomes that the psychology to which we appeal here, as well as the reference scheme or theory of reference that grows out of it, must be considered part of the all-inclusive ideal theory itself. As such, the scheme will again assign referents so as to have the theory come out true by its own lights. But for Putnam this means true *tout court*, since there is no way to step outside the theory, including the theory of reference, so as to say that its assignments are wrong. Whatever "natural" relations the theory takes to ground reference (whether the simple causal chains between objects and names of the causal theory or the more indirect causal-functional grounding to salient properties, as in my view), these relations must themselves be interpreted according to the scheme of the ideal theory. That is, they must be interpreted within a metalanguage that operates under the same constraints. These relations will themselves then be interpreted so as to hold the overall theory true.

At this point we should notice again a remarkable resemblance between the present debate on the nature of reference and the older clash between the realist and nonrealist over the relation of perception to its objects. The older nonrealist claimed that, since it is impossible to step outside our percepts in order to compare them with transcendent objects, it can make no sense to speak of the latter or to think of accuracy of perceptual representation in transcendent terms. The realist countered that features internal to the structure of experience can provide reason to explain that experience by appeal to real objects that cause it. Such objects must have properties independent of our perceptual experiences of them. Similarly, the new nonrealist points out that we cannot stand outside our practice of assigning referents and ascribing truth to beliefs in making such assignments.[20] The realist reply is predictable. He sees reference as grounded in a natural relation between terms and objects (or, on my view, between properties of objects, percepts, concepts, and terms), such that an assignment of objects for terms can itself go wrong. Rather than reference's being determined a priori by the overall theory in which the theory of reference is embedded, the theory infers to actual referents for

terms inductively. Actual reference must satisfy the real relation to which we infer in explaining verbal behavior. (How this
constraint is compatible with speakers' intentional control over
reference will be shown in the next chapter.)

Once more, inference to a real relation is taken to explain
human responses—here verbal behavior as well as perceptual
experience, most deeply. But the reality of the relation entails
that our theories can get it wrong. Even an ideal theory can
attempt to assign referents in a way that does not wholly succeed. The replica example once more illustrates this possibility.
The ideal theory or set of beliefs in his world assigns a supposed
referent for his term 'childhood experience', when none exists.
Both the grounding of reference in real (perceptual) contexts
and the social character of language, which prevents a private
mapping of terms onto objects so as to make each individual's
belief system maximally true, account for the possible lack of
requisite correspondence between relations among objects and
properties in the world and inferential relations among terms
in an operationally and theoretically ideal theory. For example,
real relations determine that a dated proposition false at one
time cannot be true at another, while the evidence for it, and
hence its inferential relations to the contents of other beliefs,
may change. Correspondence or truth for the realist requires
not simply a one-to-one mapping of terms onto objects but a
mapping of real properties and relations, a mapping grounded
in a natural relation between these relata in the world and our
uses of terms. Truth in this sense cannot be guaranteed by the
constraints we place upon evaluations of our theories, including
our theory of reference. It could be so guaranteed only if the
objects of our beliefs were created in the acts of assigning them
as referents, a creation countenanced (although not in such
bald terms) by the nonrealist[21] but not by the realist. Appeal to
such ideal objects could explain verbal behavior no better than
it could explain perception, that is, ways of appearing.

Putnam's "internal realism" reflects a desire to have it both
ways—to explain verbal behavior by appeal to inputs from the
environment and to render reference within a scheme unproblematic or transparent by guaranteeing that the objects
assigned by our interpretations are genuine referents. This is a

new attempt at Kantianism without the thing-in-itself. But, as argued earlier, the noumenon was no accident or oversight in Kant's philosophy, but instead a profound recognition of the implication of the thesis that our minds or theories impose whatever structure we find in the world we confront. In the present context we cannot appeal to inputs from real objects or to a natural relation to them in explaining verbal behavior, and hence reference, without recognizing that this relation, interpreted as it is within our theory of reference, may fail to be satisfied by that theory's purported assignment of referents. (Of course the same point applies, from the realist's point of view, to our reference to that relation itself.) Putnam's mapping of his ideal theory onto the world can then fail to capture genuine reference, as grounded in such a relation, and his argument against realism fails. Granted that the failure of reference would be revealed only from a transcendent point of view. The question boils down once more to whether appeal to transcendent or independent objects enters into deepest explanations in the domain, an argument that need not be reiterated further.

Before moving on I should dispel a possible tension between a claim made in the previous chapter, that we can know a priori that 'lemon' refers to lemons, and my claim here that we must infer inductively to proper assignments of real objects as referents for our terms. Viewed in terms of the descriptive theory of reference I shall suggest, there is no contradiction here. While it is contingent that objects appear as they do, we will generally apply natural kind terms such as 'lemon' to whichever objects appear in certain ways to us (in various conditions including experimental and counterfactual contexts). Reference to appearances will be prominent in the privileged descriptions that determine reference to objects of natural kinds. We can therefore know by understanding the term that lemons (are those objects that) appear in certain ways and not in others and that the term 'lemon' will apply to such objects, if any. As pointed out earlier, this does not afford us a priori knowledge of the real properties of lemons, properties only contingently related to the ways they appear. Nor does it guarantee that there are lemons. It is therefore more precise to say that we know a priori that 'lemon' applies to lemons *if* there exist any such objects.

The qualification was not of major importance in the earlier discussion but is highly relevant here. It, together with the merely contingent relation between real and apparent properties, shows why we must infer inductively to the referents of our terms and how we can err in such inferences, as in the replica case.

UNDERSTANDING AND TRUTH

We are now free to extend the local implication of the replica story, the claim that an operationally and theoretically ideal set of beliefs can contain *some* falsity, to the possibility of global falsity in any set of beliefs. As noted earlier, once we admit that maximally coherent beliefs can be false for failing to correspond, once coherence fails to entail truth, we cannot set a priori limits to the number of false beliefs in any set. As also noted, while we will generally ascribe mostly true beliefs in interpreting verbal behavior, this ascription does not entail its own correctness. Nor does the goal of explanation always call for such ascription as means. In the brains-in-vats case, for example, we will explain verbal output in totally nonreferential terms (by appealing directly to the electrical inputs from the programming apparatus). In light of the brains' firm realist beliefs—for example, that the objects referred to in their other beliefs exist when unconceived by them—it seems maximally coherent to consider them to fail in specific references, and hence to have mostly false everyday beliefs, rather than true beliefs about phenomenal objects. (In fact for them, as for us, there may be no phenomenal objects, only ways of appearing. See the earlier argument on sense data.) This case also shows, then, that understanding others does not require agreement with them, let alone their beliefs' being true in the realist sense. Finally, given that we can imagine global falsity in the everyday beliefs of other possible subjects, we can picture as well distortion in the sources of our beliefs that would render them mostly false. Thus the distinction between coherence and truth, forced upon us in the local case, defeats all the global antirealist arguments as well.

We have now answered the first of Dummett's questions. We

have seen how we can extend our notion of truth beyond that acquired in learning contexts in which language use and beliefs are corrected in relation to evidence. The task is accomplished by extending our notion of error to that of locally coherent but false belief, and then to the conceivability of globally false belief. We have illustrated the possibility of ultimately warranted assertibility without truth. The converse, truth without assertibility, is easier to establish, at least if we take assertibility conditions to entail both intelligent experiences and language. A prelinguistic world with dinosaurs is different from one without them; a world of two hydrogen atoms is different from a world with only one. If we take these differences to entail differences in assertibility conditions *for us,* despite our absence from these worlds, it is nevertheless clear that we posit the latter conditions only from our transcendent point of view. Yet again the notion of truth as correspondence does the work in leading us to ascribe a difference in assertibility.

We can be much briefer with Dummett's remaining questions. The second was, 'In what can knowledge of verification-transcendent truth conditions consist?'. The first part of the answer may be indicated by pointing out that for a large class of statements, those referring to observables, many philosophers would equate knowledge of truth conditions with knowledge of verification conditions. (I would couple the latter at least with knowledge that various counterfactuals obtain.) To deny this equation may be to assume that, in learning the connections between words and objects, we have access only to our experiences and not to the objects themselves. There is no reason to suppose so, and a direct realist adverbial account of perception, such as that offered in Part II, denies it. I have also acknowledged, however, that our knowledge of appearances is more immediate than our knowledge of the real properties of objects, and that we appeal to the former in validating the latter. This priority led me to argue earlier that appearances constitute verification conditions for statements about physical objects. Nevertheless, unless Dummett's skeptical position is to entail metaphysical phenomenalism, rather than, say, Putnam's sort of Kantian antirealism, he must take conditions in which we warrantedly assert perceptual knowledge of objects to include not only appearances or experiences but the experienceable presence of the objects themselves.

Thus it is only in regard to unobservables that knowledge of verification conditions must be taken to diverge from knowledge of truth conditions. Our use of analogy, our understanding of causal relations, and our grasp of inferential relations among statements containing terms for unobservables allow us to refer by using such terms. Reference here is determined, as I shall argue in the next chapter, by actual satisfaction of (privileged) descriptions specifying properties conceived in the ways just indicated. Knowledge of such properties and of how they could be instantiated allows us to refer to whatever actually does instantiate them.

If knowledge of such truth conditions, constituting understanding for the realist, must be expressed in verbal terms, it can be so expressed in Tarski-type sentences (suitably strengthened, perhaps, so as to guarantee that the sentence on the right of the schema translates the designated sentence, and suitably weakened to allow for vagueness). Dummett points out that one must understand the designated sentence in a Tarskian sentence before one can understand the whole. We therefore cannot impart the meaning of the designated sentence by using this device. But this point appears relevant only if we fail to draw the distinction between the use of Tarskian sentences to express what a language user knows when he understands meanings and the use of them to teach meanings.[22] That they are unsuitable for the latter use does not imply that they cannot serve the former. Since the sentence inserted in the right side of the Tarskian schema is used rather than designated or mentioned, it does not matter whether it is formed by disquotation. The resulting Tarskian sentence can express what a language user knows when he understands the designated sentence, since the former does not simply state that he knows the sentence in question but rather states that he knows its truth condition. Meanings captured by the Tarskian schema can be taught originally in relation to verification conditions, or by appeal to observables and causal relations, or by definitions using terms learned originally in those ways, or by appeal to analogies with observables. Terms for observables can come to be understood in terms of verification-transcendent truth conditions—as the concept of error becomes distinguished from that of lack of coherence—and then generalized. Terms for unobservables must always be understood in that way, if they are not short-hand for terms referring to observables.

Dummett argues further that we cannot use Tarskian sentences to explain both meaning and truth without circularity. If we explain truth by noting that ascribing truth to a statement is the same as asserting the statement, then we cannot explain meaning in terms of truth.[23] Rather than giving the meaning of an assertion, such an explication will accomplish no more than simply restating the assertion itself. This argument is more subtle and may appear more to the point. But all it shows, I believe, is that knowledge of truth conditions must sometimes be direct. It does not show that truth and meaning are not intimately connected, only that not all semantic notions can be taught purely linguistically without circularity. Any successful set of complete definitions can be challenged on the same ground, since all such sets will be circular (or incomplete in allowing primitives). This is obvious in regard to meaning apart from this argument regarding the explication of truth. Some statements must be taken initially to be directly verifiable, although their truth too can be questioned later, once the distinction has been drawn between truth and verification. Again the requirement relates to teaching and learning meanings, not to the knowledge that constitutes understanding them.

There may be yet another kind of circularity or regress in the account of understanding meanings as knowing truth conditions, represented by Tarski-type sentences. To know or understand a particular sentence of this type, for example, ' "Snow is white," is true iff snow is white', it seems that one must be able to represent the truth condition, here the fact that snow is white. If this representation is itself verbal, indeed accomplished by producing a token of the designated sentence, then we again face circularity or regress in the account.[24]

In responding we might be tempted toward a behaviorist line. We might want to claim that understanding requires no propositional knowledge at all, only knowledge how to produce appropriate sentences in appropriate circumstances. This response certainly does not help the realist, if his notion of understanding is to be distinct in appealing to truth conditions. It is to be rejected on other grounds as well. Understanding others requires knowing what they mean, that is, what they refer to and when their sentences are true. Indeed, I must have this knowledge in relation to my own thoughts and beliefs also, if they are genuine thoughts and beliefs and if I am to understand them correctly. Beliefs that qualify as knowledge, however, can sometimes be unpacked in dispositional terms and need not therefore involve occurrent representations. We will in fact attribute knowledge of truth conditions for statements when subjects seem to know when to assert them, how to gather evidence for them, and so on; that is, when they manifest certain types of practical knowledge. It may be, however, that part of the disposition we attribute in attributing such knowledge of truth conditions is the disposition or capacity to represent these conditions appropriately; and representing still seems to be more than simply producing noises, which might be produced accidentally or pathologically. If so, we are back where we started in regard to the charge of circularity.

In the end I believe we must admit circularity or incompleteness in the verbal expression of understanding similar to that encountered in offering verbal definitions. In neither case is the circularity vicious, as long as the expression is properly grounded in perceptual inputs and behavioral outputs. One indication of the perceptual grounding in the case of statements referring to observables is our tendency to represent truth conditions by visual images. (Think of your understanding of the sentence 'Snow is white' and of how you would represent its truth condition to yourself.) This tendency is probably part of what misled earlier philosophers into construing meaning itself as a relation to such images. In any case the circularity involved in verbally expressing understanding as knowledge of truth conditions is not of a nature to defeat the realist's account. How could verbal understanding in itself not be circular or incomplete (especially if knowledge of verification conditions in some cases just is knowledge of truth conditions)? If the truth condition for a statement must itself be represented verbally, then the circle is likely to be quite narrow. But we have seen that there are sometimes other ways to represent it and that some of these other ways express a grounding in perception that removes the viciousness of the circularity.

The only remaining question from Dummett is how the realist's notions are manifest in practice. Arguments evidencing a logic that contains the principle of bivalence do not provide the answer, as some philosophers believe. We saw that the principle fails to hold for certain ranges of predicates (that rarely affect the validity of everyday arguments); also that it is neither necessary nor sufficient for realism. The distinction between truth and warranted assertibility is itself implicit in certain general linguistic practices, however. (I argued above that we need not distinguish the meaning of every sentence separately on this ground.) It shows up first in the way that referents are assigned and understood. We may take ourselves to be speaking of the same unobservable objects, whether gods or quarks, even if we disagree about what would verify or falsify their existence or presence. Second, we can accept evidence, even complete evidence as in the replica case, without taking it to entail truth. Realism manifests itself in a willingness to acknowledge skeptical possibilities, in a healthy sense of our own fallibility and limited place and point of view in the world. Dummett might argue that such practices indicate our general intention to refer transcendently but that they cannot help to specify particular transcendent objects or states of affairs that we can understand to be referents. This objection is overcome by construing reference as actual satisfaction (of certain privileged associated descriptions) and construing the understanding of predicates in the way indicated above.

It remains only to add some flesh to this suggestion regarding reference in order to vindicate fully our ordinary linguistic intentions against Dummett's challenge.

16
TOWARD A DESCRIPTIVE ACCOUNT OF REFERENCE

The epistemologist who is a physical realist requires an account of reference to show how he can refer determinately to independent objects. The scientific realist requires an account of reference that will allow for some common referents across changes in theory, so that not all progress need be viewed as improved ontology. (It is more difficult to show such improvement than it is to show correction in beliefs about the same theoretical entities.) The first requirement can be satisfied by an account of reference firmly grounded in perceptual contexts, such that a basic set of terms is linked independently of scientific and metaphysical theories to perceived objects or to ways they naturally appear. In the absence of such anchoring we have seen that permutations of referents, all of which preserve assignments of truth to statements, can block the realist from demonstrating knowledge of real objects. The second requirement calls for reduced dependence of reference on beliefs about referents, so that scientists, for example, can hold mostly false beliefs about theoretical entities to which they nevertheless refer. In the discussion of Kuhn we saw that a descriptive cluster account of reference, which takes the referents of theoretical terms to be whichever unobservables fit most of the beliefs (especially regarding laws) expressed in the theories containing them, does not allow such cross-theoretical identification.

THE CAUSAL THEORY

The causal theory of reference has seemed an alternative to the descriptive cluster account suitable for both aims of the realist.

According to this alternative, we refer to objects to which we are causally linked through chains of communication and perception. The account satisfies the first requirement for the realist in a most obvious way: it typically grounds acts of referring in direct perceptions of objects and in those causal relations according to which the perceptions are said to be of those objects. Such links seem to leave little room for indeterminacy, at least on the level of observables (although, as I shall argue later, we still need descriptions to distinguish reference to rabbits, for example, from reference to rabbit parts, to which we are equally causally related). I argued above that determinacy there solves the problem of inscrutability for theoretical terms, given that we conceive their referents by analogy and via causal relations to observables.

The second requirement, the reduction of the dependence of reference on true beliefs, appears to be met fully as well. In the causal account it does not matter if I hold mostly mistaken beliefs about Aristotle, for example. I can refer to him as long as there is a chain of communication stretching back through my source of his name to the man himself or to dubbing acts in perceptual contexts. In the case of theoretical terms, there may appear to be a difficulty, since there are no direct perceptual causal chains to unobservable entities. But we need only extend acceptable chains from the perceptible effects of theoretical entities to the entities themselves in order to extend the account to them. Then once more it will not be required that beliefs of scientists about such unobservables be mostly correct in order for them to be about those unobservables. Cross-theoretical reference and correction of false beliefs about such things as atoms becomes possible. These advantages to the realist of the causal account are not nullified by Putnam's recent observation that causal relations themselves must be interpreted, so that assignments of referents under an interpretation remain relative to the theory or conceptual scheme in which the interpretation is given.[1] As argued earlier, for the realist the (theory-independent) relation that determines reference in general also determines reference to itself.

Despite these promising features of the causal account, I do not view it as the answer that we seek to the semantic antirealist.

Too many problems stand in the way. First, there are those that led Frege and Russell to reject the Millian view of names, according to which they refer without having sense or semantic content. These problems include that of empty or fictional names, the informativeness of certain identity statements linking two names, and the nonsubstitutivity of names in some belief contexts. If any singular terms fit the causal account, it would seem that names (as opposed to definite descriptions, for example) should. Names at least do not wear descriptive content on their sleeves. Yet even here the problems with the Millian view, adopted by the causal account, have been long notorious.

In the case of fictional names, causal chains of communication begin with acts of fictional creation, but we do not refer to those acts in using the names. Rather, we refer either to fictional characters, to whom we cannot be causally related, or to nothing. In the latter case our statements seemingly about these characters still have sense, and it is difficult to see how, if the names in question themselves lack sense or associated descriptions that could contribute to the sense of the statements. Suppose, for example, that a child believes that Santa Claus will bring him presents. What is it that he believes? Neither that no one nor that a fictional character will bring him presents, but that a real fat man in a red suit, etc., will do so, a fat man to whom the child could not in fact be causally related. If there is a causal chain extending from the use of the name beyond the act of fictional creation to a real person, it extends to a real saint, once more not the referent of the child's term. Consider a similar situation involving an adult whose use of the name 'Moses' causally connects to the real historical figure, but who intends to refer to the fictionalized hero of the Bible (to the one who brought the Ten Commandments down from Mount Sinai, etc.). Again the reference appears to be determined by the associated description, not by the causal connection. (Some causal theorists would call this an attributive use of the name, thereby admitting a limitation to their own account.)

In regard to identity statements, the causal theorist has a hard time explaining how some of these have informational content, while others do not. If names themselves lack both content and associated descriptions that could contribute to the content of statements containing them, it is difficult to say how 'John Dickson Carr is identical to Carter Dickson' could differ from 'John Dickson Carr is identical to John Dickson Carr'. The causal theorist must say that, whereas the first statement unites two different causal chains, the second does not.[2] But since these chains will be inaccessible to average, and perhaps to all, speakers, at least beyond the first link or two, this claim seems irrelevant to the difference in informational content. (Suppose, for example, that the person from whom I learned the name 'John Dickson Carr' is the same person from whom I learned the name 'Carter Dickson'. The two identity statements still differ in content for me.) If we accept some sort of associated description account of names, however, it will not be necessary that one associate such descriptions as 'author of *The Crooked Hinge*' and 'author of *A Graveyard to Let*', that is, descriptions with high informational content, in order for the identity statements to differ in content. Descriptions as weak as 'bearer of the name "John Dickson Carr" ' will suffice.

It is true that the associated descriptions that help to specify the content of a speaker's expressed belief or the informational content of a statement for him need not all be those that determine the referents of the belief or statement for him. A causal theorist might therefore admit the need for associated descriptions in explaining the informational content or beliefs expressed by certain identity statements. He must deny only that such descriptions help to fix the referents of the names contained therein. But if we require descriptions to be associated with names for the former purpose, this renders a descriptive account of reference for names both more economical and more plausible. A principal argument in favor of such an account is that it contributes to a broader and more unified semantic theory.

When we turn more specifically to belief contexts, a similar explanation seems available for our inability to substitute 'John Dickson Carr' into 'Agatha believes that Carter Dickson wrote *Fear is the Same*'. The problem is that Agatha may assent to the sentence 'Carter Dickson wrote *Fear is the Same*' and dissent from the sentence 'John Dickson Carr wrote *Fear is the Same*'. If, however, she associates descriptions with the two names and

these descriptions are connected for her in some identity statement (belief about identity), then substitution becomes possible.
Substitutivity therefore seems to depend on there being linked
associated descriptions for a speaker, and nonsubstitutivity on
there being no links between associated descriptions.

In an important, recent paper Saul Kripke has denied that
the so-called problem of substitutivity arises (only) from substitution of names in belief contexts and that the problem can be
solved by appeal to associated descriptions.[3] The problem in the
form of a paradox can arise not from substitution but from
translation, as when Pierre, a partial bilingual, assents to 'Londres est jolie' but dissents from 'London is pretty'. Here Pierre
appears to believe a contradiction, although he has made no
error in logic. The same problem can arise even from disquotation alone, as when Peter, hearing of both Paderewski the
statesman and Paderewski the musician but not linking them,
assents to both 'Paderewski had musical talent' and 'Paderewski
had no musical talent'. Kripke, of course, has argued that
names can refer when their users lack any accurate identifying
descriptions. In this example certain descriptions that Peter
could use to fix his reference do not help to dissolve the paradox. He might specify the referent of the name in both cases as
'the person referred to by the source from whom I learned the
name'.

It seems to me nevertheless that Kripke's puzzle cases may be
solved more easily by appeal to associated descriptions than by
means of any resources available to the causal theorist. In
Pierre's case the puzzle seems to arise from the fact that the
descriptions 'city named "London" ' and 'city named "Londres" ' are not linked for him. While it is not necessary that a
normal French speaker link the two names or descriptions associated with them in order for us to translate his statements and
beliefs containing (tokens of) 'Londres' into statements and beliefs about London, in Pierre's case his being bilingual and ex-
pressly denying (if asked) that 'Londres' is the name of London
may block that translation. In the case of Peter, there are different descriptions associated with different uses of 'Paderewski'
that again fail to be linked, for example, 'the statesman' and 'the
musician'. It is true that these descriptions do not fix his refer-

ence when he uses the name, but once more the need for such descriptions to specify the contents of beliefs renders the appeal to the same or to other associated descriptions that can fix reference more attractive. Thus, whether Kripke's kind of puzzle arises from substitution or just from translation or disquotation, it seems to lend additional support to descriptive views of names, despite his denial that this is so.

Changes of referents for names used at different times also pose a problem for the causal account. Suppose, for example, that I name my newborn son after my grandfather. To the extent that I am caused to use this name (normally we would say that I choose to do so), the causal chain extends back to my grandfather (and perhaps to his grandfather . . .). Yet most of my future uses will refer to my son, only some continuing to refer to my grandfather. The causal theorist must posit multiple causal chains here, some grounded in the dubbing act for my son and not extending to the cause (insofar as there was one) for that act, and some extending to applications of the name to my grandfather. He must also explain why some of my uses invoke one type of chain and some the other. Given that none of these uses may be literally caused, the crucial factor seems to be my intention to apply the term in one way rather than another. But this intention lends itself to descriptive rather than causal analysis. The way I would describe my referent can differentiate my use; appeal to causality cannot.

Even more obvious cases illustrate the same point. Consider the case of identical twins whose names at birth are later inadvertently switched. The causal theorist must say that certain subsequent uses of their names constitute new casual groundings that fix reference for subsequent utterances. But why do these later uses in perceptual contexts constitute new groundings rather than invocations of the causal chains extending to the normally significant (for the causal theorist) dubbing acts? Again, if there are causes for the uses of the names, they continue to derive from these acts. The shifts in referents rather derive from later intentions of the parents in perceptual and then nonperceptual contexts, intentions expressible by certain associated descriptions. Another case mentioned earlier was the shift in referents of 'Santa Claus' from a real saint to a fictional character. Here there may not have been an act of fictional creation initiating a new series of causal chains but rather a gradual development of a legend until a change in referents for most uses of the name occurred. There was no new causal grounding by which to explain this shift, only changes in intentions and descriptions that express them.

A final word on names and the causal connections that are supposed to determine reference for them. Such connections, when present, appear to be insufficient for fixing reference, even apart from the problem of changes in referents just described. Someone's simply hearing a name and acquiring no other information about its referent does not seem sufficient for his using that name to refer in the same way in the future, although it would establish a causal connection of the usual type. If I overhear the name 'Frank' in a conversation, pick up no other information, or forget entirely the remainder of the conversation, it does not seem that by uttering the name in the future I thereby refer to the person mentioned in the conversation. At least I do not refer to him unless I can describe him, for example as the person mentioned in the conversation. I require at least the intention to refer to whomever my source for the name referred to, and this intention requires some such descriptive resources.

All these cases constitute problems for a nondescriptive theory of reference for names, the terms for which a causal account is most plausible. (It is especially plausible in those cases in which the user of a name has mostly mistaken beliefs about (or descriptions of) its referent. It remains to be seen whether a descriptive account can handle such cases.) More obvious is the fact that the causal theory lacks scope or generality. First, we can refer to many kinds of things to which we lack causal connections: not only fictional characters but numbers and other abstract objects, future beings, alien beings from other galaxies, and so on. I acknowledged the partial success of the causal account in regard to reference to theoretical entities, but the power of the account to capture this important class of cases fully may also be questioned. We can pick out many theoretical entities by means of description schemas such as 'cause of such and such observable effects'. When our theories go deeper, extending for example to quarks, we may require another layer of descriptions of this sort, since these entities are not linked directly to observable effects. In such cases, while reference to effects in our descriptions may be crucial for picking out the entities in question, direct causal links between our uses of terms to refer to them and the entities themselves are doubtful. Neither perceptions of quarks nor perceptions of effects of quarks ground uses of the term 'quark'.

Second, when we turn our attention from names to kind terms and referring terms such as definite descriptions, the limitations of the causal account become more marked. Some definite descriptions must be taken at face value. 'The tallest man is less than twelve feet' refers to the tallest man, whoever he is, a man to whom I am not causally related when I utter this statement. It is because we can refer to whatever satisfies certain of our descriptions without being required to interact causally with things to which we refer that even brains in vats can have beliefs about real objects (as argued in the previous chapter). Causal theorists contrast such "attributive uses" of referring terms with "referential uses," for which their account was designed. An example of the latter involving a definite description would be the statement 'The man drinking the martini is bald', referring to a man seen at a party who is fact drinking only water.[4] But while, as we shall see, a sophisticated descriptive account can handle the latter example, a causal account cannot accommodate the former. If there are not in fact two radically different mechanisms of reference at work in these two cases, if a unifying theory of general scope capable of accommodating both types of cases is preferable to two very different accounts for the same domain, then we are driven again toward a descriptive account.

Kind terms pose another problem: that the application of the causal theory once more requires supplementation of the appeal to causal relations. Furthermore, unlike the case of names, once this need for supplementation is recognized for kind terms, the importance of the causal relations themselves in determining reference diminishes to the vanishing point. According to this account, mass kind terms such as 'water' or 'gold' refer to samples of substances of the same kind as certain paradigms to which their uses are causally related in perceptual contexts. General kind terms such as 'rabbit' refer to individuals of the same kind as paradigms to which users are causally related. But appeal to these causal relations must be supplemented in order to determine both the proper paradigms and the relevant similarity relations of other individuals or samples to the paradigms.

In regard to the former paradigms, even dubbing acts in the presence of perceived objects cannot fix reference on the basis of perceptual causal chains alone. Why, for example, does the term 'rabbit' refer to rabbits rather than to rabbit parts or stages, to which perceivers stand in identical causal relations (perceptually)? Given the sameness of the perceptual causal relations, the answer must lie in the way the objects are naturally conceptualized and described, based in turn on how they naturally appear (as whole, subsistent objects). It is true that in perceptual contexts one can conceptualize or describe the perceived object wrongly yet still perceive and refer to it. As in the case of the man with the martini, one may mistake a rabbit for a dog yet still perceive and refer to it. But it is doubtful whether one can refer to a perceived rabbit if one does not at least conceptualize it as an object, and it remains the case that the term for rabbits refers to them (in its general use) rather than to their parts or stages because of how we conceptualize and describe the ways they appear.

In the case of mass terms such as 'gold' and 'water', whatever tests or descriptions we take to be crucial for determining sameness of substance or the full extensions of the terms in their general uses also must determine proper paradigms for the causal account. Suppose, for example, that the original "paradigms" to which ancient fools applied the term 'gold' (or its translation in their older language) were in fact iron pyrites. Such dubbing acts and paradigms would be dismissed as irrelevant to the reference of current uses, since their objects do not satisfy accepted tests or descriptions for being in the extension of 'gold'. What counts as a paradigm must itself satisfy these descriptions. But then the descriptions alone specify the extensions of the mass terms, all paradigms becoming superfluous (all applications of the terms acquiring the same importance).

What really matters is the way that we determine the similarity relations among samples that places them in the same kind. Once more this is a matter of their satisfying certain descriptions or having certain properties, not a matter of their being causally related to speakers in any particular way.

Paradigms may still seem to play an important role in fixing the reference of mass and general kind terms in that, by appealing to them, we seem to avoid having to specify in more precise descriptions those similarity relations that determine membership in the kinds or extensions of the terms. We can simply say that something is gold if it is of the *same* substance as *this* (pointing to a paradigm), and that something is a tiger if it is of the *same* species as *that*. Such an account allows scientists to refer across theories that may specify criteria for membership in the kinds differently. What matters is what *really* determines such membership, not what they think does so. But, even aside from doubts whether there is only one way to divide real kinds, and aside from the more serious problem of fool's gold and fool's tigers (Disney World robots)—that is, the problem of wrong paradigms—there is a price to pay for such complete intertheoretical reference. When appeal is made not to any theoretical or observable criteria but rather to an unspecified sameness relation, we cannot be certain that we (even collectively) can identify members of the relevant class and distinguish them from nonmembers in practice. We may not be able to pick out what we commonly refer to by such terms as 'gold' or 'water'. Such inability may be a reasonable price and its ascription plausible in some contexts, especially theoretical contexts at admittedly primitive stages of theorizing. But not in all contexts. It is plausible for certain uses of terms such as 'water' and not for other uses.

Putnam sees appeal to paradigms as essential also for bringing out what he takes to be the irreducibly indexical or contextual element in fixing the reference of kind terms. He assumes that our counterparts in the possible world Twin Earth, where lakes and seas are filled with liquid observationally indistinguishable from our water but of chemical structure XYZ rather than H_2O, refer to a different kind when they use the term 'water'. Their descriptions may be the same as ours (and were before either of us developed chemical theory); what differentiates their referents are contextual factors that distinguish referents of indexicals, that is, different causal relations to paradigms.[5] As I hinted above, my intuitions do not match Putnam's here. It seems to me that some uses of our term 'water' (and some of our counterparts' uses) refer to stuff of which lakes in both worlds are samples, that is, to anything satisfying descriptions of the distinguishing phenomenal properties of water. Other of our uses refer to whatever passes our scientists' tests for being H_2O, and still others to ..hat meets the theoretical criteria of some distant or ideal successor to current chemical theory (which might again group purported H_2O and XYZ together). Of paramount importance once more are those descriptions that we intend to determine the kind of stuff we pick out, not simply causal relations together with similarity relations beyond our recognition. (Despite my disagreeing with Putnam in such cases, indexicals—but not paradigms—will be prominent in the account of reference I shall suggest as well, and I shall have more to say about them in a moment.)

A MODIFIED DESCRIPTIVE THEORY

Assuming that the two types of accounts considered here exhaust the alternatives, one of sufficient scope must then appeal prominently to descriptions associated with referring terms rather than (directly) to causal connections. But the objections of such philosophers as Kripke, Putnam, and Keith Donnellan to standard descriptive or descriptive cluster accounts seem equally telling. According to these accounts, a speaker refers to those objects that satisfy a certain portion of all the descriptions that he associates with his referring terms. But given the objections, we seemingly cannot equate the meanings of all referring terms with descriptions that fix their reference, and we cannot fix their referents as whichever objects satisfy all or a certain fraction of the descriptions with which particular speakers associate them.

The first problem for this account is its failure to allow a sufficient degree of error or ignorance on the part of speakers. A person can believe that Einstein was the inventor of the atom bomb, have no other individuating beliefs about him, yet refer to him in expressing that false belief. Most of the descriptions that we associate with names of people we know or have heard of fail to describe uniquely and many describe falsely, so that reference cannot be determined through satisfaction of such descriptions. As speakers we are not limited to referring to what uniquely satisfies our own true descriptions. In the case of kind terms, especially those referring to theoretical kinds, we have seen that the descriptive cluster account prohibits identification across theories. Failing to allow for widespread false beliefs about theoretical entities makes it more difficult to demonstrate progress as those beliefs are corrected in light of new evidence or theory.

These initial problems are handled by moving to a different sort of descriptional account. We must specify a certain privileged class of descriptions as fixers of reference, ones that allow for error and are lower in content than all those combined that speakers associate with their referring terms. Such privileged descriptions can divide authority for fixing reference across members of a linguistic community, so that uniquely identifying descriptions need not be possessed by each speaker. They can compensate for reduced content also by containing indexicals that relate objects uniquely to community members with the authority to specify them as referents. Permitting indexicals in the class of identifying descriptions also solves other problems that arise from Putnam's Twin Earth examples. Genuine problems here relate to singular, not kind terms. It may be that, in the absence of indexicals, my replica on Twin Earth and I share all ways of describing our respective wives, even though I refer to mine alone and he to his. But since my wife is uniquely related to me and his to him, we do have unique ways of picking them out by appeal to these relations, perceptual and otherwise. Allowing indexicals in our identifying descriptions permits us to appeal to such unique relations and avoid Putnam's objection to the older descriptive account.

But the presence of indexicals in many of our privileged descriptions, it will be objected, renders the descriptive account impure.[6] It can be held to reintroduce causal factors into the heart of the theory. I am not concerned to expunge causal elements entirely. We have noted that appeal to causes, where it works, serves the realist's purposes unproblematically. I previously appealed to causal relations, at least indirectly, in the account of primitive reference to naturally salient properties that anchors the entire realist theory and renders reference determinate. I would therefore be happy with a purely causal account of the reference of indexicals (which is assumed if the causal theorist raises the objection here). A satisfactory account of that sort has not been provided, however, and I have none to offer.

It was noted above that a causal theorist must recognize some purely descriptive or attributive uses of referring terms, and that his account therefore lacks scope. Here the question is whether the same is true of descriptive accounts in regard to indexicals. Before commenting further on that question, we may note another sort of term for which a similar claim can be made. Free variables seemingly come to refer by being assigned values directly, not via descriptions. Such assignment does not clearly depend on invoking causal relations, but is it nondescriptive as well? This is not obvious either, on reflection. Free variables may come to refer to objects only indirectly, via the terms that specify their assignments of objects. If the latter terms, ordinary referring terms, refer via descriptions, then so do the variables that refer through their mediation.

In regard to indexicals such as 'this', 'that', 'I', 'here', and 'now', the former two may seem to refer via direct causal relation rather than description. What distinguishes for me *this* paper before me from the one currently before my twin on Twin Earth seems to be my causal relation to the former that allows me to refer to it as *this one*. But this appeal to causality is not available in the case of the latter three indexicals, although Twin Earth cases arise for them as well (and 'this' and 'that' may be reducible to them in various contexts). 'I' refers to me here and to my twin when used by him on Twin Earth, although our self-descriptions are presumably the same. Yet there are no causal relations of me (or of my use of the term 'I') to myself or of this place to itself that distinguish my uses of 'I' and 'here', even for me. An additional point may further lessen the temptation to view this class of terms as a limitation on the scope of descriptive accounts of reference, at least in the form of an intrusion of causal factors. As

David Kaplan points out, the contents (and not simply the referents) of statements containing indexicals vary with context.[7]
Such terms may not enter directly into those contents. They may
not be genuine (directly) referring terms at all, their role rather
being to help determine the specification of contents by other
terms according to context. If so, then, if these other terms refer
descriptively, so do indexicals (indirectly), if they refer at all. (If
replaceable, indexicals would appear only in the penultimate
reference-fixing descriptions.)

But how can any descriptions distinguish my statements using 'I' from the counterpart statements of my twin on Twin
Earth? 'I' can be replaced by 'Alan Goldman', and the name
perhaps can be replaced by certain descriptions in specifying
the contents of my statements; but the same replacements, or
ones containing the same term types, will appear in the descriptions of the contents of my twin's statements and beliefs. To be
differentiated these descriptions themselves will have to be indexed to our respective worlds. The question then becomes
whether these worlds can be descriptively distinguished. If both
worlds (planets) were actual, then of course they would occupy
different spatial positions and could be distinguished, at least
from an ideal vantage point, in that way. But Twin Earth can be
just like real Earth except for being merely possible. If pure
actuality alone can therefore distinguish possible worlds, if actuality itself is not a property captured by a description, and if
certain reference-fixing descriptions must be indexed to worlds
in order to differentiate their referents (I assume here that we
can refer to merely possible objects, *pace* the causal account),
then descriptive accounts of reference are incomplete.[8] But so
are causal theories in the same way. Furthermore, there is no
reason to think that this gap is damaging to the realist position
defended here. The variation of reference with context, captured by the use of indexicals, does not obviously or directly
depend on causality. Nor does it render reference indeterminate or restrict it to phenomenal objects. On the contrary, such
variation seems to indicate again the grounding of reference in
perceptual situations that renders it determinate in relation to
physical objects.

Before specifying the character of reference-fixing descriptions further, we may note another shortcoming of the descriptive cluster criterion of reference. The traditional descriptive account generates counterintuitive implications regarding analyticity and a prioricity. If we equate the senses or meanings of names with descriptions associated with them by particular speakers, then certain apparently empirical facts become true by virtue of meaning. If, for example, the name 'Einstein' is associated with such descriptions as 'responsible for relativity theory' and 'leading critic of quantum theory', and if these descriptions specify the sense of the name, then it becomes analytically true and knowable a priori that Einstein developed relativity and held quantum mechanics to be incomplete. But statements to that effect are neither analytically true nor knowable a priori. Hence proper names cannot have senses specified by such descriptions.

The response of the descriptionist is to deny that names as terms in a language are synonymous with descriptions with which particular speakers associate them. Descriptions can fix the referents of names in particular uses without being strictly synonymous with them and without ascribing properties necessarily or on the basis of linguistic rules alone. A difficulty for this response lies in the requirement we noted in explaining uses of fictional names, informational contents of certain identity statements, and nonsubstitutivity of coreferential names in some belief contexts—the requirement that descriptions specify the contents of speakers beliefs. If descriptions help to express the contents of speakers' beliefs when they use names in statements, then how can they not also specify the meanings of the names, that is, the contributions the names make to the meanings of statements in which they function? The answer lies in a distinction similar to one often drawn between speaker's reference on particular occasions and the semantic reference or extension of a term in its general use in a language. If descriptions specify the contents of speakers' beliefs, then they also reveal the meanings of the terms those speakers' use. That is, descriptions help to specify what speakers mean by particular statements, which meaning may be equated with the contents of those beliefs that the statements express.[9] But a speaker's meaning or belief content on a particular occasion may not be identical to the combined normal meanings of his terms as terms in the language of his linguistic community. (Nor, in communicating his beliefs, need a speaker intend his entire audience to grasp all those beliefs that he might express.) While the latter is an abstraction from many instances of the former, given enough diversity in associated descriptions, no description will be synonymous with the name with which it is associated. Those descriptions that fix the reference and express the meaning of a name for one speaker need not be the ones that serve that function for another; nor need speakers intend that these all be identical.

The above points apply to so-called attributive uses of names, for which Kripke's modal problem appears to arise, as when I use the name 'Moses' to refer to the person who led the Jews out of Egypt (whether or not he was the historical figure named Moses). If I use the name in this way, then I might be said to know a priori that Moses led the Jews out of Egypt. But I will not know a priori that an actual person did so. My statement that Moses led the Jews out of Egypt, if I associate no other descriptions as fixing my reference, will embody the much more trivial knowledge that, *if* an actual person led the Jews out of Egypt, then, whoever that person was, he led the Jews out of Egypt. It will certainly not be true that necessarily an actual person did this; nor will it be knowable a priori that this was done.

So-called referential uses of names do not even appear to give rise to a similar problem. The reason is that the descriptions that express the meanings and fix the referents of names used in such contexts may be of such low content as 'bearer of the name "Alexis" ' or 'person referred to by source for the name "Alexis" '. The latter type of description will be replaced for some speakers by descriptions containing prominent first-person indexicals, such as 'person at whom I am now looking' or 'object appearing mostly white in the center of my visual field'. Such descriptions as these do not generate the modal problem, since they rarely appear in the predicate position of actual statements; and when they do, they do not generate problematic claims to a priori knowledge. No one would be disturbed at my claiming to know a priori that, for example, Alexis is the bearer of the name 'Alexis', or that Alexis is a person referred to by my source for the name 'Alexis'. Here we appeal to the points of the previous paragraph only in the case of the final reference-fixing, perceptual-indexical descriptions, such as 'person at whom I am now looking'. In this case it is clear that my descriptions of that form, which fix referents of certain names for me and help to express the contents of my expressed beliefs, are not synonymous with the names as terms in the language or with other descriptions used similarly by others.

In regard to kind terms, a similar problem does arise, but it applies more acutely to the causal account, in its appeal to samples or individuals *of the same kind* as paradigms. Here, whatever is taken to determine relevant similarity will be ascribed necessarily to all members of the class or kind, and there will be no relevant variation according to use or associated description. Kripke, of course, is perfectly willing to accept that water, for example, is necessarily H_2O. This does not follow strictly from his theory of reference alone. But it does follow from it together with the assumptions that sameness of substance is determined by chemical structure and that water has the chemical structure H_2O.[10] The point is that whatever *really* determines sameness of substance must be ascribed necessarily to all samples of a kind on this account. In my view, on the other hand, uses of 'water' will vary in their implicit bases for determining extensions for those particular uses. The a priori knowledge possible in such cases is of the harmless kind noted above. It does not imply the ascription of necessary properties (a posteriori) to real objects or substances that should excite metaphysicians.

We may now be more precise in specifying descriptions taken to determine reference. Our criterion is as follows. In specifying the referent of a term in a particular use, we always begin with an associated description by a speaker, but it must be a description from which he would not retreat if certain possible errors in his beliefs were pointed out to him. In the face of possible error a speaker often will delegate linguistic authority elsewhere, and there are several standard ways in which this could be done. First, in using particular terms like names, he could intend to use the referring term as those from whom he picked it up used it. His description for specifying the referent of his term would then be something like: 'whomever the sources for my use of the name referred to'. Authority typically would be delegated back through a chain of speakers until some speaker was reached who would specify an indexical description (for example, 'person appearing—to me') from which he would not retreat. Such chains would be typical in cases covered by the causal theory. In those cases in which we referred to historical figures, final authorities would be currently non-existent. (Authorities are ideal in this sense in cases in which referents are neither described nonindexically nor indicated indexically by living persons.) Second, a speaker could intend to use a name to refer to whomever those in a given community refer, as when I use the name 'Feynman' to refer to the physicist to whom most physicists refer when they use that name.

Third, for some uses of kind terms, such as 'chairs' or 'water', speakers could intend to refer to what the majority of other speakers would refer to by using such terms indexically, or to what satisfies certain phenomenal descriptions (appearing odorless, tasteless, etc.). 'Chairs' typically refers to whatever speakers apply the term 'chair' to pick out when in the presence of the objects in question. Here again the delegation of authority ends in such indexical contexts. For other uses of natural kind terms, speakers could intend to refer to what passes the tests of experts within a present scientific or technical subcommunity, or to what will meet the tests of future experts. (Putnam's criterion matches my account in deferring to those at the Peircean end of inquiry.)

The criterion proposed is a descriptive one, but the descriptions are relativized to relevant authorities, rather than to speakers or to random groups of speakers. For the extensions of some natural kind terms (tokens), authorities are those who apply currently acknowledged best theories for determining natural kinds. For other kind terms, linguistic authority resides in the community as a whole. For yet others the relevant authorities are currently nonexistent, so that we lose the ability to identify samples with certainty but gain the ability to refer across indefinitely many theories. This criterion has the virtue of allowing for falsity in speakers' associated descriptions or beliefs, while freeing us from the shackles of mythical histories in our current uses of terms, except in certain rare cases of reference to historical figures. It accepts the 'linguistic division of labor' of which Putnam speaks, making more explicit what that is to imply. It accepts also his Principle of the Benefit of Doubt (that speakers recognize the fallibility of some of their central beliefs or theories about things to which they refer)[11] where applicable, while dropping talk of "real" similarity relations determining the extensions of terms in relation to original historical paradigms. (The problem there is not that similarity relations are not real but rather that too many of them are real.)

The diversity among allowable descriptions gives the account its scope. It is intended to cover both "referential" and "attributive" uses of definite descriptions, for example. The latter wear their reference-fixing descriptions on their sleeves; the former typically transform into indexical descriptions. There are not radically different mechanisms of reference here, only an important difference in detail. Regarding kind terms, descriptions that determine reference need not be in particular speakers' heads. But they must be at least counterfactually attributable to some language users. There are no "magical" links of referring terms to objects independent of all conceivable linguistic intentions. But since language is a social institution, neither are we limited in our abilities to talk about things by our meager individual stores of knowledge.

The main problem I see with this criterion, apart from its lacking the simplicity and intuitiveness of the causal and traditional descriptive accounts, derives from the implausibility of attributing actual descriptions of the types I have indicated to particular speakers, for example, descriptions that would delegate linguistic authority elsewhere. Speakers may well lack the conceptual and semantic sophistication to avail themselves in this way of the benefits of dividing linguistic labor. Much earlier I accused certain metatheories of knowledge of being unfair to children and ingenues. To avoid the same objection here we must speak of descriptions that *would be* offered given sufficient conceptual sophistication and awareness of possible errors. Deferring to the wrong authorities, a related worry, does not strike me as a serious problem, since relevant authorities can be described, for example, as members of the dominant scientific community or as the sources for particular speakers' uses of particular terms. They need not be specified personally. Regarding the lack of intuitiveness, this, if a fact, is compensated both by gain in scope and by the clear indication in the account of the social nature of language use and reference.

The criterion, if basically sound, remains to be specified more precisely and defended against more specific objections elsewhere. My purpose here is more limited, namely, to suggest a plausible account of sufficient scope that will fit the realist's epistemological program. The account I have suggested does so fit, first because of its grounding in primitive reference to naturally salient properties, described in earlier chapters. There it was held that primitive representations upon which language acquisition and use builds stand in functionally for certain perceptual appearances and thereby refer to those objects to which the appearances are causally related in perception. Somewhat more precisely, they refer to those apparent properties for which they substitute functionally and to those objects that cause such properties to appear. (There is no differentiation of reference to properties from that to objects at this stage.) Reference to other properties must be developed in stages from primitive reference to naturally salient ones, not through definition but through the grasp of webs of relations—analogical, causal, etc.—in principle captured by descriptions. Later sophisticated and differentiated reference, under the more or less intentional control of associated descriptions, does not lose this grounding, which can be induced to render reference in general determinate. One may wonder why, in an account that claims uniformity and scope as virtues, the characterization of primitive reference is quite distinct. The answer is that any realist descriptive account must appeal to nondescriptive factors, presumably causal ones, at some point in order to anchor the entire structure to real objects and properties via perception. (And any descriptional account of object referring terms must at least begin to suggest how reference to properties originates.) I have argued that an indirect, functionally mediated connection, relating initial representations to naturally salient properties, is more plausible than a simple link between objects and (object) referring terms in mature language use.

This descriptive account serves the realist also because of

the variety of descriptions that relate referring terms to objects and the prominence of appeal to apparent, as opposed to real, properties in many ultimate reference-fixing descriptions. The traditional descriptive account, as noted, implied necessary real properties of objects that could be known a priori, simply by understanding terms that refer to those objects. On the present account, in contrast, we find out in learning how to use referring terms only that their objects are those that typically appear in certain ways (and not in others in counterfactual situations). When we instead use such terms attributively to refer to whatever actually has certain properties, we must still induce on the basis of appearances that there are such objects, that our reference succeeds. (This is not to say that we normally infer such beliefs in forming them.) Because of these features, the meanings of such terms, including those aspects of meaning captured by associated descriptions that fix referents, consist in their contributions to the specification of truth conditions. Beliefs that such conditions obtain must be validated by inferences to best explanatory accounts.

Appendix
Psychology and Epistemology

This afterword will attempt to clarify (though still by way of a conceptual map outlining only the broad contours of the territory) the relations between epistemology, as construed above, and cognitive psychology, especially psychological theories regarding perception. The account of these relations implicit in the epistemological theory articulated in this book contrasts with two more extreme views prominent in recent literature. The first, that of Quine, Jerry Fodor, and Jean Piaget for example, holds that psychology can and should simply take over what is intelligible in traditional epistemological questions regarding perception and cognition. The second position, that of British Wittgensteinian philosophers including D. W. Hamlyn, Alan White, and Godfrey Vesey, maintains that epistemological questions are conceptual, that skepticism is to be answered by pointing out what is implicit in our concepts of objects and their properties, and that psychological data and causal theories remain irrelevant to that analysis. Both these views fail to cohere with the task of the epistemologist as pursued in this book.

PSYCHOLOGY AND FOUNDATIONS

Epistemology has been viewed here in the traditional way, as concerned with the validation of claims to empirical knowledge in light of skeptical challenge. Our presentation has followed a fixed order reflecting justificatory relations among types of beliefs. Those empirical beliefs most immediately validated—the foundational beliefs—have functioned in the validation of commonsense and theoretical beliefs about the real properties of objects. The set of foundational beliefs referred to ways objects appear. Such beliefs need not be viewed as infallible or incorrigible in order to be taken as grounds for epistemic inferences to beliefs regarding objective properties. Nor need beliefs about properties of objects normally be inferred from beliefs about appearances in order to be validated in this way. It is sufficient that the latter be self-explanatory and that the former enter into best explanations for appearances as conceived in beliefs about them.

Some philosophers have thought that psychological fact and theory call into question right off the possibility of this foundational role for beliefs about ways things appear. Ways objects appear are affected by a variety of subjective factors, knowledge of which emerges only through sophisticated psychological experiment. Epistemologists cannot begin their account of validation with appearances projected directly from objects uncontaminated by subjective factors. There are no such appearances. Furthermore, beliefs about ways things appear are conceptually sophisticated and late to develop. We do not conceptualize those appearances of which we are aware *as* appearances until our epistemic concepts have become relatively mature. Indeed, in order even to formulate beliefs about sequences of appearances, we seem to require reference to the realm of physical objects and their properties. How then can sophisticated beliefs about subjectively relative appearances serve as foundations for empirical beliefs regarding objective qualities?

I have maintained that the denial that they can serve this function results from confusion between relations that are conceptual and causal and those that are epistemic. The fact that ways things appear are not "theory-free" or "given," and the fact that they are rarely conceptualized as appearances, do not alter the status of beliefs about appearances as natural empirical premises for validating inferences. Causal influences upon ways things appear do not affect the validation of beliefs about how they appear. If I believe that I am appeared to redly, I can be justified in this belief irrespective of the causes of my being appeared to in that way. What is altered by recognizing causal influences upon appearances is our view of the relation of ways of appearing to objective physical properties, and our view of the warrant for beliefs about such real properties. But the fact that our theory of this relation is subject to change with sophisticated evidence does not render sets of beliefs regarding appearances less suitable for initiating the chain of inferences that leads to theoretical beliefs in the reconstruction of epistemic warrant.

We have seen that the relative sophistication in concepts of appearances and the fact that they presuppose concepts of objects and their properties are equally irrelevant to the status of beliefs about appearances as initial epistemic premises. That concepts of objects and their properties are fundamental for us does not in itself show that they are instantiated. Showing this requires appeal to ways things appear and to the best explanations for the ways they appear. In demonstrating the justification for empirical beliefs, the epistemologist is not required to follow the order in which concepts of objective properties and appearances are initially acquired. Sophisticated concepts enter into beliefs that are more immediately validated than others involving simpler concepts. That concepts of objective properties are presupposed in the formation of beliefs about appearances does not imply that the latter are inessential to the validation of beliefs involving the former.

Some philosophers, noting the various influences on ways of appearing, question more deeply the suitability of beliefs about appearances as epistemic data. According to them our view of what constitutes data, itself theory-laden, should alter with developments in theory regarding the nature of data, that is, inputs to the cognitive system. From my point of view it is obvious that physical inputs to the sensory system, the "data" for the brain, are not to be identified with epistemic data. I have viewed the temptation to make this identification as a new version of the old longing for data projected directly in sensory stimulation uncontaminated by subjective factors. There are no such data available to the subject. This is one reason for taking appearances of which the subject is aware, or beliefs about appearances that he can form once he has the requisite concepts, rather than physical stimulation, as the source of evidence for beliefs about physical objects and ultimately for inferences in science. Physical input is not available to us in everyday contexts when appealing to evidence to justify our naive beliefs about physical objects, but the inductive reasoning that leads ultimately to scientific theory begins in such contexts.

More important, first-person beliefs about (some) appearances are more immediately validated and less subject to revision than are beliefs about the physical properties of sensory stimulations. Properties of both distal and proximal stimuli are ascribed in relation to complex measuring instruments and theories of matter and light from physics. Causally basic stimuli are theoretical posits of science, justified at the level of sophisticated theory from an epistemological viewpoint. If it is natural to begin the (demonstration of the) justification of empirical beliefs by appealing to ways things appear, and if beliefs about appearances are not validated in turn by appeal back to physical properties (they are causally explained, but not justified best in this way), then proximity to the proximal stimulus cannot be equated with epistemic priority.[1] We cannot look to psychology (or physics) for a description of epistemic data.

We saw earlier that philosophers such as Paul Churchland view the discrepancy between data with which psychologists begin their causal reconstructions and data to which we naively appeal in attempting to justify perceptual beliefs in a different light. For them our ways of categorizing appearances themselves represent a primitive theory, a part of what they call "folk psychology."[2] These categories are seen as the results of the ways we have learned to make noninferential responses to physical stimulation. In this account we have learned to report appearances as we do because of the way such reports fit into primitive explanations for such phenomena as perceptual errors. If this is so, then we ought to alter our view of the data to accord with more sophisticated and more successful theory when it becomes available. We ought to bring our view of the data more into line with that of science, rather than taking the traditional epistemologist's notion of data as sacrosanct.

We also saw, however, that the evidence does not support this thesis of the radical relativity of ways things appear to theoretical categories imposed from without. While such factors as expectations can affect appearances, especially in ambiguous situations and under poor viewing conditions, knowledge of the nature of the stimulus, or theories or sets of beliefs that categorize it in various ways, generally have little effect on its appearance for the subject. The latter seems to be more a matter of hard wiring than soft programming. If that conclusion derives from the psychological evidence, then we must also conclude that psychology has little more to offer us regarding our beliefs about appearances and their suitability as epistemic foundations. Our beliefs about (some) ways of appearing are best explained by appeal to the appearances themselves, rather than by appeal to the ways we have been taught to respond to stimulation or by appeal to the causal chain investigated by psychologists.

Psychologists can perhaps teach us more of positive epistemic significance about the relations between appearances and objective properties.

PSYCHOLOGY AND INFERENCES FROM FOUNDATIONS

In order to see the relevance of psychology, we must first dismiss again the view that the relation between ways things appear and their objective properties is determinable a priori or "conceptually." Scientific accounts of perception would be epistemologically irrelevant if there were a conceptual or logical, rather than an empirical or contingent, connection between the qualities of objects and the ways they appear in normal conditions. If it were an a priori truth that F things normally appear F, in that we simply chose to call things F that appear so to normal observers, we might still require of scientific theory a causal explanation of why they appear F. But if there were this a priori connection, then the causal theory and variables it isolated would be epistemologically beside the point, no matter how central to scientific understanding. There would be no doubt about our being warranted in believing things to be F on the basis of their normally appearing to be so. Thus, given that beliefs about the properties of things are to be validated by appeal to beliefs about ways they appear, we must construe this religion as contingent if we are to maintain the relevance of psychological data and theory to this process of validation.

The principal argument for the opposing view began with the premise that, where F is a perceptible property, say red, we can identify F things only by the ways they appear. But the continuation of the argument rested on either a mistaken theory of reference or an implicitly nonrealist conception of properties. There is no reason why one cannot pick out a class of things on the basis of something in common in the ways they appear, yet mistakenly ascribe some nonrelational property to the things on the basis of the similarity in appearance. We may call things F on the basis of their appearing F to us in certain conditions; but if we take F to be an intrinsic property of the things themselves, rather than a relational property qualifying only the way they appear, then it does not follow that we have described them correctly by calling them F.

The agreements in judgment necessary for consistent use of property terms need consist only in rough agreements regarding ways things appear under a variety of conditions (the roughness sometimes being hidden by broadness and vagueness in the terms or concepts). The extent of such agreement is to be determined by psychologists using precise matching tests. As long as there is rough agreement regarding appearances, we can ascribe perceptible properties more or less consistently. The epistemically interesting and still open question is whether we are warranted in naively believing these to be intrinsic properties of physical things themselves. This question cannot be settled a priori, and scientific evidence is therefore relevant to its answer. The question is how psychological theories of perception fit into those inferences to the best explanations for ways of appearing that validate beliefs about objective properties.

In answering it is necessary first to provide a brief characterization of the form of such theories. While there may be less controversy concerning the proper characterization here than in the case of epistemology, we nevertheless find a bewildering array of seemingly incommensurable theories and data. The tasks that provide what unity there is to the discipline that began with Hermann von Helmholtz and then progressed to Gestalt theory have been those of isolating variables that causally influence the ways we perceive things and of designing functional models that incorporate these variables. Psychologists are to determine the relations of inputs, in the form of irradiations from objects, to outputs, in the form of perceptual beliefs (both about objective properties and about appearances).

Several types of influence upon perception are widely recognized in addition to measurable physical properties of discrete parts of the distal and proximal stimuli. These include (in physical terms) structural relations among elements in the stimuli, the state of adaptation or inhibition of various types of neurons in the sensory system, eye movements and the direction of attention; (in functional terms) familiarity or expectations of the subject derived from past experience, motivation, and the coordination of visual perception into purposive activity involving the other sense modalities. Even this short list represents a very mixed bag: not all these causal factors are expressed in the same theoretical language. Those expressed in purely functional terms must be embodied somewhere in the nervous system. Psychologists differ, however, not only with respect to members of the list of significant variables and in regard to the importance of each, but more prominently with respect to functional or physiological models to incorporate them, and with respect to the type of experimental research best suited to the isolation of variables and development of models. The factors mentioned above are incorporated into models of neural systems as information processors, or into purely functional models referring to hypothesis formation and inference, or into models for the abstraction of higher-order structural stimulus invariants, etc.

For the physiologically oriented psychologist the problem is to determine how the firings of different types of neurons from the retina to the brain can result in our picking up all the information we do about our environment, information about relatively constant objects. This constitutes an interesting problem because of the fact that the neural systems in which must be encoded information leading to the perception of such properties as colors and shapes seem to lack elements structurally analogous to those properties themselves. The absence of obvious isomorphisms indicates the enormous complexity of the neural code, which remains in part mysterious, although the functions of various stages are beginning to be understood. The relevant evidence consists in various types of inhibitions and firings that appear to be independent of certain discrete proximal stimulus variables, as stimulus energy is converted to electrical impulses transmitted in stages to relevant areas of the brain. It is generally agreed, for example, that certain types of cells are innately sensitive to different types of structural relations in stimulus patterns, but that such sensitivity can alter with experience and learning.

Theories of this type attempt to map functional descriptions, often couched in intentional terms, onto the physiological sequences. It is common to speak of the causal sequence from retina to perceptual beliefs encoded in the brain in terms of data and sequences of inferences or hypotheses.[3] Thinking of the brain in this way as a reasoner or "reasoning instantiator" is suggested to psychologists by their recognition of the influence of subjective factors, including (neural patterns developed from) prior experience, upon the formation of perceptual beliefs. One can summarize the effects of such factors by saying that the subject (or the subject's brain) formulates perceptual hypotheses on the basis of physical inputs insufficient in themselves to determine appearances and beliefs. As the physiological stages of the causal sequence are isolated, one can map functional stages onto them which further suggest the structural analogy of hypothesis formulation, testing, and correction as subjective factors enter and eventually (possibly) come under the control of further physical inputs. On the basis of cues or clues from the physical data, the brain is said to generate representations of the physical environment. These representations can then be seen to result from inferences or hypotheses drawn on the basis of past commerce with the environment (although very little on the basis of sophisticated verbal learning) in addition to present stimulation.

Such talk of physical data and neural inference may suggest again that contemporary psychology of perception fills the role that epistemologists used to play from their armchairs, namely, that of relating perceptual data to beliefs about physical objects in the environment. Certainly psychologists do attempt to perform a task that was crucial also for the traditional enterprise of epistemology: that of separating subjective from objective factors in the generation of perceptual beliefs. Indeed, earlier epistemologists always had to assume or borrow from physical science and psychology in their attempts to solve this problem. But while psychologists are properly represented as having the last word, that is, as completing the causal explanatory account of the generation of perceptual beliefs, the relation of psychological theory to epistemology, as described earlier in this book, is not one of identity; nor do psychologists provide empirically verifiable and hence preferable versions of epistemological theories. The inferences presumed to be instantiated in the brain during the causal sequence initiated by sensory stimulation do not in any sense parallel the series of explanatory inferences that expose the structure of validation for empirical beliefs.

It is first of all somewhat problematic to take literally the description of the brain as inferring a representation of the environment as the best explanation for its physical data. I did take seriously, in the earlier section on natural selection, the analogy between this sequence of physical processes and the structure of explanatory inference. But literal talk of hypothesis and inference at this level suggests a neural language in which such hypotheses are formulated,[4] and the representation in this language of various possibilities *to a subject*. Reference to a language suggests (or perhaps, more strongly, presupposes) a language user, one for whom the symbols of the language are meaningful. There must be a temptation here then to introduce a little person in the brain, a ghost in the machine who can entertain various perceptual hypotheses, retaining some and dismissing others. Nevertheless, it should be clear that the symbolic content of these physical causal sequences (and of similar sequences in the brains of animals) is such only *for us*. Talk of inference and hypotheses in these cases is a heuristic way to summarize the effects of intervening variables and feedback mechanisms. (In the same way we may talk of turntables as hypothesizing the presence of another record to be played.)

It is true that when we do reason from premises, the conscious processes must be instantiated somehow in our brains. It is also true in the case of the enormously complex causal sequences leading to perception of the environment that investigators can begin to grasp the nature of these processes only by analyzing them in functional or teleological terms.[5] Assignment of content to neural processes is therefore not to be avoided. What is to be avoided is confusion between the causal process from stimulation to perceptual belief on the one hand and on the other hand the sequence of epistemic inferences from immediately justified or self-justified beliefs to empirical knowledge embodied in theoretical concepts of physical objects—the sequence that exposes the structure of validation for that empirical knowledge. If there is a fixed natural order to the epistemic sequence, as described earlier, then this order is not isomorphic or analogous to that of the physical causal sequence.

I distinguished in the previous section between physical stimulation itself, the beginning of the physical causal chain, and beliefs about ways of appearing, the starting point for the epistemological reconstruction (and one type of culmination of the causal chain). Beyond that distinction, it must be admitted also that the details of the inner physiological causal process involved in perceiving, whether described in physical or functional terms, cannot in themselves be crucial for the validation of particular perceptual beliefs about objective properties. The functional stages of processing between irradiation and perceptual belief are filled in only in relation to theories regarding the nature of the stimuli and behavioral tests of the contents of the resultant perceptual beliefs. From these tests alone, that is, from a comparison of input with output, one can recognize in advance which features of the stimulus must be encoded and transmitted over the whole process, which features will be lost or ignored, and which will be augmented by inputs later in the sequence from the nervous system. Recognition of the augmentation and loss of possible information in the proximal stimulus, or, in more traditional terms, of the separation of subjective from objective causes for perceptual beliefs, does not await the details of the stages between retina and brain. It is derivable from descriptions of stimulus properties and final beliefs alone.

From the psychologist's point of view, these descriptions function as premises or data from which the full psychological-physiological causal theory is constructed. Such data, drawn from physical theory and from behaviorally tested variations in perceptual beliefs in relation to physically interpreted stimulus variables, have import for the epistemologist too, in revealing these relations between input and output in the perceptual process. Beyond the data, it is the fact that psychologists can approach the completion of the causal account of everyday perceptual beliefs, thus further vindicating the scientific theory of objects by showing why we naively believe as we do in perceptual contexts, that it is important for an epistemology of empirical knowledge. That one can approach completing the explanation for perceptual beliefs about objective properties and appearances when one begins from the physical theories of matter and light is crucial to the full justification of those theories and to the final judgment of naive perceptual beliefs in relation to them. But the details of the inner perceptual process that emerge are not crucial to the justification of particular perceptual beliefs. It is not so much the particular inner causal story produced that is epistemically important as it is the fact that psychologists can produce some explanatorily coherent and plausible story of this type.

This last point is supported by the possibility that empirical knowledge arises not only from disparate physical sequences but from different functionally described sequences as well. It is possible that someday sophisticated empirical knowledge could be imparted to subjects in one fell swoop by direct alteration of the brain through probes or pills. While some causal sequence linking subject to object may still be necessary for empirical knowledge, it is clear from this possibility that no particular physiological or functional specification of discrete steps in the sequence can be necessary. Mature knowledge that requires chains of inference to demonstrate its justification can be acquired in one step, without the possibility of separating discrete functional stages in any way isomorphic to steps in the relevant validating inferential sequences. Thus no such specification can be required for validation.

The possibility that causal sequences all lead to empirical knowledge yet differ in proper functional description exists even given identical input and output. This means that the "inferences" that we might be inclined to ascribe to the brain on the basis of direct comparison of input with output in the form of perceptual beliefs might not map neatly onto discrete events in the physiological sequence. Collateral information necessary for acquiring correct perceptual beliefs about objects in the environment on the basis of stimulation need not be introduced in discrete steps in the neural processing. For example, when a subject (or subject's brain) perceives an apple we might ascribe to him the following inferential pattern: 'Certain patterns of stimulation are arriving that signal red, round shapes.' (This might summarize many steps or represent an intermediate lemma in the sequence.) 'These are generated by apples or wax imitations, etc. There is no reason to suspect wax imitations, etc., in this context. So take the cause of this stimulation to be an apple'. But the steps that consist in ruling out alternative explanations for stimuli need not correspond to any actual events in the processing. Certain paths may lead directly to output in the absence of contrary signals. These steps may be crucial nevertheless to the validation of the perceptual belief.

It follows from the lack of isomorphism between perceptual causal sequences, which we may describe functionally as inferential, and sequences of justificatory explanatory inferences that psychological theories do not duplicate epistemology and that psychologists cannot simply take over the epistemologist's role as construed here. Nevertheless, the construction of psychological theory in this domain is important to an epistemological overview in helping to complete the best explanatory account for ways of appearing as posited in beliefs about appearances. The psychologist's theory, rather than replacing the epistemologist's, fills in part of the explanatory account to which the epistemologist appeals in validating certain empirical beliefs and dismissing others.

PSYCHOLOGY AND REALISM

We may summarize the relations, implicit in our earlier descriptions, between epistemology and the psychology of perception. I argued at the beginning that, in order for a perceptual belief about an objective property to constitute knowledge, the object's having the property in question must enter prominently into the best explanation for the subject's having the belief that it has that property. By isolating the variables that affect ways objects appear and the formation of perceptual beliefs, psychologists call into question the degree to which an object's having particular physical properties does enter into the causal explanations for certain of these beliefs. Physical theory regarding matter and media such as light is presupposed in this procedure (but must not be by the epistemologist). But physics and psychology together represent our best (and for the time being) final inferences regarding relations of perceivers to physical objects, against which initial perceptual beliefs are to be evaluated. Psychological data and theories are parts of the overall scientific picture that best explains perceptual beliefs about objects. This picture shows that the ultimate inferences to best explanations for perceptual beliefs do not warrant the ascription to physical objects of all qualities that we are inclined to ascribe in initial perceptual beliefs.

I have represented the task of the epistemologist as that of developing an overview, of providing a unified outline of validation that incorporates and reveals the warrant for the most basic as well as the most sophisticated empirical beliefs. Theories of psychology and the physics assumed by them lie at the frontier of this account, presupposing for their warrant the realm of beliefs about appearances and many naive perceptual beliefs. The traditional philosophical problem of perception was to justify (or dismiss) perceptual beliefs about objective qualities in light of discrepancies between ways objects appear and spontaneous perceptual beliefs on the one hand and theoretical inferences regarding the nature of objects on the other. The account of warrant for perceptual beliefs in terms of inference to the most consistent and coherent explanatory systems of belief inclines the resolution of that problem toward a thorough scientific realism.

The most coherent and complete explanations for perceptual beliefs available at a given time presumably will consist in the physical and psychological-neurophysiological theories accepted by the scientific community at that time (supplemented by deeper appeals to natural selection, etc.). The concept of objects defined by those theories can, of course, differ in significant respects from the commonsense concept. But if the structure of epistemic validation is represented as proceeding first from beliefs about appearances to naive beliefs about objects, and then to scientific theories as more fully coherent and refined accounts of why objects appear as they do, then it is clear that any conflict regarding objective properties (but not appearances) must be resolved in favor of the latter. The fact that inferences typical even on the frontiers of scientific theorizing conform to the explanatory paradigm for the validation of beliefs at every level guarantees that science will constitute the last word on empirical knowledge of physical objects.

Epistemology, as represented here, presents an overview of the structure of empirical knowledge and the warrant for empirical beliefs, a unified account with scientific theory lying at the frontier yet secured by the cumulative force of the whole series of explanatory inferences. This epistemological view, in which inferences to theoretical descriptions are taken to correct more naive perceptual beliefs when conflicts occur, becomes less problematic and counterintuitive once the naive beliefs are causally explained within the broad context of physical theory, the type of explanation at which the contemporary psychologist ultimately aims. Once we grasp these causal explanations, we understand why we are initially inclined to ascribe properties to physical objects that physical theory does not ascribe to them.

Psychologists are concerned to describe the causal sequence from the projection of sensory stimuli from objects as described by physics to the appearances of objects and the formation of perceptual beliefs. This is part of the explanatory account to which epistemologists infer as well (a relatively late part). Because of their exclusive concern with this type of explanation, psychologists aim at a causal account rather than an account of justification. The latter is in my view required for explanatory coherence within the entire system of empirical beliefs, as anchored by beliefs about appearances. The psychologist's account, given its place in that system and despite its presently fragmentary state, provides part of the best explanation for perceptual beliefs about objects that is available.

Epistemologists provide a theory of warrant (I have used the term 'validation' to contrast with a looser, ordinary, quasi-moral notion of justification). This account demonstrates how we are immediately warranted in holding beliefs about appearances, how these beliefs warrant an initial picture of objects that provides an initially plausible explanation for ways things appear, and how this naive view is modified into physical theory that extends explanatory inferences to deeper levels. The psychology of perception cannot be identified with epistemology, since it is concerned not with validation but with causal explanation of perceptual beliefs. In explaining these beliefs it is willing to take for granted much of physics and biology. But if validation proceeds by inferences to best explanations, the psychology of perception is crucial to the full justification of a thorough scientific realism. For by showing how naive perceptual beliefs are themselves best explained in the context of physical theory, psychology renders the latter more explanatorily coherent. Perceptual beliefs are absorbed into the scientific image via psychological theory, and they become then a support for, rather than a threat to, the thoroughgoing realist view.

Notes

INTRODUCTION

1. See, for example, D. W. Hamlyn, *The Theory of Knowledge* (New York: Anchor, 1970); John L. Pollock, *Knowledge and Justification* (Princeton, N.J.: Princeton University Press, 1974).

2. Prominent examples are D. M. Armstrong, *Perception and the Physical World* (London: Routledge and Kegan Paul, 1961); George Pitcher, *A Theory of Perception* (Princeton, N.J.: Princeton University Press, 1971).

3. For example, see Michael Dummett, *Truth and Other Enigmas* (Cambridge, Mass.: Harvard University Press, 1978); Hilary Putnam, *Reason, Truth and History* (Cambridge: Cambridge University Press, 1981).

4. There are, of course, differences among semantic antirealists. Dummett, for example, appears to be an atomistic verificationist rather than a coherentist.

5. See Putnam, op. cit.

6. Thomas Kuhn, *The Structure of Scientific Revolutions* (Chicago: University of Chicago Press, 1970).

CHAPTER 1. THE ANALYSIS

1. This way of describing the form of inference originates with Gilbert Harman, "Inference to the Best Explanation," *Philosophical Review* 74 (1965): 88–95.

2. Alvin Goldman, "A Causal Theory of Knowing," *Journal of Philosophy* 64 (1967): 357–72.

3. This partial analysis resembles that of Wesley Salmon, "Theoretical Explanation," in *Explanation*, ed. S. Körner (New Haven, Conn.: Yale University Press, 1975), except that I take it to be necessary that the explanans raise the antecedent probability of the explanandum. Compare also Patrick Suppes, *A Probabilistic Theory of Causality* (Amsterdam: North-Holland, 1970).

4. See, for example, Kevin Saunders, "A Method for the Construction of Modal Probability Logics," Ph.D. dissertation, University of Miami, 1978.

5. Compare Illka Niiniluoto, "Statistical Explanation Reconsidered," *Synthese* 48 (1981): 437–72, esp. p. 439.

6. A good recent discussion of this problem is found in Nancy Cartwright, *How the Laws of Physics Lie* (Oxford: Oxford University Press, 1983), essay 1.

7. This example was given to me by Peter Railton.

8. For a recent discussion, See Bas C. van Fraassen, *The Scientific Image* (Oxford: Oxford University Press, 1980), chap. 5.

9. Wesley Salmon, *Statistical Explanation and Statistical Relevance* (Pittsburgh, Pa.: University of Pittsburgh Press, 1971), p. 64.

10. The need for the condition became clear from some of Alvin Goldman's objections to an earlier version of this chapter.

CHAPTER 2. TEST CASES

1. Edmund Gettier, "Is Justified True Belief Knowledge?" *Analysis* 23 (1963): 121–23.

2. The examples are from Alvin Goldman, "Discrimination and Perceptual Knowledge," *Journal of Philosophy* 73 (1976): 771–91.

3. Keith Lehrer, *Knowledge* (Oxford: Oxford University Press, 1974), p. 178.

4. Actually, the truth of the theorem helps to explain the possibility of proofs for it, and the proofs help to explain the beliefs of the mathematicians. The shift in modalities is typical for knowledge of necessary truths.

5. The example is from Marshall Swain, *Reasons and Knowledge* (Ithaca, N.Y.: Cornell University Press, 1981), p. 209.

6. These examples were suggested to me by Howard Pospesel.

7. Swain, op. cit., pp. 151–52.

8. Alvin Goldman objected in this way.

9. The example is from Gilbert Harman, *Thought* (Princeton, N.J.: Princeton University Press, 1973), pp. 143–44.

CHAPTER 3. OTHER ANALYSES

1. Compare Laurence Bonjour, "Externalist Theories of Empirical Knowledge," *Midwest Studies in Philosophy* 5 (1980): 53–73, p. 70.

2. See D. M. Armstrong, *Belief, Truth and Knowledge* (Cambridge: Cambridge University Press, 1973).

3. Lehrer, op. cit.; Swain, op. cit.

4. This example resembles one in Robert Shope, *The Analysis of Knowing* (Princeton, N.J.: Princeton University Press, 1983).

5. Keith Lehrer, paper read at the Chisholm Conference, Brown University, 1986.

6. Fred Dretske, "Conclusive Reasons," *Australasian Journal of Philosophy* 49 (1971): 1–22; Alvin Goldman, "Discrimination and Perceptual Knowledge"; Robert Nozick, *Philosophical Explanations* (Cambridge, Mass.: Harvard University Press, 1981), chap. 3.

7. This move was suggested to me by Frederick Schmitt.

8. Nozick, op. cit., p. 264.

9. Ibid., p. 284.

CHAPTER 4. THE NEED FOR FOUNDATIONS

1. See, for example, van Fraassen, op. cit., pp. 97–98.

2. James Cornman, *Skepticism, Justification, and Explanation* (Dordrecht: Reidel, 1980), pp. 136–37.

3. See Michael Williams, *Groundless Belief* (New Haven, Conn.: Yale University Press, 1977), pp. 106–7.

4. This does not rule out a concept of moral truth as coherence within a set of shared or agreed judgments. Nor does it preclude rational argument in ethics in terms of analogies and disanalogies between controversial judgments and the shared body of data, argument designed to show such coherence or the lack of it. For an account of moral truth within a relativist framework, see Alan Goldman, *Moral Knowledge* (London: Routledge and Kegan Paul, 1988).

5. See Laurence Bonjour, *The Structure of Empirical Knowledge* (Cambridge, Mass.: Harvard University Press, 1985), chap. 6.

CHAPTER 5. APPEARING AS IRREDUCIBLE

1. Examples are Armstrong, *Perception and the Physical World*, and Pitcher, op. cit.

2. This is a simplification of Pitcher's analysis, op. cit., pp. 85–130.

3. The first analysis is Pitcher's, the second Armstrong's.

4. See Fred Dretske, *Seeing and Knowing* (Chicago: University of Chicago Press, 1971), chap. 1.

5. Armstrong, *Perception and the Physical World*, pp. 118–19.

6. See, for example, Jean Piaget, *The Construction of Reality in the Child* (New York: Basic Books, 1954).

7. Compare Dretske, *Seeing and Knowing,* p. 10.

8. Compare Hamlyn, op. cit., p. 54.

9. See, for example, Jean Piaget, *The Origins of Intelligence in Children* (New York: W. W. Norton, 1963).

10. See Armstrong, *Belief, Truth and Knowledge,* p. 61.

11. Fred Dretske, *Knowledge and the Flow of Information* (Cambridge, Mass.: MIT Press, 1981).

12. Ibid., pp. 157–58.

13. Ibid., p. 219.

14. Compare Frank Jackson, *Perception* (Cambridge: Cambridge University Press, 1977), pp. 34–35.

15. Compare Sydney Shoemaker, "The Inverted Spectrum," *Journal of Philosophy* 79 (1982): 357–81.

16. This is Pitcher's analysis, op. cit., pp. 208–10.

17. Ivo Kohler, *The Formation and Transformation of the Perceptual World* (New York: International Universities Press, 1964); see also James Taylor, *The Behavioral Basis of Perception* (New Haven, Conn.: Yale University Press, 1962).

18. Armstrong, *Perception and the Physical World,* p. 82.

CHAPTER 6. THE NATURE OF APPEARING

1. The argument derives from Kant. For a more recent version see Wilfrid Sellars, "Phenomenalism," in *Science, Perception, and Reality* (New York: Humanities, 1963).

2. This use is criticized, for example, in Roderick Chisholm, *Perceiving: A Philosophical Study* (Ithaca, N.Y.: Cornell University Press, 1957), chap. 4.

3. See for example C. W. K. Mundle, *Perception: Facts and Theories* (Oxford: Oxford University Press, 1971); Jackson, op. cit.

4. See E. H. Land, "The Retinex Theory of Color Vision," *Scientific American* 237 (1977): 108–28.

5. Compare Thomas Nagel, "What Is It Like to Be a Bat?" *Philosophical Review* 83 (1974): 435–50.

6. Compare A. Olding, "Frank Jackson and the Spatial Distribution of Sense Data," *Analysis* 40 (1980): 158–62.

7. This argument appears in D. M. Armstrong, "Perception, Sense-data and Causality," in *The Nature of Mind* (Ithaca, N.Y.: Cornell University Press, 1981).

8. The argument is Jackson's, op. cit., chap. 3.

9. This is Sellars's view. See Wilfrid Sellars, "The Adverbial Theory of the Objects of Sensation," *Metaphilosophy* 6 (1975): 144–60.

10. For expansion on this objection, see Panayot Butchvarov, "Adverbial Theories of Consciousness," *Midwest Studies in Philosophy* 5 (1980): 261–80.

CHAPTER 7. KNOWLEDGE OF APPEARING

1. The distinctions are drawn nicely in N. M. L. Nathan, *Evidence and Assurance* (Cambridge: Cambridge University Press, 1980).

2. This view of phenomenal terms is that of Pollock, op. cit., p. 76.

3. Such is the response of Cornman, op. cit., pp. 69–73.

4. Bayes's theorem (simplified) for changing belief in light of evidence, $p(h/e) = p(h) \cdot p(e/h) / p(e)$, where $p(h/e)$ is the probability of h given e and $p(h)$ is the antecedent probability of h, captures part of this idea, in that the lower the antecedent probability of e, the greater is its confirmational power. I will, however, later point out difficulties in applying this theorem to the cases in which we are interested.

5. The claim is made by Williams, op. cit., pp. 62, 76.

6. See Donald Davidson, "Mental Events," in *Essays on Actions and Events* (Oxford: Oxford University Press, 1980).

CHAPTER 8. LIMITATIONS AND COUNTERARGUMENTS

1. To be grue is to be green when observed and blue when unobserved. See Nelson Goodman, "The New Riddle of Induction," in *Fact, Fiction, and Forecast* (Indianapolis, Ind.: Bobbs-Merrill, 1965).

2. Compare Nathan Stemmer, "Non-Linguistic Factors in Language," *Communication and Cognition* 6 (1973): 45–52.

3. Compare Nathan Stemmer, "Projectible Predicates," *Synthese* 41 (1979): 375–95.

4. See, for example, Piaget, *The Origins of Intelligence in Children* and *The Construction of Reality in the Child.*

5. Contrast Jerry Fodor, *The Language of Thought* (New York: Crowell, 1975).

6. The classic description is by Grace de Laguna, *Speech: Its Function and Development* (Bloomington: Indiana University Press, 1963).

7. Saul Kripke, *Wittgenstein on Rules and Private Language* (Cambridge, Mass.: Harvard University Press, 1982).

8. Ludwig Wittgenstein, *Philosophical Investigations,* trans. G. E. M. Anscombe (New York: Macmillan, 1953), sections 143ff.

9. Ibid., e.g., sections 186–88, 190.

10. Ibid., sections 197, 631ff.

11. Wilfrid Sellars, "Scientific Realism or Irenic Instrumentalism," in *Philosophical Perspectives* (Springfield, Ill.: Charles Thomas, 1967); Richard Rorty, "Mind-Body Identity, Privacy, and Categories," *Review of Metaphysics* 19 (1965): 24–54; Paul Feyerabend, "Explanation, Reduction, and Empiricism," in *Scientific Explanation, Space, and Time*, ed. H. Feigl and G. Maxwell, vol. 3 of Minnesota Studies in the Philosophy of Science (Minneapolis: University of Minnesota Press, 1962); Paul Churchland, *Scientific Realism and the Plasticity of Mind* (Cambridge: Cambridge University Press, 1979).

12. Churchland, op. cit., pp. 10–12.

13. James Cornman, *Perception, Common Sense, and Science* (New Haven, Conn.: Yale University Press, 1975), pp. 72–73.

14. One summary of experimental work on the subject is given by Eleanor Gibson, *Principles of Perceptual Learning and Development* (New York: Meredith, 1969), pp. 64–73, 154–60.

15. Ibid., pp. 66, 158.

CHAPTER 9. THE INFERENCE TO PHYSICAL REALITY

1. See again Sellars, "Phenomenalism," and his "Empiricism and the Philosophy of Mind," also in *Science, Perception, and Reality*.

2. Compare Mundle, op. cit., p. 121.

3. Compare Don Locke, *Perception and Our Knowledge of the External World* (New York: Humanities, 1967), pp. 55–60.

4. Compare James Cornman, *Metaphysics, Reference, and Language* (New Haven, Conn.: Yale University Press, 1966), pp. 205–9.

5. Roderick Chisholm, *Theory of Knowledge* (Englewood Cliffs, N.J.: Prentice-Hall, 1977).

6. Ibid., p. 67.

7. Compare Gilbert Harman, *The Nature of Morality* (Oxford: Oxford University Press, 1977), pp. 6–9.

8. Colin McGinn, "An A Priori Argument for Realism," *Journal of Philosophy* 76 (1979): 113–33.

9. Michael Dummett, "Realism," in *Truth and Other Enigmas*.

10. The claim is made by Michael Devitt, "Dummett's Anti-realism," *Journal of Philosophy* 80 (1983): 73–99.

11. Such a justification is provided by Michael Slote, *Reason and Scepticism* (New York: Humanities, 1970).

12. To move from beliefs about particular appearances to beliefs about sequences of them, one needs to justify belief in the soundness of one's memory. But, for memories of properties recently perceived, the validating argument against skeptical alternatives closely parallels the

argument regarding beliefs about particular appearances. For the sake of space I therefore omit further detail on this step in the argument.

13. See, for example, Jean Piaget, *The Mechanism of Perception* (New York: Basic Books, 1969).

14. See, for example, C. A. Hooker, "Philosophy and Metaphilosophy of Science," *Synthese* 32 (1975): 177–231, pp. 218–23.

15. Compare Pollock, *Knowledge and Justification*, p. 118.

16. See Salmon, "Theoretical Explanation."

17. Gilbert Harman, "Enumerative Induction as Inference to the Best Explanation," *Journal of Philosophy* 65 (1968): 529–33.

CHAPTER 10. SCIENTIFIC REALISM AND UNOBSERVABLES

1. See, for example, van Fraassen, *The Scientific Image*, p. 6.

2. Nancy Cartwright, *How the Laws of Physics Lie*; Geoffrey Joseph, "The Many Sciences and the One World," *Journal of Philosophy* 77 (1980): 773–90.

3. For a clear statement of the proof, see Hilary Putnam, "Craig's Theorem," in *Mathematics, Matter and Method* (Cambridge: Cambridge University Press, 1975).

4. See Richard Boyd, "Realism, Underdetermination, and a Casual Theory of Evidence," *Nous* 7 (1973): 1–12.

5. See, for example, Wilfrid Sellars, "The Language of Theories," in *Science, Perception, and Reality.*

6. See Cartwright, op. cit., and Joseph, op. cit.

7. Cartwright, op. cit., p. 4.

8. Wesley Salmon pointed out this relation in a lecture to the University of Miami Philosophy Colloquium, 1982.

9. Ian Hacking, *Representing and Intervening* (Cambridge: Cambridge University Press, 1983).

10. Salmon borrows this example from Jean Perrin in the lecture cited in note 8 for this chapter.

11. Compare Michael Friedman, "Review of van Fraassen, *The Scientific Image*," *Journal of Philosophy* 79 (1982): 274–83.

CHAPTER 11. RELATIVITY AND QUANTUM MECHANICS

1. We can instead define a substitute for velocity in coordinate-free terms, as was shown to me by Stephen Leeds.

2. See Hans Reichenbach, *The Philosophy of Space and Time* (New York: Dover, 1958); Adolph Grünbaum, *Philosophical Problems of Space and Time* (New York: Knopf, 1963); Wesley Salmon, *Space, Time, and*

Motion (Minneapolis: University of Minnesota Press, 1980). For Reichenbach, the need for coordinative definitions in geometry is a special case of a more pervasive need for conventions whenever direct verification or observation is impossible. Grünbaum's argument is based rather on what he takes to be intrinsic to space-time (topology), as opposed to the external imposition of coordinates that define properties of measuring instruments. The latter for him do not alter space-time itself, only our view of it.

3. Albert Einstein, "On the Electrodynamics of Moving Bodies," in *The Principle of Relativity* (New York: Dover, 1952), pp. 38–40.

4. Reichenbach, op. cit., p. 27.

5. The point is made by Geoffrey Joseph, "Conventionalism and Physical Holism," *Journal of Philosophy* 74 (1977): 439–62.

6. Hans Reichenbach is more consistent in this regard than later defenders of geometric conventionalism, since he also takes it to be a matter of convention whether, for example, objects exist unperceived. See his *Philosophic Foundations of Quantum Mechanics* (Berkeley, University of California Press, 1944), chap. 1.

7. We may grant the observationality of this result for the sake of argument. In fact, however, only signals sent round-trip along the same circular paths in different directions could be observed to travel at the same average speed. This would not itself establish the independence of round-trip speed from direction along different paths. The paths would have to be assumed (conventionally defined?) to be equal in length. Thus there may be a problem of consistency for those who take the round-trip velocity (in all directions) but not the one-way velocity to be observational. There may be another such problem for those who take geometric but not causal relations to be conventional. David Malament has shown that, for Minkowski space-time—the structure of special relativity—causal relations (distinctions between timelike, spacelike, and lightlike relations) uniquely determine standard simultaneity relations (equivalence relations corresponding to planes orthogonal to time axes). See his "Causal Theories of Time and the Conventionality of Simultaneity," *Nous* 11 (1977): 293–300.

Other geometrical relations central to relativity theory can be generated in this coordinate-free way as well. (This was also shown to me in a course by Stephen Leeds.) My brief presentation of some of relativity theory's basic features at the beginning of this section was in the more intuitive and common terms of features of various possible measuring devices. That derivation suffices to raise problems regarding measurable properties of objects in space-time.

8. We could also argue, following Clark Glymour, that the standard theory, in which no mysterious forces need be combined with the metric, is better tested than alternatives, since tests provide no separate values for the forces. But either this is one more inductive criterion that, like the others, must be shown to connect with truth or, more likely, it is equivalent to such criteria as simplicity, intuitiveness, or naturalness of expression. See his "The Epistemology of Geometry," *Nous* 11 (1977): 227–51.

9. There are, of course, numerous introductions to quantum theory as well as historical treatments. Two of the latter that focus on philosophical implications are Max Jammer, *The Philosophy of Quantum Mechanics* (New York: John Wiley, 1974), and Edward MacKinnon, *Scientific Explanation and Atomic Physics* (Chicago: University of Chicago Press, 1982).

10. See, for example, Jammer, op. cit., p. 165.

11. In the final essay of her recent book (op. cit.), Cartwright claims to have solved the problem of measurement by showing that the wave packet reduces in contexts other than that of measurement. But this is not a solution if measurement itself is not always interpretable in physical terms, as I argued it is not, for example in Einstein-Podolsky-Rosen contexts.

12. Albert Einstein, Boris Podolsky, and Nathan Rosen, "Can Quantum Mechanical Description of Physical Reality Be Considered Complete?" *Physical Review* 47 (1935): 770–80.

13. For a clear derivation of the inequalities, see Bas C. van Fraassen, "The Charybdis of Realism: Epistemological Implications of Bell's Inequality," *Synthese* 52 (1982): 25–38; also Bernard d'Espagnat, "Quantum Theory and Reality," *Scientific American* 241 (1979): 158–81.

14. See d'Espagnat, op. cit.

15. Nancy Cartwright urged this approach to the measurement problem in "Superposition and Macroscopic Observation," in *Logic and Probability in Quantum Mechanics*, ed. P. Suppes (Dordrecht: Reidel, 1976). She has since given up the approach as failing to account for the evolutions of macrosystems following measurements.

16. See the following articles in *Synthese* 42 (1979): Arthur Fine, "How to Count Frequencies," pp. 145–54; Allen Stairs, "On Arthur Fine's Interpretation of Quantum Mechanics," pp. 91–100; and Bas C. van Fraassen, "Hidden Variables and the Modal Interpretation of Quantum Theory," pp. 155–66.

17. Hilary Putnam, "The Logic of Quantum Mechanics," in *Mathematics, Matter and Method*.

18. Michael Gardner, "Is Quantum Logic Really Logic?" *Philosophy of Science* 38 (1971): 508–29.

19. This is argued by Paul Teller, "Quantum Mechanics and the Nature of Continuous Physical Quantities," *Journal of Philosophy* 76 (1979): 345–61.

CHAPTER 12. FURTHER PROBLEMS FOR SCIENTIFIC
REALISM

1. The example is from W. V. O. Quine, "On Empirically Equivalent Systems of the World," *Erkenntnis* 9 (1975): 313–28.

2. Hilary Putnam, "Equivalence," in *Realism and Reason* (Cambridge: Cambridge University Press, 1983).

3. I am speaking here of later positivism and of contemporary offshoots in the philosophy of science, not of those earlier purists who sought to unpack observations and observation statements in terms of sense data. While the latter are more consistent, the former, who restrict their instrumentalism to science, are less the straw men at present. The more thoroughgoing semantic verificationism suggested by Dummett will be addressed in the following section.

4. Compare Lawrence Sklar, "Saving the Noumena," in *Philosophy and Spacetime Physics* (Berkeley, Los Angeles, London: University of California Press, 1985).

5. The point derives from Clark Glymour, "Theoretical Realism and Theoretical Equivalence," *Boston Studies in the Philosophy of Science* 8 (1971): 275–88.

6. Putnam, "Equivalence," op. cit.

7. Thomas Kuhn, *The Structure of Scientific Revolutions* (Chicago: University of Chicago Press, 1970).

8. A more complex method for isolating tested hypotheses is provided by Clark Glymour, *Theory and Evidence* (Princeton, N.J.: Princeton University Press, 1980).

9. See, for example, Ernest Nagel, *The Structure of Science* (Indianapolis, Ind.: Hackett, 1979), chap. 11.

10. Kuhn, op. cit., pp. 206–7.

11. For a summary of different confirmational algorithms, see Henry Kyburg, "Recent Work in Inductive Logic," in *Recent Work in Philosophy*, ed. K. Lucey and T. Machan (Totowa, N.J.: Rowman and Allenheld, 1983).

12. Kuhn, op. cit., pp. 101–2.

13. My sample for this general claim consists, as is perhaps all too common, in physicist friends who report secondhand on other physicists.

14. Saul Kripke, "Naming and Necessity," in *Semantics of Natural Language*, ed. D. Davidson and G. Harman (Dordrecht: Reidel, 1972).

15. Arthur Fine, "How to Compare Theories: Reference and Change," *Nous* 9 (1975): 17–32.

16. Compare Larry Laudan, "A Confutation of Convergent Realism," *Philosophy of Science* 48 (1981): 19–49.

17. The standard argument is that of J. J. C. Smart, *Philosophy and Scientific Realism* (New York: Humanities, 1963), pp. 39–49. For a more recent statement, see Richard Boyd, "On the Current Status of the Issue of Scientific Realism," *Erkenntnis* 19 (1983): 45–90.

18. Compare Laudan, op. cit.; Boyd, op. cit.

19. See, for example, W. H. Newton-Smith, *The Rationality of Science* (Boston: Routledge and Kegan Paul, 1981).

20. The reader will notice that I have left the nature of this "suggestion" or analogy unspecified. I have no analysis, but a philosophy of science that views the structure of theoretical explanation in a similar way should certainly seek to provide one.

21. Wilfrid Sellars, "Philosophy and the Scientific Image of Man," in *Science, Perception, and Reality*, pp. 25–31; Bruce Aune, *Knowledge, Mind, and Nature* (New York: Random House, 1967), p. 172.

22. Land, op. cit.; see also Keith Campbell, "The Implications of Land's Theory of Colour Vision," unpublished.

23. R. Burnham, R. Hanes, and C. J. Bartleson, *Color: A Guide to Basic Facts and Concepts* (New York: John Wiley, 1963), pp. 7–8.

24. Ibid., pp. 56–57.

25. Ibid., p. 53.

CHAPTER 13. THE PRINCIPLE OF INFERENCE

1. Compare Harman, *Thought*, pp. 118–20.

2. Carl Hempel, "Recent Problems of Induction," in *Mind and Cosmos*, ed. R. Colodny (Pittsburgh, Pa.: University of Pittsburgh Press, 1966).

3. Mary Hesse, *The Structure of Scientific Inference* (Berkeley, Los Angeles, London: University of California Press, 1974), pp. 142–43.

4. Examples are provided by Hacking, *Representing and Intervening*, pp. 196–98.

5. This is argued by Donald Campbell, "Evolutionary Epistemology," in *The Philosophy of Karl Popper,* ed. P. Schlipp (LaSalle, Ill.: Open Court, 1974).

CHAPTER 14. CRITERIA

1. See, for example, Rogers Albritton, "On Wittgenstein's Use of the Term 'Criterion'," *Journal of Philosophy* 56 (1959): 845–57; Hamlyn, op. cit.; Anthony Kenny, "Criterion," *The Encyclopedia of Philosophy* (New York: Collier, 1967); William Lycan, "Non-Inductive Evidence: Recent Work on Wittgenstein's Criteria," *American Philosophical Quarterly* 8 (1971): 109–25.

2. Compare Ardon Lyon, "Criteria and Evidence," *Mind* 83 (1974): 211–27.

3. There may appear to be a problem with the scope of the modal operator here. Compare 'Normally, $\Box$ (x's being yellow indicates that x is a lemon)' and '$\Box$ (Normally, x's being yellow indicates that x is a lemon)'. My argument so far refutes the latter. The former is handled in the following paragraph, since it requires what I there call a circular definition of normality. Richard Sharvy encouraged me to make this distinction more explicit.

4. There are, of course, other uses of 'real' as well. The real color of Paul Ziff's hair may not be the color that it appears in daylight. (The example is Sharvy's [I would have used Pete Rose], deriving from J. L. Austin, who points to yet other meanings, including 'not from California'.)

CHAPTER 15. SEMANTIC ANTIREALISM

1. Michael Dummett, "Realism," in *Truth and Other Enigmas*; see also "Preface," "The Reality of the Past," and "Truth," in the same collection.

2. Ronald Dworkin, *Taking Rights Seriously* (Cambridge, Mass.: Harvard University Press, 1977), chaps. 2–4.

3. Compare Simon Blackburn, "Truth, Realism, and the Regulation of Theory," *Midwest Studies in Philosophy* 5 (1980): 353–71.

4. W. V. O. Quine, "What Price Bivalence?" *Journal of Philosophy* 78 (1981): 90–5.

5. Dummett, "Truth," p. 362.

6. Michael Dummett, *Frege: Philosophy of Language* (London: Duckworth, 1973), p. 458.

7. Michael Dummett states the argument, among other places, in "What Is a Theory of Meaning (II)," in *Truth and Meaning,* ed. G. Evans and J. McDowell (London: Oxford University Press, 1976), p. 70.

8. Dummett, *Frege,* pp. 420–21, 449–50.

9. Robert Brandom, "Truth and Assertibility," *Journal of Philosophy* 73 (1976): 137–49.

10. Compare David Papineau, *Theory and Meaning* (London: Oxford University Press, 1979), p. 91.

11. Dummett, "What Is a Theory of Meaning (II)," pp. 98–99; *Frege,* p. 465.

12. This claim is compatible with one made in an earlier chapter that particular hypotheses tested by scientists are those they would relinquish in the face of negative results.

13. One might assume a realist position for certain propositions (by holding that their truth conditions transcend verification procedures) without countenancing the possibility of global skepticism. But once truth as correspondence is distinguished from coherence, it certainly appears logically possible that most of our coherent beliefs might fail to correspond.

14. Putnam, *Reason, Truth and History,* chap. 1.

15. This possibility was pointed out to me by Eddy Zemach.

16. Putnam, *Reason, Truth and History,* chap. 3.

17. Ibid., chap. 2, Appendix.

18. See, for example, Peter Smith, *Realism and the Progress of Science* (Cambridge: Cambridge University Press, 1981), pp. 33–46.

19. See Hacking, *Representing and Intervening,* chap. 7, p. 130; also Alvin Plantinga, "How to Be an Anti-Realist," *Proceedings of the American Philosophical Association* 56 (1982): 47–70.

20. See Hilary Putnam, "Why There Isn't a Ready-Made World," in *Realism and Reason* (Cambridge: Cambridge University Press, 1983), p. 207; see also the Introduction to that volume, p. viii.

21. Compare Putnam, *Reason, Truth and History,* p. 54.

22. Compare John McDowell, "Truth Conditions, Bivalence, and Verificationism," in *Truth and Meaning,* ed. G. Evans and J. McDowell (London: Oxford University Press, 1976), pp. 55–56.

23. Dummett, *Truth and Other Enigmas,* p. 7.

24. Compare Gilbert Harman, "Language, Thought, and Communication," in *Language, Minds, and Knowledge,* ed. H. Feigl and G.

Maxwell, vol. 7 of Minnesota Studies in the Philosophy of Science (Minneapolis: University of Minnesota Press, 1975), p. 286.

CHAPTER 16. TOWARD A DESCRIPTIVE ACCOUNT OF REFERENCE

1. Putnam, *Reason, Truth and History*, p. 66.
2. The most detailed attempt by a causal theorist to handle this and related problems is Michael Devitt, *Designation* (New York: Columbia University Press, 1981).
3. Saul Kripke, "A Puzzle About Belief," in *Meaning and Use*, ed. A. Margalit (Dordrecht: Reidel, 1979).
4. The distinction and the example are from Keith Donnellan, "Reference and Definite Descriptions," *Philosophical Review* 75 (1966): 281–304.
5. Hilary Putnam, "The Meaning of 'Meaning'," in *Mind, Language and Reality* (Cambridge: Cambridge University Press, 1975).
6. The notion of an impure description is derived from Nathan Salmon, *Reference and Essence* (Princeton, N.J.: Princeton University Press, 1981), pp. 61–69.
7. David Kaplan, "Dthat" and "On the Logic of Demonstratives," *Midwest Studies in Philosophy* 2 (1979): 383–94 and 395–412. The suggestion below regarding descriptions is not in the spirit of Kaplan's account, since he does not think it possible to replace indexicals by descriptions. In the end, I don't either.
8. Another example in the literature is that of a person who knows a complete (identifying) description of himself but does not know who he is (that he is the person described). Here again it seems that no further description can be used to identify him to himself, but only an irreducibly indexical expression.
9. This equation of meaning with content is appropriate for first-person meaning. A notion of meaning as a function from context to content might be more appropriate for listeners' interpretations of speakers' contents. I do not interpret meaning here in the Gricean fashion, in terms of speakers' intentions to have certain effects on listeners. For one thing, that interpretation is inappropriate for the primitive representations that ground reference. In my view such intentions are not the source of meaning but expressions of it.
10. For an extended discussion see Nathan Salmon, op. cit.
11. Putnam, "The Meaning of 'Meaning'," also "Language and Reality," in *Mind, Language and Reality*.

APPENDIX: PSYCHOLOGY AND EPISTEMOLOGY

1. Contrast W. V. O. Quine, "Epistemology Naturalized," in *Ontological Relativity and Other Essays* (New York: Columbia University Press, 1969).

2. See, for example, Paul Churchland, *Matter and Consciousness* (Cambridge, Mass.: MIT Press, 1984).

3. See, for example, R. L. Gregory, *The Intelligent Eye* (London: Weidenfeld, 1970); Harman, *Thought,* chap. 11; Fodor, op. cit.

4. Fodor, op. cit.

5. Compare D. C. Dennett, *Content and Consciousness* (London: Routledge and Kegan Paul, 1969), chaps. 3, 4.

Index

Analysis of knowledge: causal, 22, 43–44, 51–52; counterfactual, 31–32, 57–63; defeasibility, 54–57; explanationist, 21–25, 30–37, 39–54, 59–67; goals of, 20–22; intuitions and, 20–21, 38, 44, 66; normative epistemology and, 12–14, 19–20, 54, 59; reliability, 52–54; skepticism and, 20–21, 59–64; traditional, 19, 22, 42

Analyticity. *See* Truth, analytic

Anti-realism, semantic: answer to, 7, 328–330, 336, 341–350; defined, 5–6, 309, 321, 325; skepticism and, 5, 309, 331–346

Appearing: causes of, 108, 110, 113, 118, 120, 124, 133, 150, 190, 285, 374–379; concepts of, 114–117, 119–121, 143, 152–155, 174–184, 190, 284, 374; connection to real properties, 2–5, 9, 12, 65–66, 76, 78, 101, 112–113, 116–118, 121, 146, 154–155, 178, 184–186, 190–203, 310–313, 317–320, 346, 374, 377; as evidence, 109–112, 133, 317, 375; explanation for, 205–215, 223, 280–281, 377; foundations and, 65, 75–80, 84, 87–88, 118, 120, 134, 138–143, 149–151, 178–185, 203–204; irreducible, 4, 88–113, 122–123; necessary for perception, 102–113; nonepistemic, 75, 114, 148, 159; vs. sense data, 124–133; structure within, 191–192, 207–209, 374; sufficient for perception, 99–103

Aristotle, 269

Attention, 92–94

Aune, Bruce, 284

Bayes' Theorem, 273–274, 289, 393 n. 4

Behaviorism, 103–108, 339, 348

Beliefs: acquisition of, 92–99, 109, 115, 176; dispositional, 92, 98, 103, 107; false, 82–83; foundational, 5, 75–76, 79–80, 119–120, 136–151, 184, 374; incorrigible, 139; infallible, 10,

65, 136, 139, 140–143; perceptual, 3–4, 71–80, 86–99, 104–105, 109–113, 134, 148–149, 179–180, 380–382, 386; systems of, 80, 86–87, 150–151

Bell, J. S., 248, 253–254

Berkeley, George, 12, 13, 112, 191, 200, 205, 211

Bivalence, 322–324, 350

Bohr, Niels, 245, 250–251

Born, Max, 246

Brandom, Robert, 327

Carr, John Dickson, 354

Cartwright, Nancy, 224

Causal theory of knowledge. *See* Analysis of knowledge

Causal theory of reference. *See* Reference

Causation, 33; common, 133, 225; mental, 127–128, 133–134; in perception, 1, 79, 88, 100, 109, 113, 117–118, 128, 133–134, 150–151, 173; reference and, 156–158, 276–277; by unobservables, 224–230, 279

Chisholm, Roderick, 194–198

Churchland, Paul, 173–177, 183–184, 376

Coherence: within belief systems, 80–87, 150–151; justification and, 6, 11–12, 40, 81, 86–87, 137, 197, 213, 292, 296, 304; realism and, 87, 177, 195–197, 213, 306; truth and, 5, 54, 82–87, 136–137, 196–198, 213, 292, 296, 304–306, 331–333, 345–346

Coherence theory of truth. *See* Truth

Coherentism: defined, 136; objections, 80–87, 136–138, 306

Colors, 8, 102–107, 122–124, 131, 155, 177–178, 183, 223, 239, 281–288

Concepts: of appearances, 114–117, 119–121, 142–143, 148, 152–155. 174–184, 190, 319, 374; defined, 95–98, 142, 319; innate, 96–98, 114, 154; learning of, 6, 95–99, 102 114–115, 154–161, 176, 180–181, order among, 10, 115–116, 119,

Designer: U.C. Press Staff
Compositor: Huron Valley Graphics, Inc.
Text: 11/13 Baskerville
Display: Baskerville
Printer: McNaughton & Gunn, Inc.
Binder: John H. Dekker & Sons

DATE DUE

APR 0 3 2001 APR 0 3 2001			
OCT 0 9 2006			
GAYLORD			PRINTED IN U.S.A.